COLLECTED LETTERS OF
SAINT THÉRÈSE OF LISIEUX

GW00503619

Collected Letters

St Thérèse of Lisieux

Translated F. J. Sheed

Sheed and Ward
London

PROLOGUE

God had given St. Thérèse of the Child Jesus "a Father and a Mother worthier of Heaven than earth".[1]

Born at Bordeaux, on 22 August 1823, her father, LOUIS JOSEPH ALOYS STANISLAS MARTIN, at first thought of the priesthood, but realised that God had other designs for him,[2] and on 13 July 1858 married Mlle ZÉLIE GUÉRIN in Alençon.

She had been born at Gandelain, near Alençon, on 23 December 1831. She too had thought of the religious life.[3] Having borne nine children, she died a holy death at Alençon, on 28 August 1877, of a painful illness heroically endured.[4]

M. Martin died on 29 July 1894, at the Château de la Musse, near Evreux. He had lived many years at Lisieux.

MARIE, their eldest daughter, was born on 22 February 1860.[5] She was in charge of the home after her mother's death, was Thérèse's godmother, and had sole charge of her after her sister Pauline's entry into Carmel; she herself entered on 15 October 1886, taking the name of Sister Marie of the Sacred Heart. She died 19 January 1940. She was one of the principal witnesses of her goddaughter's life and gave evidence at the Process of her Beatification.

PAULINE, the second daughter, was born 7 September 1861. Upon Mme Martin's death, Thérèse chose her for her "Little Mother."[6] She entered the Lisieux Carmel, 2 October 1882, taking the name of Sister Agnes of Jesus. The position of Prioress, which she filled several times from 1893 onwards, was given her "for life" by indult of the Holy See in 1923, on the occasion of Thérèse's Beatification. She was one of the key witnesses at the Process.

LÉONIE, the third child, was born 3 June 1863. After several unsuccessful attempts at the religious life, she entered the Convent

---

[1] Letter CCXXXI, from Thérèse to Abbé Bellière.
[2] Piat, *Histoire d'une famille*, ch. ii.
[3] Ibid., ch. ii.
[4] Ibid., ch. x.
[5] Like all the other Martin children, she was born in Alençon. All received Our Lady's name at Baptism.
[6] *Histoire d'une âme*, ch. ii.

1

of the Visitation in Caen, 28 January 1899, and remained there till her death in 1941.

HÉLÈNE, the fourth child, born 13 October 1864, died at the age of five and a half. JOSEPH LOUIS and JOSEPH JEAN BAPTISTE only survived a few months.

CÉLINE was born 28 April 1869. She entered the Lisieux Carmel 14 September 1894, having stayed with her father till his death. She brought to the Process a very explicit deposition upon the way of spiritual childhood taught her by Thérèse when she was a novice under her. Thérèse called her "the sweet echo of my soul". She was author of the portraits which popularised the appearance of "the child the whole world loved".

MÉLANIE THÉRÈSE was born in 1870 and died the same year. On 2 January 1873 came the ninth child MARIE FRANÇOISE THÉRÈSE. She was baptised two days after her birth at the church of Notre Dame d'Alençon, entered the Lisieux Carmel at fifteen, died there 30 September 1897. She was raised to the altar by Pius XI— his first Beata, then his first Saint, named by him the Star of his Pontificate and Patroness of Missions for the whole world.

For her earliest years there is no substitute for the first two chapters of the *Histoire d'une âme* and chapter ix of the *Histoire d'une famille*. Here we shall simply note the dates of the principal events of her childhood. We shall also give the first "writings" of little Thérèse, as a baby who could not yet handle a pen unaided.

Soon after her birth, it was found necessary to put her to nurse with Rose Taillé, a farmer's wife of Semallé, near Alençon. She remained with her till 2 April 1874. In this same year—the second year of her life—she uttered her first prayer. She was barely twenty-two months when she offered her love to *the good Jesus* in terms and with an intensity that enchanted her mother; but she had stammered the name of Jesus before then.

The "event" of 1875 seems to have been Thérèse's journey with her mother to the Visitation Convent at Le Mans, at the beginning of April, to see Mme Guérin's elder sister, Sister Marie-Dosithée,[1] and Thérèse's own sisters Marie and Pauline, who were boarders in the school. On 4 April Sister Marie-Dosithée gave a description of the visit to her brother's wife, Mme Guérin: "On Easter

---

[1] She had entered on 7 April 1858, aged twenty-nine. She died on 24 February 1877. She could not remember having committed, deliberately, the slightest fault.

PROLOGUE

Monday I had a delightful little visit I was not expecting. Zélie brought me her little Thérèse, thinking I would enjoy seeing her. She is a darling little girl, remarkably obedient; she did whatever she was told at once, and was so sensible that she would have sat still all day. I was very pleased to see her." Mme Martin wrote to M. and Mme Guérin: "I took little Thérèse to my sister. . . . The Superior came to see her and gave her some small gifts. I said to her 'Ask the good Mother to bless you.' She did not understand, and said 'Mother, will you come and visit us.'[1] Everyone had to laugh."

For 1876, one may quote this from a letter written 14 May by Mme Martin to her daughter Pauline (Thérèse was three): ". . . she has a remarkable intelligence and a heart of gold; she is very affectionate[2] and very open." Nothing was said to the child, but they marvelled at a piety beyond her years. For several months now she had heard God's call:

"When I had just begun to speak and Mamma asked me 'What are you thinking about?' my answer was always the same, 'About Pauline.' Sometimes I heard them say that Pauline was to be a nun; then, without much idea of what it meant, I would think 'I'll be a nun too!' That is one of my earliest memories and I never changed my resolution. So it was her example that drew me, when I was only two, to the Spouse of Virgins."[3]

"The dear little thing," wrote Mme Martin to Pauline (4 March 1877), "is our joy. She will be good, you see the germ of it already: she talks only of the good God; not for the whole world would she miss saying her prayers. I wish you could hear her telling little stories. I have never seen anything so pretty. She makes up for herself the tone and expression that are required. It is most noticeable when she says

> "Petit enfant à tête blonde
> Où crois-tu donc qu'est le bon Dieu?
> —Il est partout dans tout le monde
> Et puis là-haut dans le ciel bleu.

"When she comes to the last words, she turns her gaze upward with an angelic expression. We never tire of getting her to say it,

[1] The confusion was between " bénir " (to bless) and " venir " (to come).
[2] " Caressante."
[3] *Histoire d'une âme*, ch. i.

3

it is so beautiful; there is something so heavenly in her look that we are entranced."

Thérèse's first "letter" is in 1876. She was three. Céline, aged six and a half, wrote to her sister Marie, who was away from Alençon:

"Thérèse would like to write you a little letter, I'll help her to write you one, to please you." Then comes

My darling Marie,
I kiss you with all my heart, and Pauline too.

Thérèse.

Her second letter was early in 1877. At the age of four she wrote to her cousins Jeanne and Marie Guérin:[1]

My darling Cousins,
As Céline is writing to you, I want to write to you too, to tell you I love you with all my heart. I do wish I could see you and kiss you.

Goodbye, darling cousins, Marie won't guide my hand any more, and I can't write by myself.

Thérèse.

It amused Pauline, when she was on holiday, to have Thérèse write like this to various of her school friends. Of these early letters, only one has been given to the Lisieux Carmel. Before we come to it, it is worth seeing what Pauline wrote herself, or at least the long passage in which she speaks of little Thérèse. It was during the Easter vacation of her last year at the Visitation. She wrote to her friend Louise Magdelaine:

Wednesday, 4 April 1877.

Darling Louise,
    . . . I profit by a lucky moment which, perhaps, won't come again for the whole vacation. Thérèse and Céline are in the garden, amusing themselves blowing bubbles. Mamma is busy lecturing Léonie, Marie has just this moment gone to work downstairs. Papa is at the Pavilion;[2] so I am in complete solitude, and I hear

---

[1] Jeanne was then nine and Marie seven. They were living at this time in Lisieux.
[2] A place in the Rue des Lavoirs, where he kept his fishing tackle and often went to read and meditate.

no sound but my pen running across the paper; I can therefore think at my ease of my dear Visitation and talk to my little Louise. . . .

What do you do with your days? I hope you often see Sister Marie de Sales, I want you to tell her that in a few years she will have a future novice, guess who? Like Madame de Sévigné I give you ten guesses, thirty, even a hundred. Marie? no. . . . Léonie? no. . . . You, then? . . . Nor you either. . . . Very well, the new postulant is, is, is . . . Mademoiselle . . . Thérèse Martin. . . . Listen to the motives which will bring her. Yesterday evening she gave me her whole confidence, I could have died laughing: "I shall be a nun in a convent because Céline wants to go, and then too, Pauline, people must be taught to read, don't you see? But I won't take the class, it would be too much of a nuisance, Céline will, I shall be the Mother; I shall walk round the convent all day and then I'll go with Céline, we'll play in the sand and then with our dolls". . . . I speedily brought down her castles in Spain: "Do you really think, my poor Thérèse, that you will be talking all day? Don't you know there has to be silence?" "Has there? . . . Ah well, so much the worse, I shan't say a word." "What will you do, then?" "That's no great trouble, I shall pray to the good Jesus; but then how can I pray to Him without saying anything, I really don't know, and who will there be to show me, as I'll be the Mother, eh?" I had a frightful desire to laugh. But I kept serious. She looked at me thoughtfully. Her little face had so candid an expression, all she said to me came from so deep in her heart, that it was impossible not to be interested. At last, having reflected a few moments, she fixed her big blue eyes on me and with a mischievous smile she made gestures with her little arms like a grown-up and said: "After all, my little Pauline, it isn't worth while tormenting ourselves now, I am too little, don't you see, and when I'm big, like you and Marie, before I go into the convent, they will tell me what to do?" "That's right, baby dearest," I answered, covering her with kisses, "now it's late, let's go to sleep, I'll undress you. . . . You can still spend a few nights before calling yourself Sister Marie Aolysia² (that's the name she has chosen), you've still got time to think about it." Then we both went upstairs. I put her to bed,

---

¹ This was what Thérèse made of the name Marie Aloysia, borne by Pauline's class mistress.

and with no further thought of what she had said to me, she went off to sleep in peace. . . . *How* I wish the little angel need not grow up, a little soul that has never offended the good God is so lovely. . . . I love having my Thérèse with me, I feel that, with her, no harm can touch me. . . .

Pauline, enf. de Marie.

Thérèse sends you a little letter, she is enchanted with it and thinks herself very learned.

The "letter" added by Thérèse is a quarter sheet of small notepaper; but, as it is folded in two, it gives the regulation four pages—though they are very narrow pages.

Darling Louise,
I do not know you but I love you very much all the same. Pauline told me to write to you, she is holding me on her knees because I can't hold a pen by myself, she wants me to tell you that I am an idle little girl, but it is not true because I work all day playing naughty tricks on my poor little sisters, in fact I am a little imp, always laughing. Goodbye, little Louise, I send you a big kiss, give a big hug for me to the Visitation, that is to Sister Marie Aloysia and Sister Louise de Gonzague, because I don't know anyone else.

Thérèse.

The "naughty tricks", of which Pauline dictated the confession, were not very naughty. Pauline—like her Mother telling of Thérèse's "misdeeds"—exaggerated a little for the pleasure of having something piquant to make the guilty one write about herself.[1]

A few months later, Thérèse experienced her first real grief, one of the greatest of her life: she lost her mother. "The moving ritual of Extreme Unction," she wrote later,[2] "impressed itself on my soul. I still see the spot where I was told to kneel, I still hear the sobs of our poor father. . . . I do not remember that I wept much. I spoke to no one of the profound feelings which filled my heart; I looked and listened in silence."

After Mme Martin's death, her husband decided to come to Lisieux to live. He sacrificed all that bound him to Alençon in

[1] See *Novissima Verba*, p. 17.　　　[2] *Histoire d'une âme*, ch. ii.

order to have his daughters near their mother's people, above all to have Mme Guérin guide his elder daughters in the upbringing of their younger sisters.

The following lines were written by Thérèse to Marie Guérin, at the end of a letter of Pauline's, late in September 1877 (the departure for Lisieux had been fixed for November):

Darling Marie,
I kiss you with all my heart. Your letter gave me great pleasure. It gives me great pleasure to be going to Lisieux.

> Your little cousin,
> *Thérèse.*

In the margin Pauline added: "Thérèse said the words of this letter, I guided her hand in writing it."

M. Martin and his five daughters settled in at Lisieux—at "Les Buissonnets"—in November 1877. The Saint tells us herself that after her mother's death her personality had changed completely: "I, who had been so lively, so forthcoming, became gentle and shy, excessively sensitive; a look was often enough to make me melt into tears. . . . I could be gay only in the intimacy of my family."[1]

The next letter shows the child happy and very much herself with her aunt. The latter had written to Pauline, then visiting the Paris Exhibition with her father and her sister Marie; she says: "Thérèse's goodness simply enchants me, she was very anxious to write to you, so you are to receive a beautiful letter *in her own hand*. . . ."

My dear Pauline,
Marie Guérin has been in the country since Monday, but I am enjoying myself so much all alone[2] with Aunt. I went shopping for grey stockings with Aunt, and the lady gave me some beads. I made myself a ring with them.

Goodbye, little Pauline, give Papa and Marie a big kiss for me. I kiss you with all my heart.

> Your little sister,
> *Thérèse.*

[1] *Histoire d'une âme*, ch. ii.
[2] Léonie and Céline were pupils at the Benedictine Convent, with Jeanne Guérin.

7

Mme Guérin goes on: "She will be delighted to see her father and sisters again, but she is gay, very gay; she laughs so heartily that she starts me laughing."

Soon after, in the autumn of that year 1878, Thérèse made her first confession. In the pages of her Autobiography addressed to Mother Agnes of Jesus, she recalls that "very sweet memory": "You said to me, dearest Mother: 'Little Thérèse, it is not to a man but to the good God Himself that you are going to confess your sins.' I became so convinced of this that I asked you seriously if I must not tell M. Ducellier[1] that I loved him with all my heart."

The next year, 1879, was marked by the prophetic vision of her father "bent, aged, his head covered with a thick veil."[2]

What wonderful pages the grievous trial then foreshadowed was to move the saint to write! Many letters, in this present volume, bear witness to the heroism with which she bore the great sorrow when it came. But in 1879 she did not know what the vision meant, and the only "Letter" remaining to us from this period is an evidence of her love for Céline.

The notepaper, very small size, had been cut, folded and sewn to make a booklet by Thérèse herself; she wrote one word to the page, in her big child's writing, and brought the missive to her sister:

Darling Céline,
You know I love you a lot. Goodbye, darling Céline.
Your little Thérèse who loves you with all her heart.

Thérèse Martin.

Thérèse was not yet going to school. She was the pupil of her sister Pauline, to whom she wrote, 2 December 1880, from Lisieux:

My dear Pauline,
I am very pleased to be writing to you, I asked my aunt if I could, I make a lot of mistakes but you know your little Thérèse,

---

[1] The Abbé Ducellier, assistant at the Cathedral of Saint-Pierre, was then spiritual director to M. Martin and Pauline. He was Thérèse's confessor till she became a pupil at the Benedictine Convent in October 1881. He preached at the Clothing and the Taking of the Veil for both Pauline and Céline. He left Lisieux to be parish priest of Mathieu and later of Trévières; he was later made Archpriest of Saint-Pierre of Lisieux and died in 1917. He was a witness at his former penitent's Beatification Process.

[2] *Histoire d'une âme*, ch. ii.

8

so you know I am not very clever. Will you please kiss Papa for me. I got four good marks the first day and five the second.

Give Mademoiselle Pauline[1] a big kiss for me. I am enjoying myself so much, because, you know, we are at Aunt's. While Marie does the accounts,[2] I have fun colouring little pictures my Aunt has given me.

Goodbye, darling Pauline, your little *Thérèse* who loves you.[3]

And again from Lisieux in July 1881:

Dear Pauline,

I am very pleased to be writing to you. I wish you a happy feast for you know I couldn't give you the wish on Wednesday, the day of the feast.[4]

I hope you are having a lot of fun at Houlgate. Do tell me if you have ridden on a donkey.

Thank you very much for letting me off lessons while you are at the seaside. It would be very nice, if you were writing to Marie, to write me a little note too.

If you knew ! On the feast of St. Domitia,[5] Aunt put a pink sash[6] on me, and I threw flowers for St. Domitia. . . .

Don't show anyone my letter.

Goodbye, darling Pauline, I kiss you with all my heart. Give a big kiss for me to Marie Thérèse and little Marguerite.[7]

Your little *Thérèse* who loves you.

On 3 October 1881 Thérèse entered as a daily boarder at the Benedictine Convent in Lisieux. A year later, 2 October 1882, Pauline entered the Carmel at Lisieux, and became Sister Agnes of Jesus.

It was an immense grief for Thérèse—"I wondered how the sun could go on shining on the earth."

[1] Mlle Romet, Pauline's godmother.
[2] Marie Martin was helping Mme Guérin with the year's accounts. She spent the days at her Aunt's house and went back with Thérèse in the evenings to Les Buissonnets.
[3] The spelling is pleasing—conais, abile, cinc, tu sait, contes (for comptes), himages.
[4] 29 June, feast of SS. Peter and Paul.
[5] A child martyr whose shrine was held in much veneration at the Benedictine Convent in Lisieux.
[6] It is in the Relic Room in the sacristy at the Lisieux Carmel.
[7] Marie Thérèse Pallu du Bellay had been in the same class as Pauline at the Visitation at Le Mans. Marguerite was a much younger sister.

Soon after—towards the end of 1882—she wrote to the Prioress, Mother Marie de Gonzague, the following letter:

My dearest Mother,

I have not seen you for such a long time, so I am very pleased to be writing to you to tell you my small affairs.

Pauline told me that you were in retreat, so I ask you to pray to the Child Jesus for me, because I have many faults and I should like to be cured of them.

I must make you my confession. For some time now, I always answer back when Marie tells me to do anything.[1] It seems that when Pauline was little and was making some excuse to my Aunt at Le Mans, Aunt said "Every hole should have its peg", but with me it is much worse still. So I want to be better and in every hole put a pretty little flower, which I shall offer the Child Jesus in preparation for my first Communion. You will pray for that, won't you, my dearest Mother? Yes! that wonderful moment will come very soon, and how happy I shall be, when the Child Jesus comes into my heart, to have so many lovely flowers to offer Him.

Goodbye, dearest Mother, I kiss you very tenderly, the way I love you.

Your little girl,
Thérésita.[2]

"At the end of this year 1882," writes Thérèse, "I found myself with a headache, continuous though not unbearable; it did not prevent me going on with my studies; this lasted till Easter 1883."[3]

Soon after, the condition of her health grew worse. A momentary improvement made it possible for her to go to Pauline's Clothing, 6 April 1883; the next day, as she tells us in her third chapter, "there was a violent attack, and the illness became so grave that, by all human probabilities, it was incurable".

[1] As on other occasions, Thérèse, in her humility, is here confessing the *interior* struggle she had to overcome. Unanimously the depositions made at her Process by witnesses under oath show that she always had enough self-control never to object when an order was given.

[2] As early as October 1882 Thérèse had told Mother Marie de Gonzague of her desire to enter Carmel; and for a while the Reverend Mother had thought of giving her the name of Thérésita of the Child Jesus when she came to the Convent—in memory of a niece of St. Teresa of Avila, Teresita of Jesus, who entered very young.

[3] This and the remaining passages quoted in this Prologue are from the *Histoire d'une âme*, ch. iii.

PROLOGUE

Her illness "certainly came from the jealousy of the devil; furious at this first entry into Carmel he chose to take his revenge" on little Thérèse, "for the very great harm her family was to do him in the future. . . . A great miracle was needed to give her back to life, and this miracle Our Lady of Victories worked most thoroughly", during a novena of Masses offered at her shrine in Paris on M. Martin's request. On 13 May—the feast of Pentecost—a statue of the Immaculate Virgin, especially venerated in the Martin home, came to life and moved toward the child. . . . "The Virgin Mary grew beautiful, so beautiful that I shall never find words to express that divine beauty. In her countenance was sweetness, kindness, unutterable tenderness; but what pierced me to the depths of my heart was her enchanting smile!" Thérèse was cured. "And the Virgin Mary's flower grew so strong that, five years later, it blossomed upon the fertile mountain of Carmel."

Observe how the series of Letters and Notes published in this book end with a cry of love to Her who had given back to Thérèse the health which made life in Carmel possible.

CHILDHOOD 1884–1885–1886

8 May 1884 : Thérèse makes her First Communion, at the Benedictine Convent in Lisieux, where she is a day-boarder. On 14 June she is confirmed in the Convent.

21 May 1885 : Solemn renewal of her First Communion. During the retreat in preparation, she is assailed by "the terrible disease of scruples", from which she continues to suffer till October 1886.

31 May 1886 : Becomes a Child of Mary.

15 October 1886 : Her sister Marie enters the Carmelite Convent of Lisieux. Shortly after, Thérèse is delivered from her scruples through the prayers of her four little brothers and sisters who had died in infancy.

25 December 1886 : A Christmas gift from God—what she called her "conversion". The Child Jesus heals her of her undue sensitiveness and "girds her with His weapons".

I

To her sister, AGNES OF JESUS

*To thank her
for a little book of preparation for
First Communion*

February 1884.

My darling Pauline,

Of course I meant to write and thank you for your adorable little book,[1] but I thought it was not allowed during Lent; now that I know it is allowed, I thank you with all my heart.

You don't know the happiness I felt when Marie[2] showed me your lovely little book. I found it entrancing; I had never seen anything so beautiful, and I could not take my eyes off it. What lovely prayers at the beginning ! I said them to the little Child Jesus with all my heart. Every day I try to do all the "practices"

---

[1] The book alluded to has been republished as *Deux mois et neuf jours de préparation à ma Première Communion, d'aprés la méthode suivie par sainte Thérèse de l'Enfant-Jesus.* The method consists in sacrifices and short prayers for each day, symbolised by flowers and their scents.

[2] Her eldest sister and godmother.

I can, and I do my best not to let any opportunity pass. From the bottom of my heart and as often as possible I say the little prayers : they are sweet-scented like roses.

What a beautiful picture in the front! It is a little dove giving its heart to the Child Jesus. That's what I'll do with mine ! I intend to adorn it with all the lovely flowers I find, so as to offer it to the Child Jesus on the day of my first Communion; and truly, as it says in the little prayer at the beginning of the book, I want the Child Jesus to be so happy in my heart that He won't think of going back to heaven . . .

Do give my thanks to Sr. Thérèse of Saint Augustine for her dear little rosary of practices, and for embroidering the beautiful cover for my book.

Please kiss Mother Marie de Gonzague for me, and tell her that her little daughter loves her with all her heart.

Léonie and Céline send kisses too. Goodbye, my darling Pauline. I kiss you with all my heart.

Your little daughter who loves you *so*,

Thérésita.

II

To MME GUÉRIN[1]

May 1885.

My dear Aunt,

You told me to write and let you know how I am. I am better than on Sunday, but I still have a bad headache. I hope that you are well, Jeanne too; and that Marie is now completely well again.

I think of you very often, and I remember how good you have been to me. Nor do I forget my darling cousins; please tell Marie that I am not writing to her today, but that I shall write to her next time, so as to have more things to tell her.

I go into retreat[2] on Sunday evening, my first Communion being still fixed for the 21st; it is now certain that it won't be changed.

---

[1] She was at the seaside with her daughters Jeanne and Marie.
[2] A retreat made between the First Communion and the second. "During the retreat before my second Communion I was assailed by the terrible disease of scruples" (*Histoire d'une âme*, ch. iv)—This was a few days after the writing of this letter.

Goodbye, dear Aunt, give Jeanne and Marie a big kiss from me and keep the biggest kiss for yourself.

Thérèse,
Child of the Holy Angels.

III

To her father, M. MARTIN
Who was then travelling in Central Europe.
He received this letter in Vienna

Here a flower is sewn on to the notepaper,
surrounded by the words: "Reseda picked in my garden"

25 August 1885.

My darling Father,

If you were in Lisieux, today is the day you would be getting wishes for your feast; but, since you aren't, I want all the same, and more than ever, to wish you much pleasure on your journey. I hope, darling Father, that you are enjoying yourself a lot and very pleased with your trip. I think of you continually and I ask God to give you much pleasure and bring you back soon in good health.

My dearest Father, Pauline made some lovely verses to recite to you on your feast-day; but since I can't, I am going to write them to you:

[Here follow fifty-two lines headed "Wishes of a Little Queen for the Feast of the King, her Father".]

Goodbye, my beloved Father,

Your Queen who loves you with all her heart,

Thérèse.

IV

To her cousin, MARIE GUÉRIN[1]

Les Buissonnets, Saturday, 26 June 1886.

My darling Marie,

I am most grateful to you for being nice enough not to be annoyed with me for not writing: so I make all haste to answer

[1] Then at Trouville.

your charming little letter, you can't imagine what pleasure it gave me.

I am very pleased that you are better and are enjoying yourself a lot. I can't think of anything new at Lisieux to tell you about, I only know that we are all well.

You ask me in your letter to give you news of Madame Papineau,[1] she's very well and often asks how you are. As for the lessons, for some time I have been having more; that is why I couldn't write to you on Sunday.

I am very pleased, because I shall be in white tomorrow for the procession, Marie has tried my things on me and they look very nice.

My darling Marie, please give my kind Aunt and my dearest little Jeanne a big kiss from me.

Goodbye, darling cousin, forgive me if my letter is badly arranged and badly written. I am writing in a great hurry and hadn't time to make a rough copy first. Céline asks me to send a big kiss to you and Jeanne and my Aunt.

Your little cousin who loves you with all her heart,

Thérèse.

V

To MARIE GUÉRIN

Les Buissonnets, Thursday, 15 July 1886.

My dear Marie,

Thank you for writing, I enjoyed your letter so much. I am very pleased that you go such lovely walks as the one you describe, I was much interested.

Yesterday we went for the afternoon to Madame Maudelonde,[2] and I had much fun with Céline and Hélène.[3]

Madame Papineau has let me off lessons for tomorrow in honour of the Feast of Our Lady of Mount Carmel, so that I can be at the sermon.

You see, my Marie, that I haven't any very interesting things to write of, I haven't had a wonderful walk like yours to tell you about, but I hope all the same that my poor little letter will please you a tiny bit.

[1] She gave Thérèse lessons when she left the Benedictine Convent.
[2] Mme Guérin's sister.
[3] Mme Maudelonde's daughters.

15

Goodbye, Marie darling, give my Aunt and Jeanne a big kiss from me.

Your little sister who loves you a lot, such a lot,

Thérèse.

VI

To her sister, MARIE

Travelling with their father to Calais and Dover to meet Père Pichon, S.J.,[1] on his return from Canada. Through a misunderstanding she had to come back without meeting him

Saturday, 2 October 1886, 6 p.m., Feast of the Holy Angels.
My darling Marie,

We have just had the telegram, I'm very pleased, because I think it means that you have seen the Father at Dover; he sent you a letter on Wednesday to tell you to be there to meet him today. You can't imagine how worried we were; Céline sent letters to Dover and Calais, poste restante.

The Blessed Virgin has had a candle every day, and I have prayed and implored her so hard that I simply can't believe you could fail to discover that the Father was getting back today. Monsieur Pichon[2] also sent a letter to Papa, we didn't like to open it. Pauline told us that we had better, because there might be something urgent in it, but it was only to say that Monsieur Pichon did not yet know the day the Father would be getting back and that he was going to write to the Superior to find out.

O my little Marie, if you knew how true I find what you told us—the good God spoils us, but you can't imagine what it means to be separated from a person one loves as I love you. If you could see all that is in my mind—but I can't say it to you, it's too late and I've written my letter all crooked because I wasn't paying enough attention.

My darling Godmother, I asked Pauline if the small bottles of gold-bronze were for water-colour painting, she said no, they

---

[1] Born at Carrouges, near Alençon, in 1843. He was spiritual director of Marie Martin from before her entry into Carmel, and later of her younger sisters. He died on 15 November 1919.
[2] Père Pichon's brother.

were for painting statues: I am telling you this so that you shan't buy me any as a souvenir. Please don't buy me anything, I should be really hurt. Léonie sends kisses to you and Papa.

Goodbye, my dearly loved Marie, give my darling Father a great big kiss from me.

Your own little daughter who loves you as hard as it is possible to love,

Thérèse.

Special—don't forget our commission and the stool for Aunt. Félicité[1] sends you many messages, she has been in the best of moods since you left. Aunt, Uncle, Jeanne and Marie send you many messages.

We haven't yet taken the telegram to Carmel.

[1] A servant of the Martins.

1887

FIFTEENTH YEAR

29 May: Whit Sunday: Thérèse wins her father's consent to her entering Carmel.

July: One Sunday, at the sight of an image of Jesus crucified, she receives a definitive grace of zeal for the salvation of souls.

31 August: She obtains, by her prayers, the conversion of Pranzini, a criminal under sentence of death.

October: Permission to enter Carmel granted by M. Guérin, her uncle and guardian.

31 October: Visit to Mgr Hugonin, Bishop of Bayeux, to ask his authorisation to enter Carmel.

4 November: Departure for Rome with her father and her sister Céline, and pilgrimage to the shrine of Notre Dame des Victoires in Paris.

20 November: Audience with Pope Leo XIII, whose permission she asks to enter Carmel at fifteen.

VII

To MARIE GUÉRIN

Les Buissonnets, Monday, 27 June 1887.

My dear little invalid, how are you this morning? did you sleep well last night? is your tooth still aching? There, Marie darling, are all the questions I'm asking myself this morning; but alas, no one can answer me and I'm obliged to settle them for myself, so I'm doing it in the way that suits me best—I see that you are very much better.

I find I must turn the page, for I've just noticed that I was writing all crooked, it's so long since I've held a pen that it strikes me as very funny.

I am just back from Carmel; I told Marie and Pauline how ill you were, and they are going to pray to the good God that He may make you better and that you may enjoy your time at Trouville.

I've still got many things to write to you about, but I haven't

18

time for I must write a word to Jeanne,[1] and besides I'm afraid I should make your eyes sore, my letter is a horrid scribble and I don't know how I dare send it to you like this.

I leave you now, with a kiss not on your two cheeks—for fear I might hurt your teeth—but on your nice little forehead.

Thérèse, e.m.[2]

PS. I specially beg my dear little Loulou not to give herself the bother of writing to me, I shall keep on writing to her all the same. My little Loulou must deserve the name, by eating like a real wolf.

VIII

To MARIE GUÉRIN

Les Buissonnets, 14 July 1887.

My darling little Marie,

I've just this moment received your dear little letter and I'm still laughing at the thought of all you tell me. All the same, I must begin with a scolding: why have you taken your face back to the "sculptor"[3]? He has made a fine job of it ! . . . I am desolated to learn that your horrid little cheeks have swollen up again like balloons: experience should surely have taught you better. It seemed to me that you'd had enough the first time !

I am very pleased that my dear Aunt is better, I was dismayed when I learnt that she was ill; truly God is sending you many trials this year.

This week is not gay at Les Buissonnets either; it's the last our dear Léonie spends with us,[4] the days run away so fast, she has only two days more to be with us.

But after all, my poor darling, what of it ? My sorrow is mingled with a kind of joy to see my dear Léonie at last where she belongs; yes, I don't believe she will be truly happy anywhere else, at the Visitation she will find all that the world cannot give her.

[1] This letter or note has disappeared.
[2] Enfant de Marie.
[3] The dentist, of course.
[4] She was entering the Visitation at Caen, 16 July.

Céline is in mourning for her two little blue birds,[1] the male went to join his mate yesterday morning, and now the mortal remains have gone off to be stuffed.

My wish, darling, is that the end of your stay at Trouville may be gayer than the beginning; I hope that God, having tried you so much, may now give you much joy.

Céline is sorry not to be able to write to Jeanne; but she is so rushed because of all the business of Léonie that it is really impossible. Tell Jeanne she couldn't believe how touched Léonie was by her letter—yours too—she kisses you and my darling Aunt with all her heart.

Give Jeanne a big kiss for me, tell my Aunt how much I love her, and keep a good share of my kisses for yourself. (I have heard about the letter from Carmel, it seems to have been very amusing.) Papa sends his greetings to you all, especially his dear god-daughter.

Thérèse.

IX

To her cousin, JEANNE GUÉRIN[2]

My darling Jeanne,

Not having the artist Darel to draw me a boat, but wishing to have one at the top of my letter all the same, I had to scrawl one myself.[3]

And now, my dear Jeanne, I shall waste a few minutes of your time, I hope your migraine is completely gone; now that——[4] has left, you won't be so worried, and certainly everybody will be much better.

I fancy you must be very pleased not to be hearing my sermons on death, not to see my eyes "fascinating you", not to keep being pushed on your way to the demoiselles Pigeon. . . .

I have to announce the death of eight of my silkworms: I've only four left, Céline has lavished such attentions on them[5] that

[1] Thérèse had bought them for Céline at the Exhibition in Le Havre.
[2] Elder daughter of the Guérins. Born at Lisieux, 24 February 1868, she died (having survived her husband, Dr. La Néèle) 25 April 1938. This letter is not dated. It was probably written in July 1887.
[3] Not a scrawl, but quite a careful drawing of a ship with all sails set and flag flying. Thérèse had just left the Guérins, after staying with them at Trouville.
[4] A person who had been rather a nuisance on the beach.
[5] Having no mulberry-tree at Les Buissonnets to feed the silk-worms, Céline had tried the leaves of all the trees in the place.

she has managed to make them nearly all die on me from worry or apoplectic strokes; I am very much afraid the four that survive have caught the germ of their brothers' disease and will be following them into the kingdom of moles.

It feels very strange to find myself back at Les Buissonnets: this morning I was quite startled to see Céline at my side. We spoke to Papa of the kind suggestion my dear Aunt made,[1] but it is quite impossible, because Papa leaves on Wednesday and will be staying a very short while in Alençon this time.

Goodbye, my dearest Jeanne, I love you always with all my heart.

Thérèse, e.m.[2]

X

To MARIE GUÉRIN

Les Buissonnets, 18 August 1887.

Darling Marie,

Uncle has just told me you are ill, you little wretch: as soon as you could have a little enjoyment, you rush off to be ill. It's very lucky for you that I am not with you, otherwise you would certainly have had me to reckon with.

And my dear Aunt, how is she, better and better, I hope?

Alas! how differently things happen from how one imagines! From here I saw you running gaily in the park, looking at the fish, having loads of fun with Jeanne, in fact I saw you living like the lady of the château: but instead of that sort of life, you're living the life of a sick girl! Ah, my poor darling, I pity you with all my

---

[1] For Thérèse and Céline to come and spend a few days more at Trouville, while M. Martin was away.

[2] There is a striking contrast between the cheerful commonplaces of this letter and the profound graces the Saint has told us of in ch. v of the *Histoire d'une âme*. It was in this very month of July that she had her heart "cloven with sorrow to see the precious blood of Jesus falling to earth with no one bothering to gather it up". "Jesus' dying cry, 'I thirst,' sounded at every moment in my heart and enkindled in it a new and very vital fervour. I longed to give my Beloved to drink; I felt that my thirst for souls was devouring me and at all costs I wanted to snatch sinners from the eternal flames."

It was at this period—spring and summer of 1887—that Thérèse and Céline had their conversations in the top room at Les Buissonnets. "I feel," says the Saint, "that we received great graces. In the words of the *Imitation*, 'God communicates Himself sometimes in the midst of dazzling splendour, sometimes sweetly veiled under shadows or figures' (bk. iii, ch. xliii, 3). Thus He deigned to manifest Himself to our hearts; but how light and transparent the veil was! Doubt would have been impossible; already faith and hope were passing from our souls: love was bringing us here below to Him we sought."

heart, but you mustn't be depressed, you still have time for walks and fun, all you have to do is leave your bedroom soon. Though it's a lovely gilded room it's nothing but a beautiful cage for the little bird that wants to hop about in the sun.

Yes, my dearest little Sister, what you really need is the fresh air in the park, like the little birds. When you come back to us, you must be fresh as a lovely rose just opened. Oh! my dear, speaking of roses makes me want to kiss your pretty cheeks. They are not rosy, I know, but I like a beautiful white rose as much as a red one.

Try to get some colour into your little cheeks, and ask Jeanne to give them a kiss from me, tell her that I think of her a great deal too, and send her a kiss with all my heart. Marie dear, I have let my pen run on, and the things it has written are not very easy to read: I beg you to put the blame on it, but what I don't want you to credit *it* with is the affection your little sister bears you.

Give dear Aunt a big kiss from me, I love her with all my heart.

Goodbye, dear little Sister, I send you a loving kiss and advise you to get well very quickly so as to have a little fun.

Your sister who loves you,
Thérèse, e.m.[1]

XI

To SISTER AGNES OF JESUS

To tell her of her conversation with their uncle and guardian, M. Guérin,[2] *whose permission she had asked to enter Carmel*

Saturday, 8 October 1887.

My darling Sister,

Since Wednesday I have been looking for an opportunity to talk to my Uncle; this morning the opportunity came. He was very

[1] Speaking of the great grace she had received on Christmas Eve 1886, Thérèse wrote: "Charity entered my heart with the need to be ever forgetful of self, and from then I have been happy" (*Histoire d'une âme*, ch. v). There is a proof of her statement in this letter. It reflects nothing but her concern for her cousin's health; yet—as we know from the *Histoire d'une âme*—throughout August 1887 she was praying ceaselessly for the conversion of the murderer Pranzini—"using all the spiritual means imaginable" to that end. A similar remark could be made about more than one of the letters in this volume. Thérèse's aim was to give pleasure to the recipients, not to talk of herself.

[2] Mme Martin's brother. Born near Alençon, 2 January 1841; in 1866 opened

kind; I had been afraid, as it was a Saturday, that he would not be pleased, for on that day he is very busy: but as soon as I asked him to come, he looked very serious and left his reading at once.

He told me that for some time he had suspected that I had something to say to him; then he gave me a *most affectionate* little sermon, which I was expecting; he told me he was very sure of my vocation, that was not what kept him from letting me go; only the world, I fancy, is an obstacle. It would be a real *public scandal* to see a *child* entering Carmel, I should be the only one in the whole of France, etc. Still if God wants it, He will find a way to show it; meanwhile Uncle told me that according to the rules of human wisdom, I must not think of entering before seventeen or eighteen, and even that will be too early.

Uncle said a good deal more to the same effect, but it would take too long to tell; as you may imagine, I did not mention any date. Pauline darling, I am very pleased that at least Uncle found no objection apart from the world. I fancy that God will have no great trouble in showing Uncle, when He chooses, that it is not for the world to keep me from entering Carmel. You realise, my dearest little Sister, Uncle said many very kind things besides, but I'm telling you only the obstacles he saw. Fortunately they are not obstacles for God.

O my dearest Pauline, I cannot tell you today all the things that fill my heart, I cannot get all my ideas in order. In spite of everything, I feel full of courage, I am quite sure God is not going to abandon me now; as Uncle said, my time of testing is about to begin. Oh! pray for me, pray for your Thérésita; you know how she loves you, for she tells you everything. What I really need is to see you, but this is one more sacrifice to make to Jesus. Oh! I want to refuse Him *nothing;* even when I feel sad and solitary on this earth, He still remains to me, and didn't St. Teresa say "God alone suffices". . . .

Forgive me, Pauline dearest, for sending you this letter, or rather scrawl: the ideas don't even follow on. It's so badly written that I don't know if you will be able to read it, but my heart had so many things to say to you that my pen could not keep up. Tell my dear Godmother that I think of her often during her retreat, ask her not to forget her goddaughter.

---

a chemist's shop in Lisieux; married Mlle Céline Fournet the same year. Died 28 September 1909.

I shall see you soon, my dearest Sister; once more, you won't be annoyed with me for sending you this letter? I haven't the heart to begin it all over again.[1]

Your little
Thérésita.

(Tell my dearest Mother that her little Thérésita loves her with all her heart. I am sending you your small pen-holder.)

XII

To FATHER ALMIRE PICHON, S.J.[2]

Reverend Father,[3]

I thought, as you have concerned yourself with my sisters, that you would be kind enough to take on the youngest too.

I wish I could tell you all about myself, but I am not like my sisters, I am not very good at expressing all I feel in a letter.

I believe, Father, that you will read me aright all the same.

When you come to Lisieux, I hope that I may be able to see you at Carmel and open my heart to you.

Father, God has lately granted me a great grace: for a long time now I have wanted to enter Carmel: I think the moment

[1] Two weeks later—on 22 October—Sister Agnes of Jesus wrote to M. Guérin: "Our poor little Benjamin of a Thérèse was so pale, sad, and wretched this morning that the cause must be told . . . a whole week of agony. . . . In her eyes—so loving but so tearful—I thought I detected something more than a child's trouble: 'What is the matter? Are you ill?' 'No, Pauline, but I have never suffered like this; if it goes on, I shall die of anguish; I can see that Uncle is waiting for a miracle, but of course God won't work a miracle for me. They say it's extraordinary to enter Carmel at fifteen. It's most unfortunate that it should be extraordinary; but it seems to me that the good God never asks the impossible, and He is asking this of *me*. . . . O Pauline, I have but one hope, prayer; I pray, if you could know how ardently I pray! Every day I say to the good God: My God, You are almighty and my Uncle always listens to You. When You are in his heart, do tell him that You want me without delay. I have been greatly tried this week, and have suffered greatly, give me a ray of hope. . . . The journey to Rome is a burden to me, unless You tell me that it is my wedding journey. . . . O Jesus, take me for Christmas!'" (from an unpublished letter). That very day, M. Guérin gave his consent (see *Histoire d'une âme,* ch. v).

[2] This letter is copied from Thérèse's rough draft, preserved at the Lisieux Carmel. The letter actually sent to Père Pichon was destroyed by him, as has been told in the Preface to this volume. Thérèse had written to him, just before her first Communion, to commend herself to his prayers, saying that soon she would be a Carmelite and that then he would be her director. He had replied, under date 7 May 1884 (the eve of Thérèse's first Communion and Pauline's Profession): "To-morrow I shall go to the altar for you and Pauline."

[3] Undated, written 23 October 1887.

has come. Papa is willing to let me enter at Christmas. Oh ! Father, how kind the Child Jesus is to take me so young, I don't know how to thank Him.

My Uncle thought me too young, but yesterday he told me that he only wanted to do God's will.

Father, I ask you please to pray for your youngest child. I am just back from the Convent : my sisters there told me that I could write and tell you quite simply all that was going on in my heart. You see, Father, I have done so, hoping that you will not refuse to take me as your little daughter.

Bless your second little lamb,

Thérèse.

⸰ XIII

To her Carmelite Sisters,
MARIE OF THE SACRED HEART and AGNES OF JESUS
From the first stop on the Italian journey[1]

Paris, Hôtel de Mulhouse, 6 November 1887.

My darling Sisters,

Céline didn't want me to write to you today, but I wouldn't like you to get a letter from her without a word from your little Thérésita. I see my writing's like a little cat-scratch, but I hope you won't be annoyed with me, because I am quite exhausted : things are going round and round.

Tomorrow we shall be out of France. I am worn out by all I am seeing ; we have seen beautiful things in Paris, but all this is not happiness. Céline will tell you, if she likes, of the marvels of Paris ; but, for me, all I have to tell you is that I *keep* thinking of you ; the beauties of Paris do not win my heart in the least.

I am a little like my dear Godmother, I am in constant fear of being squashed to death : every moment I seem to be completely surrounded by vehicles.

O my darling Sisters, all these beautiful things I see do not bring me happiness ; I shall only have that when I am where you are now.

---

[1] M. Martin, with Céline and Thérèse, was on pilgrimage to Rome, for the golden jubilee of Leo XIII's priesthood (cf. *Histoire d'une âme*, ch. vi, and *Histoire d'une famille*, pp. 286–97).

I was very happy at Notre Dame des Victoires,[1] I said many prayers for you and my dearest Mother.[2]

I should like to write to my little cousins, but it must be another time, for I still have to write to Léonie.[3]

What is happening to poor Léonie ? Please tell my cousins that I think of them often. I prayed for the "favour" for Jeanne at the Sacré-Coeur at Montmartre. I think she will understand. And don't forget my kind Uncle and my dear Aunt.

Goodbye, my dear Godmother and my darling confidante,[4] pray for your little daughter.

Thérésita.

I hope you will realise that I have written this letter in the evening and very weary, otherwise I wouldn't dare to send it.

Kiss my dearest Mother for me.

XIV

To MARIE GUÉRIN

Venice, Thursday, 10th (evening).

My darling Marie,

At last the moment has come when I can write to you, we are not going out for a walk this evening, I thought it would be nicer just to be with you and relax.

Please tell my dearest Aunt that she cannot possibly imagine how her letter touched me; I should like to write and thank her, but I hope she will excuse her little girl and know without telling what my heart would say. You see, I have only a very short time, for Céline doesn't want me to stay up too late.

You can form no idea, my darling Sister, of all that we see; it is really marvellous; I had never imagined we would see such lovely things; there are so many that I must not even attempt to tell them; I shall do it better when I am in my darling Lisieux, which all the beauties of Italy cannot make me forget.

---

[1] "I cannot express what I experienced in her shrine," writes Thérèse in her *Histoire d'une âme* (ch. vi). "The graces she granted me were like those of my first Communion : I was filled with peace and happiness. . . . It was there that my Mother, the Virgin Mary, told me plainly that it was she who had smiled at me and cured me."
[2] Mother Marie de Gonzague.
[3] Then at the Visitation in Caen.
[4] Sister Agnes of Jesus.

Dearest little Sister, how are you, how are all of you ? Well, I hope. Are you as gay as when we left ?

O Marie, if you knew how often I think of you all ! In the beautiful churches we visit, I do not forget you. I have thought of you also in presence of the wonders of nature, amid those Swiss mountains that we crossed; one prays so well then; one feels that God is there !

How small I seem beside those gigantic mountains !

This land of Italy is very beautiful; we are now enjoying its lovely blue sky. This afternoon we visited the monuments of Venice in a gondola; it was enchanting.

It seems to me very odd to hear the language of Italy spoken all round us. It is very beautiful, very harmonious. The hotel people call me Signorella, it's the only word I understand, it means "little lady".

I should like to write often, but it is incredible how full our days are, one can write only very late at night.

I am much ashamed of my letter, I have written it very fast and the ideas don't follow properly; I see I haven't even begun to tell you what I wanted to . . . I have so many things to tell you, so many to ask you ! . . . If I followed my own wish, I should keep on for a very long time, but Céline wouldn't let me finish; she has even made me hurry over this.

Thank Uncle for the kind little message he sent us, we were all delighted. Give him a big kiss from me. Don't forget my little Jeanne. I often think of her.

Goodbye, dearest little Sister ! Think sometimes of your little Thérèse who thinks so often of you.

(You know, I haven't forgotten what you did for me one Sunday.)

Your little
Thérèse.

Papa is well, he sends you all many messages. Say good-day for me to Marie and Marcelline.[1]

Monday, 14th.

Dearest little Sister,

You see the date of my letter. I thought Céline had sent it: I thought you had received it long ago. . . . You will surely think I am forgetting you !

[1] Servants of the Guérins. See note to Letter XCIX.

O, little Sister ! how your letter pleased me. In it I found my little Marie again.

Thank you ! . . . Goodbye, I'm sending you this ancient letter, remember it should have gone four days ago.

XV

To her Carmelite Sisters,
MARIE OF THE SACRED HEART and AGNES OF JESUS
From Rome

14 November 1887.

My dearest Godmother,

You were definitely guilty of rash judgment in thinking I would read Pauline's letter before yours, it was just the other way round. . . .

Yes, Marie, you told me so much in this evening's short note. My heart understood all. . . . What pleasure that short message gave me !

When I read the letters you write me, I feel an indescribable sweetness filling my heart.

Papa is well. He is very pleased with your letters.

I asked at the monastery if I could not have some relics of St. Agnes; it is impossible.[1]

Your *Thérèsita* loves you with all her heart.

Pauline dearest,

I simply must thank you for all you do for me. Oh ! do pray to the good God for me; since Monseigneur is opposed,[2] the last resource I have left is to speak to the Pope; so that has to be possible; the Child Jesus must make all the preparations, so that His *little ball* need only roll where He wishes. If you knew how the Loretto letter pleased and consoled me ! O, Pauline, continue to protect me : I am so far from you ! I cannot tell you all I think, it's not possible.

Jesus' *little toy*,

Thérèsita.

[1] Ch. vi of *Histoire d'une âme* tells how Thérèse got her relic.
[2] To her entry.

28

XVI

To her Aunt, MME GUÉRIN

Monday, 14 November 1887 (evening)

My darling Aunt,

If you knew how happy your little girl would be if she could be with you to wish you a Happy Feast,[1] but, since this joy is denied her, at least she would like a little word from her heart to start off over the mountains to take her place. Poor little word, how inadequate it will be to tell my dearest Aunt all the affection I have for her !

How happy we were this morning to get your dear letters. O Aunt, if you knew how good I think you ! . . .

We have received all the letters from Carmel, not one has gone astray. I shall do as Pauline told me in her letter (Hôtel de Milan).[2]

I don't know how I shall get to speak to the Pope; truly, if God did not make the whole thing His affair, I don't know how I should manage, but I have such great confidence in Him that He cannot abandon me; I put everything in His hands.

We do not yet know the day of the audience. It seems that to speak to everyone, the Holy Father passes before the faithful, but I don't think he stops: in spite of all, I am fully resolved on speaking to him: before Pauline wrote to me, I was thinking of it, but said to myself that if God wanted me to talk to the Pope, He would let me know clearly. . . .

Dear Aunt, I wish I could let you read my heart, there you would see much better than in my letter all I wish you for your feast. I am far, very far, from you, darling Aunt, but it's incredible how close to you I seem tonight. I wish I could tell you how I love you and how often I think of you, but there are things that cannot be said, they can only be guessed.

Dear Aunt, please thank my dear little Marie for her charming and affectionate little letter, it gave me intense pleasure. Thank my little Jeanne also for thinking of her little sister.

[1] It was the custom in the family to treat the Feast of St. Elizabeth, 19 November, as that of Mme Guérin (whose names were Céline Elisa) and her mother Mme Elizabeth Fournet.

[2] The letter addressed to the Hotel di Milano, in Rome. Most of the Lisieux pilgrims were in this hotel and the Martins had expected to be there too; but they were sent to the Hotel del Sud, via Capo le Case.

Goodbye, little Aunt, please kiss my dear Uncle for me. I send you, dear Aunt, the best wishes I've ever addressed to you for it is when separated from those we love that we realise all the affection we have for them.

Your little girl,
Thérèse.

XVII

To MARIE GUÉRIN

Rome, Saturday, 19 November 1887.

My darling Marie,

It is tomorrow, Sunday, that I shall speak to the Pope. By the time you get my letter, the audience will be over. I find that the mail does not send letters fast enough, for when you get this letter, you will know nothing. . . . I am not going to write to Carmel this evening, but tomorrow I shall tell what the Holy Father has said to me. O my dearest little Sister, if you knew how *hard* my heart beats when I think of tomorrow !

If you knew all the thoughts in my mind this evening ! I wish I could tell them to you, but no, I find it impossible, I see Céline's pen racing over the paper, mine stops, it has too much to say. . . .

O my little Marie, I don't know what you're going to think of your poor Thérèse, but tonight she really can't describe her journey, she will leave the task to Céline.

I hope that you are well, and still playing lovely music. In Italy one hears plenty. You know it's the land of artists : you would be better able than I to judge of what is beautiful, for I am no artist : Jeanne would see very lovely paintings ; you see, little Sister, there is nothing for me in Rome ! Everything is for the artistic ! If only I could have a word from the Pope, I should ask no more of Rome.

Today is the feast of my dear Aunt, I keep thinking of her, I hope she has received our letters. Dearest little Sister, give a big kiss from me to all those I love. I often think of my darling Jeanne. Thank you for your letter, you don't know the pleasure it has given me, it was like a ray of joy.

Goodbye, little Sister, pray for me.

Your little
Thérèse.

XVIII

To SISTER AGNES OF JESUS

Account of the Audience with the Pope

20 November 1887.

My darling Pauline,

The good God is making me pass through many trials before bringing me into Carmel. I shall tell you how the visit to the Pope went. O Pauline, if you could have read my heart, you would have seen great confidence; I think I have done what God wanted of me, now nothing remains for me but to pray.

Monseigneur[1] was not there, the Abbé Révérony[2] took his place; to have an idea of the audience, you would have had to be there.

The Pope was sitting on a great chair; M. Révérony was near him; he watched the pilgrims kiss the Pope's foot and pass before him, and spoke a word about some of them. Imagine how my heart beat as I saw my turn arrive, but I didn't want to come back without speaking to the Pope. I spoke, but I did not get it all said, because M. Révérony did not give me time: he said immediately: "Most Holy Father, she is a child who wants to enter Carmel at fifteen, but its Superiors are considering the matter at the moment." I would have liked to be able to explain my case, but there was no way. The Holy Father said to me, simply: "If the good God wills, you will enter." Then I was made to pass on to another room. Pauline, I cannot tell you what I felt, it was like annihilation, I felt deserted, and then I am so far, so far. . . . I could weep as I write this letter, my heart is so full. Still God cannot be giving me trials beyond my strength. He gave me the courage to sustain this one. Oh! it is a very great trial, but, Pauline, I am the Child Jesus' *little ball*; if He likes to break His *toy*, He is free to; yes, I do indeed want what He wants.

I haven't written at all what I meant to: I cannot write things, I have to speak them; and anyhow you cannot read my letter for

---

[1] Mgr Germain, Bishop of Coutances, who led the pilgrimage.
[2] Vicar-general of Bayeux.

three days. Pauline, I have nothing but God, alone, alone. Goodbye, dearest Pauline, I cannot go on telling you, I'm afraid Papa may come and ask to read my letter, and that is impossible.[1]

Pray for your little girl

Thérésita.

I should very much like to write to my dearest Mother, but I cannot tonight, ask her in her kindness to pray for her poor Thérésita.

Give my dear Marie a big kiss from me, I have written this letter for her too, but I prefer to speak to one person only; I hope she will understand.

I haven't the time to read my letter over, it is quite certainly full of faults; excuse me.

Your little

Thérésita.

XIX

To MARIE GUÉRIN

On the way back to France[2]

Florence, Friday, 25 November 1887.

My darling Marie,

A few days more and we shall be together, I hope we shall be with you in a week.

I assure you I'm leaving all the wonders of Italy with pleasure; it's all very beautiful, but I cannot forget those I have left in Lisieux, it is as if a magnet were drawing me. So I shall be delighted to be back.

You don't know the joy your nice letter gave me ! I was very happy that you told me of my dear Aunt's feast. I was with you all in spirit. At that moment, there was no distance at all between Rome and Lisieux.

You were right to tell me of the present Aunt gave you, for I'd never possibly have guessed it; what a surprise !

I say nothing of my visit to the Sovereign Pontiff, I imagine

---

[1] She feared her letter would cause him pain.
[2] They arrived in Paris on the night of 1 December.

you have had news of it through Carmel; I have had many trials, but since it is God's will ! . . .

I hope, dearest little Sister, that you are going to keep on praying for me, I have great confidence in your prayers, I feel that the good God can refuse you nothing.

You are sorry that your letter was badly written: I must say, if you are as hard to please as that I shall not dare to go on sending mine, which are sheer scrawls. I think of you, of all of you, very often, so often that I dream of you at night. I wish I could be with you now.

It is a long time since we have had news from Carmel, I fear letters may have gone astray.

Yesterday, we were at Assisi; coming back from a church, I found myself all alone and the coaches gone, the only one left was M. Révérony's; he made me get in with him; he was very kind and would not let me pay my share. . . .

Thank Aunt for her letter, it touched me more than I can express. Give all those I love a kiss from me.

Goodbye, dearest little Sister, I hope to see you very soon.

Thérèse.

XX

To His Excellency, MONSEIGNEUR HUGONIN[1]
Bishop of Bayeux and Lisieux
*This letter, copied from a draft in St. Thérèse's
handwriting, was not sent to Monseigneur Hugonin.
M. Guérin thought it should be corrected. For the
letter as actually sent, see below (XX bis)*

16 December 1887.

Monseigneur,

I write to ask Your Excellency to be kind enough to give me the answer I have so long desired.

Monseigneur, I put all my hope in your paternal kindness, I believe it is through you that Jesus means to carry out His promise.

---

[1] He had been Bishop since 1867. He confirmed Thérèse on 14 June 1884. He received her and her father in audience, 31 October 1887, and granted her the authorisation solicited in this letter. As it turned out, the Saint could not profit by it, as the Prioress had postponed her entry till after Easter. He presided at her Clothing, 10 January 1889. He died in 1898, aged seventy-four, soon after having given permission to print *Histoire d'une âme.*

O Monseigneur, it is said that trials are a sign of vocation; so indeed they are; you know that the good God has not spared me trials, but I felt that I was suffering for Jesus, and not for a single instant did I cease to hope. The Child Jesus has made me so strongly feel that He wants me at Christmas, that I cannot resist the grace He is giving me. . . . It is true that I am very young, but, Monseigneur, since God calls me and Papa is in favour. . . .

I hope that the Abbé Révérony has been kind enough to speak of me to Your Excellency; on the journey to Rome he promised me that he would; I shall never forget his kindness to me.

O Monseigneur, Christmas is drawing near; but I await your reply with great confidence.

I shall never forget that it is to Your Excellency that I shall owe the accomplishment of God's will.

I beg you to bless your child, Monseigneur.

I am Your Excellency's most grateful little daughter,

Th. Martin.

XX bis

To His Excellency, MONSEIGNEUR HUGONIN
Bishop of Bayeux and Lisieux

*The letter as corrected by M. Guérin; it reached
the Bishop in this form*

16 December 1887.

Monseigneur,

I write humbly to remind Your Excellency of the request I have had the honour to address you for authorisation to enter Carmel.

I await with confidence, Monseigneur, this most signal favour from your fatherly kindness. I believe it is through you that Jesus means to carry out His promise.

It is said that trials are a sign of vocation; you know, Monseigneur, that the good God has not spared me trials, but I felt that I was suffering for Jesus, and not for a single instant did I cease to hope.

The Child Jesus has made me so strongly feel that He wants me at Christmas, that I cannot resist the impulsion of the gentle violence He is putting upon me.

It is true that I am very young, but, Monseigneur, since the good God calls me and Papa is in favour ! . . .

All the distractions of my journey to Rome, the beautiful things I admired, could not drive from my mind for one instant the ardent desire I have to be united with Jesus. May I hope that the frequent contacts I had during my journey with M. Révérony (which enabled me to appreciate his kindness) were for him an opportunity to judge of the genuineness of my vocation, and a motive to plead my cause with Your Excellency ?

Christmas is drawing near, Monseigneur, and I am waiting with great confidence, because I remember the promise Jesus made me in the depth of my heart.

I shall never forget that it is to Your Excellency that I shall owe the accomplishment of God's designs for His little servant. Nevertheless, I do not fear to affirm that, whatever pain a refusal would cause me, I should accept it with the most entire submission, as coming from God Himself.

I venture to call myself, Monseigneur,

Your Excellency's smallest daughter and most obedient servant,

Thérèse Martin.

XXI

To the ABBÉ RÉVÉRONY
Vicar General of Bayeux

Lisieux, 16 December 1887.

Monsieur le Vicaire Général,[1]

I have just written to Monseigneur. Papa and my Uncle gave me permission.

I continue to await with confidence the "Yes" of the Child Jesus.

Monsieur l'Abbé, it is now only a week to Christmas. But the closer the time comes, the more hopeful I am ; perhaps it is temerity, yet it does seem to me that it is Jesus speaking within me. All the distractions of the journey to Rome could not drive from my mind for one instant the ardent desire I have to be united with Jesus. Ah ! why should He call me so powerfully, if I am to be made to languish far from Him ?

---

[1] Only the rough draft of this letter has survived.

Monsieur l'Abbé, I hope you have pleaded my cause with Monseigneur, as you promised me. If Jesus has consoled me for my trials, it is through your agency; and if I enter Carmel, I know that I shall owe it to you: but I am not ungrateful, and all my life I shall remember it.

I ask you humbly, Monsieur le Vicaire Général, to be so good as to bless

Your very respectful and grateful little child

Thérèse Martin.

1888

SIXTEENTH YEAR

9 April : Thérèse enters the Carmel at Lisieux.
22 May : Her sister Marie of the Sacred Heart is professed.
End of June : M. Martin's health, which has been causing anxiety since
  May 1887, grows suddenly worse.

XXII

To SISTER MARIE OF THE SACRED HEART

Tuesday, 21 February 1888.

My dear Godmother,

I have not forgotten that tomorrow is your birthday. I have been thinking of it for a long time. I should be very happy if I could see you to congratulate you on being twenty-eight, but since it is Lent, one must, of course, make sacrifices.

Darling Marie, on Ash Wednesday Papa gave me a present. If I gave you a hundred, or even a thousand guesses, I'm sure you would never guess it. Imagine, dear Marie, in the bottom of Papa's big bag, the sweetest little curly lamb. That kind little Father told me as he gave it that he wanted me, before I entered Carmel, to have the pleasure of owning a little lamb. Everybody was happy, Céline was enchanted, that we had a day-old lamb; what moved me most was Papa's kindness in giving it—and then, a *lamb*, it's so symbolic ! it set me thinking of Pauline.[1] . . .

So far all is excellent, delightful; but wait till you hear the end. Already we were building castles in Spain with the lamb; we were looking forward to seeing it leaping about us in two or three days. But alas! the pretty little creature died in the afternoon; it had been too cold in the cart it was born in. Poor little thing! barely born, it suffered, and it died.

[1] Her name in religion was Agnes.

37

The little lamb was so darling, it looked so innocent, that Céline drew its portrait; then Papa dug a grave and the little lamb was laid in it: it looked as if it were asleep. I did not want it to be covered with earth; we threw snow on top of it, then all was over.

You don't know, dear Godmother, what food for reflection the death of the little creature gave me. Oh ! truly, on earth we must be attached to nothing, not even to the most innocent things, for they fail you just when you least expect it. Only the things that are eternal can content us.

Marie dear, I see that I've spent all the time talking of nothing but the lamb,-and now Léonie[1] wants me to leave her a little bit of my letter.

Tomorrow I shall offer my Communion for my dear Godmother. Embrace my dear Mother Prioress[2] for me, and Pauline, too; tell her I am well.

I have said many prayers for M. de Virville.[3] Goodbye then, dear Godmother. Your little girl who loves you much more than you can have any idea

Thérésita.

XXIII

To SISTER AGNES OF JESUS

March 1888.

My darling Pauline,

I should have liked to write to you immediately to thank you for your letter, but it wasn't possible, I had to wait till today.

O Pauline! It is surely true that a drop of gall must be mingled in every cup, but I find that trials help us to detach ourselves from the earth; they make us look higher than this world. Here below nothing can satisfy us; one cannot enjoy a moment's rest save in constant readiness to do the will of God.

My little boat has much trouble making harbour. For a long time I have seen the shore, but I keep on finding that I'm further from it; still Jesus is steering my little ship and I am sure that on the day of His choosing He will bring it happily to port. O Pauline ! When Jesus has set me down on the sacred shore of

[1] Léonie had come back to her home after trying her religious vocation at the Visitation Convent in Caen.
[2] Mother Marie de Gonzague.
[3] Mother Marie de Gonzague's brother.

Carmel, I want to give myself to Him wholly, I want to go on living for Him only. Oh! no, I shall not fear His blows, for even when the pain is bitterest, one always feels that it is a loving hand that strikes. I felt it in Rome, even at the moment when I thought the earth would give way beneath my feet.

I desire one thing only when I am in Carmel, and that is to suffer for Jesus always. Life passes so quickly that it is obviously better to have a most splendid crown and a little suffering, than an ordinary crown and no suffering. When I realise that one will love the good God better for all eternity, because of suffering borne with joy—! And, by suffering, one can save souls. Ah! Pauline, if, at the moment of my death, I could have a soul to offer to Jesus, how happy I should be! There would be a soul snatched from the fire of hell and blessing God for all eternity. . . .

My darling Sister, I see I've said nothing so far about your letter, though it gave me great pleasure. O Pauline, I am so happy that the good God has given me a sister like you; I hope you will pray for your little girl, that she may correspond to the graces Jesus in His goodness loves to give her; she has great need of your aid for she is only very slightly what she wants to be.

Tell my dear Godmother that I think of her often, we should like to know when she will make her Profession within the enclosure.[1]

Céline sends you a kiss; poor little sister, she has a sore foot, I fancy she won't be able to go to Vespers. Almost everybody is ill at Uncle's house. Truly life is not gay, it is very difficult to be attached to it.

Goodbye, my dearest Pauline, my *confidante*. Till Easter Monday,[2] above all till 9 April[3]. . . . Kiss our Mother[4] for me.

Thérèse.

[1] As distinct from the ceremonies of Clothing and Taking the Veil which are public ceremonies.
[2] The next visit to the Parlour.
[3] The day fixed for Thérèse's entry into Carmel.
[4] Mother Marie de Gonzague.

XXIV

To SISTER AGNES OF JESUS

Tuesday, 27 March 1888.

My darling Sister,

I have just sent Monseigneur the letter you advised me to write,[1] thank you so much. Oh! how lovely your painting[2] is. It is a marvel. . . .

I am sending you this brief word straight away to find out if you want me to mention to the Guérins that you painted the picture and that I have written. . . . I shall tell them too that it is for the 9th. As it is on Thursday that we are visiting Uncle, I should be glad if you would leave a little note at the turn,[3] Papa could pick it up tomorrow morning.

O Pauline, I want always to be a *little* grain of sand——— Your letter has done me so much good. If you knew how it has been in the depth of my heart. I should like to say many things about the little grain of sand, but I haven't time. . . . *I want to be a saint.*

The other day I saw words which greatly please me, I don't recall which saint said them—"I am not perfect but I want to become so".

What a jumble of words, forgive me, dearest little Sister, I am in a great rush.

Till the 9th of April.

Thérésita.

[1] This letter has not been preserved.
[2] Picture Sister Agnes had painted for Mgr Hugonin. It was attached to Thérèse's letter.
[3] A turning-cupboard, near the door of Carmel.

XXV

To M. MARTIN

*This letter is the first written by Thérèse from Carmel;
she entered on 9 April*[1]
J. M. J. T.[2]

Jesus †   Carmel, Sunday, 29 April 1888.

My darling Father,
   How good you are to your *little Queen* ! Hardly a day passes
but she receives some gift from her King !
   Thank you for them all, little Father. If you knew how the
little *Orphan of the Berezina*[3] loves you ! but no, you will discover
that only in Heaven. There indeed we shall see lovely *statues*
on lovely *cornices*, then we shall really be able to go into an ecstasy.[4]
And then, what a *guide* will be there, to show us the wonders of
Heaven ! I fancy many saints will have a *Byzantine* cross in their
halo. We shall see everything but *sarcophaguses*, for there will
be no tombs in Heaven.
   My darling Father, I see that it's getting late, I must leave you,
but first I send you a kiss with all my heart.
   Your little *fine Pearl*[5] kisses you. O Papa, if you knew how
precious your fine Pearl is. . . . The shining *Diamond*, the *Gypsy*[6]
kisses you also with all her heart.
   Goodbye and thank you, little Father, your *little Queen* "drawn
out" at last "from under the cart".[7]

Thérèse of the Child Jésus,
post. carm. ind.[8]

---

[1] *Histoire d'une âme*, ch. vii.
[2] Initials of Jesus, Mary, Joseph, Teresa of Avila. By a Carmelite custom Thérèse
headed her letters with them. She usually added the name of Jesus with a small
cross. The letters she wrote to her Carmelite Sisters are headed more simply, as
will appear later.
[3] Nickname given Thérèse by her father.
[4] Thérèse writes *Estatues, Cornichons* and *estasaison*, words invented by their
Italian guide. *Histoire d'une âme*, ch. vi.
[5] Nickname used by M. Martin for Pauline.
[6] These are Marie's nicknames.
[7] A local expression, used by M. Martin when his children's future was decided
upon. It means that one is now free to go on one's way.
[8] Abbreviations for "unworthy Carmelite postulant".

XXVI

To her sister, CÉLINE

J. M. J. T.

8 May 1888.

I send you, my little Céline, two little cloths to hemstitch on the machine. I know that you are terribly busy, but you cannot refuse your little Thérèse this favour. I think that two rows would be right, one has too small a hem, you might make the second row wider. I should like to have them by after dinner tomorrow at the latest, for Thursday is Ascension Day.

Four years ago today I made my First Communion, do you remember ? How many graces the good God has given me since.

My dearest Céline, there are moments when I ask myself can it be true that I am at Carmel ; sometimes I can't believe it ! Alas, what have I done for God that He should so fill me to over-flowing with His graces?

Tomorrow, I shall have been away from you for a month, but I feel as if we were not separated, no matter where we may be ! . . . If the ocean lay between us, we should still be united, for our desires are the same and our hearts beat as one. . . . I am sure you understand me. "After all, what does it matter, whether life is cheerful or sad, either way we shall come to the end of our journey here below." A day passed by a Carmelite without suffering is a day lost ; it is the same for you, because you are a Carmelite in your heart.

Kiss Léonie for me.

Your little
Thérèse of the Child Jesus.

XXVII

To M. [MARTIN

J. M. J. T.

Jesus †   Carmel, 8 May 1888.

My darling Father,
Your lovely little candles have given me so much pleasure that I must write a word to thank you. *Jesus' messenger*[1] is very kind to provide his little *Queen* with the means of making such beautiful illuminations.[2]

The *Queen* thinks continually of her King, and anyhow the *messenger of the good Jesus* comes so often bringing messages that it would be impossible to forget him.

My darling Father, honestly I almost think you will ruin yourself, but I shall surprise you by saying that I don't worry very much. After all you have so many resources, that you will never be short . . . even famine would not alarm you. Do you remember what you used to say ? "We shall eat this or that in the *famine* . . ." or again, "We'll do that when we are *ruined*." With such an outlook, no adversity can frighten you.

Thank you for the fish, dearest Father. Thank you, thank you, you give us so many things that I must simply make one thank-you cover everything, but all the same each separate thing gives its own pleasure.

Goodbye, my dearest *King*, your *Diamond* and your *Pearl* thank you as well as your *Queen*.

Thérèse of the Child Jesus.

[1] "Le facteur de Jésus," M. Martin himself.
[2] In honour of the Child Jesus, whose statue she was decorating.

XXVIII

To SISTER MARIE OF THE SACRED HEART
During her retreat before Profession[1]

May 1888.[2]

The Solitary of the Heart of Jesus has given a very sweet pleasure to her little girl, she has read her heart! . . . So Jesus *does* speak when one is in retreat ? I am so filled with fragrance by your little note[3] and by the most charming way in which it was presented to me,[4] that I simply must answer tonight, soon the bell will ring, it . . .[5]

I stopped my little note short, just at the moment when I would have liked to say so much. . . .

Life is full of sacrifices, truly ! But what happiness ! Given that our life is "a night spent in a bad inn",[6] isn't it better that it be spent in an inn that is *wholly* bad rather than one that is only *half* bad. . . .

If you knew how I LOVE you. When I meet you, you seem to me an angel . . . You, who are an EAGLE called to fly in the upper air and gaze upon the sun, pray for the little weak reed in the depths of the valley, the least puff of wind bends it over. Oh ! pray for her on the day of your Profession.

Pray that your little girl may remain always a little grain of sand, very obscure, hidden from all eyes, that Jesus alone may be able to see it. Let it become smaller and smaller, let it be reduced to a *nothing*. . . .

Forgive me all the hurt feelings I have caused you. If you knew

[1] On 22 May took place "The beautiful feast of the Profession of Marie"—the eldest daughter—"whom Thérèse the Benjamin had the privilege of crowning with roses on the day of her mystical espousal". After her own entry, the Saint's "letters" to her sisters in the convent are usually short notes scribbled in haste, with no thought of style, on scraps of paper (more often than not with writing on the other side), used envelopes, mourning cards, and in a very fine writing: all for the sake of poverty.

[2] This note was written between 12 May and 21 May, within which dates Sister Marie was on her retreat before Profession.

[3] The note was published in *Les Annales de sainte Thérèse de Lisieux*, v. xvi (1940), p. 211. It is signed : "A little solitary to whom Jesus said all this in a whisper."

[4] With a violet : Thérèse alludes to it again at the end of her letter.

[5] In the strictness of her obedience, the Saint stopped writing at the first sound of the bell—she had written " elle son " (meaning to write "elle sonne"—it is ringing) and the word remained unfinished. She did not think to add the two letters when she resumed writing.

[6] St. Teresa of Avila, *Way of Perfection*, ch. xlii.

44

how I repent of having told you that you were sending for me too often.[1] Oh ! after your Profession, I shall never cause you any trouble. Goodbye, forgive me.

Pray for your little girl.

I have had your little violet dried *so* carefully.

XXIX

To MARIE GUÉRIN

J. M. J. T.

Sunday, 13 May 1888.

My darling Sister,

If you have "Pott's disease[2] at the tip of your tongue", you certainly haven't it in your mind, or your finger-tips either. What a delightful letter ! If it was your object to make me laugh, you certainly succeeded ! You little wretch, fancy you with a sore foot. It's most extraordinary, for your feet are so tiny that surely there isn't room.

Fortunately it will soon be Pentecost, the Holy Ghost will certainly repair a serious omission He made on the day of your Confirmation. He gave you all His gifts, but unfortunately He forgot a gift that would be very useful to you. You guess which ? I'm going to beg Him during my retreat[3] that on Pentecost day you will be as *strong* as a little Samson. . . .

Last night I kept dreaming of Jeanne;[4] since I've been at Carmel, it's incredible how often I dream of her. Give her a big kiss from her little Thérèse.

What lovely weather! The sun is very bright, it is certainly more brilliant than the one that was drawn on your letter, which did not give much light to the earth. If today's sun were like that, I should be obliged to use the lamp[5] you gave me.

[1] Sister Marie had been charged to initiate Thérèse in the ways of Carmel. Thérèse, in fidelity to the rule of silence, told Sister Marie that she could prepare her books for the recitation of divine office without assistance.
[2] Marie Guérin had made a jest about this disease--there was some fear that she might be getting it.
[3] The whole community was in retreat every year from Ascension Day to Whit Sunday, in preparation for the coming of the Holy Spirit, following the example of the Blessed Virgin and the disciples in the Upper Room.
[4] Thérèse jestingly uses a local expression—"rêver dans".
[5] A mineral oil lamp Marie Guérin had got for her. Later, the mechanism wore out and Thérèse had to draw the wick up with a pin.

We shall meet before long, I hope, my dearest sister. Kiss my nice Uncle for me, tell him that we shall not forget his advice. A thousand kisses to my dearest Aunt.

(Your strength must be not in your hair, but in your foot.)

I kiss you warmly.

> Your little sister,
> *Thérèse of the Child Jesus.*

Our big sister is making her retreat before Profession, she has her white veil drawn down, she looks like an angel. She will pray for her little Marie.

XXX

To M. MARTIN[1]

J. M. J. T.

My dearest King,

I know that the *Diamond* has written you a brief word, so I'm not going to write at length, for your poor *Queen* would be eclipsed by the splendours of the *Diamond*.

Thank you, my darling Father, for all you have given me: the lovely spade and all the rest. . . .

Do you remember, Papa, when at Geneva we stalked M. X. and the others?[2] Oh! What fun we had! The remembrance of that lovely journey with my darling Father will stay with me always.

I kiss you, my dearest King.

Your *Queen of France and Navarre*,[3]

> *Thérèse of the Child Jesus,*
> *p. c. ind.*

---

[1] Letter undated, probably May or June 1888.
[2] A game invented by M. Martin, acting as if they were on the track of a thief.
[3] Another of M. Martin's jesting names for Thérèse.

XXXI

To CÉLINE

J. M. J. T.

Sunday, 17 June 1888.

(In haste)

My dear Céline,

Would you be very kind and send me as SOON as possible the material you bought to make yourself an apron. . . . Send me all the clean white ribbons you have, there is one I had round my head the day of my First Communion . . . All this is to represent St. Agnes. . . .[1]

Dearest little sister, isn't the good God good to you ! If you could see what a grace you received on Friday ![2] I think it must surely be the grace you were waiting for. You know you said to me : " But *I* have received no decisive grace. " I am convinced that this is the one. Now you must belong wholly to Jesus, more than ever He is wholly yours. He has already placed on your finger the mysterious ring of the espousals. He wills to be the one only Master of your soul.

Dearest sister, we are SISTERS indeed in all the force of the word. Goodbye, my heart reads yours from afar off.

> *Thérèse of the Child Jesus,*
> *p. c. ind.*

Kiss my incomparable King for me.

XXXII

To CÉLINE

J: M. J. T.

Jesus Alone †   Carmel, Monday, 23 July 1888.

Dearest Sister,

Your Thérèse understands your whole mind ; she has read even more of it than you wrote to her. I understood Sunday's

---

[1] For the feast of the Prioress.
[2] See *Histoire d'une famille* (p. 302), how Céline told her father of her desire to be a nun, and how nobly he received her confidence.

sadness, I have felt it all. . . . It seemed to me as I read that the same soul animated us, there is between our souls something so evident and so alike. Always we have been together, our joys, our griefs, have all been shared. Ah ! I know that this will continue at Carmel, never, no never, shall we be separated. You know, only the yellow lily[1] could have made some slight separation; I tell you so, because I am sure that a white lily will always be your lot, since you have chosen it, and it first chose you. Do you understand these lilies ?

I used sometimes to wonder why Jesus took me first. Now I understand. You see, your soul is a Lily-Immortelle,[2] Jesus can do whatever He will with it. It makes little difference whether it is in this place or that. Always it will be—an *Immortelle*. The wind cannot scatter the yellow of the Lily's stamens over its fragrant white calyx. Jesus made it so, He is free and none can ask Him why He gives His graces to one soul rather than another.

Alongside this lily, Jesus placed another, its faithful companion. They grew up together, but one was *Immortelle*, the other was not; and Jesus had to take His lily before the blossom began to open, that both lilies might be for Him. . . . One was frail, the other strong. Jesus took the weak, and left the other to grow to a lovelier flowering. . . . Jesus demands ALL of His two lilies, He wills that they keep nothing but their white garment. . . . ALL, has the *Immortelle* understood its little sister? . . .

Life is often a burden: such bitterness, but such sweetness ! Yes, life *costs*, it is *hard* beginning a day's work, the frail bud has known it and so has the beautiful lily. . . . If only one felt Jesus close at hand ! Oh ! One would do all for Him . . . but no, He seems a thousand leagues away, we are alone with ourselves; oh ! how wearisome is company when Jesus is not there !

But what can that loving Friend be doing ? Doesn't He see our anguish, the weight that is crushing us ? Where is He, why does He not come to console us, since we have no Friend but Him ?

Alas ! . . . He is not far off, He is here, close, looking at us, begging us to offer Him this grief, this agony[3]. . . . He needs it

---

[1] Symbol of marriage.

[2] Thérèse unites the symbol of virginal purity, the lily, with the unfading quality of the immortelle.

[3] This allusion is to M. Martin's illness. From 1 May 1887 he had had a series of paralytic strokes; in the June just past he had had one much worse (see *Histoire d'une famille*, pp. 312 ff.).

for souls, for our soul: He means to give us so splendid a reward !
His ambitions for us are so great.

But how will He say "My turn now !"[1] if we haven't had our
turn, if we haven't given Him a thing? Alas ! it is great pain
to Him thus to fill our cup with sorrows, but He knows that it is
the only way to prepare us "to know Him as He knows Himself,
to become gods".[2] Oh ! What a destiny ! How great a thing is
our soul! Let us lift ourselves above all that passes, not stay
close to earth; higher, the air is pure ! Jesus is hidden, but one
senses Him. . . . Shedding our tears, we dry His, and the Blessed
Virgin smiles; poor Mother ! She has had so much trouble on
our account ! It is just that we should console her a little by
weeping and suffering with her.

This morning I read a passage in the Gospel where it is said:
"I am come not to bring peace but a sword."[3] All that remains for
us then is to fight. When we have not the strength, it is then that
Jesus fights for us. Together let us put the axe to the root of the
tree. . . .[4]

What a poor muddler is Thérèse—such a letter, such a fuss !
Oh, if I had been able to say all I think, how long it would have
taken Céline to read. . . .

Jesus is good to have brought us to such a Mother[5] as we have !
she is a treasure ! little Sister, if you had seen her bringing me your
letter, at six this morning . . . I was deeply touched.

Jesus asks of you ALL, ALL, ALL, as He does of the greatest
saints. . . .

Your poor little sister,

Thérèse of the Child Jesus,

p. c. ind.

[1] Abbé C. Arminjon, *Fin du monde Présent et mystères de la vie future*, p. 290.
The Saint had deeply enjoyed this work, especially the passage from which she
quotes here (cf. *Histoire d'une âme*, ch. v).
[2] 1 Cor. xiii. 12; Ps. lxxxi. 6; cf. Arminjon, loc. cit.
[3] Matt. x. 34.
[4] Matt. iii. 10; Luke iii. 9.
[5] Mother Marie de Gonzague.

XXXIII

To M. MARTIN

J. M. J. T.

Carmel, 31 July 1888.

My dearest King,

If you knew the pleasure your *monster* of a carp gave us: dinner was put back half an hour. It was Marie of the Sacred Heart who made the sauce, it was delicious, one might have been in some great hotel.[1] It was even better than the rich cookery of Italy, and that is saying a lot, for what feasts we had ! . . . and what company, do you remember, little Father ? . . . But that isn't always what gives appetite, at least to me: I have never eaten so much as since I have been in Carmel. I feel I am exactly where I belong: if Mlle Pauline[2] were here, she would say that "I have found my way".

When I remember that in a week I shall have been four months in Carmel, I can't get over it ! I feel as if I had always been here, and in another way I feel as if I had only entered yesterday. How everything passes ! . . . It's very true what you so often said to us : "Vanity of vanities, all is but vanity, vanity of the life that passes."[3] The longer I live, the truer I find it that all is vanity upon earth, and also, my darling Father, the longer I live, the more I love you. I don't know how it can be, but it is the truth; I wonder what it will be by the end of my life . . . !

When I think of you, little Father, I naturally think of the good God, for it seems to me impossible to find anyone on earth holier than you. Yes, you are quite certainly as much of a saint as St. Louis himself, and I feel the need to keep telling you that I love you, as if you didn't know it already. Oh ! how proud I am to be your *Queen*—I hope always to deserve the title. Jesus, the King of Heaven, in taking me for Himself, has not taken me from my saintly *King* in this world.

Oh, no ! always, if my dearest little Father is willing and finds me not too unworthy, I shall continue to be "*Papa's Queen*" !

[1] Thérèse's phrase is "cela sentait la cuisine du monde".
[2] Mlle Pauline Romet, of Alençon, Pauline's godmother.
[3] Eccles. i. 2.

Yes, I shall always remain your little *Queen* and I shall try to be your glory by becoming a great saint.

Your *Diamond* cannot write to you, for she is doing the washing, but that does not prevent her thinking of you, my dearest little Father; she kisses you with all her heart. You know your *Big One's* heart is not small.

The *fine Pearl* sends you a great big kiss.

Goodbye for the present, my dearest Father.

Your little *Queen,*
Thérèse of the Child Jesus,
p. c. ind.

XXXIV

To M. GUÉRIN

On the occasion of the illness of one of his relations

J. M. J. T.

Jesus †   Carmel, 22 August 1888.

My dear Uncle,

We have just had a letter from Aunt, in which she tells us all your bad news. Though not with you, your little niece shares in your sorrow, she would like to be with her kind Uncle to console him, but alas! what could she do? No, it is better for her to be at Carmel; there at least she can pray as much as she will, to Him who alone can give consolation, that He may pour an abundance of it into her dear Uncle's heart.

The state of poor Monsieur David[1] grieves us greatly; I realize, my dear Uncle, how you must be suffering, for there is nothing so painful as to watch those we love suffer. Still I thank God with all my heart for the great grace He has in His goodness granted to that beautiful soul. In what a disposition he appears before God; it is truly admirable. All that our dear Aunt has told us has touched me profoundly.

It was quite impossible, Uncle, for God not to grant you this consolation, seeing all you do for His glory! Ah! I feel that

[1] Mme Guérin's cousin. He was mortally ill. M. Guérin brought him back to God on his deathbed.

51

the crown laid up for you is very beautiful! It cannot be otherwise, since your whole life is one perpetual cross, and God acts thus only with great saints. What a happiness to think that in Heaven we shall be united, never again to part! Without that hope, life truly would not be bearable. . . .

Dear Uncle, I don't know what you are going to think of your poor little niece, she lets her pen run on without taking much account of what she says; her heart, if it could write, would say quite other things, but it is obliged to rely upon this cold pen, which cannot express what the heart feels. I must leave it to my good Angel, I think a heavenly messenger would execute my commission aright, I send him to my dear Uncle to pour into his heart as much consolation as our soul can contain in this valley of exile. . . .

Goodbye, dear Uncle, please remember me to Madame Fournet, I do indeed share in her sorrow; to you, Uncle, I send all the tenderness my heart holds and I shall continue to pray without ceasing for poor Monsieur David.

Your little niece, who wishes she could lighten your trouble a little,

Thérèse of the Child Jesus.

XXXV

To MME GUÉRIN

J. M. J. T.

Jesus †   Carmel, 23 August 1888, 6 o'cl.

My dear Aunt,

Yesterday evening we learned of the death of poor M. David. Though we were expecting every moment to hear the sad news, I was much moved on learning the actual fact; I pray that God may take that holy soul into His Paradise; perhaps it is there already, for with dispositions so perfect, one can go straight to Heaven.

I ask the good God to pour consolation into your heart, dear Aunt. Already He has been so very good, to grant all the prayers you had offered to win Him the soul of your dear relative. If, from the depths of her solitude, your little girl could hope that she had had some small part in it, she would be very happy.

I find, dear Aunt, that in these moments of great grief, one feels the need to look up to Heaven; there they are not weeping, but all are joyful because Our Lord has one more among His elect, a new sun brightens the forecourt of Heaven with its rays, all are in the rapture of divine ecstasy, they marvel that we can give the name of death to the commencement of life. To them, we are in a narrow tomb, whereas their souls can fly out to the far bounds of "ethereal shores, horizons infinite".[1] Dearest Aunt, when we look upon the death of the just man, we cannot but envy his lot. For him the time of exile is no more, there is now only God, nothing but God.

O Aunt ! what things your little girl could say to you, her heart has such deep thoughts; this morning, she is all lost in the thought of the death of the saints; but I haven't time to finish my little scrawl, I must stop, for the bell has just warned me that it is time to finish. I offer this small sacrifice to Jesus that He may deign to console you with His tender hand.

Your little girl, who is with you, and her dear little sisters,[2] in heart.

Thérèse of the Child Jesus,
p. c. ind.

XXXVI

To M. MARTIN

J. M. J. T.

Jesus †   Carmel, 25 August 1888.

My darling Father,
    The day has at last arrived on which your Queen can wish you from Carmel a happy feast with all the honours, because she is at Carmel along with your jewels, the *Diamond* and the fine *Pearl*.
    Poor *little Queen*, she really should withdraw and yield place to the splendid gems of the King, but truly she cannot resign herself to that, for she, too, has her title, she can show it to whoever wishes

---

[1] From *Une Voix de Prison*, by Lamennais. Thérèse had heard it from her mother.
[2] Her cousins, Jeanne and Marie Guérin.

to see it, it is signed with her *King's* own hand : *Queen of France and of Navarre.* She has nothing else, but it seems to me that this is sufficient to secure her admission into his presence ; in any event, no one ventures to contest her right, even abroad it is recognised. In Italy, in Rome, they knew the *Queen* was there !

My dearest *King*, your little *Queen* wishes she had magnificent gifts to offer you, but she has nothing ; besides, she would be too hard to please. For her *King*, all the palaces of the Vatican crammed with presents would not be fine enough, she dreams of something more kingly, he must have treasures immeasurable, limitless horizons. What she would like to give her *King* is not found upon earth, Jesus alone possesses it, so she is going to pray to Him to fill her *King* to overflowing with heavenly joys. For a father who is not of this world, nothing worldly could be enough.

You see, darling Father, that while I seem to be giving you nothing, I am giving you a magnificent present ; if it does not charm your eyes, at least your heart will realise it, for I hope that God will grant my prayer.

Yet, dearest little Father, though I say that it is only your heart that I want to please, I am giving you a little painting made by your *Queen.* I hope that, in spite of my want of talent, it will give you pleasure, the *fine Pearl* was kind enough to help me with her artistic advice and she drew the charming design, but she was firm that I should colour it myself. It is of no great merit, but my powerlessness is so great and my *King* so indulgent that I hope I may cause him a little pleasure by giving him this little picture.

Goodbye for now, darling Father, if the *Queen* is not with you today, she is, really, in mind and heart ; she wishes you the best feast you've ever had in all your life and kisses you with all her heart.

Your *little Queen*,
Thérèse of the Child Jesus,
p. c. ind.

SIXTEENTH YEAR

XXXVII

To MARIE GUÉRIN

J. M. J. T.

Jesus †   Thursday, September 1888.

My dearest little Sister,
    I had begun to write to you Tuesday evening, a while ago I meant to continue that letter, but the things I said are not the ones I want to say today, so I decided to begin all over.
    Thank you for your delightful letter; if Mme de Sévigné had written to me, she would certainly not have given me so much pleasure.
    If my little cousin often thinks of me, I am often with her in spirit too, I feel the need to hear her talked of often and still more to talk of her myself. I satisfy my need by talking about my dearest little sister to God, I never have the least fear that He may find me talking of her at too great length, for I am sure that my little Marie is deep in His Heart.
    What a lot of things to say, but time passes rapidly, I see it slipping away from me at frightening speed, it is late, I am writing by the light of your dear little lamp,[1] you observe that my writing shows how rushed I am. What consoles me for having such ugly writing is to remember that in Heaven we shall no longer need this means of conveying our thoughts, which is certainly lucky for me.
    Yesterday I had visitors. I give you a hundred guesses . . . a fine society lady, her dear husband, a grown-up young lady of sixteen, a gentleman of fourteen. . . . Have you guessed ? Mme X. She was accompanied by her niece and nephew. Society, if you like. If you had seen her in the parlour—she was almost singing "Que mon coeur, que mon coeur a de peine",[2] at seeing me behind the grille.
    It's time for my nonsense to stop, yet I've said nothing of any interest to my darling cousin, but what can you expect from a person like me who writes without even noticing that her paper is filling up with trivialities when she has so many serious things to say. Forgive me. . . .

[1] See note to Letter XXIX.
[2] From a song they used to sing at Les Buissonnets.

55

I close, darling Marie, by asking you a favour: it would be very kind if you could, while walking in your beautiful grounds,[1] find some dry mosses, bark of trees, etc. They would do to make little things like cribs, for example. If it's a nuisance, don't bother to send them; it is only if you find such things on your walks.

I am much concerned that my dear Aunt is ill, I think of her often and pray continually for her speedy cure. Give her a great *big* kiss from her little girl, not enough to hurt her of course!

Also give kisses from me to my dear little Jeanne, Céline and Hélène Maudelonde from me. I have no pity for them, they not being ill, so please kiss them as hard as you can.

I see, darling Marie, that all my kisses are not done with, I am not at the end after all, for I've given none to you, who are charged to distribute the whole lot, so I beg all the dear people to whom you are giving them to pay you back to the best of their power. I doubt if my wishes will be carried out, so I embrace you with all my heart, but very hard, so hard that if you had a gland it would be pierced, like before the journey to Rome.

Your little sister,

Thérèse of the Child Jesus.

XXXVIII

To M. MARTIN

J. M. J. T.

Carmel, 30 September 1888.

My dearest King,

Your *little Queen* is loaded down with the weight and magnificence of her gifts, it is plain that they are the gifts of a King to his *Queen.*

First there is the *point d'Alençon,*[2] which I've seen arrive, it is indeed absolutely *regal.* I don't know how to thank you for such lovely presents—where is the time when your *little Queen* jumped for joy at a gift worth a halfpenny from her King! Now her heart would still be happy, but her *King's* heart feels the need to

---

[1] At La Musse, a property left by M. David to the Guérin and Maudelonde families.

[2] Lace for the ceremony of Clothing (see *Histoire d'une âme,* ch. vii).

give more. That is why he offers his *Queen* lace worthy of *The Queen of France and Navarre.*

It is true, darling Father, that even if your *Queen* is not worthy of such rich things, they are not too beautiful for God's *Spouse* to whom you have given them; that is why I shall be happy to wear them, otherwise truly I should not dare, for I am still only the *orphan of the Berezina*, not till the day of my Clothing will I deserve my title of *Queen.*

I have one other pleasant mission to discharge—to thank you, in my name as *Queen*, and in the name of the *Diamond* and the *Fine Pearl*, for an avalanche of pears, onions, plums, apples, pouring out of the turn as from a horn of plenty. Where did it all come from?—an old fellow says it was a gentleman who lived by the Jardin de l'Etoile. It could be no one but you. So, darling Father, what you provided has been warmly accepted, no one had to be asked twice to give it a good reception. A funny thing—it had less trouble to enter than your *Queen*, who had to go to Rome to get the door opened for her. . . .

The enormous onions gladdened my heart, they make me think of the ones in Egypt, we shall not, like the Israelites, have to sigh after them. I thought also of the onions of Lyons which cost 50 centimes and are so big.

Well, my *King*, I fear your *Queen* will weary you with her babble, but she is so pleased that she simply has to tell you. She thanks you for everything, and embraces you with all her heart.

Thérèse of the Child Jesus,
p. c. ind.

XXXIX

To M. MARTIN

J. M. J. T.

Jesus †   Carmel, October 1888.

My dearest Father,

I should like to write you a long letter, but I am in retreat, so it is impossible. You don't know how much your little Thérèse loves you ! . . .

As I was under the necessity of sending a letter[1] to the King's daughter, Princess Léonie, I thought I could not deliver my missive to her save through the King himself, so it is for this reason that I address myself to *His Excellency the King of France and Navarre.* If his dignity is not apparent to the eyes of men, I at least know full well that in Heaven it will be plain to the eyes of God. Then *the least of the elect will be like the chief of a most strong nation*[2] and, my *King* . . . oh ! what a place will be his !

Thérèse of the Child Jesus.

XL

To CÉLINE

For her feast

J. M. J. T.

Jesus †   Carmel, 20 October 1888.

My dearest Céline,

As tomorrow is your feast day,[3] oh ! how I should like to be the first to wish you a happy feast ; if that is not possible at least I can do so in my heart. For your feast, what would you like me to give you ? If I followed my own wish, I should ask Jesus to send me all the sorrows and troubles of my dearest Céline's life, but you see I don't, for I should be afraid that Jesus might tell me I'm selfish : I should be wanting Him to give me all the best things, leaving none for the small spouse He loves so dearly. It is to prove her His love that He makes her feel the *separation*, so I cannot ask that of Jesus. And then, He is so rich, so rich, that He has plenty to enrich us both. . . .

When one remembers that if the *good* God gave us the entire universe, with all its treasures, it would not be comparable to the *slightest* suffering ! What a grace, when in the morning we feel no courage or strength for the practice of virtue—then is the moment to put *the axe to the root of the tree.*[4] Instead of wasting time

---

[1] This letter has been lost.

[2] Suggested by Isa. lx. 22, quoted *Imitation of Christ*, bk. iii, ch. lviii, Lamennais's translation.

[3] 21 October, St. Céline, Virgin, Patron of Meaux, a companion of St. Geneviève (*not* St. Célinie, mother of St. Rémy, mentioned in the Roman Martyrology on the same day). From earliest childhood Céline and Thérèse had given each other presents on their feast-days.

[4] Matt. iii. 10 ; Luke iii. 9.

picking up little bits of straw, one can dig for diamonds. What profit at the end of the day ! . . . It is true that now and then we feel, for some instants together, that our treasures are not worth the trouble of amassing; that is the difficult moment, one is tempted to drop the whole thing; but in an act of love, even *not felt*, all is restored, and more. Jesus smiles, He aids us without seeming to, and the tears the wicked make Him shed are dried by our poor weak little love. Love can do all; "the most impossible things do not seem difficult to it".[1] "Jesus regards not so much the greatness of acts", nor even their difficulty, "but the love which leads us to do them".[2]

I found, a while back, a very beautiful passage. Here it is, I think it will give you pleasure: "Resignation is still distinct from the will of God, there is the same difference as between union and unity; in union, we are still two, in unity we are but one."[3] Oh ! yes, let us be but one with Jesus. Let us see all that passes as naught. Our thoughts should be of Heaven, since there Jesus dwells. It struck me the other day that we must not become attached to what surrounds us, since we might easily be in a different place from where we are : our affections and desires would not be the same . . . I can't explain my thought to you, I am too stupid for that, but when I see you I'll tell it to you.

Why have I told you all these things that you know *much better* than I ? Forgive me. I felt I needed once more to have a conversation with you like those we used to have; but the time has not really passed, we are still just the SAME SOUL and our thoughts are still the *same* as they were at the windows of the top room.[4]

I rejoice to think of the day when we shall wish you a happy feast in the heavenly city.

Your little sister,
Thérèse of the Child Jesus.

Oh ! yes, it is very sad to think that Père Pichon[5] is off to Canada, but Jesus is with us still.

[1] Cf. *Imitation of Christ*, bk. iii, ch. v, 4.
[2] St. Teresa, *Interior Castle*, bk. vii, ch. iv.
[3] Mme Swetchine.
[4] See *Histoire d'une âme*, ch. v.
[5] Ibid., ch. vii.

XLI

To M. MARTIN

Who has just had another paralytic stroke[1]

J. M. J. T.

15 November 1888.

My dearest King,

How good the good God is to have cured you ! I assure you your *little Queen* was terribly worried, and with every reason, for you have been very ill. All Carmel was praying, so God at last heard their sighs and has given me back my King !

But you know, dearest little Father, now that the good God has done all that we desired, it is your turn to make us all happy, so the *orphan of the Berezina* asks you to take as much care of yourself as you should, you know that *Intrepid No.* 2[2] is very skilful at it. . . . So, please, pay attention to her right (conferred by the King himself) to take all necessary care of you.

Your *little Queen* is always with you in heart, how could she forget her most kind *King* ? And then it seems to me that affection is still greater, if possible, when one has suffered so ! . . .

Goodbye, dearest *King*, and *don't forget*, take care of yourself to please your *Queen*.

Thérèse of the Child Jesus,
p. c. ind.

XLII

To MME GUÉRIN

For her feast

J. M. J. T.

18 November 1888.

My dear Aunt,

Permit your little girl, too, to offer you her poor little good wishes. They will seem to you a very small thing, compared with

[1] Twelve days earlier, at Le Havre, where he had gone with Père Pichon, who was on his way to Canada (see *Histoire d'une famille*, p. 314).
[2] Nickname for Céline. Marie was *Intrepid No.* 1.

those you have already received, but no matter, her heart simply must tell her dearest Aunt how much she loves her.

This morning, at Communion, I prayed hard to Jesus to fill you to the full with His joys. . . . Alas, joys are not what He has been sending us for some time, it is the cross, only the cross,[1] that He gives us to rest upon. . . . Oh ! my dearest Aunt, if it were only I that must suffer, I should not mind, but I know the great part you take in our trial, I should like to take every sorrow from you for your feast, to take all your burdens to myself. That is what a moment ago I was asking of Him whose Heart was beating in unison with mine. I felt then that suffering was the very best gift He had to give us, that He gave it only to His *chosen* friends ; this answer made clear to me that my prayer was not granted, for I saw that Jesus loved my dear Aunt too much to take away her cross! . . .

I am indeed touched, Aunt, at the lovely cake you have sent us. Instead of our wishing you a Happy Feast, you are doing it to us, really it is too much ! I have nothing to give my dearest Aunt but a poor little picture,[2] but I hope in her kindness she will see only her little girl's intention.

Goodbye, dearest Aunt, it seems to me that while the trial lasts, you are still closer to your little girl.

Thérèse of the Child Jesus,
post. carm. ind.

Sister Marie of the Sacred Heart's letter was finished when we received the cake. She asks me to thank you very much.

XLIII

To M. MARTIN

J. M. J. T.

Carmel, 25 November 1888.

My darling Father,

Your *Queen* thinks of you continually and prays for you all day. I am very happy in the sweetness of Carmel and have no further desire upon earth save to see my little Father completely

[1] M. Martin's illness.
[2] Mother Marie de Gonzague has added the following lines, unsigned, to Thérèse's letter : "Sister Agnes has not touched this picture, the little one has done it all herself."

cured, but I know why the good God sends us this trial, it is that we may gain Heaven and its beauty. He knows that our dearest Father is all that we love upon earth, but He knows too that one must suffer to gain eternal life and that is why He tries us in all that is dearest to us.

I feel also that the good God means to give my *King* a magnificent throne in the Kingdom of Heaven, so beautiful and raised so high above all human thoughts that one can say with St. Paul: "Eye hath not seen nor ear heard nor hath it entered into the heart of man what God hath prepared for those He loves."[1]

Is there anyone on earth that God loves more than my darling Father? . . . Truly I cannot believe it. Today, at least, He is giving us the proof that I am not wrong since God always tests those He loves. I am quite sure that God makes people suffer so on earth in order that Heaven may seem better to His elect. He says that at the last day He will wipe away all tears from their eyes,[2] and surely the more tears to wipe away, the greater the consolation.

Goodbye, my dearest *King*, your *Queen* rejoices to think of the day when she will reign with you in the beautiful and only true kingdom of Heaven.

Thérèse of the Child Jesus,
post. carm. ind.

XLIV

To MARIE GUÉRIN[3]

J. M. J. T.

I cannot resist my desire to thank you for your letter, it gave me great pleasure. You cannot imagine how often I think of you. My little Marie is always coming into my mind; in any case, even if I wanted to forget my darling cousins, I couldn't, my pretty little lamp[4] lights up so well !

Thérèse is asking you for another favour: Sister Agnes says I need a pair of fur-lined slippers[5] like those I often saw you

---

[1] 1 Cor. ii. 9. St. Paul writes "those who love Him" (ceux qui l'aiment), where Thérèse has "those He loves" (ceux qu'il aime).

[2] Apoc. xxi. 4.

[3] This undated letter is of October or November 1888.

[4] See note to Letter XXIX.

[5] Thérèse did not wear them long: after her Clothing, 10 January next, she wore only the alpargates (hemp sandals) prescribed by the Constitutions of Carmel.

wearing in winter. If my Aunt would be kind enough to buy them for me, I should be very pleased. Jeanne could try them on, she has exactly the same foot as I.

I have a good deal to tell you, but they're waiting for this little note. I must leave you till Thursday. Meanwhile I send a big kiss to my dearest Aunt, my kind Uncle and my dear little Jeanne. For my Loulou,[1] I cannot tell her how much I love her, my heart is too full of affection for her.

If I could have the slippers this afternoon, I should be very glad. You cannot imagine how perfectly one is looked after at Carmel: I have to be eating, and warming my feet, all the time.[2]

Till Thursday, my darling. I am *very, very* happy, to the limit of my desires.

Thérèse of the Child Jesus.

I often think of my dear Marcelline.[3]

XLV

To M. MARTIN[4]

J. M. J. T.

The *messenger of the Child Jesus* is very good, I send him all my tenderness and my kisses. I shall be happy to take the wine[5] he gives me, regarding it as coming from the Child Jesus' cellar.

My darling Father, you are indeed *Jesus' messenger*, I know. Oh ! thank you, how good you are to me. Yes, I shall remain ever your *little Queen* and I shall try to bring you glory by becoming a great saint.

THÉRÈSE OF THE CHILD JESUS, the *brilliant Diamond* and the *little fine Pearl*, send you many kisses.

[1] Nickname for Marie Guérin.
[2] A jest not to be taken literally ! Thérèse knew her cousin would understand. Because she was so very young, she was the object, while a postulant, of special solicitude on the part of the Prioress and the Mistress of Novices. But it is worth noting that the more abundant, though still frugal, nourishment allowed her did not always agree with her stomach (cf. *Histoire d'une âme*) and that she could warm her feet only at the small fire that burned, in winter-time, in the community recreation-room.
[3] Servant of the Guérin family. See Letter XCIX.
[4] Undated: it belongs to November or December 1888.
[5] A tonic wine prescribed for Thérèse.

They have just been in to show me the birds.[1] Oh ! Father darling, how good you are. There is a bird for the *Diamond*, one for the *Fine Pearl*, and one for *Papa's little Queen* ! She will try to do her best to be a little like her *King*.

XLVI

To MOTHER SAINT-PLACIDE[2]

J. M. J. T.

Jesus †   Carmel, December 1888.[3]

My dear Mistress,

I am much touched by your kind attention. It gave me great pleasure to get the dear circular of the Children of Mary. Certainly I shall not fail to be present in heart at this beautiful feast. For was it not in that hallowed chapel that the Blessed Virgin in her goodness adopted me as her child, on the lovely day of my First Communion and of my reception into the Congregation of Children of Mary ?[4]

Never could I forget, dear Mistress, how good you were to me at those great epochs in my life, and I cannot doubt that the signal grace of my religious vocation took its origin on that happy day when, surrounded by my good mistresses, I made the consecration of myself to Mary at the foot of her altar, choosing her specially for my mother, when I had received Jesus for the first time that morning. I like to think that she did not consider my unworthiness, but that in her great kindness she chose to consider the virtue of the dear mistresses who had with so much care prepared my heart to receive her divine Son. I like to think that this is the reason why she chose to have me become still more perfectly her child, by giving me the grace to lead me to Carmel.

[1] Moorhens, which did not break the community's abstinence.
[2] In charge of the boarding school of the Benedictine Convent in Lisieux. She died 10 December 1909.
[3] Early in the month. This letter, and other objects connected with Thérèse kept by the Benedictine Nuns, disappeared in the bombardment which destroyed their convent in June 1944.
[4] The Abbey of Benedictine Nuns at Lisieux was preparing to celebrate, on 13 December 1888, the twenty-fifth anniversary of the Foundation of the Association of Children of Mary among its pupils. Thérèse, like all ex-pupils who had been members, received a card of invitation.

I believe, my dear Mistress, that you know about the illness of my beloved Father. For some days I was afraid that the good God might take him from my tenderness; but Jesus has deigned to grant me the favour of restoring him for the moment of my Clothing.

Every day I kept meaning to write to you, to inform you of my reception in Chapter,[1] but, not knowing the time Monseigneur would fix upon,[2] I went on waiting.

I hope, my dear Mistress, that you have not taken my delay for indifference. Oh ! no, my heart is still the same, and I think that, since my entering Carmel, it has become still tenderer and more loving. So I often think of all my good mistresses, and I love to name them one by one to Jesus during the blest hours I pass at His feet. I am venturing to ask you, my dear Mistress, if you will kindly be my spokesman to them, and recall me to their religious memory, in particular to that of Mother Prioress, for whom I retain the most filial and grateful affection. Please also remember me to my happy companions, whose little sister in Mary I still remain.

Goodbye, my dear Mistress. I hope you will not forget in your prayers one who is and will always be your grateful child,

Sister Thérèse of the Child Jesus,
post. carm. ind.

XLVII

To MME GUÉRIN

J. M. J. T.

Jesus †   28 December 1888.

My darling Aunt,

I was so very sorry, last night, I did not know my sisters were going to write to you, I slept like a lazy girl.[3] This morning I have only a little time . . .

Dear Aunt, I should like to be the first to wish you a happy new year for 1889. When I remember, dearest Aunt, that your little girl will soon be in Carmel nine months,[4] I can't get over it, it seems to me that only yesterday I was still with you. How quickly

[1] It was the Conventual Chapter that decided who should be admitted to Clothing.
[2] Mgr Hugonin was to preside at the ceremony.
[3] French Carmelites are allowed to rest in the hour of free time before Matins.
[4] For the delay in Thérèse's Clothing, see note to Letter L.

life passes, already I am sixteen years on earth, oh! soon, we shall all
be together in Heaven. I greatly love this phrase from the Psalms :
"A thousand years in the sight of the Lord are as yesterday which
is past."[1] What speed, oh ! I mean to work hard while it is still
the daylight of life, for then comes the night when I shall be able
to do nothing.[2] Pray for your little daughter, dear Aunt, that she
may not abuse the graces that God lavishes on her in the fertile
valley of Carmel.

I can't help laughing when I look at this letter, it isn't really a
new year's letter, but, darling Aunt, with you I am like a child who
lets her heart run on without thinking out what it is going to say!

If you knew, Aunt dearest, all I shall ask for you and my dear
Uncle on New Year's Day ! . . . No, you do not know it, and I
shan't try to tell you, it would bore you for it would be too long.
And my little cousins (my dearest little sisters), how I shall pray
for them !

Goodbye, dear Aunt, please tell Uncle how much I love him;
I should have written to him at the same time as you, dearest Aunt,
but I am too stupid to talk to two people at the same time. I beg
him to forgive me and I send you both the best kiss from your
little Benjamin.

Thérèse of the Child Jesus,
post. carm. ind.

I have just remembered that I haven't even thanked my dear
Aunt for the wreath she is so kindly giving me for my Clothing.
Oh ! if she could know how grateful I am, and also how dear the
remembrance of it will be to the heart of her little girl !

XLVIII

To M. MARTIN

J. M. J. T.

Jesus †   30 December 1888.

My dearest King,

What a happiness to be able this year to send you my new year
wishes from the *Kingdom* of Carmel. Never has your *little Queen*

[1] Ps. lxxxix. 4.   [2] John ix. 4.

been able to offer her affection with more joy, she feels so close to her King, so close that nothing can possibly separate her from him.

The Kings of the earth are most happy when they succeed in contracting noble alliances for their daughters, and what gratitude these children feel to their parents ! . . . For your little Queen it is a very different matter ; you, *as father* and truly *as King*, chose to entrust her to no other than to the King of Heaven, Jesus Himself ; from *Orphan of the Berezina* I have passed to the most noble title of Carmelite.

How I ought to love a father who has chosen to gain me so great a happiness, and how I do love him ! . . . If our Roman guide were here, he might say : "*Messieurs les Abbés*, I am going to show you such a Father as you have never seen, there is that in him which will make you fall down in wonder."[1] Isn't it true, darling Father, that more you could not do for your *little Queen* ! If she isn't a saint, it will certainly be her own fault, for with a Father like you, she has the means ! . . .

Dearest Father, the day is ending, I must leave you, but to find you again at Jesus' side, your rightful place.

Soon the day without shadows will dawn for us, and then we shall never break off our conversation.

Happy New Year, my dearest *King*, thank you for all the gifts you have spoiled us with this week and throughout the year !

May Jesus load you with His blessings, may He give you, as He has promised, a hundredfold in this life and the beauty of His Heaven in the next. There you have the wish of your *little Queen*, who loves you more than ever Queen has loved her King.

Sister Thérèse of the Child Jesus,
post. carm. ind.

[1] "Emerveillaison" : see note 4 to Letter XXV.

1889

SEVENTEENTH YEAR

10 January : Thérèse takes the habit.
12 February : M. Martin's health gets worse ; he has to be placed in
*   a mental home at Caen. This trial (which Thérèse called " our*
*   great riches") threw its sad shadow over the whole of this year of*
*   novitiate.*

XLIX

To MME GUÉRIN

To thank her for a gift on the occasion of
Thérèse's Clothing

J. M. J. T.

Jesus †   2 January 1889.[1]

My dearest Aunt,
    Your little girl is at the highest peak of joy ! . . . How good
you are to her ! Truly it is too much . . . how can she thank
you ? But surely a mother can read the heart of her small daughter,
so I am not going to worry, I know you will realise how grateful
I am.
    The lilies[2] are utterly delightful, they look as if they had just
been picked ! How dear of my little sisters to give them to me;
it will be a great joy for me, on the day of my Clothing, to
remember that it is they who have adorned me for my coming
to my divine Spouse. These flowers will speak for them to Jesus,
and I know He will fill them to overflowing with His graces, and
you too, dearest Aunt.
    If you knew how happy I was to have the enormous toffee-
apple to give our Mother[3] : in that I saw the hand of my dearest

---
[1] Thérèse's sixteenth birthday.
[2] To be carried at her Clothing, 10 January.
[3] The Prioress was subject to bronchial attacks, and such things helped.

Aunt, who is always on the lookout for whatever will give most pleasure to her little girl. My joy was no less great at sight of the lovely package of gingerbread; I was full of pride in the refectory when our Mother told the whole community that you were giving us this treat in honour of my sixteenth birthday.

Thank you, dearest Aunt, if you only knew how good I think you! On the day of my Clothing, I shall indeed pray for you, and for my dear Uncle, because I know that all the lovely presents I've been given this evening are from him too.

Our dearest Mother thinks the wreath quite lovely, and so do the whole community. I have never seen flowers that please me so much, there is such purity in lilies! It is my hope that my soul will be all adorned with them as I go to Jesus, for it is not enough to wear them in my hair, the eye of Jesus always sees the heart.

Goodbye and thank you, dearest Aunt, pray that your little girl may be as well adorned inwardly as outwardly. . . .

Sister Thérèse of the Child Jesus,
post. carm. ind.

L

To SISTER AGNES OF JESUS[1]

During Thérèse's retreat before Clothing

J. M. J. T.

Jesus †

This morning I was in trouble[2] with Sister X. and came away close to tears.

What is there in you that so draws my soul? You cannot imagine what a privation I feel it not to be able to speak to you.

There is something, which I wonder if you realise, in the way

[1] This letter, undated, was written by the Saint at the beginning of her retreat before Clothing, 7 or 8 January. At that time Postulants made this retreat for three days only. Each day they saw, and were instructed by, their Mother Prioress or Mistress of Novices. The Prioress, Mother Marie de Gonzague, gave Thérèse permission to unburden herself, in writing, to her sisters who were in the order, during the retreats before Clothing and Profession. It was a very exceptional permission; Thérèse used it with simplicity, but did not ask for its prolongation. Referring to the first years of her religious life, she said later to Mother Agnes'of Jesus, then Prioress: "Oh, little Mother, how I suffered at that time! . . . I could not open my heart to you, and I thought you no longer knew me" (see *Histoire d'une âme*, ch. xii).

[2] One of the "pin-pricks" Thérèse refers to in the next letter.

Jesus treats us. You remember I said that children don't know what they want; that's how Jesus treats his "little ball". . . .[1] I suppose he found that the 9th delighted it too much.[2] He wants it to have nothing to delight in ! . . . And I know why, because He alone is delight in the full force of the word, and He wants to show His *little ball* that it would be a mistake to look elsewhere for a shadow of beauty which it might take for Beauty itself. He who will soon be my Spouse is so good to me, so divinely lovable in His determination not to let me attach myself to ANY created thing ! He knows of course that if He let me have the bare *shadow* of HAPPINESS I should cling to it with all the energy, all the strength of my heart: this shadow He refuses me ! . . . He would rather leave me in darkness than give me a false light that would not be *Himself.*

Since I can find no created thing to content me, I will to give all to Jesus, I will *not* to give to a creature[3] even an *atom* of my love, may Jesus grant me always to realise that He alone is perfect happiness, even when He seems to be absent ! . . .

Today more than yesterday, if that be possible, I have been without any consolation. I thank Jesus, since He sees that that is good for my soul; perhaps, if He gave me consolations, I should rest in their sweetness, but He wants *all* to be for Him! Good ! then all *shall* be for Him, all ! Even when I feel nothing that can be offered to Him, I shall (as tonight) give Him that

[1] As soon as she entered Carmel, Thérèse had offered herself to the Child Jesus as a *little toy* for Him to play with, a "ball of no value" (see *Histoire d'une âme*, ch. vi, and Letter XVIII).

[2] Three unpublished letters (one of Mgr Hugonin, two of M. Delatroëtte) leave no doubt that Thérèse was regularly called to receive the Habit, after six months as a postulant, round October 1888. Only the health of her father—whom they wanted to have present at the ceremony—imposed a delay. The date then fixed, 9 January, had seemed to Thérèse a delicate compensation for the delay she had suffered. For 9 January was exactly nine months from 9 April, the day of her entry into Carmel: on that day was celebrated the Feast of the Annunciation, postponed because 25 March fell that year in Holy Week. The nine months of waiting represented to Thérèse the exact time Jesus was in the womb of His Mother. . . . But Mgr Hugonin found that he could not preside on 9 January and the ceremony was postponed until the following day.

[3] As the starting-point of this aspiration must be seen Thérèse's desire to live in perfect detachment with regard to the Prioress, Mother Marie de Gonzague. Later she confided to her the struggles this had caused her to undergo. "I remember that when I was a postulant, I had often such violent temptations to seek my own satisfaction and find some drops of joy, that I was obliged to hurry past your cell and cling tight to the banisters to keep from retracing my steps. There came into my mind any number of permissions to ask, a thousand pretexts to give way to my nature and let it have what it craved: How happy I am now that I denied myself at the very beginning of my religious life!" (*Histoire d'une âme*, ch. x).

nothing ! . . . If Jesus does not give me consolation, He gives me a peace so great that it does me more good !

What of the Father's letter ?[1] I find it heavenly, my heart finds most lovely things in it—but happiness ? Oh no ! not happiness. . . . Happiness lies only in suffering, and in suffering with no consolation !

Little Sister, my own Mother,[2] what will you think of your little daughter ? Oh ! if it were not you, I should not dare to send these thoughts, the most intimate of my *soul*. I *beg* you, tear up these papers when you have read them.

Pray that your little daughter may not withhold from Jesus an *atom* of her heart.

Thérèse of the Child Jesus.

LI

To SISTER AGNES OF JESUS

During Thérèse's retreat before Clothing[3]

J. M. J. T.

Thank you, little Lamb[4] beloved of Jesus ! . . . If you knew what pleasure your brief message gave me.

Ask Jesus that I may be very generous during my retreat: He RIDDLES me with *pin-pricks*, the poor *little ball* can take no more ; all over it are tiny holes which cause it more suffering than if it had but one great gash ! . . . Nothing from Jesus. Dryness ! . . . Sleep ! . . . But at least there is silence ! Silence does good to the soul. . . . But creatures ! *creatures* ! . . . The *little ball* shudders at the thought of them . . . Realise that it is Jesus' *toy*. When it is that loving Friend who pierces His *ball* Himself, suffering is only sweetness, His hand is *so sweet* ! . . . But creatures ! . . . Those who surround me are good, of course, but there is a touch of something in them that repels me ! . . . I can't explain it to you, but do understand *your* little soul. All the same I am VERY *happy*, happy at suffering what Jesus wants me to suffer. If He does not Himself pierce His *little ball*, it is He who guides

[1] A letter from Père Pichon, S.J.
[2] Thérèse says "Maman".
[3] Undated, probably 8 January.
[4] Thérèse loved to call her sister by this symbolic name.

71

the hand that pierces it ! . . . Jesus chooses to sleep, why should I keep Him from sleep ? I am too happy that He does not put Himself to any trouble about me, He shows me that I am not a stranger by treating me like this: for I assure you He simply doesn't bother to make conversation with me !

If you knew how great is my wish to be indifferent to the things of this world ! What matter all created beauties to me ?

Possessing them, I should be utterly unhappy, my heart would be so empty ! . . . It's incredible how big a thing my heart seems when I consider the world's treasures . . . since all of them massed together could not content it . . . but how small a thing it seems when I consider Jesus ! . . . I want to love Him *so* ! . . . To love Him more than He has ever been loved !—My sole desire is to do the will of Jesus always, to dry the tears that sinners cause Him to shed . . . Oh! I want Jesus to have NO pain the day of my espousals, I wish I could convert *all* the sinners on earth and bring all the souls in purgatory to heaven !

The Lamb of Jesus will laugh to see such a wish from the small *grain of sand* ! . . . I know that it is foolishness, but still I wish that it could be so, that Jesus might not have a single tear to shed.

Pray that the *grain of sand* may become an ATOM, which only the eyes of Jesus can see.

Thérèse of the Child Jesus,
post. carm. ind.

LII

To SISTER MARIE OF THE SACRED HEART

During Thérèse's retreat before Clothing[1]

J. M. J. T.

Jesus †

Dearest sister of Jesus, the *baby lamb* has great need to borrow a little strength and courage from you, the courage which brings one through *everything*. The poor *baby lamb* cannot say a thing to Jesus, yet Jesus says absolutely nothing to her; pray for her that her retreat may all the same be pleasing to the Heart which alone reads the deepest depth of the soul.

Why look for happiness upon earth ? I confess to you that my

[1] Undated; written 7 or 8 January.

heart has a burning thirst for happiness, but well it sees, poor heart, that no creature can slake its thirst. It is exactly the reverse: the deeper it drinks at that enchanted spring,[1] the more burning its thirst becomes.

I know another spring, the spring "where after drinking one thirsts still"[2]—but with a thirst not feverish but very sweet because it has that which can satisfy it: that spring is suffering when none but Jesus knows it ! . . .

Dearest sister, I have much to tell you, but I haven't the time. Read the heart of your little girl, as you so well know how ! . . .

Thérèse of the Child Jesus,
post. carm. ind.

LIII

To M. MARTIN[3]

Written during Thérèse's retreat before Clothing, to thank him for gifts sent in view of the coming ceremony

J. M. J. T.

Jesus †   Carmel, 8 January 1889.

My Incomparable King,

If you could know how touched I am by your kindness ! . . . a melon ![4] champagne ! . . . Oh ! it would make we want to weep if I did not control myself : but I do, and I am wonderfully happy about Thursday's lovely festival.

Normally a queen's wedding is celebrated with great rejoicings. That, I imagine, is why the *Queen of France and of Navarre* will have fireworks. It is the *King* who provides all this for the *Queen* and he is skilled at giving surprises ! The little *blonde scatterbrain* can only thank him !

If on Thursday there is to be a grand festival upon earth, I imagine it will be more magnificent still in Heaven, the angels

[1] The "enchanted spring" of love for creatures. The allusion is to her filial affection for Mother Marie de Gonzague. See note 3 to Letter L.
[2] Eccles. xxiv. 20.
[3] This is the last letter sent by Thérèse to M. Martin at Les Buissonnets. The rare later letters have not been preserved.
[4] A mechanical trick: it exploded when a lighted match was put to it and threw out a shower of bonbons.

will be lost in wonder at a father so pleasing to God, and Jesus will prepare a wreath to add to all those that that incomparable father has already woven.

No, the festivals of earth will never be as ravishing as the festivals of Heaven! Yet it seems to me impossible to find one more heavenly than is being prepared for me. And I have done nothing to be worthy of so great a grace; but the good God has willed to look upon the merits of my dearest father, that is why He grants me this wonderful favour.

I am now in retreat, and writing is not allowed in retreat, but our Mother has given me permission to send you this brief word to thank you, you are so good to your *Queen*! After all, writing is only forbidden so as not to disturb the silence of the retreat, but can one disturb one's peace by writing to a saint?

Until Thursday, dearest Father, your little Queen kisses you in her heart, until she can kiss you in fact.[1]

Thérèse of the Child Jesus,
post. carm. ind.

LIV

To SISTER AGNES OF JESUS

During Thérèse's retreat before Clothing[2]

J. M. J. T.

Jesus †

I have not seen the *Lamb of the day*, but I know it has a very bad headache! This grieves the *baby lamb* who is in great fear that Jesus may cause wings to grow on His *Lamb*. . . .

What a ravishing little note! . . . .It is quite heavenly, it has the feel of our true Homeland[3]. . . . The *Lamb* is in error in thinking that Jesus' toy is not in darkness, she is plunged in darkness. Perhaps, as the baby lamb realises, the darkness is luminous, but none the less it is darkness . . . her *sole* consolation is a very great strength and peace, and in this she hopes to be as Jesus wills; that is her joy, for all else is sadness.

---

[1] At this time novices came out of the enclosure for the ceremony and could embrace their family.

[2] Undated; written 9 January.

[3] "La Patrie": Heaven, of course. Cf. "Qui vitam sine termino nobis donet in patria".

With our Mother I am always being interrupted,[1] and then, when I have an instant, I cannot tell her what is going on in my soul. I come from her joyless as I go to her joyless !

I believe that Jesus' effort, during this retreat, has been to detach me from all that is not He. . . .

If you knew how great is my joy at having no joy, to give pleasure to Jesus ! . . . It is essence of joy (but wholly unfelt).

Dearest *Lamb*, one day to go and I am Jesus' spouse ! . . .

Do not die right away. Wait till the *baby lamb* has wings to follow you.

> *Thérèse of the Child Jesus, Jesus' little toy,*
> *post. carm. ind.*

Would you like (1) to give me your Chinese ink and gold leaf; (2) to tell me if for the little Clothing cards the responses of St. Agnes will do; (3) to slip open our door at 6 if you're there, otherwise I must wake myself up. If all these things are a nuisance, don't give me anything. I can very well do without.

LV

To SISTER MARIE OF THE SACRED HEART

During Thérèse's retreat before Clothing

J. M. J. T.

Jesus †

Dearest sister, your little note has given GREAT PLEASURE to your little girl's heart. . . . Thank you ! . . . How good you are ! . . . Oh ! how I wish I were like you ! But *Jesus' toy* is weakness itself; if Jesus does not carry it, or throw His *little ball*, it stays there, inert, on the one spot. One day to go, and I am Jesus' spouse. What a grace ! . . . What can I do to thank Him, to make myself less unworthy of such a favour ?

Oh ! "La Patrie . . . La Patrie !"[2] . . . How I thirst for Heaven, where we shall love Jesus with the whole of our being. But we must suffer and weep if we are to get there; so—I am

---

[1] By the Sisters who came to speak to Mother Prioress.
[2] Reminiscence of a dialogue sometimes recited at Les Buissonnets.

willing to suffer all that Jesus pleases, to let Him do as He likes
with His *little ball.*

Thérèse of the Child Jesus,
post. carm. ind.

LVI

To SISTER MARTHE OF JESUS

Her fellow novice[1]
Lines written in pencil on the back of a small picture
of the Child Jesus in the crib

10 January 1889.

To my dearest little Sister in memory of my beloved Clothing.

Soon the divine spouse of Thérèse of the Child Jesus will be
the spouse of Marthe of Jesus too.

Ask Jesus that I may become a great saint. I shall ask the same
grace for my darling companion !

Sister Thérèse of the Child Jesus of the Holy Face,
nov. carm. ind.[2]

[1] Sister Marthe of Jesus had entered the Carmel at Lisieux, 23 December 1887,
as a lay-sister. Thérèse describes in the *Histoire d'une âme* how she was led to help
Sister Marthe detach herself from too natural an affection for the Prioress, 8
December 1892 (see ch. ix of that book, and Letter CXLVI, below). As lay-sisters
are postulants for a year, Marthe's Clothing could have taken place at Christmas
1888, but was postponed to 2 May 1889.

[2] Abbreviation for "unworthy Carmelite novice". This is the first time that
"of the Holy Face" appears in Thérèse's signature. She had obtained permission
to add it to her name, as from her Clothing, in consideration of the great sufferings
undergone by her father, which reminded her of the humiliations of Jesus during
His passion. Devotion to the Holy Face was held in high honour at the Lisieux
Carmel, which had it from the Carmel at Tours, where Sister Marie de Saint-Pierre
had her communications from Our Lord on the cult of the Holy Face. The foundress
of the Lisieux community, Mother Geneviève of St. Teresa, had approached the
ecclesiastical authorities of the town to obtain from the Bishop the erection of the
Archconfraternity of Reparation in the Parishes of Lisieux. She installed in her
Convent chapel a reproduction of the Veil of Veronica, devotion to which was
being spread at the time by the Holy Man of Tours, M. Dupont.

It was at the threshold of her life as a nun that Thérèse, encouraged by Mother
Agnes of Jesus, awoke to this devotion, which rapidly took a very individual, very
profound, orientation in her soul (see *Histoire d'une famille,* pp. 327 ff.). Note that
when she includes "the Holy Face" in her signature, she nearly always signs *"Thérèse
of the Child Jesus of the Holy Face"*, only occasionally *"Thérèse of the Child Jesus
and the Holy Face"*.

LVII

To CÉLINE

A few days after Thérèse's Clothing

J. M. J. T.

January 1889.

Jesus and His Cross ! . . .

Dearest Sister,

Yes, my heart's *dearest*, Jesus is there with his Cross ![1] You have the privilege of His love, and He would make you like to Himself: why should it frighten you that you cannot bear His cross without weakening ? On the way to Calvary Jesus fell three times; and you, a poor little child, would not be like your *Spouse*, would not fall a hundred times, if need be, to prove Him your love by rising up again with more strength than before your fall ! . . . Céline . . . Jesus must love you with a very special love to try you like this. Do you realize that I am almost jealous ? To those who love *more*, He gives more suffering, to those who love less, less. . . .

But you do not *feel* your love for your *Spouse*, you would like your heart to be a flame mounting upward without a trace of smoke. . . . Do grasp this, that the smoke that wraps you round is simply for your own good, to hide from you wholly the sight of your love for Jesus. The flame is seen by Him alone, in that way at least He has it all; for when He lets us see a little of it, self-love comes rushing in like a deadly wind, extinguishing it wholly ! . . .

At this moment I see you as a person surrounded by immense riches . . . as far as the eye can see, and beyond. This person would like to turn her back because—she says—too many riches would be a nuisance, she would not know what to do with them; better let them be lost, or even taken over by someone else ! . . . But this someone else will not come, for the riches are prepared for Jesus' spouse and for her alone ! . . .

---

[1] Their father's malady was growing rapidly worse: the burden fell especially upon Céline. Thérèse's Clothing was for M. Martin "his triumph, his last feast here below" (see *Histoire d'une âme*, ch. vii).

77

"God would turn the world upside down to find suffering to give to a soul upon which His divine gaze is fixed with ineffable love."[1]

What do the things of this world matter to us? Could this *slime*, so unworthy of an immortal soul, be our Homeland? And why should we care that wretched human creatures reap the *musty harvests* that grow from the slime. The more our heart is in heaven, the less we feel these pin *pricks*.[2] . . .

But don't think it isn't a *grace*, and a *great* grace, to feel them; for then our life is a *martyrdom*, and one day Jesus will give us the palm. Oh "to suffer and be *despised*!"[3] What *bitterness*, but what glory! That is the motto of the *Lily-Immortelle*,[4] and none other would become her.

My heart goes with you in the *noble task* Jesus has entrusted to you.[5] You are not a soldier but a General! . . . To suffer, still, always. . . . But everything passes.[6]

LVIII

To CÉLINE

J. M. J. T.

Jesus †   February 1889.[7]

My dearest Céline,

I cannot tell you the good your dear little note has done me! . . . Now you are really the *Lily-Immortelle* of Jesus,[8] oh! how pleased He is with His lily, with what love He looks upon His beloved flower, now that it has no wish but *Him alone*, no desire but to console Him. . . .

Each new suffering, each heart's pain, is a gentle wind to bear to Jesus the fragrance of His lily; then He smiles lovingly, and

[1] A thought of Père Pichon, S.J. Thérèse liked to quote him in her letters to Céline, knowing it would please her sister, whose spiritual director he was.

[2] The allusion is to certain humiliating comments on their family distress, rather like the consolations offered by Job's friends.

[3] Wish expressed by St. John of the Cross, and, in imitation of him, uttered many times by Thérèse and Céline in the evening at the windows of the top room.

[4] See Letter XXXII.

[5] Céline had to take charge of her father.

[6] This letter is unsigned.

[7] Early in the month.

[8] See note 4 on this page.

immediately makes ready a new grief, fills the cup to the brim, for He knows that the more His lily grows in love, the more it must grow in suffering too.

What a privilege Jesus gives us in sending so great a SORROW ! Ah ! ETERNITY will not be too long to thank Him. He fills us to overflowing with His favours, as He filled the greatest saints : Why are we so chosen out ? That is a secret Jesus will lay bare to us in our Homeland, on the day when "He will wipe all tears from our eyes."[1]

It can only be to *my soul*[2] that I speak like this, otherwise I should not be understood ; but it *is* to her that I speak, and all my ideas have been anticipated by her ; yet, what perhaps she does not realise is the love Jesus bears her, a love that asks ALL. Nothing can be impossible to Him, He wills to set no limit to the SANCTITY of His lily. . . . Her limit is to have no limit ! . . . Why should she ? . . . We are greater than the whole universe. One day we shall have, even *we*, a divine existence. . . .

Oh ! how I thank Jesus for thus giving a lily to be with our dearest Father, a lily which nothing affrights, a lily which would *die* rather than desert the *glorious* field in which Jesus' love has placed it ! . . .

Now, we have nothing left to hope on earth, nothing but suffering and more suffering. When we have finished, suffering will still be there holding wide its arms to us ; oh ! how enviable is our lot. . . . In Heaven the cherubim envy us our good fortune.

This is not why I set out to write to my dearest Céline, but to ask her to write Mlle Pauline[3] the misfortune that has come upon us in our Father's malady. It's your turn to laugh at your poor Thérèse for arriving at her subject at the end of her letter !

Poor Léonie, I love her deeply too, she is less fortunate than we, Jesus has given her less. But "unto whomsoever much is given, of him much shall be required".[4]

Your little sister,

Thérèse of the Child Jesus,
nov. carm. ind.

[1] Apoc. xxi. 4.
[2] No phrase could better express the intimacy of her union with Céline.
[3] See note to Letter XXXIII.
[4] Luke xii. 48.

LIX

To CÉLINE

Then at Caen, with M. Martin, whose condition had
grown worse

J. M. J. T.

Jesus †   Carmel, 28 February 1889.

My dearest Céline,
    Is it possible that I am writing to you at Caen? I wonder if
I am dreaming or awake?[1] . . . But no, it's real.
    I shall surprise you, darling Sister, when I say that I am far
from pitying you; you know, I find your lot actually enviable.
    Jesus has designs of love ineffable for you. He means to have
His *"Lily-Immortelle"* all for His own. But He is giving her the
beginning of her novitiate Himself, it is His divine hand that
adorns His bride for her wedding-day, His beloved hand is un-
erring in the garb it bestows. . . . Jesus is "a betrothed in
blood".[2] . . . He wills for Himself *all* her heart's blood.
    Oh! *what* it costs to give Jesus what He asks! What HAPPINESS
it costs! What unutterable joy to bear our crosses FEEBLY!
    Does the *Lily-Immortelle* understand the poor *grain of sand*?
. . . Your novitiate is the novitiate of sorrow, a privilege so far
beyond understanding! . . .
    Ah! darling Sister, far from complaining to Jesus of the cross
He sends us, I cannot fathom the *infinite* love which has brought
Him to treat us so. Our dearest father must indeed be loved by
Jesus, to have to suffer like this! But doesn't it strike you that
the ill with which he is stricken is the exact complement of his
beautiful life? I feel, little *Lily-Immortelle*, that I am talking
sheer foolishness, but no matter, I think many other things of the
love of Jesus which are perhaps much stranger. . . . What a

---

[1] M. Martin had been transferred to the Hospital of the Holy Saviour at Caen
on 12 February. Léonie and Céline went to Caen to be with him and lived with
the Sisters of St. Vincent de Paul. They were there for three months (see *Histoire
d'une famille,* pp. 318 ff.). Because of all this, Mother Marie de Gonzague gave
Thérèse permission to write Léonie and Céline fairly frequent letters to strengthen
and encourage them. Those to Léonie have been destroyed.
[2] Exod. iv. 25—often quoted by Père Pichon, S.J.

happiness it is to be humbled ! It is the one way that makes saints !
. . . Can we now have any doubt of Jesus' will for our souls ?
. . . Life is only a *dream*, soon we shall awaken, and what joy . . .
the greater our sufferings, the more limitless our glory. . . . Oh !
don't let us waste the trial Jesus sends us, it is a gold-mine we
must exploit, shall we let the chance slip ? . . . The *grain of sand*
would set herself to the task without *joy*, without *courage*, without
strength, and all these *conditions* will make the enterprise easier,
it wants to work for love.

What is beginning is *martyrdom*; let us enter the arena together,
if in her kindness the *Lily-Immortelle* does not disdain

the poor grain of sand.

LX

To MME GUÉRIN

Mme Guérin had paid for a picture painted by Thérèse,
who thanks her

J. M. J. T.

Jesus †   Carmel, 12 March 1889.

My darling Aunt,

I find it quite impossible to obey you, for it would be too
difficult not to say thank you. How small a thing are these five
letters[1] to express my gratitude; but, dearest Aunt, I beg you,
realise all that your little girl cannot say. O Aunt, how good you
are ! How I am going to pray for you ! It is true, alas, that I am
incapable of doing anything of value. Instead of making money,
I can only waste it; so the delicate attention of my darling Aunt
has touched me keenly. I could not get over finding myself so
rich, without having done anything to earn so much money !
I can't help smiling at the thought that, thanks· to my kind
relation, I shall be the one to provide the fish for the whole community. I hope, darling Aunt, that you will thank my dear Uncle
for me and tell him all my gratitude. Dear Aunt, God must
indeed love you to make you suffer so, but if He listened to my
prayers, you would never be ill again, for I should be happy if
He willed to send me all the pains He has in store for you.

[1] M-e-r-c-i.

Alas, dearest Aunt, how little my letter can convey to you the feelings of my heart ! I wish I could make you see all my gratitude. How kind Jesus is to leave us, in the cruel trial He sends, the consolation of seeing our sorrow shared and understood, by our kind relations! With all my heart I kiss my little Jeanne and also my little lady of the house.[1]

Goodbye, darling Aunt, I thank you again, and Uncle too; and I kiss you tenderly.

Your grateful little girl,

Sister Thérèse of the Child Jesus,
nov. carm. ind.

LXI

To CÉLINE

J. M. J. T.

Carmel, 12 March 1889.

"Jesus for ever ! how good it is to vow oneself to Him, sacrifice oneself for His love."[2]

Céline !—the dear name echoes softly in the depths of my heart ! . . . Surely our two hearts beat in perfect harmony.

This evening, I feel a need to plunge with my Céline into the infinite ˙. . . a need to forget the earth; here below everything wearies me, everything is an effort, I find only one joy, to suffer for Jesus. . . . But this *unfelt* joy is above every joy. Life passes . . . eternity comes to meet us with great strides. Soon we shall be living with the very life of Jesus. Having drunk deep at the source of all bitterness, we shall be deified in the very source of all joys, of all delights.[3] . . .

Soon, little sister, with a single glance we shall be able to take in what is happening in our inmost being !

" The fashion of this world passes away"[4] . . . soon we shall see new heavens, "a sun more radiant shall lighten with its splendours ethereal seas, horizons infinite. . . ."[5] Immensity

[1] Her cousin Marie Guérin.
[2] Père Pichon, S.J.
[3] This is not a verbal quotation, but has evidently been inspired by many passages of Arminjon, *La Fin du monde présent*, etc. (pp. 297, 298, 315).
[4] 1 Cor. vii. 31.
[5] From *Une Voix de Prison* by Lamennais.

will be our abode . . . we shall be no more prisoners on this earth of our exile, *all* will have PASSED AWAY! With our heavenly Spouse, we shall skim over lakes with no shore. . . . "The infinite has neither bounds, nor bed, nor shore. . . ."[1] "Courage, Jesus hears our sorrow even to its last echo."[2] "Now our harps are hung up on the willows by the river of Babylon",[3] but on the day of our deliverance, what harmonies shall we not draw from them! With what joy shall we set all the strings of our instruments vibrating ! . . .

Jesus' love for Céline cannot be understood save by Jesus. . . . Jesus has committed *follies* of love for Céline. . . . Let Céline commit *follies* for Jesus. . . . "Love is paid by love alone",[4] and "love's wounds are healed by love alone".[5]

Let us offer our sufferings to Jesus to save souls; poor souls ! . . . they have fewer graces than we, yet all the blood of a God has been shed to save them. . . . Jesus has chosen to make their salvation depend on a sigh of our heart. . . . What a mystery is there ! . . . If a sigh can save a soul, what cannot sufferings like ours do ? . . . Let us refuse Jesus nothing ! . . .

There is the bell, and I have not yet written to my poor Léonie ; give her my greetings, kiss her and tell her that I love her. Let her be *very faithful* to grace, and Jesus will bless her. Let her ask Jesus to tell her what I would say to her. I charge Him with my messages.

Goodbye for the present ! . . . Oh ! Heaven ! Heaven ! When shall we be there?

Jesus' little grain of sand.

---

[1] Arminjon, loc. cit., p. 300.
[2] Père Pichon, S.J.
[3] Cf. Ps. cxxxvi. 2.
[4] St. John of the Cross, *Spiritual Canticle*, strophe ix, from the translation by the Carmelites of Paris, published by Douniol, 1875.
[5] Ibid., strophe xi.

LXII

To CÉLINE

J. M. J. T.

Jesus †

15 March 1889.

Thank you for your letter, it made the little *grain of sand* glad.

In one of your letters, you said recently that you were *my shadow*. Alas! it would be very sad if that were so, for what is the shadow of a poor little *grain of sand*?

I have thought of something better for my dearest Céline. The idea of a shadow pleased me, I said to myself that Céline must indeed be the shadow of something—but of what? I can find nothing in creation to satisfy the idea I have of the reality whose faithful shadow my dearest Céline should be—it is Jesus Himself who must be that *divine reality*.

Yes, Céline must be *the little shadow of Jesus*. . . . How lowly, yet how glorious a title. For what is a shadow? . . . But Jesus' shadow, what glory! . . .

What things I could say to the *little shadow of Jesus* about all this, but I have too little time, it's impossible.

My Céline's dream is very lovely,[1] perhaps one day it will come true . . . but meanwhile let us begin our martyrdom, let us allow Jesus to rend away from us all we cling to most, and refuse Him nothing. Before we die by the sword, let us die by pin-stabs. . . . Does Céline understand?

The *little grain of sand* is united in suffering with the *little shadow of Jesus*.

Sister Thérèse of the Child Jesus of the Holy Face,
nov. carm. ind.

[1] Céline had dreamt that she was being martyred.

LXIII

To CÉLINE

J. M. J. T.

Carmel, 4 April 1889.

Jesus ! . . .

My darling Céline,

Your letter has brought my soul great sadness ![1] . . . Poor little Father. . . . No, Jesus' thoughts "are not our thoughts— His ways are not our ways"[2]. . . .

He offers us a cup so bitter that our feeble nature cannot bear it. Let us not draw back our lips from the cup prepared by the hand of Jesus. We must see life in its true light. . . . It is an instant between two *eternities*. Let us suffer in *peace* ! I admit that the word peace struck me as rather strong, but the other day, thinking over it, I hit upon the secret of suffering in peace. The word *peace* does not mean *joy*, at least not *felt joy* ; to suffer in peace, it is enough to will whatever Jesus wills.

To be the spouse of Jesus, one *must* be like Jesus ; Jesus is all bloody, crowned with thorns ! . . .

"A thousand years in thy sight, Lord, are as yesterday, which is PAST."[3]

"By the rivers of Babylon, there we sat and wept ; when we remembered Zion. On the willows in the midst thereof we hung up our instruments. . . . For there they that led us into captivity said : 'Sing us a hymn of the songs of Zion.' How shall we sing the songs of the Lord in a strange land ?" (Ps. of David[4] . . .)

No, let us not sing the songs of Heaven to creatures . . . but, like Cecilia, *let us sing in our heart*[5] a melodious song to our Well-Beloved !

The song of suffering in union with His sufferings is what most delights His heart. . . .

Jesus burns with love for us—look at His adorable Face. . . . Look at His glazed and sunken eyes ! . . . look at His wounds.

---

[1] Because of what it told of M. Martin's health.
[2] Isa. lv. 8.
[3] Ps. lxxxix. 4.
[4] Ps. cxxxvi. 1–4. The reference in the text is as St. Thérèse wrote it.
[5] From the office of St. Cecilia.

. . . Look Jesus in the face ! . . . *There, you will see how He loves us.*

Sister Thérèse of the Child Jesus of the Holy Face,
nov. carm. ind.

LXIV

To MARIE GUÉRIN

J. M. J. T.

Jesus †   Wednesday, 24 April 1889.

My darling Sister,
I write to ask you a favour; and I address myself to you, for I know that Les Buissonnets, now alas deserted, was once your home.
Do you remember a book Mme Tifenne[1] gave me on my first Communion? It was entitled "Le Bouquet de la jeune fille". This book is probably in one of the drawers of my poor little Father's chest-of-drawers. I should be very glad to have it as soon as possible, and also another, smaller book which the mesdemoiselles Primois[2] gave me. It's a brown book, surrounded by a design in gold, I think it contains meditations on the Eucharist. This book is on one of the shelves of the cupboard in Céline's bedroom (the one near the door).[3]
Darling Sister, pardon me for asking you this favour. It might be possible to explain to the maid what you want, without yourself going to Les Buissonnets.
It is incredible how tight the links that bind us are drawn now; it seems as though after our terrible trial we are even more *sisters* than before. . . . If you knew how I love you, how I think of you all. Oh ! it helps so much, when one is suffering, to have loving hearts to echo back our grief ! . . . I thank Jesus so much for having given us such good relatives, such kind little sisters. Our poor little sisters *over there*[4] simply could not weary, the other day, of telling us all the kindnesses you have shown them. I saw that my little Marie's *heart* had touched my Céline's *heart*

[1] Intimate friend of the Martins, at Alençon; Léonie's godmother.
[2] Friends of the family at Lisieux.
[3] These books were given to Mother Marie de Gonzague's family.
[4] Léonie and Céline, then at Caen.

and this gave great joy to my poor *heart*, I love my Marie so ! Whatever compliments they pay her can hardly measure up to what I think of her myself.

I am rushing on without remembering that my poor pen is quite unable to do justice to my heart, and that I shall almost certainly have the embarrassment of being unreadable.

Darling Sister, give a kiss from me to all those I love so dearly, thank them for spoiling us at Easter with the nice chocolate and the nice fish. Oh ! I cannot bear to think of the fish[1] . . . Uncle had something so fatherly about him that day, something out of the ordinary, I shall never forget that "parlour".

Your little sister who loves you,
Sister Thérèse of the Child Jesus.

LXV

To CÉLINE

For her twentieth birthday

J. M. J. T.

Jesus †   Carmel, 26 April 1888.

Jesus has made it his own personal task to bring greetings for His spouse's twentieth birthday[2] . . . What a year the twentieth has been, fertile in sufferings, in special graces ! Twenty ! O age full of illusion, tell me what illusion do you leave in my Céline's heart ? . . .

What memories between us ! . . . A whole world. . . . Yes, Jesus has His preferences, in His garden are fruits that the sun of His love ripens almost in the twinkling of an eye. . . . Why are we of their number ? . . . A question full of mysteries. . . . What reason can Jesus give us ? . . . His reason is that He has no reason. . . . Céline ! . . . let us make use of the preference shown us by Jesus, who has taught us so much in few years, let us not neglect anything that can give Him pleasure. . . . Ah ! let us be made golden by the Sun of His *love*—it is a burning sun—let us be consumed with *love* ! . . .

[1] M. Guérin's gift reminded Thérèse of her father, who used to give the Community the fish he caught.
[2] Céline's birthday was 28 April.

St. Francis of Sales says: "When the fire of love is in a heart, all the furniture flies out the windows."[1]

Oh ! let us leave nothing . . . nothing in our heart save Jesus.

Let us not fancy we can love without suffering, without suffering deeply. Our *poor nature* is there, and it is not there for nothing ! It is our wealth, our livelihood ! It is so precious that Jesus came on earth on purpose to make it His own. Let us suffer bitterly, that is without courage ! . . . "Jesus suffered with *sorrow*: could the soul be suffering if there were no sorrow ?"[2] And here are we wanting to suffer generously, greatly. . . . Céline ! . . . What folly ! . . . We want never to fall ?—What does it matter, my Jesus, if I fall at every instant, for thereby *I see* my weakness, and that for me is great gain. Thereby *You see* what I can do, and so You will be more moved to carry me in Your arms. . . . If You do not, it is because it pleases You to see me *on the ground* . . . so I am not going to be disquieted, but shall go on stretching out to You arms of supplication and of love ! I cannot believe You would abandon me ! . . . "When the saints were at Our Lord's feet, that is when they found their cross."[3] Dearest Céline, *sweet echo of my soul* ! . . . If you knew my misery . . . oh ! if you knew ! Sanctity lies not in saying beautiful things, or even in thinking them, or feeling them: it lies in truly willing to suffer.

"Sanctity ! it has to be won at the point of the sword, one must *suffer* . . . agonise !"[4]

A day will come when the shadows will vanish away; then there will remain only joy, ecstasy. . . .

Let us turn our single moment of suffering to profit, let us see each instant as if there were no other. An instant is a treasure . . . a single act of love will teach us to know Jesus better, will bring us closer to Him for all *eternity*.

Sister Thérèse of the Child Jesus of the Holy Face,
nov. carm. ind.

---

[1] Quoted by Père Pichon in a retreat given at the Lisieux Carmel in October 1887, second instruction of the seventh day.
[2] Père Pichon.
[3] Père Pichon.
[4] Idem.

LXVI

To CÉLINE

J. M. J. T.

For 28 April 1889.[1]

I want once again to wish a happy birthday to my dearest Céline; I am sending her a little bouquet, from the Child Jesus; He thanks her for all the lovely flowers she has given Him.

Alas, these flowers are not very brilliant, the child Jesus of Carmel is poor, but in Heaven He will show us His riches and I know upon whom He will lavish them. . . .

Tomorrow I shall receive my Jesus,[2] oh! how I shall speak to Him of my Céline, the other *me*. I shall have many things to tell Him, but I shall not find it difficult, a single sigh will tell Him all.

What a little scrawl! but I'm going so fast that you must excuse me.

I wish that my heart, and all it holds for you, could be known by you, but there are things that can't be written, only the heart comprehends them.

(Jesus' bouquet has spent several hours before Him, in a vase even poorer than He was Himself! . . .)

Céline dearest, one day we shall go to heaven, for ever; then there will be neither day nor night, as on this earth . . . Oh! what joy! let us go forward in peace, our eyes upon Heaven, the ONE ONLY goal of our labours.

The hour of rest approaches. Give my Léonie, whom I love so, a big kiss from me. I shall not forget her twenty-sixth birthday.[3] Since I have been in Carmel, I have a great memory for dates.

Goodbye for the present, my Céline, Jesus' *immortelle*.[4] . . . I love you more than I could possibly say.

Your little sister,

Thérèse of the Child Jesus.

[1] The letter was written 27 April.
[2] At this time daily Communion was not the custom, even in Carmelite convents. This privation was a martyrdom for St. Thérèse (see *Esprit de Ste Thérèse de l'Enfant-Jésus*, pp. 67 ff.).
[3] 3 June.
[4] See Letter XXXII.

LXVII

To SISTER AGNES OF JESUS

During her annual retreat[1]

J. M. J. T.

The bleating of the *Lamb* beloved of Jesus has sounded in the ears of the *baby lamb* like sweet music ! . . . Where could the *Lamb* have learned Saint Cecilia's melody ?
Eternity ! . . . Oh ! the *baby lamb* is plunged in it; following the *Lamb*, it tries to bound onwards, but the way has to be opened for it by the music of the sweet *Lamb*.

In spite of its littleness, the *grain of sand* wants to make a glorious eternity for itself, wants also to make a glorious eternity for the souls of sinners, but alas ! it is not yet small enough or light enough.

Lamb and *baby lamb* must win the palm of Agnes; if not by blood, then certainly by love. . . .

That is the *grain of sand's* dream !

Jesus alone ! . . . Nothing but Him ! The *grain of sand* is so small that if it wished to have any other[2] in its heart beside, there would be no room for Jesus. . . .

The white *Lamb* must pray for the obscure *grain of sand* that in eternity it may grow brilliant and luminous.

The little Reed of Jesus.[3]

[1] This undated letter was written by Thérèse to her sister during one of the latter's annual retreats, in all probability in May 1889. According to the custom of Carmel, these annual retreats are spent by each sister separately, in a total solitude lasting ten days; during this period, in the interests of a more absolute silence, any communications permitted are made by writing. Sister Agnes of Jesus was in the habit of making her retreat about the time of her Profession, that is to say, in the month of May.

[2] See note 3, page 70.

[3] The Carmelites mark certain of their clothes with a symbol, instead of a number as is customary in other congregations. The Reed was the symbol allotted to Thérèse. It gave her great pleasure, for she placed it in her mystical coat-of-arms.

LXVIII

To SISTER AGNES OF JESUS

During her annual retreat[1]

Thanks to my dearest *Lamb* for having let the *baby lamb* hear once more the music of Heaven. It was a gentle breeze which set the *little reed* gently waving. . . .

It was nine o'clock when the *reed* noticed the darling little paper;[2] it had no light of this world, but its heart, rather than its eyes, was able to decipher the music of St. Cecilia. It did not lose a single word ! . . .

Yes, I do desire these griefs in the heart, the pin-stabs of which the *Lamb* speaks. What does it matter to the *little reed* if it bends ? It is in no fear of breaking, for it has been planted on the edge of the waters. Instead of touching the earth when it bends, it meets only a pleasant wave which gives it new strength and makes it long for another storm to break over its frail head. It is its weakness that gives it all its confidence. It could not possibly break since, whatever happens to it, it wills to see only the gentle hand of its Jesus. Sometimes small puffs of wind are more insupportable to the *reed* than great storms; for in the storms it is bowed down to soak in the stream that it loves, but the small puffs of wind do not bend it so low. They are the pinpricks.

But nothing is too much to suffer to win the palm. . . .

LXIX

To SISTER AGNES OF JESUS

During her annual retreat[3]

What a happiness tomorrow to see the sweet face of the *Lamb* once more ![4] But the *baby lamb* begs the Lamb not to go bounding

[1] This note is neither signed nor dated. It was written, in all probability, in May 1889.
[2] A note written to her by Sister Agnes of Jesus.
[3] This note is neither signed nor dated. It was certainly written a few days after the preceding note.
[4] During their private retreat the Carmelites keep their veil lowered whenever they

on to Heaven. If her place is already prepared, let her think of the poor *baby lamb* and wait a little until the *baby lamb* can bound along with her, then both will go together to their Homeland. Their heart, which never knows total satisfaction on earth, will slake its thirst at the very source of love. Oh ! how lovely that feast ! What a joy to see God, "to be judged by Him whom we have loved above all things".[1] I have dreamed that the *Lamb* would soon be flying off to her Fatherland, but I hope that she will stay still a little while in exile to guide the poor *baby lamb*.

LXX

To SISTER MARIE OF THE SACRED HEART[2]

During her annual retreat

J. M. J. T.

Jesus †

Dearest Sister, thank you and thank you again ! . . . What would you like the poor *baby lamb* to say to you ?[3]

Wasn't *it* taught by *you* ? Remember the time when, sitting on the *big chair* and holding me on your knees, you spoke to me of Heaven. . . .

I can still hear you saying to me : "Look at the shopkeepers, how much trouble they give themselves to make money, whereas we can amass treasures for Heaven at every instant without giving ourselves so much trouble; all we have to do is gather diamonds with a RAKE."

And off I went, my heart filled with joy, overflowing with good resolutions. Perhaps, but for you, I should not be in Carmel ! . . .

Time has passed since the happy moments that flowed by in our pleasant nest. Jesus has paid us a visit . . . and found us worthy to pass through the crucible of suffering.

Before my entry into Carmel, our *incomparable* Father said, as

---

are at the Community exercises. Sister Agnes was to come out of retreat the following day.

[1] St. Teresa of Avila, *Way of Perfection*, ch. xlii.

[2] This undated note was written at the end of May 1889.

[3] Sister Marie of the Sacred Heart had written to her : "A little message, please, for your poor big sister. Sister Marie of the Angels [their novice mistress] has given permission, console me a little, my heart is full when I think of our darling father."

he gave me to God: "I wish I had something better to offer the good God." Jesus heard his prayer. . . . The something better was *himself*! . . . What joy, for a *moment* of suffering. . . . "This is the Lord's doing . . ."[1] and the Lord loves our Father incomparably more than we love him. Papa is the good God's little child.

To spare him *great* suffering, God wants us to suffer for him ! . . . It is for us to thank Him !

Dearest Sister, life will pass very quickly. In Heaven, it will be of no importance to us whether all the relics of Les Buissonnets have been taken to one place or another.[2] What does earth matter ? . . .

Your little girl, whom you brought up !

Sister Thérèse of the Child Jesus of the Holy Face,
nov. carm. ind.

LXXI

To MARIE GUÉRIN

To encourage her to receive Communion in spite
of her scruples

J. M. J. T

Jesus †
Thursday, 30 May 1889.

My dearest little Sister,

You did well to write to me,[3] I understood everything, everything, everything ! . . . You have not committed the *shadow* of *sin*, I know so well what temptations of this kind are, that I can give you the assurance without fear; besides, Jesus tells me so in the depth of my heart. . . . We must disregard all these temptations, pay no attention to them.

[1] Ps. cxvii. 22.

[2] Léonie and Céline, after a stay of three months in Caen, near the mental home where M. Martin had been since 12 February 1889, had returned to Lisieux on 14 May. Beginning from 7 June, they went to board with M. Guérin. The lease of Les Buissonnets was given up.

When Les Buissonnets was furnished again in 1913, pieces of furniture that had been dispersed were brought back. Thérèse had thought of them as "relics" of her father.

[3] About her scruples.

I think I must tell you something that has caused me *great* pain.

It is that my little Marie is not receiving Communion . . . on Ascension Day or on the last day of Mary's month. . . . Oh! what pain that gives to Jesus ! . . .

The devil must indeed be clever to deceive a soul like that ! . . . But surely you know, darling, that that is the one goal of his desires. He realises, treacherous creature that he is, that he cannot get a soul to sin if that soul wants to belong wholly to Jesus, so he only tries to make it *think* it is in sin. It is already much for him to have put confusion into that soul, but his rage demands something more ; he wants to deprive Jesus of a loved tabernacle ; since he cannot enter that sanctuary himself, he wants at least to have it remain *empty* and without master ! . . .

Alas ! what will become of that poor heart ? . . .

When the devil has succeeded in keeping a soul away from Holy Communion, he has *gained all* . . . and Jesus weeps ! . . .

O my darling, do you realise that Jesus is there in the tabernacle expressly for you, for *you alone*, He burns with the desire to come into your heart . . . don't listen to the demon, laugh at him, and go without fear to receive the Jesus of peace and love ! . . .

But I hear you say : "Thérèse says this because she does not know . . . and anyhow I cannot receive Communion, for I believe that I should be committing a sacrilege, etc. . . ." Yes, your poor little Thérèse does know, I tell you that she sees it *all* ; she assures you that you can go without fear to receive your one true Friend. She also has passed through the *martyrdom* of scruples ; but Jesus gave her the grace to receive Communion all the same, even at the time when she thought she had committed grave sins . . . so ! I assure you that she realises that it was the only way to get rid of the demon ; for when he sees that he is wasting his time, he leaves you in peace ! . . .

No, it is not possible that a heart "that finds no rest save in the sight of the tabernacle" should offend Jesus enough to be unfit to receive Him. What offends Jesus, what wounds His heart, is want of trust ! . . .

Little Sister, before I got your letter, I had a presentiment of your anguish, my heart was united with your heart ; that night I dreamt that I was trying to console you, but alas I could not succeed ! . . . I shall be no more fortunate today unless Jesus and the Blessed Virgin come to my aid; I hope that my desire will be realised and that on the last day of her month the Blessed Virgin will cure my dearest little sister. But for that, prayer is necessary, *much prayer*; if you could light a candle at Notre Dame des Victoires![1] . . . I have such confidence in her . . . Your heart is made to love Jesus, to love Him passionately; pray hard that *the most beautiful years of your life* may not be spent in imaginary fears.

We have only the brief moments of this life to love Jesus, the devil is well aware of it, so he tries to consume it in futile occupations. . . . Dearest little Sister, *receive Communion often*, very often . . . there you have the *sole remedy* if you want to be cured, Jesus has not put this attraction into your heart for nothing (I think He would be glad if you could make up your two lost Communions, for then the demon's victory would be less, since he would not have managed to keep Jesus from your heart).[2] Do not be afraid of loving the Blessed Virgin *too much*, you will *never* love her enough, and Jesus will be glad of your love for her because the Blessed Virgin is His mother.

Goodbye, little sister, excuse my scrawl; I can't even read it over, I haven't the time; kiss all my relations for me.

Sister Thérèse of the Child Jesus,
n.c.i.

LXXII

To MARIE GUÉRIN

On vacation at La Musse

Jesus †   Sunday, 14 July 1889.

My darling Sister,
    Since you have the humility to ask advice from your little Thérèse, she cannot refuse you; but, a poor little novice without

[1] In Paris, where the Guérins, accompanied by Léonie and Céline, were at that time visiting the great Exhibition.

[2] This letter, with its accurate eucharistic teaching, a teaching largely forgotten at the time when it was written, was to win the admiration of Pius X. "Oportunissimo! Oportunissimo!" he cried out as the opening lines were read; then, addressing Mgr de Teil, Vice-Postulator of her cause: "Oh! this is a great joy to me . . . we must make this process *quickly*!"

experience, she might well be afraid of making a mistake, and you too might have doubts upon what she tells you. But today have no fear, it is the reply of Jesus Himself that I bring you. . . . Oh! how happy I am to convey it to you. . . .

This morning I asked our good Mother[1] what answer I should send you about what you told Céline. If you do what that dearest Mother told me you ought to do, you need have no fear of doing wrong, for God has put into her heart a profound knowledge of souls and all their miseries; she knows *everything, nothing* is hidden from her, your little soul is known to her perfectly.

This is what she told me to say to you *as from Jesus*: "You did quite right to tell Céline everything,[2] yet it is better not to converse of such things, it is better to pay no attention at all to them, for our Mother is sure that you are doing no wrong." There, are you reassured? It seems to me that if I were you, and the same thing had been said to me, I should be completely cured and should let myself be led like a blind man, for that is the one means to have peace and above all to give pleasure to Jesus.

Even if you were sure that you were doing evil, there is still no danger, since *our Mother*, who has (I imagine!) more experience than *you*, tells you that you are not. . . .

Oh! Marie, how lucky you are to have a heart that can love so . . . thank Jesus for having made you so precious a gift, and give Him your heart *whole and entire*. Creatures are too small to fill the *immense void* that Jesus has hollowed out in you, give them no place in your soul. . . .

The good God will not catch you in His nets, for you are already wholly caught up in them. . . .

Yes, it is surely true that our affection is not *of this world*, it is too strong for that, death itself could not break it. . . .

Do not be worried at feeling no consolation in your communions; that is a trial that must be borne with love, do not waste any of the *thorns* that you meet every day; with one of them you can *save a soul*! . . .

Ah! if you knew how the good God is insulted! Your soul is so well made to console Him . . . love Him, even to folly, for all those who do not love Him! . . .

[1] Mother Marie de Gonzague, then Prioress.
[2] It was on the advice of Père Pichon, S.J., that Marie Guérin had confided in Céline.

Little Sister, after its mad course, my pen must stop. I have five letters[1] to write today, but I began with my little Marie. I love her so, and so supernaturally.

Give Uncle and Aunt and dear Jeanne a kiss from me and tell them that I love them.

And do you, little one so favoured by Jesus, pray that your unworthy little sister may be able to LOVE as much as you if that is possible.

Sister Thérèse of the Child Jesus of the Holy Face,
nov. carm. ind.

LXXIII

To CÉLINE

Then at La Musse with the Guérins

J. M. J. T.

Jesus †

Carmel, 14 July 1889.

My dearest Céline,

My soul never leaves you. It suffers exile with you ! . . . Oh ! what it costs to go on living, to remain upon this earth of bitterness and anguish. . . . But tomorrow . . . in an hour, we shall be in harbour, what happiness ! Ah ! how good it will be to contemplate Jesus *face to face* for *all* eternity ! Always, always more love, always joys more intoxicating . . . bliss unclouded.

What then has Jesus done, so to detach our souls from every created thing ? Ah ! He has struck us a great blow, but a blow of love. . . . God is admirable, but above all He is lovable, so let us love Him . . . let us love Him enough to suffer for Him whatever He chooses, even griefs of soul, aridities, anguish, seeming frigidities. Ah ! that is indeed a great love, to love Jesus without feeling the sweetness of that love, there you have martyrdom. . . . All right ! *let us die martyrs !*

Oh ! my Céline . . . sweet echo of my soul, do you understand ? . . . Martyrdom unrealised by men, known to God alone,

---

[1] One of these five letters was to Céline (see next letter). The recipients of the other three letters are not known.

undiscoverable by the eye of any creature, martyrdom without honour, without triumph. . . .

There you have love pushed even to heroism. But one day "a grateful God will cry out: 'My turn now'".[1] Oh! what shall we see *then*? What is that life, to which there shall be no end. . . . God will be the soul of our soul. Mystery beyond sounding! "The eye of man has not seen the uncreated light, man's ear has not heard the incomparable harmonies, his heart cannot have any fore-notion of what God has prepared for those He loves."[2] And all this will happen soon, yes soon. Let us hasten to make our crown, stretch out our hand to grasp the palm; and if we love much, if we love Jesus with passion, He will not be so cruel as to leave us long in this land of exile. . . .

Céline, during the *brief moments* that *remain to us*, let us not waste our time . . . let us save souls . . . souls "*are lost like snow-flakes*"[3] and Jesus weeps, and we are thinking only of our own sorrow instead of consoling our Spouse! Oh! my Céline, let us live for souls, let us be apostles, especially let us save the souls of priests, souls which should be more transparent than crystal. . . . Alas! how many bad priests there are, how many who are not holy enough! Let us pray, let us suffer for them, and on the last day Jesus will be *grateful*.[4] We shall give Him souls! . . .

Céline, do you understand the cry of my heart?

Together . . . always together,

Céline and Thérèse of the Child Jesus of the Holy Face,
nov. carm. ind.

P.S. Sister Marie of the Sacred Heart cannot write to you, because the letter would be too heavy.

---

[1] C. Arminjon, op. cit., p. 290.
[2] Cf. 1 Cor. ii. 9. St. Paul wrote "Those who love Him" (ceux qui l'aiment); Thérèse writes "those He loves" (ceux qu'il aime).
[3] St. Teresa of Avila.
[4] C. Arminjon, op. cit., p. 290.

LXXIV

To CÉLINE

To thank her for her feast wishes and gifts

J. M. J. T.

Jesus †   15 October 1889.

My dearest Céline,

If you knew how you have touched Thérèse's heart . . . your little flower-pots[1] are ENTRANCING. YOU DO NOT KNOW the pleasure they have given me ! . . . Céline, your letter gave me great, great pleasure, I felt how much our souls are made to understand each other, to advance along the same road. . . . Life . . . ah ! It is true that for us it has no more charm . . . but I am wrong, it is true that the charms of this world have vanished for us, yet it is a mist . . . and the reality remains to us, yes, life is a treasure . . . each instant is an *eternity*, an eternity of joy for Heaven, an eternity . . . to see God *face to face* . . . to be simply one with Him . . . only Jesus *is*: everything else *is not* . . . let us love Him then to the point of folly, let us save souls for Him.

Ah ! Céline, I feel that Jesus is asking us two to slake *His thirst* by giving Him souls, souls of *priests* above all, I feel that Jesus wants me to tell you this, for our mission is to *forget* ourselves, to annihilate ourselves . . . we are so small a matter . . . yet Jesus wills that the salvation of souls should depend on our sacrifices, our love, He is a beggar begging us for souls . . . ah ! let us understand the look on His face ! So few can understand it. Jesus does us the marvellous favour of instructing us Himself, showing us a *hidden light*.

Céline . . . life will be short, eternity has no end. . . . Let us make of our life a continual sacrifice, a martyrdom of love to console Jesus. He wants only a *look*, a *sigh* from us, but a look and a sigh that are for Him *alone* ! . . . Let every instant of our life be for *Him alone*. Let creatures touch us only in passing. . . .

There is but one sole thing to do during the night of this life, that single night which will come but *once*, and that is to love, *to*

---

[1] A gift from Céline to Thérèse for her feast.

love Jesus with all the strength of our heart, and to save souls for Him that He may be *loved.* . . . Oh ! to make men love Jesus !

Céline ! How easily I speak to you. . . . It is as though I were speaking to my soul. . . . Céline, I feel that to you I can say all. . . .

(Thank you again for your pretty little flower-pots, the Child Jesus looks *radiant* at so much ornament.)

Sister Thérèse of the Child Jesus of the Holy Face,
nov. carm. ind.

LXXV

To MME GUÉRIN

To thank her for feast gifts

J. M. J. T.

Jesus †   15 October 1889.

My dear Aunt,

I cannot tell you how touched I am at all the ways you spoil me. I am asking my holy patroness to thank you by loading you, and my dear Uncle, with her favours. Will you please give my thanks to my dear little sisters Jeanne and Marie for their pretty bouquets and their delicious grapes ?

My letter was interrupted at this point by the arrival of a new gift: two magnificent plants for the Child Jesus. Really I am utterly overwhelmed, I should be much embarrassed if it were not all to adorn the altar of the Child Jesus, and of course *He* will see to the payment of my debt to my dear relations. I do not know who the person is who has made this lovely gift to St. Teresa's Jesus; if you know it, dear Aunt, I beg you to convey my gratitude!

Oh ! Aunt, how I am begging St. Teresa today to repay you a hundredfold all that you do for me. In her feast letter, Céline spoke of your kindness to her; I was very much touched, but not surprised, for I know all the lovely motherly feelings you have for us.

Dear Aunt, I have a heart full of pleasant things that I should like to be able to tell you, but I must leave you and go to Vespers.

I send you, and Uncle too, and my four little sisters, my best kisses.

Your very grateful little girl,

Sister Thérèse of the Child Jesus,
nov. carm. ind.

LXXVI

To CÉLINE

On the day after her feast

J. M. J. T.

Jesus †

Carmel, 22 October 1889.

My dearest Céline,

If you could know how grieved I am ! . . . When I realise that I let the 21st pass without wishing my Céline a happy feast ! . . . Could Céline have doubted Thérèse's heart ? . . . You know she was thinking of this cherished feast for a very long time, but the life of Carmel is so eremitical that the poor little solitary never knows what date it is.

Céline, I feel this oversight in my heart, but, you see, I think that this year Jesus wanted our feasts to be the same day, for is not today the octave of St. Teresa ? Yes, Céline, St. Teresa is your patroness too, since you are already her beloved child. If you knew how I look upon the sorrow I feel today as willed by Jesus, for it pleases Him thus to sow our life with small sorrows. . . .

I am sending you a lovely picture of the Holy Face which our Mother gave me some time ago. I find that it goes so well with Marie of the Holy Face[1] that I cannot keep it for myself; for a long time now I have been thinking of giving it to my Céline, *my* Céline. Let Marie of the Holy Face be another Veronica,[2] wiping away all the blood and tears of Jesus, her *sole* beloved ! Let her

---

[1] This name, chosen spontaneously by Thérèse for her sister, was the one borne by Céline from her entry into Carmel until her Clothing (14 September 1894–5 February 1895). Letter CLIV of January 1895 tells how her superiors changed her name.

[2] Veronica means literally "true likeness". It is most remarkable that Thérèse should have given this name to her sister Céline, who was later, under her inspiration, to reproduce so faithfully the true likeness of Our Lord, as it appears on the Holy Shroud of Turin.

It was *immediately* after Thérèse's death that this precious relic was at last shown for what it was. The hour had come when the secrets hidden in its folds were to be

win Him souls, especially the souls she *loves*![1] Let her boldly face the soldiers, that is to say the world, to come to Him. . . . Oh! how happy she will be when one day she gazes in glory upon the *mysterious* draught with which she has slaked the thirst of her heavenly spouse, when she sees His lips, once parched, open to utter for her the *unique* and *eternal* word of *love*! The *thank-you* which will have no end. . . .

Goodbye for the present, dearest *little Veronica*; tomorrow doubtless the Beloved will ask a new sacrifice, a new relief for His thirst; but what matters—"let us die with Him".[2]

Happy Feast, dearest Céline. . . .

> Your poor little sister,
> *Thérèse of the Child Jesus of the Holy Face,*
> *nov. carm. ind.*

P.S. Do not forget to pluck a little Céline-flower,[3] it will be my heart offering it to you.

LXXVII

To MME GUÉRIN

For her feast

J. M. J. T.

Jesus †   Carmel, 18 November 1889.

Darling Aunt,

How time passes. Already it is two years since I sent you feast wishes from Rome, and it seems like only yesterday.

---

revealed to the world. When the solemn exposition was made in 1898, no one had seen the Holy Shroud for thirty years. Then was made clear, by the positive film of photography, the mysterious negative imprint of the body of Jesus, which until then had puzzled men of science, and the majestic face of Christ appeared; but not having yet been clearly shown photographically life-size, the contours were vague and the features smudged. It was then necessary to redraw the Holy Effigy with more clarity to present it to the piety of the faithful.

The deeply moved welcome given by Pope Pius X to the Holy Face of the Lisieux Carmel is well known, as are the many indulgences he attached to it, showing plainly his desire "that it should have its place in all Christian homes".

An indulgence of three hundred days, toties quoties, was at the same time granted to a prayer to the Holy Face composed by St. Thérèse which accompanies the picture painted by her sister.

[1] The souls of priests.
[2] John xi. 16.
[3] This is the name Thérèse gave to the white asters, which bloom in October at Les Buissonnets, whose name she did not know. She gave them to her sister every year for the feast of St. Céline.

During these two years, many things have happened, God has granted me great graces. . . . He has also visited us with His cross, and at the same time has revealed to us all the tenderness He has put into the heart of our dearest Aunt.

What memories for me on this date, 19 November. What joy when I used to see the moment arrive ! It is still with the same happiness that I now tell my dear Aunt again all the wishes I form for her ; but I am foolish, I shall not waste my time enumerating them, for I believe a whole volume would not be enough.

If you knew, darling Aunt, how your little girl is going to pray for you on the day of your feast. Alas ! I am so imperfect that I imagine my poor prayers have not much value, but there are beggars who get what they desire by sheer importunity; I shall do as they do, and the good God simply will not be able to send me away empty-handed. . . .

There is four o'clock sounding, I must leave you, darling Aunt, but I assure you that my heart stays with you still.

I beg you, darling Aunt, to remember me to Mme Fournet,[1] for I have not forgotten that it is her feast. It goes without saying that I embrace my dear Uncle and my dear little sisters with all my heart.

For you, dearest Aunt, I send the best kiss from the littlest of your seven little girls.[2]

Sister Thérèse of the Child Jesus,
nov. carm. ind.

LXXVIII

To M. AND MME GUÉRIN

New Year wishes

J. M. J. T.

Jesus †

30 December 1889.

My dear Uncle and my dear Aunt,

Your Benjamin comes in her turn to wish you a happy New Year. As each day has its last hour, so each year sees its last

---

[1] Mme Guérin's mother. She was named Elizabeth and had the same feast as her daughter.
[2] Mme Guérin's two daughters and five nieces.

evening come, and it is on the evening of this year that I feel urged to cast a glance over the past and over the future.

As I consider the time that has just gone by I thank the good God, for if His hand has held a cup of bitterness to our lips, His divine heart has supported us in the trial and has given us the strength needed to drink His cup to the dregs. For the year that is about to open, what has He awaiting us? It is not given me to penetrate the mystery, but I beg that God will reward my dear relations a hundredfold for all their most touching kindnesses to us.

The first day of the year is for me a world of memories. . . . I still see Papa showering caresses upon us. He was so good! But why recall these memories? This dearest of fathers has received the reward of his virtues. God has sent him a trial worthy of him.[1]

There is nine o'clock sounding, I must end my letter, having said nothing of what I should have said . . . but I hope my dear relations will excuse their little Thérèse, and especially pardon the unreadable writing. *Happy New Year* to my dear little sisters; above all may Marie get well soon. I shall be angry with her if influenza prevents her coming to see us.

Goodbye for now, dear Uncle and dear Aunt, your little girl wishes you a *good, good* year and kisses you with all her heart.

> *Sister Thérèse of the Child Jesus,*
> *nov. carm. ind.*

LXXIX

To CÉLINE

At the end of the year

J. M. J. T.

Jesus †   31 December 1889.

My dearest Céline,

My last goodbye of this year is for you! . . . In a few hours, the year will be gone forever . . . it will be in eternity!

---

[1] Thérèse is alluding to the great trial of her father's mental illness. He was not to die for another four and a half years.

Since my Céline is in her bed,[1] it is for me to seek her out to wish her a *Happy New Year* . . . Do you remember how it used to be?

The year that has just passed has been good, yes, it has been precious for heaven, may the one which is to follow it be like it! . . . Céline, I'm not surprised to see you in bed after such a year! At the end of such *a day* as that, you have good reason to rest. . . . Do you understand? . . . Perhaps the year that is about to begin will be the last! . . . Ah! let us profit, profit by the shortest instant, act like misers, be jealous of the smallest things for the sake of the Beloved! . . . Our New Year's Day is very sad this year. . . . It is with a heart filled with memories that I shall watch, waiting for midnight. . . . I remember everything. . . . Now we are orphans,[2] but we can say with love: "Our Father who art in Heaven." Yes, He still abides as the unique *all* of our souls! . . . One more year gone by! Céline, it is gone, gone, it will never come back. As this year has gone from us our life also will go, and soon we shall say: "It is gone." We must not waste our time, soon eternity will shine for us! . . . Céline, if you will, let us convert souls, this year we absolutely must make many *priests* who love Jesus, who *touch* Him with the same delicacy as Mary *touching* Him in His cradle.

Your little sister,

Thérèse of the Child Jesus of the Holy Face,
nov. carm. ind.

P.S. I also wish a Happy New Year to Lolo,[3] but I expect to see her. Thank Uncle and Aunt warmly, tell them that I am much moved by their gifts; also thank Jeanne and Marie, truly they are too kind.

[1] The Carmelites have the custom of staying up to spend the last hour of the year in prayer and beginning the New Year in choir before the tabernacle. Thérèse was writing to her sister after matins and before the last hour, knowing that Céline was at that time asleep in bed.
[2] Allusion to their father's illness.
[3] Her sister Léonie.

1890

EIGHTEENTH YEAR

8–24 September : Thérèse is professed and takes the veil.—M. Martin's health is still the great cross to his daughters.—It is to this year and the next that a passage in the Histoire d'une âme (*ch. 8*) *refers : " What lights did I not draw from the works of our Father, St. John of the Cross! At seventeen and eighteen, I had no other nourishment."*

LXXX

To CÉLINE

For her birthday

J. M. J. T.

Jesus †   26 April 1890.

My dearest Céline,

There was I looking forward to writing you a long letter for your *twenty-first* birthday, and here I find myself with barely a few moments ! . . . Céline, did you imagine that your Thérèse could forget the 28th of April ? . . . Céline, my heart is filled with memories. . . . I feel as if I had been loving you for centuries, and it is not twenty-one years after all. But now, I have eternity before me. . . .

Céline, the lyre of my heart will sing for you on the 28th, your name will sound again and again in the beloved ears of my Jesus. Ah ! Since our hearts are one SAME heart, let us give it whole and entire to Jesus; we must go *together*, for Jesus cannot dwell in *half a heart* ! . . . Pray that your Thérèse may not linger behind. . . .

As I looked at the image of the Holy Face, tears came to my eyes, is it not the symbol of our family ? Yes, our family is a *lily-branch*, and the *Lily without name*[1] resides in the midst, He

[1] The picture on parchment painted by Sister Agnes of Jesus represents a spray of lilies interlaced with thorns. The lilies make a background around the Holy Face. . . .

106

resides there as king and grants us to share the honours of His kingship, His divine blood flows out upon our petals, and His thorns tear us so that the perfume of our love can breathe forth. Goodbye, Céline, our conversation is about to be interrupted, understand *everything*.

Thérèse.

LXXXI

To SISTER AGNES OF JESUS

During her annual retreat[1]

J. M. J. T.

Jesus †

Light little *Lark*, my heart goes with you into the solitary place, and however high you soar, you must carry your burden with you, but a *grain of sand* is not heavy, and after all it will be lighter still if you ask Jesus. . . . Oh ! how it desires to be reduced to nothing, unknown by any creature; poor little thing, it desires nothing more, nothing but to be FORGOTTEN . . . not contempt, not insults, such things would be too much glory for a *grain of sand*. To be despised, it would have to be seen, but it wants to be FORGOTTEN ! . . . Yes, I want to be forgotten, and not only by creatures, but also by *myself*, I should like to be so reduced to nothingness as to have no desire left. . . . The glory of my Jesus, that is all ! For my own, I abandon it to Him ; and if He seems to forget me, very well, He is free to, since I am no longer mine, but His. . . . He will weary of keeping me waiting sooner than I of waiting for Him ! . . .

Dearest *Lamb*, do you understand ? Understand everything, even what my heart cannot express. You, who are a flaming torch that Jesus has given me to light my steps in the dark pathways of exile, have pity on my weakness, hide me under your veil that I may share in your light. Tell Jesus to look upon me, that the *night lilies*[2] may penetrate with their luminous rays the heart

---

Thérèse and her four sisters are represented by flowers in bloom, the four little dead brothers and sisters by buds. No names are indicated. The expression "Lily without name", referring to Our Lord, signifies that His true name is too sublime to be uttered in human words upon earth.

[1] This letter is undated, unsigned. It was written at the end of April or the beginning of May 1890.

[2] The eyes of Jesus. The allusion is to a prayer in which the Holy Face is compared to a bouquet of flowers.

of the *grain of sand*; and if it is not too much, ask also that the *Flower of flowers*[1] may open its petals and that the melodious sound that comes forth may set its mysterious teachings vibrating in my heart. . . . Dearest *Lamb*, do not forget the *grain of sand*! . . .

LXXXII

To SISTER AGNES OF JESUS

During her annual retreat[2]

J. M. J. T.

Thank you for your letter, Oh thank you ! . . .

It does not surprise me that you have no consolation, for Jesus is so little consoled that He is happy to find a soul in which He can take His rest without a mass of formalities. . . .

How proud I am to be your sister ! And your little girl, too, for it was you who taught me to love Jesus, to seek only Him.

Céline has told us of our poor little Father; she remarked that it was Saturday, the day of the Finding of the True Cross, that we too found our cross ![3] Léonie was there. She hopes to be cured either at the Holy Face or at Lourdes. She means to go down into the bath. Poor Léonie, she was very good, she was willing to forgo her visits to our parlour to give pleasure to Céline. . . . The bell has rung for vespers, I am off. I don't know when they will be at Tours, but I think they will be at Lourdes next week.[4] One must write on Monday, or before midday Tuesday, in order that the letter may arrive on Saturday.

Oh ! what an exile is this earth . . . there is no one to lean upon save Jesus, for He only is *immutable*. What a happiness to realise that *He cannot change*. . . . What a joy for our hearts to remember that our little family loves Jesus so tenderly ! That is always my consolation . . . Surely our family is a virginal family, a family of lilies ? Ask Jesus that the *smallest* and *last* may not be the *last* to love Him with all her power of loving.

[1] Allusion to the same prayer.
[2] This letter is not dated or signed. It was written early in May 1890.
[3] Allusion to M. Martin's state of health.
[4] Léonie and Céline were on the point of going travelling with the Guérins. They were to visit Tours (which has the oratory of the Holy Face), Lourdes, Gavarnie, the principal towns of the west and south of France and north of Spain.

EIGHTEENTH YEAR

LXXXIII

To CÉLINE

On tour with her family

J. M. J. T.

Jesus †   May 1890.

My dearest Céline,

Are you enjoying your tour? I hope the Blessed Virgin is filling you to overflowing with her graces; if they are not graces of consolation, they are assuredly graces of light! And the Holy Face!¹ Céline, you realize that it is a great grace to visit all these sacred spots. . . . My heart would like to go with you everywhere, but alas! I do not know your itinerary, I even thought that you would not be at Lourdes until next week.

Céline, you must be very happy to contemplate nature in her beauty, the mountains, the silvery streams, all so magnificent, so calculated to raise up our souls . . . Ah! little Sister, let us detach ourselves from the earth and fly up to the mountain of Love where grows the lovely Lily of our souls. Let us detach ourselves from Jesus' *consolations*, to attach ourselves to *Him!*

And the Blessed Virgin? Ah! Céline, hide yourself in the shadow of her virginal mantle that she may *virginize* you! . . . Purity is so lovely, so white! "Blessed are the pure in heart, for they shall see God."² Yes, they shall see Him even upon earth, where nothing is pure, but where all creatures grow limpid when we can look at them with the Face of the loveliest and whitest of Lilies between! . . .

Céline, pure hearts are often ringed with thorns, often in darkness, then the lilies think they have lost their whiteness, think that the thorns which ring them round have actually torn their petals! Do you understand, Céline? The lilies in the midst of thorns are those whom Jesus loves, it is in their midst that He takes His pleasure! "Blessed is the man that has been found worthy to endure temptation."³

Thérèse of the Child Jesus of the Holy Face.

¹ The allusion is to their stopping at Tours and their pilgrimage to the Oratory of M. Dupont, the Holy Man of Tours.
² Matt. v. 8.
³ Jas. i. 12.

P.S. I should have liked to write to my dear Léonie, but it is impossible for lack of time; tell her how much I pray for her and how much I think of my dearest godmother.[1] I meant also to write to little Marie, but I cannot; I keep praying that the Blessed Virgin may make her a *little lily* which thinks of Jesus a great deal, and *forgets itself*, and all its miseries as well, in the hands of obedience.[2] I do not forget my Jeanne.

We have had nothing from Canada.[3] Sister Agnes of Jesus cannot write because she is in retreat. If you have bought nothing for our Mother, you might bring back a statue of Our Lady of Lourdes, not painted, at four or five francs.

LXXXIV

To SISTER AGNES OF JESUS

Who was on her annual retreat[4]

J. M. J. T.

Jesus †

Darling *Lamb*, permit your poor *baby lamb* to bleat a little . . . the Lamb did me good on Sunday! There was one phrase especially in your letter that I found luminous. It was "Let us say no word that might make others think more highly of us". It is true that we must keep everything for Jesus with *jealous* care. . . . Dearest *Lamb*, how good it is to work for Jesus *alone*, for Him all ALONE. . . . Oh! then, when the heart is wholly filled, how light one feels.

Little Lamb of Jesus, pray for the poor little *grain of sand*. May the *grain of sand* be always in its place, that is to say beneath everyone's feet. May no one think of it, may its existence be, so to speak, *ignored* . . . the *grain of sand* does not desire to be humiliated, that would still be too much glory since it would involve its being noticed,[5] it desires but one thing "*to be* FORGOTTEN, counted as nought!"[6] . . . But it desires to be *seen* by Jesus.

---

[1] Léonie had been her godmother in confirmation.
[2] An allusion to the scruples from which Marie Guérin suffered (see Letter LXXI).
[3] From Père Pichon, S.J.
[4] This letter has no date or signature. It was written in all probability during Sister Agnes's annual retreat in 1890.
[5] This same wish was expressed in Letter LXXXI.
[6] *Imitation of Christ*, bk. i, ch. ii.

The gaze of creatures cannot sink low enough to reach it, but at least let the bleeding Face of Jesus be turned towards it. It desires but one look, one only look !

If it were possible for a *grain of sand* to console Jesus, to dry His tears, there is one that would so love to do it. . . . Let Jesus take the poor *grain of sand* and hide it in His adorable Face . . . there the poor atom will have nothing more to fear, it will be *sure* to *sin no more* ! . . .

At every cost the *grain of sand* wants to save souls. . . . Jesus must grant it this grace, little Veronica,[1] ask it of the *luminous* face of Jesus ! . . . Yes, the face of Jesus is *luminous*; but if it is so beautiful with all its wounds and tears, what shall it be when we see it in Heaven ? . . .

Oh ! Heaven . . . Heaven ! Yes, one day to see the face of Jesus, to contemplate the marvellous beauty of Jesus eternally, the poor *grain of sand* wants to be despised upon earth. . . . Dearest *Lamb*, ask Jesus that His *grain of sand* may hasten to save many souls in little time that it may the sooner fly where His beloved Face is. . . .

I suffer ! . . . But the hope of the Homeland gives me courage, soon we shall be in Heaven. . . . There, there will be neither day nor night any more, but the Face of Jesus will bathe all in a light like no other.

Dearest *Lamb*, understand the *grain of sand*, it does not know what it has said tonight, but quite certainly it had no intention of writing one word of all that it has scribbled.

LXXXV

To SISTER AGNES OF JESUS

Who was on her annual retreat[2]

J. M. J. T.

Jesus †

Dearest *Lamb*, one day more and you will come down again to battle in the plain ! . . . the poor *baby lamb* will have its *Mother* again, at last. How happy I am to be *forever a prisoner* in Carmel.

---

[1] So called because of her devotion to the Holy Face. She had been the promoter of this devotion in the Martin family.
[2] This letter is not dated or signed. It was written in May 1890.

I have no wish to go to Lourdes to have ecstasies. I prefer the monotony of sacrifice ! What happiness to be so well hidden that no one thinks of you ! . . . To be unknown even to the people who live with you. . . .

Dearest *Lamb*, how I thank Jesus for having given me to you, for having made you understand my soul so well . . . I cannot tell you all that I think . . . Ah ! HEAVEN ! ! ! . . . there, a single look and all will be said and understood.

Silence, that is the language which alone can tell you all that passes in my soul.[1]

LXXXVI

To CÉLINE

Back at Lisieux

J. M. J. T.

Jesus †   May, 1890.

My darling Céline,

I have been instructed to write you a brief note to tell you not to come with news of Papa during the Pentecost retreat.[2] If you liked to write us a little note, it would be very kind of you, and then on Monday[3] you could come to see us.

Céline dearest, I am happy to be made the bearer of this message, for I feel the need to tell you to what a point it seems to me that the Good God loves you and treats you as an especially favoured soul. Ah ! you may well say that your *reward* is *great* in Heaven, since it is said: "Blessed are you when they shall persecute you and falsely speak all that is evil against you."[4] Then be glad and tremble with joy ![5] Céline, what a privilege to be misjudged upon earth. Ah ! God's thoughts are not our

[1] What a power of silence Thérèse had ! During the years of her canonical novitiate, she had been authorised to open her heart to her sisters in letters written during their annual retreats (1889 and 1890). All these notes are published in this volume. Then she relapsed into silence. Apart from the letter written on the day of her sister's election as Prioress (CXIX) and the one she wrote for her feast in 1894 (CXXXV), we must wait until 1897 to find a handful of notes. . . . Thérèse then felt so close to eternity that she felt she must show her sisters the last evidences of her supernatural tenderness towards them.

[2] It was the custom in the convent to suspend visits to the parlour from Ascension Day to Whit Sunday (see note to Letter XXIX).

[3] Whit Monday, 26 May.

[4] Matt. v. 11.

[5] Matt. v. 12. Céline had been the victim of very trying malicious gossip.

thoughts.[1] If they were, our life would be one unbroken hymn of gratitude. . . .

Céline, do you think that St. Teresa received more graces than you? . . . for my part, I do not tell you to aim at her *seraphic* sanctity, but simply "to be perfect as your heavenly Father is perfect".[2] . . . Ah! Céline, our *infinite desires* are after all not dreams or fantasies, since Jesus Himself gave us this *commandment*.[3]

Céline, does it not seem to you that upon earth there remains to us *nothing*! Jesus wills to make us drink our cup to the dregs by leaving our darling father over there.[4] Ah! let us refuse Him nothing. He has so great *need of love*, He is so *parched* that He awaits a drop of water from us to refresh Him. Ah! let us give without counting, one day He will be able to say: "My turn now."[5]

Give my warm thanks to my darling Marie for her enchanting bouquet, tell her that I am giving it to Jesus from her, and that I am asking him in return to adorn her soul with as many virtues as there are rosebuds.

> Your little sister,
> *Thérèse of the Child Jesus of the Holy Face,*
> *nov. carm. ind.*

LXXXVII

To MARIE GUÉRIN

At La Musse

J. M. J. T.

Jesus †   Carmel, July 1890.

My darling Marie,

Do thank the good God for all the graces He grants you, and do not be so *ungrateful* as not to recognise them. You seem to me like a little village girl to whom a mighty king proposes marriage, and who dare not accept, because she is not rich

---

[1] Isa. lv. 8.
[2] Matt. v. 48.
[3] About this time, Thérèse had confided to the Jesuit, Père Blino, her desire to "become a Saint, to love God as much as St. Teresa". The worthy religious, far from encouraging her, did his best to moderate aspirations that he judged temerarious. The Saint found this opposition a stimulus to seek in Scripture a ground for her confidence. The few lines addressed to Céline reflect her state of soul (cf. Laveille, *Sainte Thérèse de L'Enfant-Jésus*, p. 188, note 1).
[4] In Caen.
[5] Cf. Arminjon, loc. cit.

enough, nor trained enough in the usages of the court; she does not reflect that her royal suitor knows her quality and her weakness much better than she knows it herself. . . . Marie, if you are nothing, you must not forget Jesus is *all*, so you must lose your little nothing in His *infinite all* and from now on think only of that uniquely lovable all. . . . Nor must you desire to see the fruits of your efforts, Jesus likes to keep, for Himself alone, these little nothings which console Him. . . . You are wrong, dearest, if you think your little Thérèse always marches with ardour along the way of virtue, she is weak, very weak; every day she experiences it afresh; but, Marie, Jesus delights to teach her, as He taught St. Paul, the science of glorying in one's infirmities;[1] that is a great grace, and I beg Jesus to teach it to you, for in it alone is found peace and rest for the heart. Seeing yourself so worthless, you wish no longer to look at yourself, you look only at the sole Beloved ! . . .

Darling Marie, for my part I know no other means to arrive at perfection save love. . . . Love, how evidently our heart is made for that ! . . . Sometimes I try to find another word to express love, but on this earth of exile words are impotent to render all the vibrations of the soul, so one must rest satisfied with the single word Love ! . . .

But upon whom shall our poor love-famished heart pour itself out ? . . . Ah ! who shall be great enough for that ? . . . Can a human being comprehend it . . . still more, can he return it ? . . . Marie, there is but one being who can comprehend the depths of the word Love ! . . . None but our Jesus can return us infinitely more than we give Him. . . .

Marie of the Blessed Sacrament[2] . . . your name tells you your mission. To console Jesus, to get souls to love Him. . . . Jesus is sick for love, and one must realise that "the sickness of love is cured only by love".[3] . . . Marie, give all your heart to Jesus, He is athirst for it, hungry for it; your heart, to have that is His ambition—so much so that to have it for Himself He consents to dwell in a dark and unclean corner.[4] . . . Ah ! how

---

[1] 2 Cor. xii. 5.
[2] Name chosen for Marie Guérin when she should become a Carmelite. She entered Carmel five years later and was given the name of Marie of the Eucharist.
[3] St. John of the Cross, *Commentary on the Spiritual Canticle*, strophe xi.
[4] Allusion to the church of a village near the Château de la Musse (where the Guérins spent the summer). Its tabernacle was a poor dilapidated box.

can we fail to love a friend who reduces Himself to such utter destitution, how can anyone still dare to plead her poverty, when Jesus makes Himself like His spouse . . . "being rich He became poor"[1] to unite His poverty with the poverty of Marie of the Blessed Sacrament. . . . What a mystery of love.

All my greetings to the dear colony.

My heart is always with Marie of the Blessed Sacrament, the tabernacle is love's house, wherein our two souls are enclosed. . . .

Your little sister who asks you not to forget her in your prayers,

Sister Thérèse of the Child Jesus of the Holy Face,
nov. carm. ind.

LXXXVIII

To CÉLINE

On holiday at La Musse

J. M. J. T.

Jesus †   Carmel, 18 July 1890.

Dearest Céline,

If you knew how your letter spoke to my soul ! . . . Ah ! joy flooded in on my heart like a vast ocean ! . . . Céline, all I have to tell you, you know, since you are I. . . . I am sending you a page[2] which has affected my soul deeply, it seems to me that yours will be immersed in it too.

Céline, it was *so long* ago . . . and already the soul of the prophet Isaias was immersed like ours in the HIDDEN BEAUTIES[3] of Jesus. . . . Ah ! Céline, when I read these things, I ask myself what time is ?—Time is only a mirage, a dream; already God *sees us in glory,* He *is enjoying* our *eternal beatitude* ! . . . Ah ! what good the realisation of this does to my soul ! I understand why He does not bargain with us . . . He feels that we *understand* Him, and He treats us as His friends, as His most dear brides. . . .

Céline, since Jesus "has trodden the winepress alone"[4] and gives us to drink of it, let us on our part not refuse to wear garments stained with blood, let us tread, for Jesus, a new wine

[1] 2 Cor. viii. 9.
[2] See copy of this page at the end of the letter.
[3] These two words are underlined three times.
[4] Isa. lxiii. 3.

to slake His thirst and give Him love for love. Ah! let us not lose a single drop of the wine we can give Him . . . then "looking about Him"[1] He will see that we come to give him aid! . . . "His look was as it were hidden!"[2] . . . Céline, it is still hidden today . . . for who comprehends the tears of Jesus?

Dearest Céline, let us make a little tabernacle in our heart where Jesus can find refuge, then He will be consoled, and He will forget what we cannot forget—the ingratitude of souls who leave Him alone in a deserted tabernacle!

"Open to me, my sister, my love, for my face is full of dew, and my locks of the drops of the night" (Cant. of Cant.).[3] That is what Jesus says to us when He is left alone and forgotten! . . . Céline, *forgetfulness*, I feel that that is what causes Him most pain. Papa! . . . Ah! Céline, I cannot tell you all that I think, it would take too long, and how can one say things which thought itself can hardly frame, profundities which are in the most secret abysses of the soul. . . .

Jesus has sent us the best-chosen cross that He could devise in His immense love. . . . How can we complain when He Himself was considered "as one struck by God and afflicted"?[4]

The "charm divine"[5] charms my soul and marvellously consoles it at every instant of the day! Ah! The *tears* of Jesus, what *smiles* they are! . . .

Kiss everybody for me and give them any messages you please. I think often of my dearest Léonie, my dear little Visitandine.[6] Tell Marie of the Blessed Sacrament[7] that Jesus asks much love from her, He wants reparation from her for the coldnesses He meets, her heart must be a brazier at which Jesus can find warmth. . . . She must forget herself entirely to think only of Him. . . .

Céline, let us pray for priests, ah! let us pray for them, let our life be consecrated to them. Every day Jesus makes me feel that that is what He wants from us two.

C. T.[8]

[1] Isa. lxiii. 5.
[2] Isa. liii. 3.
[3] Cant. of Cant. v. 2. The reference in parenthesis is by Thérèse herself.
[4] Isa. liii. 4.
[5] Allusion to a poetic composition of Céline's.
[6] An allusion to Léonie's persistent desire to re-enter the Visitation order.
[7] See note to Letter LXXXVII.
[8] The saint signs her letter with the initials of Céline, Thérèse, writing them immediately under the words "us two", and ringing them round with a line.

EIGHTEENTH YEAR

From the Prophet Isaias (Ch. 53)[1]

Who hath believed our report? And to whom is the arm of the Lord revealed? Christ shall grow up as a tender plant before the Lord, and as a root out of a thirsty ground. There is no beauty in Him, nor comeliness : we have seen Him, and there was no sightliness that we could be desirous of Him : despised and the most abject of men, a man of sorrows and acquainted with infirmity : His look was as it were hidden and despised. Whereupon we esteemed Him not. Surely He hath borne our infirmities and carried our sorrows. We have thought of Him as it were a leper, and as one struck by God and afflicted. But he was wounded for our iniquities : He was bruised for our sins. The chastisement of our peace was upon Him : and by His bruises we are healed.

Chapter 63[2]

Who is this that cometh from Edom, with dyed garments from Bosra, this beautiful one in His robe walking in the greatness of his strength?—I that speak justice and am a defender to save. Why then is thy apparel red and thy garments like theirs that tread in the winepress?—I have trodden the winepress alone, and of the Gentiles there is not a man with me. I looked about, and there was none to help. I sought and there was none to give aid.

Those who are clad in white robes, who are they and whence come they? These are they who are come out of great tribulation and have washed their robes in the blood of the Lamb. Therefore, they are before the throne of God: and they serve Him night and day.[3]

A bundle of myrrh is my beloved to me : he shall abide between my breasts. My beloved shines with the whiteness and the glory of his countenance, the hairs of his head are as the purple of the king.[4] *My beloved is all lovable, his countenance inspires love, and his face bowed down presses me to return him love for love.*[5]

> *My face bending over my beloved*
> *There I remained, all forgetful of myself;*
> *Everything vanished and I abandoned myself*

[1] The reference is noted by the saint herself. She quotes verses 1–5.
[2] Isa. lxiii. 1–5.
[3] Apoc. vii. 13–15.
[4] Cant. of Cant. i. 12; v. 11; vii. 5; etc.
[5] Liturgical office of the feast of the Seven Dolours of the Blessed Virgin Mary, first nocturne, first response.

LETTERS OF ST. THÉRÈSE

Leaving all my solicitudes
Lost in the midst of lilies.

(Fragment of a *Canticle* of our father
ST. JOHN OF THE CROSS.)[1]

LXXXIX

To SISTER AGNES OF JESUS

During Thérèse's retreat before Profession[2]

J. M. J. T.

Jesus †

Dearest *Lamb*, yes, joys for us will always be mingled with suffering. Yesterday's grace[3] required a crowning, and Jesus gave it to you, and then to me at the same time, for whatever causes you suffering wounds me deeply ! . . . I should very much like to know if our Mother consoled you and if you still feel hurt ? I feel that we should thank "the holy old man Simeon "[4] and tell him that his letter arrived. What do you think ?

I give you a brief note from Sister X. . . . she wrote it to me this morning. Must I do all that for her ?[5] . . . I have no models, and in any event it seems to me that the linen and the "Blessed Virgin"[6] are more urgent, but I shall do what you tell me.

Do you think Céline is really going to die ?[7] . . . I promised her yesterday to make Profession for us both, but I shall not have the courage to ask Jesus to leave her on earth if it is not His will. It seems to me that love can substitute for long life. Jesus

---

[1] *Canticle of the Soul*, strophe viii.

[2] Thérèse had received from the Mother Prioress permission to tell her intimate thoughts to her Carmelite sisters, in brief notes, during her retreats before Clothing and Profession (see note to Letter L). This letter is not dated. It was written at the beginning of the ten-day retreat in preparation for her Profession, that is to say, the last days of August 1890.

[3] We do not know what is the grace that Thérèse alludes to.

[4] Brother Simeon of the Christian Schools, founder and director of the College of St. Joseph in Rome (see *Histoire d'une âme*, ch. vi, viii and Letters XCIX and CLXXXVII, with note, in this volume).

[5] This sister was asking Thérèse for a long and difficult job of painting on statues.

[6] The linen to be mended, and ornaments to be arranged for a statue of the Blessed Virgin.

[7] Céline had heart trouble, and those about her were alarmed.

takes no account of time, since there is none in heaven. He must take account only of love. Ask Him to give me great love too. I do not desire love that I feel, but only love that Jesus feels. Oh ! how sweet it is to love Him and to make Him loved ! Tell Him to take me on the day of my profession if I am ever to offend Him again, for I want to bear the white robe of my second baptism to heaven without stain. But it seems to me that Jesus could very well give one the grace never to offend Him again, or rather to commit only faults which do not OFFEND Him, but merely have the effect of humbling oneself and making love stronger.

If you knew what things I should tell you if I had words to express what I think, or rather what I don't think but feel !

Life is very mysterious ! It is a desert and an exile . . . but in the depths of the soul one feels that there will be one day infinite DISTANCES, DISTANCES which will make us forget forever the sadness of desert and exile.

The little grain of sand.

The Abbé Domin[1] does not know that I am making my Profession, should he be told ? It occurs to me that, if our Mother has not yet written to the Abbey, she might tell the nuns to inform him.

XC

To SISTER AGNES OF JESUS

During Thérèse's retreat before Profession[2]

J. M. J. T.

Jesus †

Monday.

Here is the letter I have written for Papa.[3] If you find that it cannot go, I hope you will write a line for me, but I imagine he will not understand.[4] . . . Ah ! what a mystery is the love

---

[1] Chaplain to the Benedictine Convent at Lisieux, he was Thérèse's confessor during the years she was a student there. She speaks of him in the *Histoire d'une âme* (ch. iv). He gave evidence at her Process of Beatification, and died 13 June 1908 in his seventy-fifth year.

[2] This note, unsigned, bears no other date than the word Monday. It was Monday, 1 September 1890.

[3] This letter has not been preserved.

[4] Allusion to M. Martin's state of health.

of Jesus upon our family ! What a mystery the tears of love of that "Betrothed in blood".[1]

Tomorrow I shall go to M. Youf;[2] he has told me to make him a brief review of my life[3]—only since I have been in Carmel; pray that Jesus may leave me the *peace* He has *given* me. I was very happy to receive absolution on Saturday. But I do not understand the retreat I am making, I think of nothing, in a word I am in a very dark subterranean passage ! . . . Oh ! you who are my light, ask Jesus not to allow souls to be deprived, because of me, of the lights they need, but to let my darkness serve to enlighten them. . . . Ask Him also that I may make a good retreat and that He may be as satisfied as possible; then I too shall be satisfied and I shall consent, if it is His will, to walk all my life the dark road upon which I am, provided that one day I arrive at the goal of the mountain of love, but I think it will not be here below.

XCI

To SISTER AGNES OF JESUS

During Thérèse's retreat before Profession[4]

J. M. J. T.

Jesus †

Little Mother of mine, thank you, oh ! thank you . . . if you knew what your letter said to my soul.

But the little solitary must tell you of the itinerary of her journey. Here it is :

Before they started, it seemed that her Spouse asked her in what country she wished to travel, what road she wished to follow . . . the little bride answered she had only one desire, to come to the summit of the *mountain of Love*. To reach it, there were many

---

[1] Exod. iv. 25. Père Pichon, S.J., liked to quote this phrase.

[2] Chaplain to the Carmel at Lisieux since 1870, after having been for three years curate at the parish of St. Jacques. This pious, zealous priest gave himself utterly to the community. He had a very high opinion of Thérèse. He died a few days after her, 8 October 1897, aged fifty-five. His health had long been affected, owing to the excessive intellectual labour he had imposed upon himself at the beginning of his priestly life.

[3] That is to say, a confession.

[4] Undated, unsigned; written early in September 1890.

roads open to her, so many of them were perfect that she found herself incapable of choosing, so she said to her Divine Guide: "You know where I desire to go, You know *for whom* I wish to scale the mountains, for whom I wish to keep on to the end, You know Who it is that I love and Whom it is my sole wish to content. It is for Him alone that I undertake this journey, so lead me by the paths He loves to travel; provided He is content, I shall be at the uttermost point of happiness."

Then Jesus took me by the hand and brought me into a subterranean way, where it is neither hot nor cold, where the sun does not shine, and rain and wind do not come; a tunnel where I see nothing but a brightness half-veiled, the glow from the downcast eyes in the Face of my Spouse.

My Spouse says nothing to me, nor do I say anything to Him either, save that *I love Him* more than *myself*, and in the depth of my heart I feel that this is true, for I am more His than my own ! . . .

I do not see that we are advancing towards the mountain that is our goal, because our journey is under the earth ; yet I have a feeling that we are approaching it, without knowing why.

The road I follow is one of no consolation for me, yet it brings me all consolations because it is Jesus who has chosen it, and I desire to console Him only. . . .

Ah ! I do indeed give Him the wine of my heart, it is between the B. and the A.,[1] for I can make nothing of it myself. Above all do not forget to drink your wine,[2] drinking it you will think of your little girl, who very surely does not drink either of the good *sweet wine of Engaddi*[3] . . . pray that by saving souls she may be able to give it to her Spouse and she will be consoled. . . .

Should I write to M. Lepelletier[4] and to M. Révérony[5] that I am making my Profession ?

---

[1] It is not known what the Saint is alluding to here. To the ox and the ass (le boeuf et l'âne) of the crib ? to a child reciting the alphabet ? . . .
[2] The doctor had ordered Sister Agnes to take quinquina, a tonic wine.
[3] Cant. of Cant. i. 13.
[4] The Abbé Lepelletier, born in 1853, ordained priest in 1877, and later first assistant at the Cathedral of St. Pierre in Lisieux. Had been M. Martin's confessor. He was Thérèse's from her leaving the Abbey (early in 1886) until her entry into Carmel. The Saint has made allusion to this excellent priest (*Histoire d'une âme*, ch. v). He left Lisieux for Lion-sur-Mer in 1898, was parish priest of St. Etienne at Caen, and Canon in 1891. He died 27 November 1918.
[5] The Abbé Révérony was Vicar-General of Bayeux (see note 1 to Letter XXI).

XCII

To SISTER MARIE OF THE SACRED HEART

During Thérèse's retreat before Profession[1]

Darling Godmother,

If you knew how your song from Heaven ravished the soul of your little girl![2] . . . I assure you that she is not hearing celestial harmonies![3] Her wedding-journey is very arid! Certainly her Spouse leads her by fertile and magnificent countrysides, but the *night* prevents her from admiring anything, and, what is worse, from enjoying all these marvels.

Perhaps you will think that she is afflicted by this? But no, the very opposite, she is happy to follow her Spouse for love of *Him alone*, and not because of what He gives her. . . . He alone, He so beautiful! so enchanting! even when *He is silent* . . . even when He hides! . . .

Do you understand your little girl? She is weary of the consolations of this world; she now wants nothing but her Beloved alone. . . . Don't forget to keep praying for the little girl whom you brought up and who is yours.

XCIII

To SISTER AGNES OF JESUS

During Thérèse's retreat before Profession[4]

J. M. J. T.

I give you a letter from Rome[5] that you may give it to Céline, if you will. Perhaps Papa will not understand it, but it is not difficult to grasp, and if at moments he understood, he

---

[1] This note, undated and unsigned, was probably written 3 September.

[2] The reference is to an unpublished note of Sister Marie, dated 2 September.

[3] In her note Sister Marie makes Jesus say: "Little bride . . . do you understand the celestial harmonies which already hymn our divine union? . . ."

[4] This note, unsigned and undated, was written on 4 September or 5 September at latest.

[5] From Brother Siméon (see note to Letter LXXXIX) to Sister Agnes of Jesus.

would be so happy ! Should he also be sent my vows, that he may bless them ?[1] If you think yes, would you tell me that too to-morrow morning so that I may write them at once, they could be put with my wreath, but perhaps it would be better not to do anything about it ?

Thank you for your little letter; if you could know what pleasure it has given me ! My soul is still in the underground tunnel but it is *very happy* there, yes, happy to have no consolation, for thus I see that its love is not like the love of the world's brides who are always looking at their bridegrooms' hands to see if they bear a gift, or at his face in the hope of surprising a smile of love to enchant them. . . .

But Jesus' poor little bride feels that she loves Jesus for *Himself* alone, and wishes to look upon the face of her Beloved only for a sudden glimpse of the tears which flow from eyes that have enchanted her with their *hidden charms* ! . . . She wants to gather up these tears, to adorn herself with them on the day of her Marriage. This adornment too *will be hidden*, but the Beloved will know it for what it is.

Should Madame Papineau[2] be written to ? It seems to me not worth the trouble, she would not understand. Perhaps it will be better to wait for the taking of the veil ?[3]

---

[1] The formula of her vows. Thérèse had expressed a wish that the wreath she was to wear on the day of her profession should be blessed by her father, and that it should be placed on his brow, marking by this symbolic gesture the part he took in the oblation of his daughter. Céline carried out this double ceremony (see *Histoire d'une âme*).

[2] She had given lessons to Thérèse. See Letter IV.

[3] As the ceremony of Profession was private, Thérèse thought it would be better to inform Madame Papineau by inviting her to the public veiling ceremony.

XCIV

To SISTER MARIE OF THE SACRED HEART

During Thérèse's retreat before Profession[1]

J. M. J. T.

Jesus,

If you knew what good your brief notes do me![2] They are like music from Heaven, I feel as if I were hearing an angel's voice . . . after all, are you not the angel[3] who led me and guided me in the way of exile until my entry into Carmel? And now you go on being, for me, the angel who consoled my childhood and I see in you what others cannot see, for you are so skilled at hiding what you are that on the day of eternity many people will get a surprise.

But your little girl will be surprised at nothing; and, beautiful as your throne and diadem may be, she will not be astonished at what the Divine Spouse will give to one who formed in her own heart the same love for the Spouse of Virgins; and your little girl also hopes that in your wreath she will be a tiny flower, lending its humble beauty to the glory of the angel who was present to it on earth.

[1] This note, undated and unsigned, was written 6 September 1890.
[2] Sister Marie, in an unpublished note of 5 September, wrote: "If it is night for my little girl, it is not night for her Spouse, and it is in the sunshine of eternity that He is preparing her wedding presents."
[3] Sister Marie was in a number of ways the "angel" of her younger sister and goddaughter, for she had been given the task of initiating Thérèse in the ways of Carmel during the first weeks of her postulancy. In monastic language the nun to whom this task is entrusted is called the *Angel*.

XCV

To SISTER MARIE OF THE SACRED HEART

During Thérèse's retreat before Profession[1]

J. M. J. T.

I should like the candles of the Child Jesus[2] to be lit when I go to Chapter.[3] Will you please see about it ? Don't forget, I beg you. . . . I do not say the pink candles, for these move my heart too deeply. They burnt for the first time the day of my Clothing, then they were rosy and fresh : Papa, who had given them to me, was there and all was joy. But now the *rose* colour has gone. . . . Are there still any rose-coloured joys for his *little Queen* here below ? . . . Oh ! no, for her there are no joys left but those of Heaven . . . joys in which the whole of creation, which is nought, gives place to the uncreated, which is reality. . . .

Do you understand your little girl ? . . .

Tomorrow she will be the bride of Jesus.

Tomorrow she will be the bride of Him whose face was hidden so that men knew Him not ![4] What an alliance and what a future ! . . . Yes, I feel it, my wedding will be thronged about with angels, only Heaven will be glad and the little bride too and her dearest sisters.

XCVI

To SISTER MARIE OF THE SACRED HEART

Lines pencilled on the back of a picture of the Blessed Virgin kneeling by the Child Jesus

Souvenir of 8 September 1890.

Day of eternal remembrance on which your little girl has become, like you, the bride of Him who said : "My kingdom is not of

---

[1] Note, undated and unsigned, written 7 September.
[2] The statue of the Child Jesus of which she had the care and before which the Sisters passed in procession accompanying her to Chapter.
[3] To make her vows.
[4] Isa. liii. 3.

this world,"[1] and later: "Nevertheless, soon you shall see the Son of Man coming in the clouds of Heaven on the right hand of God."[2] For us, that is the awaited day . . . the day of the eternal Marriage, on which our Jesus "will wipe every tear from our eye,"[3] on which He will have us "sit with Him"[4] upon His Throne. . . .

Now His face is hidden to the eyes of mortals, but for us who comprehend His tears in this valley of exile, His face will soon be shown all radiant in our Homeland, and then it will be ecstasy, the eternal union of glory with our Spouse. . . .

Pray that she whom you have instructed in the ways of virtue may one day be very close to you in the Homeland.

Your little girl.

XCVII

To SISTER MARTHE OF JESUS[5]

On the back of a picture which bears the inscription:
Two inseparable devotions: the Holy Face and the
Sacred Heart

To my dear little companion, in memory of the most beautiful day of your life, the unique day on which you have been consecrated to Jesus.

Together, let us console Jesus for all the ingratitudes of souls, and, by our love, let us make him forget His sorrows.

Your unworthy little sister,

Thérèse of the Child Jesus of the Holy Face,
rel. carm. ind.[6]

---

[1] John xviii. 36.
[2] Matt. xxvi. 64.
[3] Apoc. xxi. 4.
[4] Luke xxii. 30.
[5] For her Profession, 23 September 1890. It was the day before Thérèse received the veil. See notes to Letters LVI and CXLVI.
[6] The abbreviations stand for "unworthy Carmelite religious".

EIGHTEENTH YEAR

XCVIII

To CÉLINE

On the day before Thérèse took the veil[1]

J. M. J. T.

Jesus †   Tuesday, 23 September 1890.

Oh! Céline, how can I tell you what is passing in my soul? It is all torn, but I feel that the wound is made by a loving hand, a hand *divinely jealous.* . . .

All was in readiness for my espousal; but didn't you feel that something was lacking to the feast? It is true that Jesus had already put many jewels among my wedding presents, but all the same one was lacking, of incomparable beauty; and this precious diamond Jesus gave me today. . . . Céline, when I received it, my tears flowed, they flow still;[2] and I should almost blame myself for them if I did not know that "there exists a love of which tears are the sole pledge".[3]

Jesus alone has managed the whole affair, it is He, and I have recognised His touch of *love* . . .

You know how intensely I longed to see our dearest father this morning; ah well! now I see clearly that it is the good God's will that he should not be here. He allowed it simply to try our love. . . . Jesus wants me to be an *orphan.* He wants me to be alone with Him alone, that He may be united with me more intimately; and also He wants to give me, in the Homeland, the utterly legitimate joys He has refused me in the land of exile.

Céline, be consoled, our Spouse is a Spouse of tears not smiles ; let us give Him our tears to console Him, and one day these tears will be changed into smiles of inexpressible sweetness !

Céline, I do not know if you will understand my letter, I can hardly hold my pen . . . another would give you a long

[1] For this ceremony Thérèse had hoped that her father might be present; for the moment his mind was somewhat restored. But at the last minute M. Guérin decided against, rightly fearing to subject the invalid to an emotion beyond his strength.
[2] "My tears were not understood . . ." writes the saint in her *Histoire d'une âme* (ch. viii).
[3] Quotation from a poetic composition of Céline's.

127

description of Uncle's visit, but your Thérèse can speak to you only the language of Heaven. Céline, do understand your Thérèse !

Today's trial is an affliction difficult to understand, one sees a joy offered, it is possible, natural, we stretch out our hand . . . and we cannot seize the consolation we so long for . . . but Céline, how mysterious it all is ! . . . We no longer have a shelter here on earth,[1] or at least you can say like the Blessed Virgin : "What a shelter !" yes, what a shelter . . . but it is no human hand that has done this thing, it is Jesus ! It is His "veiled glance" that has fallen upon us !

I have received a letter from the exiled Father,[2] and here is a passage from it : "Oh! my *Alleluia* is drenched with tears. Neither of your fathers will be there to give you to Jesus. Need you be much pitied here below when the angels in Heaven are congratulating you and the saints envying you ? It is your crown of thorns that makes them envious. Love these thorn-pricks as so many pledges of love from the Divine Spouse !"

Céline, let us accept with a good heart the thorn Jesus holds out to us ; tomorrow's feast will be a feast of tears for us, but I feel that Jesus will be so consoled !

I should love to tell you so much but the words fail me ! . . . I was told to write and console you, but I fear that I have not made a very good job of it. . . . Ah ! if I could convey to you the peace that Jesus put in my heart when my tears were at their worst, I ask Him to do the same for you who are me ! . . .

Céline, "the shadows retire"[3] and "the fashion of this world passes",[4] soon, yes soon, we shall see the loved unknown Countenance which ravishes us with its tears.

Sister Thérèse of the Child Jesus of the Holy Face,
rel. carm. ind.

---

[1] See note 2, page 93.
[2] Père Pichon.
[3] Cant. of Cant. iv. 6.
[4] 1 Cor. vii. 31.

XCIX

To SISTER MARIE-JOSÈPHE OF THE CROSS

Benedictine of the Blessed Sacrament at Bayeux[1]

J. M. J. T.

Jesus †   Monastery of Carmel, 28 September 1890.

My dear Sister,

I was very much touched by your letter, and I thank you for the prayers you have said for me. I have not forgotten you either, and I have commended all your intentions to God.

Now at last I belong wholly to Jesus; in spite of my unworthiness, He has chosen to take me for His little bride. Now I must give Him proofs of my love, and I count upon you, dear Sister, to aid me in thanking Our Lord.

We have both received great graces and soon, I hope, the same bond will unite us to Jesus for ever.[2]

I had the happiness of receiving the Holy Father's blessing for the day of my Profession. The religious[3] who got it for me wrote how numerous are the enemies of the Church in Rome, the warfare against our Holy Father the Pope never ceases for an instant. It is heartbreaking. . . .

How good it is to be a religious, to pray and appease the good God's justice; yes, the mission entrusted to us is indeed beautiful, and eternity will not be long enough to thank our Lord for the portion He has given us.

---

[1] Marcelline-Anne Husé, born at Saint-Samson (Mayenne) 19 July 1866, became housemaid with the Guérins on 15 March 1880 and so remained till she became a Benedictine at Bayeux, 18 July 1889. Having known Thérèse between her seventh and fifteenth year, she was called as a witness in the Process of Canonisation. She died 26 December 1935.

[2] The bond of religious profession: Sister Marie-Josèphe did not make her vows till two years later, 10 August 1892.

[3] Brother Siméon, of the Christian Schools, director of the College of St. Joseph in Rome (see *Histoire d'une âme*, ch. vi and ix, and, in this volume, Letters LXXXIX and CLXXXVII). The Holy Father's blessing, procured by Brother Siméon, helped Thérèse, the day before her Profession, to overcome a temptation against her vocation which she called the "most furious tempest of her whole life" (ibid., ch. viii).

My dear Sister, I commend to your prayers my dearest Father, who is so tried by the cross and so admirable in his resignation. I venture also to recommend myself to the prayers of your Holy Community.

Do please believe, dear Sister, in all the religious affection of one who is so happy to call herself

Your little sister,

Thérèse of the Child Jesus,

rel. carm. ind.

C

To PÉRE PICHON, S.J.[1]

September 1890.

This letter has been destroyed, but, in Père Pichon's answer, the feelings the Saint had expressed are reflected as in a mirror. In particular, it is clear that she had confided to him her desire to go to a Carmelite Convent in a missionary country. Here are extracts from the saintly Jesuit's reply.

Canada, 16 February 1891.[2]

My dear and fortunate Child in Jesus Christ,

. . . Yes . . . the alliance is concluded and it will be eternal. You have all the rights, all the privileges of a true Bride. My congratulations on your wedding-journey to Calvary ! Were you not spoilt, to get the Holy Father's blessing? . . . Oh! spoilt in so many ways.

I was much moved to learn that your wreath of white roses had been blessed by the venerated Patriarch[3] and placed on his white head.

It is the seal of the cross that makes the glory of your profession. Your sisters may well envy you and the elect in Heaven are jealous.

Jesus has given you His Childhood and His Passion. How fortunate you are.

What an incomparable dowry ! Make the Child in the crib smile and console the Crucified on Calvary. Did the Blessed Virgin have a more beautiful mission ?

[1] See note 1 to Letter VI.
[2] Père Pichon wrote to his spiritual daughters in the Lisieux Carmel every six months.
[3] M. Martin (see note to Letter XCIII).

If ever I wept for my exile and suffered from the fifteen hundred leagues of the Atlantic, it was on 8 September. But in spite of all, I was there with you, no one was more there than I, and I offered you to Jesus in the gladness of my heart.

. . . Yes, yes, let the desire to save souls, the thirst·to be an apostle by aiding the apostles, grow and develop more and more in your heart. If you knew how my Canadian apostolate relies on you, and cashes your prayers, tears and sacrifices.

I understand the silence of your soul, I see the far places of your heart. I can read and re-read the thoughts you leave unuttered.

You are blest, dearest little lamb of God, to find no pleasure now apart from Jesus. Jesus alone ! what wealth ! Do not ask martyrdom for yourself without asking it for me. That would be too selfish. Meanwhile, long live the martyrdom of the heart, the daily martyrdom by pin-stabs.

To feel our nothingness and to rejoice at being only a poor little nothing is indeed a great grace. Profit by it !

This ambition of an "exile more exiled"[1] I shall commend to our Lord. Before answering you about it, I must pray. I bless you with my whole heart.

A. P.

CI

To her Sisters in Religion and her Family

Announcement of her Spiritual Marriage

October 1890.

"A week after I took the veil," Thérèse writes in the Autobiography,[2] "our cousin, Jeanne Guérin, married Dr. La Néele.[3] On her next visit to the parlour, hearing her speak of all the trouble she took to please her husband, I felt my heart tremble:

---

[1] The Saint wrote later, in 1897 : "I dream of a monastery where I should be unknown, where I should have an *exile of the heart* to suffer" (*Histoire d'une âme,* ch. ix). What she confided to Père Pichon as early as 1890 shows how seriously we must take this other passage from *Histoire d'une âme* : "From my entry into Carmel, I have always thought that if Jesus did not very quickly sweep me off to Heaven, the lot of Noah's little dove would be mine : that one day, the Lord, opening the window of the ark, would tell me to fly far off to the shore of the infidels, bearing with me the olive branch. This thought had me soaring high above every created thing" (ch. ix).

[2] *Histoire d'une âme,* ch. viii.

[3] The marriage was on 2 October.

'It shall not be said,' I thought, 'that a woman in the world will do more for her husband, a mere mortal, than I for my beloved Jesus.' And filled with new ardour, I set myself more than ever by every action to please the heavenly Spouse, the King of Kings, who in His goodness had chosen to elevate me to an alliance with Him. Having seen the wedding announcement, I amused myself composing the following invitation which I read to the novices to show them, what had so much struck me, how small a thing is the glory of this world's unions compared to the titles of a spouse of Jesus."

.　　　.　　　.　　　.　　　.

ALMIGHTY GOD, Creator of Heaven and earth, Sovereign Ruler of the world, and the MOST GLORIOUS VIRGIN MARY, Queen of the Court of Heaven, beg to inform you of the marriage of their august Son, JESUS, King of Kings and Lord of Lords, with little THÉRÈSE MARTIN, now Lady and Princess of the realms—the Childhood of Jesus and His Passion—brought her as dowry by her divine Spouse, whence come her titles of nobility: of the CHILD JESUS and of the HOLY FACE !

MONSIEUR LOUIS MARTIN, Lord and Master of the Seigneuries of Suffering and Humiliation, and MADAME MARTIN, Princess and Lady of Honour of the Court of Heaven, beg to inform you of the marriage of their daughter THÉRÈSE, with JESUS, the Word of God, Second Person of the Adorable Trinity who, by the power of the Holy Spirit, was made Man and Son of Mary, the Queen of Heaven.

As it was not possible to invite you to the wedding-feast, which was celebrated on the Mount of Carmel, 8 September 1890—the Court of Heaven being alone admitted—you are invited to be present at the Renewal of the Nuptials which will take place to-morrow, the day of Eternity, upon which day Jesus, Son of God, will come upon the clouds of Heaven, in the glory of His majesty, to judge the living and the dead.

The hour being still uncertain, you are invited to hold yourselves in readiness and watch.

CII

To CÉLINE

On pilgrimage to Paray-le-Monial

J. M. T. J.

Jesus †   14 October 1890.

My dearest Céline,

I cannot let Marie's letter go without adding a brief word. Our dearest Mother gives me permission to say my prayers with you; don't we *always* say them together ? . . .

Céline *dearest*, it is *always* the same thing I have to say to you; ah ! let us pray for priests[1] . . . each day shows how rare are the friends of Jesus. It seems to me that that is what He must feel most . . . ingratitude, especially when He sees souls consecrated to Him giving to others the heart which belongs to Him in so absolute a fashion.

Céline, let us make our heart a little garden of delight where Jesus may come to find rest. . . . Let us plant only lilies[2] in our garden, yes lilies, let us allow no other flowers, for they can be cultivated by others . . . but only virgins can give Jesus lilies. . . .

"Virginity is a profound silence of all this world's cares," not only useless cares, but *all cares*. . . . To be a virgin one must have no thought left save for the Spouse, who will have nothing near Him that is not virginal, "since He chose to be born of a Virgin Mother, to have a virgin forerunner, a virgin foster-father, a virgin favourite disciple, and at last a virgin tomb". He also wants a little virgin bride, His Céline ! . . . Again it has been said that "every one has a natural love for the place of his birth, and as the place of Jesus' birth is the Virgin of Virgins and Jesus was born, by His choice, of a Lily, He loves to be in virgin hearts".

I seem to be forgetting your journey[3]. . . . No, my heart goes

---

[1] A number of priests in great temptation had just been recommended to the prayers of the Carmelites of Lisieux.

[2] In the fragments of letters published at the end of the *Histoire d'une âme* there was inserted at this point strophe viii of the *Spiritual Canticle* of St. John of the Cross, which Thérèse had copied and sent to her sister Céline 18 July 1890 (see this strophe at the end of Letter LXXXVIII).

[3] To Paray-le-Monial where the second centenary was being celebrated of Margaret Mary (who was not yet canonised).

with you over there, I understand all that you are feeling . . . I understand all ! . . . Everything passes, the journey to Rome with its harrowing experience *has passed* . . . the life we used to live *has passed* . . . *death* will pass too and then we shall enjoy life— not for centuries, but millions of years will pass for us like one day . . . and other millions of years will come after them, filled with repose and felicity . . . Céline. . . .

Do pray to the Sacred Heart. You know, I do not see the Sacred Heart like everyone else. I think that the Heart of my Spouse is mine alone, as mine is His alone, and then I talk with Him in the aloneness of that enchanting heart-to-heart, waiting for the day when I shall gaze upon Him face to face.

Do not forget your Thérèse, simply murmur her name and Jesus will understand. So many graces are attached to the place where you are, especially for a heart that is suffering. . . . I should much like to write to Léonie, but it is impossible, I haven't even the time to read over this. Tell her how often I think of her. . . . I am sure that the Sacred Heart will grant her many graces . . . tell her all, you understand.

Your

Thérèse of the Child Jesus of the Holy Face,
rel. carm. ind.

CIII

To MME GUÉRIN

To thank her for her feast presents

J. M. J. T.

Jesus †   15 October 1890.

My dear Aunt,

I was much moved by all you sent me for my feast, I don't know how to thank you or where to begin. First, darling Aunt, you sent me your charming Marie who wished me a happy feast in the name of all the people I love.

The two pretty pots of flowers given by my two dearest little sisters, Jeanne and Marie, gave me great pleasure; they are placed in front of the Child Jesus and at every hour of the day they beg as many graces and blessings as each bush of heather has tiny flowers. . . .

Lastly, darling Aunt, your delicious cakes came to crown the feast and fill your little Thérèse's heart with gratitude to you who spoil me with all these nice things ! I am still more touched because I know, dear Aunt, in what great pain you are; and in spite of it you still think of your little Thérèse. But if you think of her, she very often thinks of you too and never ceases to beg God that He may give you back a hundredfold all that you do for us. I pray also very often for my dear little Jeanne. May the good God make her as happy as it is possible to be on earth ! I ask Him also to console you for the great void that the departure of that dearest sister must mean, nor do I forget my dear Uncle, please give him a big kiss from me.

I now leave you, darling Aunt, or rather I leave the pen which is so unskilled to carry out the mission my heart entrusts to it. My heart, of course, never leaves you for an instant.

Your little girl,
Sister Thérèse of the Child Jesus,
rel. carm. ind.

CIV

To CÉLINE

For her feast

J. M. J. T.

Jesus †   20 October 1890.

My dearest Céline,

This is your Thérèse wishing you a happy feast ! It has been in her mind for a long time, so this year she will not be last. Céline, it may well be the last time your feast will be celebrated on earth. Perhaps ! . . . What a lovely hope ! Next year, will the little *Céline-flower*,[1] unknown upon earth, be placed upon the heart of the divine Lamb ? But the entranced eyes of the angels will then be contemplating, not a poor little flower of no beauty, but a lily of dazzling whiteness ! . . .

Céline, life is very mysterious, we know nothing, we see nothing, yet Jesus has already revealed to our souls *what the eye of man has*

[1] See note to Letter LXXVI.

not seen. Yes, our heart has a foretaste of *what the heart of man cannot conceive,*[1] since there are times when we lack the *thoughts* to express the inexpressible thing that we feel in our soul ! . . .

Céline, I am sending you two of your flowers for your feast. You will understand their language. . . . A single stalk bears them, one same sun caused them to grow together, the same ray brought them to blossoming, and surely the same day will see them die ! . . .

The eyes of creatures do not bother to pause upon a little *Céline-flower,* yet its white cup is full of mystery. It has in its heart a great number of other flowers, which are of course the children of *its soul* (souls); and then its white calyx is red within, as though it were stained with its blood ! . . . Céline, the sun and the rain can fall upon this little insignificant flower and do not wither it. No one thinks to pick it, so it stays virgin. . . . Yes, for Jesus alone has seen it, it was He who created it, and for Himself alone ! Oh ! but then it is more fortunate than the glowing rose which is not for Jesus alone.

Céline, I am wishing you a happy feast in a fashion that might seem uncommon, but you will understand the stumbling words of your Thérèse. . . .

Céline, it seems to me that God does not need years to do His work of love in a soul, a ray from His heart can in one instant bring His flower to blossoming for eternity. . . .

Your Thérèse of the Child Jesus and of the Holy Face,
r. c. ind.

CV

To MME GUÉRIN

For her feast

J. M. J. T.

Jesus †

Carmel, 17 November 1890.

My dear Aunt,

With what happiness I write to wish you a happy feast ! . . . I have been thinking of this beautiful day for a long time and I

[1] 1 Cor. ii. 9.

rejoice to be talking to my darling Aunt, telling her how much her last and smallest daughter loves her. On the whole, she likes being the last and smallest, but in affection and tenderness she will never let her elders outpass her. . . . And after all, surely it is the right of a Benjamin to love more than the others. What memories there are for me in this date of the 19th ! Long in advance I used to begin my rejoicing. First because this day was the feast of my dearest Aunt, and second because of all the nice presents and things that went with the day. Now, time is gone by, the little birds have grown, have opened their wings and flown from the most pleasant nest of their childhood. But, darling Aunt, as she has grown, your little girl's heart has grown too in tenderness for you, and now more than ever it realises what it owes you. . . . To pay my debt I have only one means; being very poor and having as my Spouse a very rich and powerful King, I charge Him to pour out the treasures of His love in profusion upon my dearest Aunt, and thus pay her back for all the maternal kindnesses with which she surrounded my childhood.

Dear Aunt, I do not say goodbye, for I mean to stay with you the whole day, and I hope that you will see deep into the heart of your little girl.

Thérèse of the Child Jesus,
rel. carm. ind.

1891

NINETEENTH YEAR

The family trial continues painful.
8–15 October : Retreat preached at the Lisieux Carmel by Père Alexis
    Prou, Franciscan Recollect, who "launches Thérèse upon a sea of
    confidence and love".
5 December : Death of the venerated Mother Geneviève of St. Teresa,
    foundress of the Lisieux Carmel.

CVI

To CÉLINE

J. M. J. T.

Jesus †   3 April 1891.

My darling Céline,
    This afternoon we saw N. . . .[1] I haven't time to talk of the
visit in detail but I cannot tell you the good it has done my soul.
. . . Ah ! how fortunate we are to have been chosen by the Spouse
of Virgins ! N. . . . has confided to us intimate secrets which she
tells to no one. We must certainly pray for her, for she is under
grave temptation . . . she says that no book does her any good,
I thought that *Les Mystères de la vie future*[2] might be good for her
and strengthen her faith which, alas, is very much in danger ! . . .
She told us that she could read books without her husband knowing
about it.
    So you must give her the book[3] and tell her we thought it

---

[1] A woman friend of the Martins.
[2] By C. Arminjon. See note to Letter XXXII.
[3] This is the list of conferences contained in the book, which has been long out
of print. (1) Of the end of the world and the signs that will precede it. (2) Persecution by anti-Christ and conversion of the Jews. (3) Resurrection of the body and
the general judgment. (4) Of the place of immortality and the state of glorified
bodies. (5) Of purgatory. (6) Of eternal punishment and the fate of the lost.
(7) Of eternal beatitude and the supernatural vision. (8) The Christian sacrifice,
means of redemption. (9) Of the mystery of suffering in its bearing upon the future
life.

would interest her, but to begin only at the third chapter where there is a small picture, because the earlier chapters would be of no interest to her. I think you had better not seem to know the book but simply to be carrying out my commission, for she would be upset if she knew we had breathed a single word of her confidences. We should prefer that Madame X. . . . and my aunt should not know that we are lending this book to N. . . . anyhow do what seems best, and tell her to keep it as long as she likes. If you cannot give it to her unobserved, it would perhaps be better to do nothing; but at least try to mention it to her.

Personally, I have a very strong wish for her to read the book, for in it she will certainly find the answer to many doubts ! . . . I think you will be doing a work very pleasing to God; it was to me He gave the idea, but you know that Thérèse can do nothing without Céline, it takes them both to do any one thing properly, so it is for Céline to finish what Thérèse has begun ! . . . Céline . . . if you could know how I love you and how pure my love for you is ! . . .

Dearest Céline, your little Thérèse is never apart from you, for you are in her heart and the half of her heart. . . .

Thérèse of the Child Jesus of the Holy Face,
rel. carm. ind.

CVII

To CÉLINE

For her birthday

J. M. J. T.

Jesus †   Carmel, 26 April 1891.

My dearest Céline,
For the fourth time[1] Thérèse writes from the solitude of Carmel to wish you a happy birthday. . . . Oh ! how little these wishes resemble those of the world. It is not health, happiness, fortune, glory, and such like, that Thérèse wishes her Céline. Oh ! no, not that at all.

Our thoughts are not in the land of exile, *our heart is where*

[1] In 1888 Céline had visited the convent on her birthday.

our treasure is,[1] and our treasure is above, in the Homeland where Jesus *prepares a place for us*[2] with Him. I say *a place* and not places, for surely one same throne is reserved for those who upon earth were ever but one single soul. . . . Together we have grown up, together Jesus has instructed us in His secrets, sublime secrets whicu *He hides from the powerful and reveals to the little ones,*[3] together too we suffered *in Rome*; our hearts then were closely united, and life upon earth would have been ideally happy even if Jesus had not come to make the bonds that bind us closer still. Yes, in separating us, He united us in a fashion till then unknown to my soul, for from that moment I have been able to desire nothing for myself alone, but only for us both.

Ah ! Céline ! . . . Three years ago our hearts had not yet been broken, happiness was still possible for us upon earth ; but Jesus cast a look of love upon us, a look dimmed with tears, and that look has become for us an ocean of sufferings but also an ocean of graces and of love. He has taken from us the one we love so tenderly, in a manner even more afflicting than when He took our dearest mother from us in the springtime of our life, but surely He did so that we might be able to say in all truth : Our Father, who art in heaven. Oh ! how consoling is that word ! What an infinite horizon it opens to our eyes ! . . .

Céline, this foreign land has for us nothing but wild plants and thorns—but is not that the portion it gave to our Divine Spouse ? Oh ! how lovely for us too is the portion which is ours . . . and who shall tell us what eternity has in store for us ? . . .

Dearest Céline, you asked me so many questions when we were little, I wonder how it happened that you never asked this one : "But why did the good God not create me an angel ?" Ah ! Céline, I shall tell you what I think ; if Jesus did not create you an angel in Heaven, it is because He wants you to be an angel on earth, yes, Jesus wants to have His heavenly court here below as well as above ! He wants angel-martyrs, He wants angel-apostles, and to that very end He created a small unnoticed flower called Céline. He wants His little Flower to save Him souls, and for that He wants only one thing, that His flower should *look at* Him while it suffers its martyrdom . . . and this mysterious gaze passing between Jesus and His small flower will work marvels and

---

[1] Matt. vi. 21 ; Luke xii. 34.　　　　[2] John xiv. 2.
[3] Matt. xi. 25 ; Luke x. 21.

will give Jesus a multitude of other flowers, particularly a certain faded, withered lily that must be changed into a rose of love and repentance.[1]

Céline dearest, don't be displeased with me for saying that in Heaven we shall have the same place—for, don't you see, it seems to me that a poor little daisy may very well grow in the same soil as a lovely lily dazzling in its whiteness, or again that a tiny pearl may be set beside a diamond and borrow of its brilliance. . . .

Oh ! Céline, let us love Jesus to infinity, and of our two hearts make but one, that it may be greater in love ! . . .

Céline, with you I should never finish, do grasp all I should like to say to you for your twenty-second birthday ! . . .

Your little sister who is but one being with you. (Do you know that we two together are forty, already ? It is not surprising that we have already experienced so much, do you think ?)

Thérèse of the Child Jesus of the Holy Face,
rel. carm. ind.

CVIII

To CÉLINE

Then at La Musse

J. M. J. T.

Jesus †   8 July 1891.

My dearest Céline,

Your short note impressed my soul deeply, it came to me like a faithful echo repeating all my thoughts. . . .

Our dearest Mother[2] is still in great pain; it is very sorrowful to see those we love suffer so. Yet, do not be too much grieved; though Jesus may well want to enjoy our dearest Mother's presence in Heaven, He cannot refuse our prayer that He leave with us still upon earth one whose maternal hand is so skilled to guide and console us in the exile of life. . . .

---

[1] The allusion is to ex-Père Hyacinthe Loyson, whose conversion Thérèse had undertaken. This unhappy man, formerly a Carmelite, had broken with the Church over the question of Papal Infallibility, and had contracted a sacrilegious "marriage".
[2] Mother Marie de Gonzague.

Oh ! what an exile it is, the exile of earth, especially in those hours when we seem abandoned by all ! . . . but it is then that it is precious, it is then that the days of salvation dawn ; yes, dearest Céline, only suffering can bring souls to birth for Jesus. . . . Is it surprising that we are so well served, we whose sole desire is to save a soul that seems forever lost ? . . .[1]

The details have interested me deeply, though they cause me great distress of heart. . . . And here are further details, no more consoling. The unhappy prodigal went to Coutances where he resumed the lectures he had been giving at Caen. It seems that he means in this way to cover all France . . . Céline . . . and at the same time, they add, it is easy to see that *remorse* is gnawing him, he goes through the churches with a large crucifix and he seems to be making great acts of adoration. His wife goes everywhere with him.

Dearest Céline, he is indeed guilty, more guilty perhaps than any sinner has ever been who yet was converted ; but cannot Jesus do what He has never done before ? And if He did not wish it, would He have put into the heart of His poor little brides a desire He could not fulfil ? . . . No, it is certain that He desires more than we to bring back this poor lost sheep to the fold ;[2] a day will come when he will open his eyes and then who knows if he will not cover all France with a very different object from the one now in his mind.

[1] The ex-priest Hyacinthe Loyson.
[2] Hyacinthe Loyson died in Paris 9 February 1912, at the age of eighty-five, under major excommunication. He was assisted at the end by a priest of the Armenian Church, a representative of the schismatic Greek Church, and three Protestant pastors. It is worth observing that the poor erring creature had never ceased to repeat the invocation: "O my sweet Jesus." Thérèse, who had prayed for him throughout her religious life, offered her last communion for him, in 1897, on 19 August, which was at that time the feast day of St. Hyacinthe.

Details given under all reserves to the Lisieux Carmel:
From the abbey of St. Maurice at Clervaux (19 August 1912):

"At the moment of the unhappy man's death, a privileged soul saw him supernaturally enlightened upon the whole extent of the sins of his life. This sight was the occasion of a terrifying temptation to despair over which, happily, he triumphed."

From Père Flamérion, S.J., grand exorcist of France (25 August 1912):

Result of an exorcism:
"You have asked us in the Virgin's name if Hyacinthe is damned, we are forced to answer you that he is saved, through the intercession of Thérèse and the prayer of Holy Souls in the cloister, saved by a glance cast upon him by Our Lord before he was judged, an instant before."

We must not grow weary of praying. Confidence works miracles and Jesus told Blessed Margaret Mary: "*One just soul* has so much power over My Heart that it can obtain from it pardon for a thousand *criminals.*" No one knows whether he himself is just or sinful, but, Céline, Jesus gives us the grace to feel in the very depth of our heart that we would rather die than offend Him. And in any event it is not our merits but those of our Spouse, which are *ours*, that we offer to our Father who is in Heaven, in order that our brother, a son of the Blessed Virgin, should come back vanquished to throw himself beneath the cloak of the most merciful of mothers. . . .

Céline dearest, I must end, guess the rest, there are *volumes* of it to guess ! . . .

Kiss everybody for me,[1] and, any messages you care to give them from me, I shall mean.

Sister Thérèse of the Child Jesus of the Holy Face,
rel. carm. ind.

CIX

To CÉLINE

J. M. J. T.

Jesus †

Carmel, 23 July 1891.

My dearest Céline,

Once again I am assigned to answer you. . . . Mother Geneviève[2] was much moved by your letter, and she has said many prayers for her little Céline; what a grace to have the prayers of such a saint and to be loved by her ! . . . Yesterday's feast[3] was enchanting, truly a foretaste of Heaven . . . all the presents gave us great pleasure—the fish, the cherries, the cakes; thank Aunt warmly and tell her whatever you like that is nicest.

Dearest Céline, your two letters have set me thinking deeply and brought tears from my eyes . . . the *suitor* made me laugh, it

---

[1] Céline was at the Château of La Musse, with the Guérins, where she was spending a few days' vacation, taking turns with Léonie, in order that one of the two sisters should always be close to their invalid father at Caen.

[2] The venerated Mother Geneviève of St. Teresa, foundress in 1838 of the Carmel at Lisieux, had often filled the office of Prioress. She died in the odour of sanctity on 5 December of this year 1891, in her eighty-seventh year.

[3] The diamond jubilee of Mother Geneviève's profession.

must be admitted that he is pretty cool to seek in marriage one who is engaged to the King of Heaven—the poor man, I suppose he did not see "the sign that the Spouse had placed upon your brow",[1] a mysterious sign seen only by Jesus and the angels who form His royal court. . . .

Céline, why this extraordinary privilege, why ? . . . Ah ! what a grace to be a virgin, to be the bride of Jesus ! It must indeed be beautiful, sublime, since the purest and most intelligent of all creatures thought it better to remain a virgin than to become the mother of a God. . . . And this is the grace that Jesus grants us, He wants us to be His brides, indeed He even promises us that we may be His mother and His sisters for He says so in His gospel : "For whosoever shall do the will of my Father, He is my mother, my brother and my sister".[2] Yes, one who loves Jesus is all His family ; in that *unique* Heart which has *no other like it*, he finds all that he desires, in it he finds his heaven ! . . .

Céline dearest, let us always remain lilies of Jesus ; the grace I ask Him is that He take His lilies from this world before the perilous wind of earth has blown the tiniest bit of pollen from their stamens, pollen that might ever so little stain with its yellow the whiteness and the radiance of the lily. Jesus must always be able to find in His lilies all that He desires, find the purity in them which seeks only Him and has no repose but in Him. . . .

Alas ! there is nothing so easy to tarnish as a lily . . . but if Jesus could say of Magdalen "that one loves more to whom more has been forgiven",[3] surely it may be said with even more reason when Jesus delivers from sins *in advance* ![4] . . . Do you understand, Céline ? After all, given that "the tears of Jesus are the smile of a soul",[5] what has she to fear ? I think those mysterious pearls have power to whiten lilies and preserve their radiance.

. . . Céline dearest, the fashion of this world passes,[6] the shadows retire,[7] soon we shall be in our native land, soon the joys of our childhood, the Sunday evenings, the intimate conversations, all

[1] Office of St. Agnes, antiphon of the first nocturn.
[2] Matt. xii. 50.
[3] Luke vii. 47.
[4] The Saint was to express the same thought in the *Histoire d'une âme*, written four years later (see ch. iv).
[5] The quotation is from a poetic composition of Céline's, which has not been preserved (see note to Letter LXXXVIII).
[6] 1 Cor. vii. 31.
[7] Cant. of Cant. iv. 6.

will be given back to us forever and with interest. Jesus will give us back the joys of which for an instant He has deprived us ! . . . Then we shall see waves of light issuing from the shining head of our dearest father, and every one of his white hairs will be like a sun pouring joy and happiness upon us ! . . . So life is a dream, is it not ? And to think that with that dream we can save souls ! . . . Ah ! Céline, we must not forget souls, but forget ourselves for them, and one day Jesus will look on us and say "How beautiful is the chaste generation of virgin souls !"[1]

I send a big kiss to my little Marie, Léonie and everybody; as for you, Céline, you know where your place is in my heart ![2] . . .

CX

To MME LA NÉELE

To thank her for her feast-gifts

J. M. J. T.

Jesus †

Carmel, 17 October 1891.

My darling Jeanne,

I don't know how to thank you for so delicate an attention.

I was very much touched to see Francis' name joined with Jeanne's to wish me a happy feast, so I send my thanks to you both.

My debt I leave my Divine Spouse to pay. Since I am poor for His sake, it is clearly just that He should not refuse the things I ask Him for those I love.

I assure you, dear Jeanne, that if you do not forget the smallest of your sisters, *she* thinks of *you* again and again; and you know that, for a Carmelite, to remember—and still more to love—means to pray. Naturally my poor prayers are not worth very much, yet I hope that Jesus will hear them, and that He will not look at the one who is offering them but will keep His eyes fixed on those who are their object, so that He will be obliged to grant me all I ask. I hope that God will soon send a small Isidore as perfect as his papa, or else a small Jeanne exactly like her mama. . . . I am also asking that his pharmacy may find a buyer,[3] I want

[1] Wisdom iv. 1.
[2] This letter is not signed.
[3] When he married, Dr. la Néele practised medicine in Caen and tried to sell his pharmacy.

nothing whatever to be lacking to the perfect happiness of my dear little sister and my good cousin. On earth, of course, there will always be some small cloud, for life cannot go along without, and only in Heaven will joy be perfect; but I want God as far as possible to spare those I love the sufferings there must be in life, even if it involves taking upon myself the trials He has in store for them.

Sister Marie of the Sacred Heart asks me to thank you for what you sent in payment for the odds-and-ends bag; it was really too kind of you, especially as our Mother was glad to be able to offer you this small object. I have only enough space left to say thank you again, for myself and my sisters, and to assure you, and our dear cousin too, of the affection of the last of your sisters, who is not the least in the love she feels for you. . . .

Sister Thérèse of the Child Jesus,
rel. carm. ind.

CXI

To CÉLINE

For her feast

J. M. J. T.

Jesus †   Carmel, October 1891.

My dearest Céline,

Now is the fourth time that I write to wish you a happy feast since I have been in Carmel ! . . . I feel that these four years have drawn still closer the bonds that already held us so close. The longer we live the more we love Jesus, and as it is in Him that we love one another, you see why our affection grows so strong that between our two souls there is rather *unity* than union ! . . . Céline, what is there that I need tell you, don't you know it all ? Yes, but I want to tell you why the célines[1] have blossomed earlier this year, Jesus put the idea into my head this morning for your feast.

You must have noticed that no winter had ever been as hard as last year's; as a result, all the flowers were late in coming out; it

---

[1] Asters; see note to Letter LXXVI.

was perfectly natural and it did not occur to anyone to be surprised. But there is a mysterious little flower which Jesus has reserved for Himself for the instruction of souls, it is the *céline-flower*. . . . As against all the others it flowered a month before its proper time. . . . Céline, do you understand the language of my dearest little flower, the flower of my childhood, the flower of so many memories ? . . .

The frosts, the rigour of winter, instead of retarding it made it grow and flower. No one paid any attention, the flower is so small, so very ordinary. Only the bees know the treasures enclosed in its mysterious calyx, composed of a multitude of small calices all equally rich. Thérèse, like the bees, has grasped the mystery. The winter is suffering, suffering not understood, hated, regarded as useless by the eyes of the profane; but fertile and of great power to the eyes of Jesus and the angels who, like vigilant bees, know how to gather the honey contained in those many mysterious calices, which stand for the souls, or rather the children, of the virginal little flower. . . . Céline, I should need volumes to write all I think about my tiny flower; for me it is so truly the image of your soul ! Yes, Jesus has let frosts come upon it instead of the warm sun of His consolations, but the result He aimed at has been achieved, the little plant has grown and flowered almost in one act. . . . Céline, when a flower has blossomed, nothing remains save to pluck it; but when and how will Jesus pluck His little flower ? . . . Perhaps the red tinge of its petals indicates that it will be by martyrdom ! . . . Yes, I feel my desires born anew; perhaps having asked, so to speak, love for love, Jesus will go on to ask blood for blood and life for life.[1] . . . Meanwhile, we must let the bees gather all the honey from the little calices, we must keep nothing, give all to Jesus, and then "like the flower we shall say in the evening of our life: Evening, it is evening".[2] Then it will be over . . . and the frosts will give place to the sweet rays of the sun, the tears of Jesus to eternal smiles. . . .

Ah ! we must not refuse to weep with Him for a day, since we shall enjoy His glory for eternity ! . . .

Dearest little flower, do you understand your Thérèse ?

---

[1] Many thought at the time that the anti-religious measures would become bloody persecution.

[2] From a poetic composition by Céline.

CXII

To MME GUÉRIN

For her feast

J. M. J. T.

Jesus †

Carmel, 16 November 1891.

My dear Aunt,

It is very sweet for your smallest girl to join with her elders in wishing you a happy feast.

Each year I delight to see the date 19 November coming round again; for me it is not only filled with sweet memories, but also rich in hope for the future.

The longer I live, the more I realise how sweet is a Mother's feast. Alas! in my childhood it seemed as if God had taken from me forever a joy I had never experienced;[1] but, from Heaven above, she who could not lavish her caresses upon me inspired in a maternal heart, a heart very dear to her,[2] a mother's tenderness for her poor little child; since then, she too has known the sweet joys of celebrating a beloved mother's feast-day.

Darling Aunt, since she has been upon Mount Carmel, your little Thérèse feels still more deeply, if possible, the affection she bears you. The more she learns to love Jesus the greater grows her love for her dearest relations.

The little gift[3] our good Mother was glad to have us make for your feast will tell you better than I, dear Aunt, what I am powerless to tell you. My heart is filled with emotion to see these poor hairs which surely have no value at all save the delicacy of the work and the grace of their arrangement, but which were loved all the same by one whom the good God has taken from us.[4]

. . . Darling Aunt, do you understand? I am happy in the thought that this hair, which he would have received with such pleasure,

[1] Thérèse had lost her mother at the age of four and a half.
[2] A profound affection united Madame Martin and her sister-in-law (see *Histoire d'une famille*, p. 63).
[3] A frame containing some of Thérèse's hair, cut off on the day of her Clothing. The hair was arranged in the shape of a spray of lilies on a cross. This most remarkable relic, later bequeathed to the Lisieux Benedictine nuns, disappeared along with their Convent under the terrible bombardment of 7 June 1944.
[4] M. Martin.

has been given to her who, after my dearest father, is dearest to me in this life.

Darling Aunt, this letter is not much like a feast letter, which should speak only of joy and happiness. But I can speak only with my heart, it alone guides my pen, and I am quite sure that the maternal heart I am addressing will understand me and indeed divine what I cannot express.

Dearest Aunt, I must end my letter, but first I want to send you all my kisses: please tell your little girls that I charge them with their delivery; I am sure they will be charmed at the mission I entrust to them and will carry it out to perfection.

Your little girl again sends you all her good wishes and begs you, darling Aunt, to believe in all the tenderness of her child's heart.

Sister Thérèse of the Child Jesus,
rel. carm. ind.

TWENTIETH YEAR

10 May : From the mental home in Caen where M. Martin, stricken
with paralysis, had been for over three years, he is brought back
to his family in Lisieux. This is a great lessening of the trial for
Thérèse and her sisters.
From this year Thérèse begins to draw mainly from Holy Scripture the
nourishment her soul needs. "It is the Gospel above all that
occupies me in my prayers. . . . I am forever discovering in it
hidden, mysterious meanings."[1]

CXIII

To CÉLINE

For her birthday

J. M. J. T.

Jesus †   26 April 1892.

My dearest Céline,
This year the Carmel meadow provides me with a symbolic
present which I am happy to give you for your twenty-third
birthday. . . . One day, amid the grass all white with single
daisies, I thought I saw one with a slender stalk, more beautiful
than the rest; coming close, I saw with surprise that it was not
one daisy, but two quite distinct ones. Two stalks so closely
united reminded me at once of the mysteries of *our souls.* . . . I
realised that if, in nature, it pleases Jesus to sow marvels so entrancing beneath our feet, it is only to aid us to glimpse the
mysteries, more hidden and of a higher order, that He sometimes
works in souls. . . .
Céline, I feel that you have already understood your Thérèse.
Already your heart has divined what is happening in that other
heart to which yours is united so closely that the sap that

[1] *Histoire d'une âme,* ch. viii.

nourishes one nourishes the other! . . . All the same, I shall talk to you of some of the mysteries hidden in my tiny flower.

To rejoice our eyes and instruct our souls, Jesus has created a multitude of little daisies. In the morning I see with wonder that their rosy petals are turned toward the dawn, they are waiting for the sun to rise. The moment that radiant star casts one of its warm beams upon them, the shy little flowers begin to open their calices, and their tiny petals form a sort of crown, which lets you see through to their little yellow hearts and thus gives these flowers a strong resemblance to the being which has touched them with its light. All through the day, the daisies never take their gaze from the sun, turning with him until evening; then, when he has disappeared, they quickly fold up their petals and from white become rosy again. . . .

Jesus is the Divine Sun and the daisies are His brides, the Virgins. When Jesus has looked upon a soul, in that act He gives it His Divine likeness, but the soul must not cease to keep its gaze fixed upon *Him alone*.

To develop the mysteries of the daisies, I should have to write a volume, but my Céline understands all, so now I want to talk to her of a pleasant fancy Jesus had. . . .

In His meadow Jesus has many daisies, but they are separate and each receives separately the rays of the sun. One day the Spouse of Virgins bent down upon the earth, bound two little barely opened buds tight together, their stalks were fused into a single stalk, and under a single gaze they grew. Together these little flowers, now *one single flower*, blossomed; and now the double daisy fixing its gaze upon its Divine Sun carries out its own unique mission. . . . Céline, only you can understand my language. To the eye of creatures our lives seem very different, totally separate, but I know that Jesus has bound our hearts together in so marvellous a fashion that whatever makes the one heart beat sets the other vibrating too. . . .

Where your treasure is, there is your heart.[1] Our treasure is Jesus and our hearts make but one heart in Him. The same gaze ravished our souls, a gaze dimmed with tears which the double daisy has resolved to dry; its humble white petals will be the chalice in which those precious diamonds will be collected to be poured in turn upon other flowers, less privileged flowers,

[1] Matt. vi. 21; Luke xii. 34.

which have not fixed their hearts' first gaze on Jesus. . . . Perhaps the petals that the daisy will present to the Divine Spouse in the evening of its life will have turned red.[1]

Goodbye, dearest Céline, the tiny flower I send you is a relic; for it has rested in the hands of our holy Mother Geneviève,[2] and she blessed Céline and Thérèse.

Thérèse of the Child Jesus of the Holy Face,
rel. carm. ind.

CXIV

To CÉLINE

At La Musse

J. M. J. T.

Jesus †
15 August 1892.

My dearest Céline,

I cannot let this letter go without adding a brief note. To do so, I must steal a few moments from Jesus, but He does not mind, for it is by Him that we speak together, *without Him no discourse has charm* for our hearts. . . .[3]

Céline! the wide spaces, the magic horizons which open before you,[4] should say profound things to your soul. I do not see any of those things but I say with St. John of the Cross:

In my Beloved I have the mountains,
The lonely wooded valleys . . . etc.[5]

And that Beloved instructs my soul, speaks to it in silence, in darkness. . . .

Recently a thought has struck me which I feel the need to tell my Céline. One day I was pondering over what I could do to save souls; a phrase from the Gospel showed me a clear light; Jesus said to his disciples, pointing to the fields of ripe corn: "Lift up your eyes and see the countries. For they are white already to

[1] Allusion to the possibility of martyrdom.
[2] See note to Letter CIX.
[3] Cf. *Imitation of Christ*, bk. ii, ch. viii, 1; bk. iii, ch. xxxiv, 1.
[4] Céline, urged by her uncle, had gone off for a short visit to La Musse leaving her father in Léonie's charge for a few days.
[5] St. John of the Cross, *Spiritual Canticle*, strophe xiv.

harvest",[1] and a little later, "The harvest indeed is great, but the labourers are few. Pray ye therefore the Lord of the harvest that He send forth labourers".[2]

How mysterious it is ! Is not Jesus all powerful ? Do not creatures belong to Him who made them ? Why then does Jesus say: "Pray ye the Lord of the Harvest that he send forth labourers . . ." ? Why ? . . . Surely because Jesus has so incomprehensible a love for us, that He wants us to have a share with Him in the salvation of souls. He wants to do nothing without us. The creator of the universe waits for the prayer of a poor little soul to save other souls redeemed like itself at the price of all His blood.

Our vocation, yours and mine, is not to go harvesting in the fields of ripe corn; Jesus does not say to us; "Lower your eyes, look at the fields, and go and reap them"; our mission is still loftier. Here are Jesus' words : "Lift up your eyes and see. . . ." See how in My Heaven there are places empty; it is for you to fill them . . . each one of you is My Moses praying on the mountain; ask Me for labourers and I shall send them, I await only a prayer, a sigh from your heart !

Is not the apostolate of prayer lifted higher, so to speak, than the apostolate of preaching ? Our mission, as Carmelites, is to form those gospel labourers, they will save millions of souls, whose mothers we shall be. . . .

Céline, if these were not the very words of our Jesus, who would dare to believe them ? . . . I find our lot most beautiful ! . . . What have priests that we need envy ! How I wish I could tell you all I think, but time is lacking, understand *all I cannot write to you* ! . . .

The day of Jeanne's feast,[3] wish her a happy feast with a small bouquet, the rule does not permit us to do so, but tell her that we shall be thinking of her all the more. Kiss everybody for me and tell them whatever nicest thing you can think of.

Your little
Thérèse of the Child Jesus,
rel. carm. ind.

If you could find some heather, I should be very pleased.

[1] John iv. 35.
[2] Matt. ix. 37, 38.
[3] Her cousin. Her feast was 21 August (St. Jeanne de Chantal).

153

CXV

To MARIE GUÉRIN

To thank her for her feast wishes and gifts

J. M. J. T.

Jesus †   Carmel, 16 October 1892.

My darling Marie,

Since it is you who have been deputed to wish me happy feast for the whole family, I imagine that it is upon you I must lay the task of thanking my dear Aunt, first for her little letter and the large package of chocolate which gave great joy to our little provisor,[1] then for the delicious coffee cream, and then, quite especially, for the dear and affectionate letter of her nurse who, I have no doubt, will soon restore my darling aunt to health. Also I ask the little *Doctor of the rue de l'Oratoire*[2] to offer my thanks to the *Big Doctor*[3] and to his most darling Jeanne[4] who thought of my feast in spite of her convalescence, which touched me deeply.

The slight relapse, which so luckily has had no ill results for Jeanne's health, gave me an idea which I shall tell my dear "little doctor". It struck me that good St. Anne was finding herself rather overlooked, so she took steps to remind people of her existence. I assure you that from that moment her memory has always been present to me. When in thought I am with my dear little sister in Caen, good St. Anne immediately comes back into my mind and I put the girl I love in her hands.[5]

I see with pleasure, dear Marie, that the air of Caen does not depress your spirits. Your gaiety, I do not doubt, even more than your skill as a doctor, will quickly restore our two dear invalids.

Patties made by a pastrycook of your distinction strike me as rather a delicate dish for Carmelites, but could you not prove your talent by making pies so light that Jeanne may not only devour them with her eyes, but even *eat* them without any ill effects?

I conclude, dear little Doctor, by praying you to excuse my

---

[1] Sister Agnes of Jesus; the provisor sees to the Community's meals
[2] Nickname for Marie Guérin.
[3] Dr. La Néele.
[4] Mme La Néele.
[5] Jeanne was praying especially to St. Anne to have a baby.

horrid handwriting. Give a big kiss for me to the whole family and thank them for all the nice things which have been sent me in such abundance that I fear I may have forgotten to mention some of them.

Tell my dear Aunt please to imprint a large kiss for me on your little cheeks, and be assured of your little sister's affection.

Thérèse of the Child Jesus,
rel. carm. ind.

CXVI

To CÉLINE

For her feast

J. M. J. T.

Jesus †   Carmel, 19 October 1892

My dearest Céline,

Long ago, in the days of our childhood, we rejoiced in our feast because of the little presents we gave one another. In those days the least object had in our eyes a value without equal. . . . Soon the scene changed, even the youngest of the birds grew wings, it flew far off from the sweet nest of its babyhood, then all illusions vanished away. Summer had taken the place of spring, life's reality of childhood's dreams. . . .

Céline, surely at that decisive moment the bonds that bound our hearts together were drawn tighter. Yes, separation united us in a fashion there are no words to express. Our childhood affection changed into a union of feelings, a unity of souls and of thoughts. But who could have wrought this marvel ? . . . Ah ! it was He who had ravished our hearts. "My beloved chosen out of thousands . . . the odour of His ointments suffices to draw us after Him.[1] Following in His steps maidens speed lightly on the way" (Cant. of Cant.).[2]

Together Jesus attracted us, though by different ways, together He has raised us above all the fragile things " of this world whose fashion passes ".[3] He has, so to speak, put *all things* beneath our

[1] Cant. of Cant. v. 10; i. 3.
[2] St. John of the Cross, *Spiritual Canticle*, strophe xxv. The reference in brackets was inserted by the Saint herself.
[3] 1 Cor. vii. 31.

feet. Like Zachaeus we "have climbed up into a tree to see Jesus".[1]
. . . So we could say with St. John of the Cross: "All is mine, all
is for me; the earth is mine, the heavens are mine, God is mine and
the Mother of my God is mine."[2]

Speaking of the Blessed Virgin, I must tell you one of the
little affectionate things I say to her; sometimes I find myself
saying: "But, good Blessed Virgin, it seems to me that I am more
fortunate than you, for I have you for Mother, and you have no
Blessed Virgin to love. . . . It is true that you are the Mother of
Jesus, but you have given this same Jesus to me whole and entire
. . . and He on the Cross gave you to us for our Mother, so we
are richer than you, since we possess Jesus and you are ours as
well ! Long ago, in your humility, your wish was that one day
you might be the little serving maid of the privileged Virgin who
should have the honour to be the Mother of God;[3] and here I am,
poor little creature, not your serving-maid but your child, you
are Jesus' Mother and you are my Mother !" I am sure the
Blessed Virgin must laugh at my simplicity; but all the same what
I say to her is perfectly true !

Céline, what a mystery is our greatness in Jesus ! That indeed
is what Jesus showed us by having us climb up into the symbolic
tree of which I spoke a moment ago. And now, what new truth is
He going to teach us.? Has He not taught us everything? Listen
to what He tells us:

"Make haste and come down, for this day I must abide in thy
house."[4]

Good ! Jesus tells us to come down ! But where must we come
down ? Céline, you know better than I; still, let me tell you where
now we must go with Jesus. At one time the Jews asked our
Divine Saviour: "Master, where dwellest Thou ?"[5] And He
answered them: "The foxes have their holes and the birds of the
air their nests but I have not where to lay my head."[6] That is

---

[1] Luke xix. 4.

[2] St. John of the Cross, *Prayer of the soul inflamed with Divine Love.*

[3] The source of this thought is in Dom Guéranger's *Année Liturgique*, on 9
December (second day within the octave of the feast of the Immaculate Conception).
There one finds these words of the most Blessed Virgin to St. Elizabeth of Hungary:
"I especially asked the Lord that He should grant me to see the time when that
most holy Virgin should live who was to give birth to the Son of God. . . . I prayed
to Him to preserve my hands to serve her . . . my feet to go upon her orders. . . ."

[4] Luke xix. 5.

[5] John i. 38.

[6] Matt. viii. 20; Luke ix. 58.

where we must come down, if we are to serve as a dwelling for Jesus: we must *be so poor that we have not where to lay our head.*

That, dearest Céline, is what Jesus did in my soul during my retreat. . . . You realise that I am talking of the interior dwelling. After all, the exterior one has already been brought to nothing by the painful affliction of Caen . . . in our dearest Father, Jesus has stricken us in the most sensitive external part of our heart, now let Him act as He will, He knows how to bring His work in our souls to completion. . . .

Jesus wants us to receive Him in our hearts; by now, doubtless, they are empty of creatures; but alas! I feel that mine is not wholly empty of me, which is why Jesus tells me to come down. . . . He, the King of Kings, humbled himself in such manner that *His countenance was hidden*[1] and no one recognised Him . . . and I too want to hide my face, I want my Beloved alone to be able to see it, Him alone to count my tears . . . that in my heart, at least, He may lay His dear head and feel that there He is recognised and understood! . . . Céline, I can't tell you all that I would, my soul hasn't the strength. . . . Ah! if I could! But no, it is not in my power . . . but why should that grieve me, don't you always think what I think? . . . So whatever I do not say, you divine, Jesus makes your heart feel it. After all, has He not taken up His dwelling in your heart to find consolation for the crimes of sinners? Yes, it is there, in the inmost recess of the soul, that He instructs us together and will show us the day that shall have no sunset any more!

Happy feast! How sweet it will be one day for your Thérèse to wish you happy feast in Heaven![2]

[1] Isa. liii. 3.   [2] This letter is not signed.

CXVII

To MME GUÉRIN

For her feast

J. M. J. T.

Jesus †   Carmel, 17 November 1892.

My dear Aunt,

The smallest of your girls feels utterly incompetent to tell you once more the love she has for you and all her wishes, but a mother's heart has no trouble in divining all that passes in the soul of her child. So, darling Aunt, I shall not try to put into words feelings you have known so long.

This year God has filled my heart with very sweet consolation in bringing back my darling father from his exile.[1] As I run over in memory the sorrowful years that have passed, my soul overflows with gratitude. I cannot regret the griefs that are past, griefs which have completed and adorned the crown God is making ready to place upon the venerable brow of one who has loved and served Him so faithfully. . . . And then, these griefs have taught me a better knowledge of the treasures of tenderness hidden within the heart of the dear relations the good God has given me. "The loveliest masterpiece of the heart of God is the heart of a mother." I feel how true that word is and I thank the Lord for giving me the sweet experience of it. Darling Aunt, if you have the heart of a mother for us, I assure you your little girl has a very filial heart, so she asks Jesus to fill you to overflowing with all the favours a child's heart can dream for its dearest mother. Often silence is the only way I have to express my prayer, but the divine Guest in the tabernacle understands all, even the silence of a child's soul filled with gratitude ! . . .

If I am not present on the day of my dearest Aunt's feast, my heart will be very near her, and no one will heap more tenderness upon her than I.

---

[1] Thérèse alludes to her father's return to his family. Brought back on 10 May to the Guérin home in Lisieux, where Léonie and Céline were, he was installed immediately, with his daughters, at 7 Rue Labbey (see *Histoire d'une famille*, p. 331).

Please, dear Aunt, kiss my kind Uncle and darling sisters for me.

I leave you, dearest Aunt, but I remain wholly united to you as a daughter to her mother.

Your child who loves you,
Sister Thérèse of the Child Jesus,
rel. carm. ind.

CXVIII

To M. and MME GUÉRIN

New Year wishes

J. M. J. T.

Jesus †   Carmel, 30 December 1892.

My dear Uncle and Aunt,

It is very sweet for your little Benjamin to be bringing you her good wishes for the new year that is about to begin.

I am not going to try to write down here all the wishes I have for my dearest relations, it would take too long and anyhow the heart so often has aspirations which speech is powerless to translate. There are desires that the good God alone can understand, or rather divine. So it is to Him that I shall confide the wishes my heart forms for those who are dear to me.

Often, when I am at the feet of Our Lord, I feel my soul overflowing with gratitude as I think of the grace He has granted me in giving me relations like those I have the happiness to possess.

I do not forget that January 2 is my dear Uncle's birthday. I am proud that I was born on the same day as he, and I hope he will not forget to pray for his little Thérèse who will soon be an old maid of twenty. How time passes ! . . . It seems like only yesterday that my dear Uncle was bouncing me up and down on his knees, singing the tale of Bluebeard with terrible eyes which had me almost dying of fright. The "petit air de Mirlitir" was more to my liking. The memory of this song is still enough to start me laughing.

You see, dear Uncle and Aunt, that the weight of years has not yet destroyed your little girl's memory; in fact, she is at an age when memories of childhood have a special charm.

Please, dear relations, give all my greetings to all I love; I am not naming anybody because the rest of my paper would not be enough; but in my heart all the names are written, and hold a great place.

Your ELDERLY Niece who loves you with all her heart,

Sister Thérèse of the Child Jesus,
rel. carm. ind.

1893

TWENTY-FIRST YEAR

20 February : Reverend Mother Agnes of Jesus is elected Prioress of the Lisieux Carmel. Shortly after, she officially assigns Sister Thérèse of the Child Jesus to aid Mother Marie de Gonzague in the direction of the novices.
23 June : Léonie enters, for the second time, the Convent of the Visitation in Caen.

CXIX

To REVEREND MOTHER AGNES OF JESUS

On the day of her election as Prioress

J. M. J. T.

Jesus †   20 February 1893.

My dearest Mother,

How lovely it is to be able to give you that name ! . . . For a long time you had been my "Mother", but it was in the secret of my heart that I gave that sweet name to one who was at once my *Guardian Angel* and my *Sister*. And now today God has *consecrated* you. . . . You are really and truly my Mother, and so you will be for all eternity. Oh ! how lovely a day it is for your child ! The veil Jesus has cast over the day[1] makes it still more luminous to my eyes; it is the seal of the adorable Face, the perfume showered upon you of the "mystic bouquet".[2] Surely it will always be so. "He whose look was hidden,"[3] He who continues hidden in His little white Host and does not communicate with souls save veiled, will spread over the whole life of the beloved *apostle* of His divine Face a mysterious veil which only He can penetrate ! . . .

[1] Certain circumstances had cast a gloom over her election.
[2] The bouquet of myrrh, emblem of suffering.
[3] Isa. liii. 3.

161

Yes, the spirit of Mother Geneviève dwells in you[1] whole and entire, and her prophetic word is fulfilled.[2] *At thirty* you have begun your public life; it was you, after all, who gave all Carmels and all pious souls the joy of having the moving and poetic account of the life of our holy Foundress. But Jesus had cast a veiled look upon my dearest Mother, and He did not let her be recognised, for her look was hidden[3]. . . .

If today is so beautiful even here upon earth, what must it be like in Heaven ? I seem to see our darling Mother, looking happily upon her Pauline (the one she loved, the one who drew her most[4]); she sees her become a Mother in her turn, the Mother of many virgins, among them her sisters ! How mysterious it is !

Now you are to penetrate into the sanctuary of souls, now you are to shower upon them the treasures of grace with which Jesus has filled you so wholly. Of course you will suffer. . . . The vessels will be too small to contain the precious perfumes you will want to put into them; but Jesus, too, has only very small instruments on which to play His melody of love, yet He is skilled to use all those that we give Him. You will be like Jesus ! . . . Little sister, dearest Mother—my heart, the heart of your child, is a lyre, a very *tiny* one; when you are tired of plucking the strings of the harps, you can pick up your *tiny lyre*, and you will hardly touch it, and it will give forth the sounds you desire . . . at the bare touch of your maternal fingers it will UNDERSTAND, and its thin little melody will mingle with the song of your heart. . . .

O Mother ! What things I want to tell you ! But no, you know *all*. . . . One day, when the shadows have passed, I shall lie at rest upon your heart and say over and over the sweet name: *my Mother*.

[1]Thérèse is alluding to the exhortation of the Superior of the Lisieux Carmel, who, immediately after the election, had said to Mother Agnes before the whole Community: "Your saintly Mother Geneviève will aid you; you must set yourself to imitate the precious example she has left you. I may tell you, without any failure of discretion, that if the majority of your sisters chose to give you their votes, it was because they saw that you were trying to reproduce the virtues you had seen her practise."

[2] Mother Geneviève (see note to Letter CIX) had announced well before that an important position would be entrusted to Sister Agnes when she was thirty.

[3] The circular letter to the Carmelite Convents, describing the life and death of Mother Geneviève, was written by Sister Agnes, but signed by Mother Marie de Gonzague, at that time Prioress.

[4] See *Histoire d'une famille*, p. 213, for Mme Martin's feelings towards Pauline.

CXX

To CÉLINE

To tell her of Jesus' designs for her soul:
written for her birthday, now very near

J. M. J. T.

Jesus †   Carmel, 25 April 1893.

My dearest Céline,

I am going to tell you a thought that occurred to me this morning, or rather I am going to tell you of Jesus' designs for your soul. . . .

When, in the presence of the *one Friend* of our souls, I think of you, what always strikes me as the distinctive quality of your heart is simplicity . . . Céline . . . *simple* little *Céline*-flower, do not envy the flowers that grow in gardens.

Jesus did not say to us: "I am the flower of the gardens, the garden rose", but "I am the flower of the fields, the lily of the valleys".[1] So—it occurred to me this morning, before the tabernacle, that my Céline, Jesus' little flower, must be and must always remain *a drop of dew* hidden in the divine cup of the lovely Lily of the valleys.

What is simpler and purer than a dewdrop? It is not formed by the *clouds*, because dew falls on the flowers when the vault of heaven is filled with stars. Rain is not to be compared with it, for it surpasses the rain in freshness and beauty. Dew exists only by night; the sun, darting its warms rays upon it, distils the lovely pearls sparkling on the tip of the blades of grass in the meadow, and the dew changes into a light vapour. Céline is a drop of dew, not formed by the clouds but come down from the loveliness of heaven, her Homeland. During the *night* of this life, it is its mission to be hid in the heart of the *Flower of the fields*; no human eye can find it, only the cup that holds the tiny dewdrop can know its freshness.

Fortunate little dewdrop, known only to Jesus, do not stay to consider the course of the mighty rivers that creatures so admire,

---

[1] Cant. of Cant. ii. 1.

do not envy even the clear brook winding through the meadow. Truly its murmur is very sweet, but creatures can hear it : nor can the chalice of the *Flower of the fields* contain it. It cannot be for Jesus alone. To be His, one must be small, small as a drop of dew ! Oh ! how few souls there are that aspire to stay so small. "But," say they "the river and the brook are surely more useful than the dewdrop ? What does it do ? It is good for nothing, save to give a few moments' refreshment to a flower of the fields which is today and tomorrow is no more".[1]

They are right, of course : the dewdrop is good for no more than that ; but they do not know the *wild Flower* which has chosen to dwell in our land of exile and remain here during the short night of this life. If they knew it, they would understand the rebuke Jesus gave Martha[2] long ago. Our Beloved has no need of our fine thoughts—has He not His angels, His legions of heavenly spirits, whose knowledge infinitely surpasses that of the greatest geniuses of our sad earth ?

So it is not intellect or talents that Jesus has come upon earth to seek. He became the Flower of the fields solely to show us how He loves simplicity. The *Lily in the valley* does not aspire to more than a drop of dew. . . . That is why He created one, called Céline ! . . . During the night of this life, she is to remain hid from every human eye, but when the shadows "begin to retire",[3] when the *Flower of the fields* has become the *Sun of justice*,[4] when He is come to run His *course like a giant*,[5] will He forget His tiny drop of dew ? . . . Oh, no ! the moment He appears in His glory, the companion of His exile will appear with Him. The divine sun will rest one of His rays of love upon her, and then, to the dazzled gaze of the angels and the saints, the poor little dewdrop will be shown forth, sparkling like a precious diamond which, reflecting the Sun of justice, has grown like to It. But that is not all. The divine Luminary, looking upon His dewdrop, will draw it upward to Him, and it will ascend like a light vapour and go where it may abide for eternity in the bosom of the glowing furnace of uncreated Love, forever united with Him. Just as, upon earth, it was the faithful companion of His exile and despised as He was, so in Heaven it will reign eternally.

[1] Reminiscence of Matt. vi. 39.
[2] Cf. Luke x. 42.
[3] Cant. of Cant. iv. 6.
[4] Mal. iii. 20.
[5] Ps. xviii. 6.

Into what astonishment will those then be plunged, who in this world had regarded the tiny dewdrop as useless. They will have an excuse, of course, the *gift* of God had not been revealed to them, they had not brought their heart close to the *Flower of the fields*, had not heard the enchanting words "Give me to drink".[1] Jesus does not call all souls to be drops of dew, He wills that there should be precious draughts appreciated by men and solacing them in their needs; but for Himself He reserves a drop of dew, that is the whole of His ambition.

What a privilege to be called to so high a mission ! . . . but to respond to it how *simple* one must remain. . . . Jesus knows that upon earth it is difficult to keep pure, so He wants His dewdrops not even to be aware of themselves; He delights to contemplate them, but only He regards them; and they, not realising their value, think themselves below other creatures . . . and that is what the *Lily of the valleys* desires. One tiny drop of dew, called Céline, has understood. . . . That is the end for which Jesus created her, but she must not forget her poor little sister, she must win for her the grace to put into action what Jesus has given her to realise, in order that one day the same ray of love may distil both and that they may go together, being but one upon earth, to be united for eternity in the heart of the Divine Sun.

Thérèse of the Child Jesus of the Holy Face.

CXXI

To CÉLINE[2]

At La Musse

J. M. J. T.

Jesus †   Carmel, 6 July 1893.

My dearest Céline,

Your two letters were like a sweet melody to my heart. . . . I am happy to see the love Jesus has for Céline. How He loves her, with what *tenderness* He *looks* upon her ! . . . So here we are, all

---

[1] John iv. 7.
[2] This letter was sent to La Musse, where M. Martin had been brought with his wheel-chair and his paralytic's bed.

five of us, on our way.[1] What a happiness to be able to say: "I am sure I am doing God's will." That holy will has manifested itself very clearly in regard to my Céline. She it is whom Jesus *chose* out of us all to be the crown and reward of the saintly old man who has enraptured Heaven by his fidelity. How could one dare to say that you have been overlooked, less loved than the others? I tell you that you have BEEN CHOSEN OUT as a privilege, your mission is all the more beautiful because, while you remain the visible angel of our dearest father, you are at the same time the bride of Jesus.

"That is true," perhaps my Céline thinks, "but after all I do less than the others for God, I have many more joys and therefore fewer merits." "My thoughts are not your thoughts,"[2] says the Lord. Merit does not consist in doing or giving much, but in receiving, in loving much. It is said that "it is more blessed to give than to receive,"[3] and that is true; but when Jesus wants to make His own the blessedness of giving, it would not be gracious to refuse. Let Him take and give what He chooses, perfection consists in doing His will; and the soul which gives itself totally to Him is called by Jesus "His mother, His sister", and His whole family.[4] And more than that: "If anyone love Me, he will keep My word (which means he will do My will) and My Father will love him and We will come to him and make Our abode with him."[5]

O Céline! how easy it is to give pleasure to Jesus, to enrapture His heart! All one has to do is love Him, not considering oneself, not examining one's faults too closely. . . .

At this moment your Thérèse does not find herself on the heights, but Jesus is teaching her "to draw profit from all, from the good and from the evil she finds in herself".[6] He is teaching her to play at love's bank or rather He plays for her, not telling her just how He goes about it—for that is His business and not Thérèse's; her part is to abandon herself, give herself over, keeping nothing for herself, not even the joy of knowing how His bank is paying. But after all she is not the prodigal son, there is no point in Jesus making her a feast since she is with Him always.[7]

---

[1] Léonie had entered two weeks earlier at the Convent of the Visitation in Caen.
[2] Isa. lv. 8.
[3] Acts xx. 35.
[4] Matt. xii. 50; Mark iii. 35; Luke viii. 21.
[5] John xiv. 23.
[6] St. John of the Cross.
[7] Luke xv. 31.

Our Lord chooses to leave in the desert the sheep that have not gone astray.[1] What deep things that tells me ! . . . He is *sure of them*, they cannot go astray now, for they are love's captives; so Jesus robs them of His visible presence to bring His consolations to sinners; or even if He does meet them upon Mount Tabor it is only for a few moments, the valleys are more often the place of His repose: "It is there that He takes His rest at noonday."[2]

The morning of our life is over; we enjoyed the scented breezes of dawn, then all smiled upon us, Jesus let us realise His sweet presence; but when the sun came up in its strength, the Beloved "brought us into His garden, made us gather the *myrrh*"[3] of trial by separating us from *all*, even from Himself. The mountain of myrrh[4] strengthened us with its bitter scents, so Jesus brought us down again and now we are in the valley. He has "led us gently beside the waters".[5]

Céline dearest, I do not see the things I am saying to you very clearly, but I feel that you will understand, that you will divine what I am trying to say. Ah ! let us always be *a drop of dew* for Jesus, there lies bliss, there lies perfection . . . fortunately I am talking to *you*, for others could not understand our way of speech, and I admit that it is true only for very few souls. Directors do in fact bring souls forward in the way of perfection by having them make a great many acts of the virtues, and they are right; but my director, Jesus, does not teach me to count my acts, but to do *everything* for love, to refuse Him nothing, to be pleased when He gives me a chance to prove to Him that I love Him—but all this in peace, in *abandonment*, Jesus does everything, I nothing.

I feel closely united to my Céline, I doubt if God has often made two souls that understand each other so well: never a discordant note. Jesus' hand, touching one lyre, instantly sets the other vibrating. . . . Oh ! let us stay hid in our divine *Flower* of the fields until "the shadows retire";[6] let us leave the *precious liquids* for the delight of creatures. Since we give pleasure to *our lily*, let us be happy to remain His drop, His single

---

[1] Matt. xviii. 12.
[2] Cant. of Cant. i. 6.
[3] Cant. of Cant. v. 1.
[4] Ibid., iv. 6: "Vadam ad montem myrrhae et ad collem thuris."
[5] Ps. xxii. 2.
[6] Cant. of Cant. iv. 6.

167

drop of dew ! . . . and in return for this drop, which will have consoled Him during our exile, what will He not give us in the Homeland ! . . . He tells us Himself: "If any man thirst let him come *to Me* and drink";[1] thus Jesus is and will be our *ocean* . . . like the thirsty hart, we thirst for that water[2] which is promised us; but great is our consolation to be in our turn an ocean for Jesus, an ocean for the Lily of the valleys ! . . .

Only your heart will be able to read this letter for I have trouble myself in deciphering it. . . . I have no more ink, I have been forced to "*spit*" into our inkwell to make some . . . that makes you laugh, doesn't it?

I embrace the whole family, but especially my dearest King, who is to receive a kiss from his Céline on behalf of his *queen*.

Sister Thérèse of the Child Jesus of the Holy Face,
rel. carm. ind.

CXXII

To CÉLINE

J. M. J. T.

Jesus †   Carmel, 18 July 1893.

My dearest Céline,

I had not expected to be answering your letter this time, but our Mother[3] wants me to add a brief word to hers. How many things I have to say to you ! But, since I have only a few moments, I must begin by assuring the "tiny drop of dew" that her Thérèse understands her. . . . After reading your letter, I took myself to prayer. Picking up the gospel, I asked Jesus to find a passage for you, and this is what I hit upon: "See the fig-tree and all the trees; when they now shoot forth their tender leaves you know that summer is nigh; so you also, when you shall see these things come to pass, know that the kingdom of God is at hand."[4]

I closed the book, I had read enough; "these things" which are happening in my Céline's soul are clear proof that the kingdom of Jesus is established there. . . . Now I want to tell you what is

---

[1] John vii. 37.
[2] Ps. xli. 2.

[3] Mother Agnes of Jesus, Prioress.
[4] Luke xxi. 29, and parallel passages.

happening in *my own* soul, I am sure it is the same thing as in yours.

You are right, Céline, the "fresh mornings"[1] are over for us, there are no more flowers left for us to pick, Jesus has taken them for Himself; perhaps one day He will make new flowers bloom, but meanwhile what must we do ? Céline, God no longer asks anything of me . . . in the beginning, He asked me an infinity of things. For awhile I thought that now, with Jesus asking nothing of me, I must go gently in peace and love, doing only the things He used to ask. But a light has been given me.

St. Teresa says we must feed the fire of love. When we are in darkness, in dryness, there is no *wood* within our reach, but surely we are obliged at least to throw little bits of *straw* on the fire. Jesus is quite powerful enough to keep the fire going by Himself, yet He is glad when we add a little fuel, it is a *delicate attention* which gives Him pleasure, and then He throws a great deal of wood on the fire ; we do not see it but we feel the *strength* of Love's heat.

I have tried it: when I *feel nothing*, when I am INCAPABLE of praying or practising virtue, then is the moment to look for small occasions, *nothings* that give Jesus more pleasure than the empire of the world, more even than martyrdom generously suffered. For example a smile, a friendly word, when I would much prefer to say nothing at all or look bored, etc. . . .

Darling Céline, do you understand ? It is not to make my crown, to gain merits, but to give pleasure to Jesus. . . . When I find no occasions, at least I want to keep telling Him that I love Him, it's not difficult and it keeps the *fire* going; *even if* that fire of love were to seem wholly out, I should throw something on it and then Jesus could relight it.

Céline, I am afraid I have not put this very well; perhaps you will think that I always act like this. Oh, no ! I am not always faithful, but I am never discouraged, I abandon myself in Jesus' arms. The "tiny drop of dew" buries itself still deeper in the calyx of the Flower of the fields and there it finds all it has lost and much more besides.

Your little Sister

Thérèse of the Child Jesus of the Holy Face,
rel. carm. ind.

[1] St. John of the Cross, *Explanation of the Spiritual Canticle*, strophe XXX.

CXXIII

To CÉLINE

J. M. J. T.

Jesus †   Carmel, 23 July 1893.

My darling Céline,

I am not surprised that you can make nothing of what is happening in your soul. A LITTLE *child all alone*, at sea, in a boat lost amid the stormy waters—could it know whether it was close to port or far off? While it can still see the shore it started from, it knows how much way it has made; seeing the land further and further away, it cannot contain its childish joy. Oh, it says, I'll soon be at the end of my journey. But the further away the shore becomes, the vaster the ocean looks. . . . Then the child's *knowledge* is reduced to nothing, it no longer knows where its boat is going. It does not know how to handle the helm; so the only thing it can do is let itself be borne along, let its sail go with the wind.

Céline, Jesus' *little child* is all alone in a small boat, *land* has vanished from its sight, it knows not where it goes, whether forward or backward. . . . Little Thérèse knows, she is *sure*, that her Céline is on the *open sea*, the boat that bears her on is speeding with all sails set towards the port; the helm, which Céline cannot even see, does not lack a pilot. Jesus is there, *sleeping* as long ago in the Galilean fishermen's boat.[1] He sleeps . . . and Céline does not *see* Him, for night has come down upon the boat. . . . Céline does not *hear* Jesus' voice. . . . The wind is high . . . she *hears* the wind . . . she *sees* the darkness . . . and Jesus *sleeps* on. Yet if He awoke only for an instant, He would have but "to command the wind and the sea, and there would come a great calm";[2] night would be brighter than day. Céline would *see* the *divine gaze* of Jesus, and her soul would be comforted. . . . But then, Jesus would be no longer asleep, and He is so WEARY.[3] . . . His Divine feet have grown weary from following after sinners, and He rests so sweetly in Céline's little boat.

The apostles had given Him a *pillow*,[4] the Gospel gives us this detail, but in His *dearest bride's* little boat Our Lord finds another

---

[1] Matt. viii. 24.   [2] Matt. viii. 26.   [3] John iv. 6.   [4] Mark iv. 38.

pillow, far softer; it is Céline's heart, there He forgets all, He is at home. . . . It is not a stone that He lays His divine head upon, the stone He longed for during His mortal life,[1] it is the heart of a *child*, the heart of a *bride*. Ah! how happy is Jesus! Yet how can He be happy when His bride is suffering, when she is *awake* while He sleeps so peacefully. Does He not know that Céline sees nothing but the night, that His Divine countenance remains hidden from her, and even, sometimes, the weight she feels upon her heart seems heavy to her. . . .

How mysterious it is! Jesus, the tiny child of Bethlehem whom Mary bore as "a light burden" grows heavy, so heavy that St. Christopher marvels. . . . The spouse of the Canticles says that "her beloved is a bundle of myrrh and He reposes upon her breast".[2] Myrrh is *suffering*, and that is how Jesus reposes upon Céline's heart. Yet Jesus is happy to see her in her suffering, He is happy to receive all from her while the *night* lasts. . . . He awaits the dawn and *then, oh! then, what an awakening will be the awakening of Jesus !!!*

Be sure, dearest Céline, that your boat is in the open sea, already perhaps very *close to port.* The wind of sorrows driving it is a *wind of love*, and that is a wind that goes faster than lightning.

How *touched* I am to see that Jesus had inspired in you the idea of small sacrifices. I had asked Him to, not expecting to be writing to you so soon. Never has Our Lord refused to inspire in you what I had begged Him to tell you. He always gives us the same graces at the same time. I am even obliged to have a rosary of practices. I made it through charity for one of my companions,[3] I shall tell you about it in detail, it is quite amusing. . . . I am caught in nets which please me not at all, but which are very useful to me in the state of soul in which I am.[4]

[1] Matt. viii. 20; Luke ix. 58.
[2] Cant. of Cant. i. 13.
[3] Sister Marthe of Jesus, one of the two novices entrusted to her charge as assistant to Mother Marie de Gonzague (see notes to Letters LVI and CXLVI).
[4] This letter is not signed.

CXXIV

To CÉLINE

J. M. J. T.

Jesus †   Carmel, 2 August 1893.

My darling Céline,

Your letter fills me with consolation, the road you walk is a royal road, not a beaten path, but a *track* made by Jesus Himself.

The bride of the Canticles says that, not finding her Beloved in his bed, she arose to seek him in the city, but in vain; it was after leaving the city,[1] that she found Him Whom her soul loved ! . . .

Jesus does not want us in repose to find His adorable presence, He hides, is wrapped in darkness; not thus did He act toward the *multitude* of the Jews, for we see in the Gospel that *the people were uplifted when He spoke to them.*[2] Jesus charmed feeble souls by His divine words. He was trying to make them strong against the day of trial. . . . But how small was the number of Our Lord's friends, when *He was silent* before His judges ![3] . . . Oh ! what a melody for my heart is that silence of Jesus. . . . He makes Himself poor that we may be able to do Him charity; He stretches out His hand to us like a *beggar*, that upon the sunlit day of Judgment, when He appears in His glory, He may be able to utter and we to hear the loving words: "Come, blessed of my Father; for I was hungry and you gave me to eat: I was thirsty and you gave me to drink: I was a stranger and you took me in; I was in prison, sick, and you came to me".[4]

It was Jesus Himself who uttered those words, it is He who wants our love, *begs* for it. He puts Himself, so to say, at our mercy. He wills to take nothing unless we give it to Him, and the smallest thing is precious in His divine eyes. . . .

Céline dearest, rejoice in our lot, it is very lovely ! Let us give, give to Jesus, let us be misers to others but spendthrifts to Him ! Jesus is a hidden treasure,[5] a good beyond price that few souls can find, for it is *hidden* and the world loves things that glitter.

---

[1] Cant. of Cant. iii. 2–4.   [4] Matt. xxv. 34–36.
[2] Luke xix. 48.   [5] Ibid., xiii. 44.
[3] Matt. xxvi. 63.

Ah ! if Jesus had chosen to show Himself to all souls with His ineffable gifts, surely not one would have spurned Him; but He does not want us to love Him for His gifts; it is *Himself* that must be our *reward*. *To find a thing hidden, we must ourselves be hidden;*[1] so our life must be a mystery ! We must be like Jesus, like Jesus whose *look was hidden.*[2] . . . "Do you want to learn something that may serve you ?" says the *Imitation*: "love to be ignored and accounted for nothing.[3] . . ." And in another place: "After you have left everything, you must above all leave yourself;[4] let one man boast of one thing, one of another; for you, place your joy only in the contempt of yourself."[5]

May these words give peace to your soul, my Céline ! You know them, but then you know all I would say to you. . . . Jesus loves you with a love so great that if you saw it, you would be in an ecstasy of happiness of which you would die, but you do not see it and you suffer.

Soon Jesus "will arise to save all the small and humble of the earth ! . . ."[6]

CXXV

To MME GUÉRIN

J. M. J. T.

Jesus †   Carmel, 10 August 1893.

My dear Aunt,

I saw with pleasure that you could read your little girl's heart. Yet I don't want my *beautiful* writing to lose the honour of being admired at the château of La Musse. So I was very happy when our good little *Mother* laid upon me the pleasant task of answering your letter.

O Aunt ! every line you have written shows me your heart, the heart of the tenderest of mothers; but your little Thérèse's heart too is that of a child full of love and gratitude.

I am asking the good God to cure my dear Uncle.[7] Truly it

[1] St. John of the Cross, *Explanation of the Spiritual Canticle*, strophe i.
[2] Isa. lii. 3.
[3] *Imitation of Christ*, bk. i, ch. ii.
[4] Ibid., bk. ii, ch. xi, 4.
[5] Ibid., bk. iii, ch. xlix, 7.
[6] Ps. lxxv. 10. This letter is not signed.
[7] M. Guérin was suffering at the time from very painful rheumatism.

seems to me that this prayer cannot fail to be granted, since Our Lord is personally interested in the cure. After all, it is for His glory that my Uncle's arm should toil on and on, writing admirable pages which must indeed save souls and make the demons tremble.[1]

I hope that our prayers are already granted and that no anxiety troubles your enjoyment of the last days you have still to spend in your lovely château. How happy Jeanne must be to be able to enjoy this vacation in Francis's company, since she has so little of it in Caen.[2] I have said many prayers that that nasty sprain may disappear completely, for it must have been a heavy cloud against the blue of my Jeanne's heaven.

I think too of my little sister Marie.[3] I fancy that since she has established her dwelling in *the treetops*,[4] I must seem to her very small and insignificant; as you get closer to heaven, you discover marvels not to be met in the lowly valley! She will say I'm teasing, which won't stop me from offering Holy Communion for *Her Grandeur* on her feast day.

I cannot tell you, dear Aunt, the happiness I feel at the thought that my darling father is with you, surrounded by all possible tenderness and care. God has chosen to act with him as with His servant Job: having first humiliated him, He showers His favours upon him; and it is through you that all these kindnesses and all this affection are given him.

Darling Aunt, I have still many things to tell you, but I've no space left and it is not respectful to end up like this, across the letter; forgive me, dear Aunt, and realise all the things I should like to write to you and the whole family.

Mother Marie de Gonzague and our Mother send you a thousand affectionate messages, they are glad to think that Mme de Virville will be making your acquaintance.[5]

I kiss you with all my heart, dear Aunt, and am always

Your respectful little girl

Sister Thérèse of the Child Jesus.

---

[1] M. Guérin devoted his pen and his fortune to the Catholic paper of the region, *Le Normand* (see *Histoire d'une famille*, pp. 63, 344).

[2] Dr. Francis La Néele, Jeanne Guérin's husband, had often to be away from home in the practice of his profession.

[3] Her cousin, Marie Guérin.

[4] One of the oaks in the park that she was specially fond of.

[5] Mother Marie de Gonzague's sister-in-law.

CXXVI

To LÉONIE

*Who had entered the Convent of the Visitation
in Caen*

J. M. J. T.

Jesus †   Carmel, 13 August 1893.

My dear Léonie,

I wonder if you think your little Thérèse has forgotten you?
Oh no! You know her heart too well to think that. I should have
liked to write to you along with our Mother and Sister Marie
of the Sacred Heart, but there was a muddle and their letter went
off earlier than I thought. Today I get the chance to take my
revenge and spend a small moment in your company.

If you knew, darling Sister, the acts of thanksgiving I send
heavenward for the favour that God has granted you! At
last your wishes are realised; like the dove that went forth from
the ark, you could not find upon the surface of the earth anywhere
to rest your foot, for a long time you flew, seeking to return tó the
hallowed place where your heart had fixed its dwelling for ever.
Jesus kept you waiting, but at last the moaning of His dove
touched Him, He stretched out His divine hand and, taking His
betrothed, placed her upon His heart, in the tabernacle of His love.

So now at last our saintly Aunt's prediction[1] is fulfilled. The
child of Blessed Margaret Mary[2] is in the Visitation, and for ever
she will be the bride of Our Lord.

Obviously my joy is wholly spiritual, since from now on I am
never again to see my dear Léonie here below, or hear her voice, or
pour out my heart in hers. But I know that the earth is the place
of our exile, we are travellers on the way to our Homeland; what
matter if we do not follow the same road, since the one end of

[1] Sister Marie-Dosithée, a Visitandine of Le Mans, Mme Martin's elder sister,
whose supernatural intuition bordered upon prophecy, had said of Léonie: "I
cannot help thinking that later on this child will be a Visitandine," though at the
time nothing humanly made it seem likely (*Histoire d'une famille*, p. 170, and notes
to Letter CXLII).

[2] At the age of eighteen months Léonie had been dangerously ill and was cured
at the end of a novena made by her aunt Sister Marie-Dosithée to Saint Margaret
Mary, not then canonised (see ibid., p. 70).

both roads is Heaven, and there we shall meet, never to part. There eternally we shall live joyously as a family, we shall find our dearest Father, and he will be ringed about with glory and honour for his perfect fidelity, and above all for the humiliation of which he has drunk so deep; we shall see our kind mother, who will be full of joy at the trials which were our lot during the exile of life, we shall enjoy her happiness as she gazes upon her five daughters in religion, and we shall join with the four little angels awaiting us there to form a crown which will encircle for ever the brow of our dearest parents.

Darling Sister, you see what share I take in your joy; I know that your joy is very great, but also that there are many sacrifices to go with it; would the religious life be meritorious without them? On the contrary, surely it is the small crosses that are all our joy, they are more commonplace than the great, and they prepare the heart to receive the great when it is our dear Master's will.

Please, dear Léonie, be kind enough to give my respectful greetings to your Reverend Mother, for whom I have retained a deeply filial affection ever since I had the honour to meet her;[1] am I not, in a very small way, a member of her family, since you are her daughter, and I your unworthy little sister?

Our Mother Marie de Gonzague and Sister Marie of the Sacred Heart also send their religious greetings to the Superior, and they send to their dear Léonie their best wishes for her happiness.

Do not forget in your prayers, dear Sister, the smallest Carmelite, who is so closely united to you in the heart of the Blessed Virgin.

Sister Thérèse of the Child Jesus of the Holy Face,
rel. carm. ind.

[1] On the occasion of a visit paid to Léonie during her first period as a nun at the Visitation Convent.

176

CXXVII

To CÉLINE

J. M. J. T.

Jesus †   Carmel, 13 August 1893.

My darling Céline,

We are much concerned about all the worries you are having with your servant. Our Mother had not meant to send you a letter before your return, but she is so kind and loves her *little Célin*[1] so much that, knowing the trouble she is in, she wants to give her a small pleasure by allowing your Thérèse to write a brief note.

We do not know what you should do about the house, you must consult Uncle, we shall be satisfied with what he may decide; in any event we shall talk about the matter when we see you.[2] Your poor servant is most unfortunate to have such an ugly fault—dishonesty is specially ugly—but perhaps you might convert her like her husband ?[3] For every sin there is mercy, and the good God is powerful enough to give *stability* of character even to people who have none at all. I shall say many prayers for her; perhaps, in her place, I should be still worse than she, equally she might be a great saint by now, if she had received half the graces God has showered upon me.

Surely Jesus is very kind to allow my poor little letters to do you good, but I assure you that I don't make the mistake of thinking that is any of my doing. . . .' 'If the Lord build not the house, they labour in vain who build it."[4] All the finest speeches of the greatest saints could not bring forth a *single* act of love from a heart not possessed by Jesus. Only He can play on His lyre, no other can set its harmonious notes vibrating, but Jesus uses all means, creatures are all at His disposal, and He loves to use them during the night of life in order to hide His adorable presence; but He does not so hide Himself that we cannot sense that He is there. I do indeed often feel that He gives me lights, not for myself but

---

[1] So her sisters often called Céline.
[2] Céline was living in the house in the Rue Labbey with her sick father and servants in whom she had not full confidence. The Guérins thought of having her and her father to live with them.
[3] He had been converted by a novena made by Céline to St. Joseph.
[4] Ps. cxxvi. 1.

for His little exiled dove, His dearest bride. This is very true, I find an example in nature.

Think of a lovely peach so sweet that no confectioner could imagine so delicious a sweetness. Tell me, Céline, was it *for the peach* that the good God created that lovely red colour, so velvety, so pleasant to see and to touch ? Again was it for the peach that He used up so much sugar ? . . . No, it was for us and not for it. What belongs to it, what makes the *essence* of its life, is its *kernel*; we can rob it of all its beauty without robbing it of *its being.*

In the same way Jesus delights to lavish His gifts upon some of His creatures, but very often He does it to draw other hearts to Himself; and then, His end attained, He lets those exterior gifts disappear, despoils completely the souls dearest to Him. Seeing themselves in such great poverty these poor little souls are afraid, it seems to them that they are good for nothing—since they receive everything from others and have nothing to give; but it is not so, the *essence* of their *being* works on in secret. *Jesus* is forming in them the seed which is to develop above, in the gardens of heaven. It pleases Him to make them see their nothingness and His might; to make His way into them He uses the *most worthless* instruments, to show them that it is Himself alone that works. He is in haste to bring His work to completion for the day when, the shadows having vanished away, He will have intermediaries no more, but a face-to-face seeing for eternity ! . . .

(Our Mother thanks Marie[1] for her note, Mother Marie de Gonzague also. They are delighted about it.)

Sister Thérèse of the Child Jesus of the Holy Face,
rel. carm. ind.

CXXVIII

To CÉLINE

For her feast

J. M. J. T.

Jesus †   1893.

My dearest Céline,

I am asking *Jesus* to bring my little sister Marie of the *Holy Face*[2] my wishes for her feast . . . *Jesus* must be the divine link

---

[1] Marie Guérin, who desired to enter Carmel.
[2] See note 1, Letter LXXVI, and Letter CLIV.

between us. He alone has the right to penetrate into the sanctuary of His bride's heart. . . . Yes, *He, only He*, hears when nothing answers us. *He*, and He alone, disposes the events of our life in exile. He it is who sometimes holds the bitter cup to our lips. But we do not see Him, He hides, He veils His divine Hand and we can see nothing but creatures; and then we suffer because the voice of our Beloved is not heard and the voice of creatures seems to misjudge us . . .

Yes, the bitterest pain is to be misunderstood. . . . But this pain will never be suffered by Céline and Thérèse, never, for their eyes see higher than the earth. They rise above the created; the more Jesus hides, the more do they feel that He is close to them. In His *exquisite delicacy* He goes on ahead removing stones from the road, driving away reptiles; what is much more, He causes the voice of friends to sound in our ears, warning us not to advance over-confidently.[1] . . . And why? Is it not Jesus Himself who has marked out our road? Does He not enlighten us and reveal Himself to our souls? . . . All things bear us towards Him, the flowers growing by the roadside do not captivate our hearts: we look at them, we love them, because they speak to us of Jesus, of His power, of His love, but our souls remain free; why thus trouble the sweetness of our peace? Why fear the storm when the sky is cloudless? . . .

O Céline! dearest Céline. . . . We have not to bother about avoiding precipices, we are in the arms of Jesus, and if the voices of friends warn us to be careful, it is our Beloved Himself who wants them to. And why? . . . Ah! in His love, He chooses the same road for His brides that He chose for Himself. He wants the purest joys to be turned into sufferings, so that, having not even time to draw breath, we shall turn our hearts to Him who alone is our Sun and our joy. . . .

The *flowers by the roadside* are the *pure pleasures* of life, there is no evil in enjoying them, but Jesus is jealous of our souls. He wants all our pleasures mingled with bitterness. . . . And yet, the *flowers by the roadside* can lead to the Beloved: but by a détour like a disc or mirror that reflects the sun but is not the sun.

I am not managing to say to my dearest Céline what I want to say to her, I explain myself so badly. Perhaps she will understand

[1] Thérèse is putting her sister on guard against the seductions of the world.

at a half phrase. Jesus is so good at executing His poor Thérèse's commissions ! . . .

I find in the *Canticle of Canticles* a passage which applies perfectly to poor little exiled Céline: "What do you see in the bride, but choirs of music in the camp of an army ?"[1] My Céline's life is indeed a battlefield . . . poor little dove "she mourns by the rivers of Babylon, and how can she sing the songs of the Lord in a strange land ?"[2] Yet sing she must, her life must be a *melody*, a "choir of music". It is Jesus who holds her captive, but He is by her side. . . . Céline is a lyre in Jesus' hand. . . . It is a poor concert when nobody *sings*. . . . When Jesus plays, must not Céline *sing* ?[3] When the tune is sad, very well, she will *sing* the song of exile, and when the tune is gay, she will sing the songs of the *Homeland*. . . . All the things that happen, all the events of life, will be but distant noises, they will not set the lyre vibrating; Jesus alone *of right* touches it with His divine Fingers, creatures are *means*, instruments He uses, but it is Jesus' hand that *governs all*. In *everything*, you must see only Him.

I cannot think without ecstasy of dear little St. *Cecilia*, what a model for Jesus' lyre ! . . . In the midst of the world, with every sort of danger ringing her round, on the point of being married to a young pagan who dreamed only of earthly love, Cecilia might well have trembled and wept . . . but no, "hearing the instruments sounding for her wedding, Cecilia was singing in her heart".[4] . . . What total trust! Surely she was *hearing* other melodies than those of earth, her divine Spouse was *singing* too, the angels set the music of their heavenly choirs sounding in Cecilia's heart. They sang as once before they had sung by Jesus' cradle: "Glory to God in the highest and peace on earth to souls of good will."[5]

The glory of God ! Oh ! Cecilia realized that her divine Spouse was athirst for souls, and she longed for the soul of the young Roman who had no thought but for this world's glory; soon she was to make him a martyr and multitudes were to walk in his steps. . . . She was not afraid, for the angels had sung "Peace to

[1] Cant. of Cant. vii. 1.
[2] Ps. cxxxvi. 1, 4.
[3] "Chanter": the word is used not only for the sounds produced by the voice, but by such instruments as the lyre. I translate "sing" in the rest of this letter.
[4] Office of St. Cecilia, first responsory to the first nocturne.
[5] Luke ii. 14.

souls of good will", she knew that Jesus was under obligation to guard her and protect her virginity, and she knew the reward !¹ . . . Yes, "how beautiful is the chaste generation of virgin souls",² the Church hymns it over and over, and the phrase is still true today as in the time of the virgin Cecilia. . . .

O my dearest Céline, what pleasure Jesus takes in His lyre ! He has so few of them in the world, let Him take His rest by you, never weary of *singing* since Jesus never wearies of playing . . . One day, there in the Homeland, you will see the fruits of your labours . . . having smiled at Jesus through your tears, you will enjoy the radiance of His divine face and He will play once more upon His lyre. For all eternity He will play new melodies that *none* can sing but Céline !³ . . .

CXXIX

To MME LA NÉELE

To thank her for feast presents

J. M. J. T.

Jesus †

Carmel, 22 October 1893.

My dear Jeanne,

It is my turn to offer excuses, for I am very late in thanking you for all your nice gifts,⁴ but I had a slight hope that I might be able to say thank you in person, and for that reason I postponed writing.

Oh ! no, I did not have the horrid thought that my little sister was forgetting me, but it seemed to me perfectly natural that she should think it enough to offer up a prayer for her little Thérèse, so I was more touched than I can say to receive your affectionate letter. My dear Cousin's⁵ good wishes also touched me deeply. And then the pots of jam came to put the crown upon all your thoughtfulness for me ; our Mother, St. Teresa, was so grateful

¹ Thérèse expresses these same thoughts in her poem "Mélodie de Sainte Cécile", composed for Céline's birthday, 28 April 1894.
² Wisdom iv. 1.
³ This letter is not signed.
⁴ On the occasion of Thérèse's feast, 15 October.
⁵ "Cousin": Jeanne's husband.

that you could win her heart with a sardine, so she says. What would she have said if she had known Francis and Jeanne?

But heaven is not so far from earth that she cannot see them and bless them. I even feel confident that she cherishes my dear Jeanne quite specially.

Our Holy Mother too had a sister named Jeanne, and I was very much touched, reading her life, to see with what tenderness she cared for her small nephews. So, without deserting good St. Anne, I address myself to St. Teresa to obtain by her intercession that I too may be an aunt.[1] I do not doubt that she will grant my prayer and send my darling Jeanne a family blessed by God which will give the Church great saints.

The delay does not discourage me, for I know that in the Roman Curia it takes a long time to make saints, and I cannot hold it against God that He should put all His care and all His love into the preparation of the small souls that He means one day to entrust to my Jeanne.

I urge you, little Sister, offer a prayer to St. Teresa, I am sure St. Anne will be delighted; union is strength, and together they will win you the favour we beg for.

Please, dear Jeanne, be my spokesman to Francis, to thank him for his good wishes. I kiss you warmly, with all the tenderness of a little sister.

Our Mother and Sister Marie of the Sacred Heart send you a thousand loving messages, they pray continually that the desires of their darling Jeanne may be abundantly granted.

Sister Thérèse of the Child Jesus,
rel. carm. ind.

CXXX

To LÉONIE

After the retreat preached to the community

J. M. J. T.

Jesus †   Carmel, 5 November 1893.

My dear Léonie,

I am so delighted at your happiness, your dear little letters are a real joy. I see, beyond the possibility of doubt, that you are

---

[1] Not exactly an aunt, of course. Jeanne had no child and was to have none.

indeed where the good God wants you to be. How good Our Lord has been to our family! He has not suffered any mortal to become the spouse of a single one of us.

We have just heard a beautiful retreat[1] in preparation for the feast of our Holy Mother. The good father spoke especially of union with Jesus and of the beauty of our vocation. He brought before us all the advantages of the religious life, of the contemplative life especially. He gave us one comparison which delighted me: "Consider the oaks of our countryside, how crooked they are; they thrust their branches to right and left, nothing checks them so they never reach a great height. On the other hand, consider the oaks of the forest, which are hemmed in on all sides, they see light only *up above*, so their trunk is free of all those shapeless branches which rob it of the sap needed to lift it aloft. It sees only heaven, so all its strength is turned in that direction, and soon it attains a prodigious height. In the religious life the soul like the young oak is hemmed in on all sides by its rule. All its movements are hampered, interfered with by the other trees . . . But it has *light* when it looks toward HEAVEN, there alone it can rest its gaze, never upon anything below, it need not be afraid of rising too high. . . ."

Darling Sister, I feel I give you pleasure by speaking of such things, for us happiness lies in talking of the soul's affairs, plunging our hearts in the infinite. . . .

Please forgive me for sending letters so *ill-written*, but you see, darling Sister, I would rather let my pen run under the impulse of my heart than turn my phrases with skill and send you *a page of writing*.

Please give my respectful greetings to the Superior. Do not forget me in your prayers, think of me by Jesus' side as often as I think of you. I leave you, dear Léonie, yet remain wholly united with you in the heart of our divine Spouse.

Your unworthy little sister,

Thérèse of the Child Jesus of the Holy Face,
rel. carm. ind.

[1] Preached by Père Lemonnier. He was a witness at the Process of Thérèse's Beatification.

CXXXI

To MME GUÉRIN

For her feast

J. M. J. T.

Jesus †   Carmel, 17 November 1893.

My dear Aunt,

How sweet your little Thérèse finds it to bring you each year her good wishes for your feast ! Yet I have nothing new to say to you, you have long known how much I love you.

Darling Aunt, in saying it again I am not afraid of wearying you, and here is the reason why. When I am before the tabernacle, I can find only one thing to say to Our Lord : "My God, you know that I love you."[1] And I feel that my prayer does not weary Jesus; knowing the powerlessness of His poor little bride, He is satisfied with her goodwill. I know too that the good God has poured into the hearts of mothers something of the love with which His own heart overflows. . . . And she to whom I speak has received so large a measure of maternal love that I can have no fear of feeling not understood. . . .

There is another thing. My powerlessness will not last eternally; in the homeland of Heaven I shall be able to tell my darling Aunt many things that cannot be uttered in human words.

Meanwhile I ask Our Lord to leave one so skilled to work for His glory long, very long, upon earth; and I desire that she may see "her children's children" ![2] Perhaps my little sister Jeanne would smile if she read these lines, but I have much more trust than she, and I go on expecting the great saint and the great bishop,[3] followed by a large number of other little angels.

My dear Aunt, tomorrow I shall offer Holy Communion for you and for Madame Fournet;[4] I think of her often and beg Our Lord to preserve her to you for a long time yet.

[1] John xxi. 15.
[2] Ps. cxxvii. 7.
[3] Allusion to a dream Jeanne had.
[4] Madame Guérin's mother. She also was called Elizabeth, so that her feast was the same as her daughter's.

Please, dear Aunt, give my kind Uncle a kiss from me; and I call upon him, and my little sisters, to shower the tenderest caresses upon you from me.

Your little *Benjamin* who is proud of her title,

Sister Thérèse of the Child Jesus,
rel. carm. ind.

CXXXII

To LÉONIE

New Year wishes

J. M. J. T.

Jesus †   Carmel, 27 December 1893.

My dear Léonie,

I am glad to be bringing you my greetings for '94. The wish I form for you by Jesus' crib is soon to see you clothed in the holy habit of the Visitation. I say to *see* you, but I know I shall have that happiness only in heaven. What a joy it will be then to meet again after the exile of life; what things to tell each other ! Here below words are powerless, but there we shall understand one another at a single glance, and I think our happiness will be still greater than if we had never been apart.

Your dear little letter gave me such pleasure, I see that you are truly happy, and I do not doubt that God is giving you the grace to remain for ever in the ark of holiness. We are reading the life of St. Chantal in the refectory; it is a real joy for me to hear it, it brings me even closer to the dear Visitation, which I love so, and again I see the intimate union which has always existed between it and Carmel, which makes me bless the good God for having chosen these two Orders for our family. The Blessed Virgin is truly our Mother, since our convents are especially dedicated to her.

Darling Sister, don't forget to pray for me during the month of the dear Infant Jesus, ask Him that I may always stay little, *very little* ! . . .

I shall offer the same prayer for you, as I am aware of your desires and I know that humility is the virtue of your special choice.

Do not forget, dear Léonie, to give my respectful greetings to your venerable Mother, and be assured of the affection of the last and *littlest* of your sisters,

Thérèse of the Child Jesus of the Holy Face,
rel. carm. ind.

CXXXIII

To M. and MME GUÉRIN

New Year greetings

J. M. J. T.

Jesus †   Carmel, 29 December 1893.

Dear Uncle and dear Aunt,

I have only a few minutes to send you my New Year greetings. Our Mother has just told me that her letter is to be taken tomorrow morning. But I don't need a great deal of time to tell my dear relations once again the wishes my heart forms for their happiness. I should like the new year to have nothing but joys in store for them if that were possible.

But alas! God, who knows what rewards He has in store for His friends, sometimes likes to let them win His treasures by sacrifices. Our Holy Mother Teresa said jestingly to Our Lord words that are very true: "O my God, I am not surprised you have so few friends, you treat them so badly."

All the same, in the very midst of the trials He sends, the good God is full of delicate consideration. My darling father's illness is a clear proof. That cross was the greatest I could have imagined, but after making us taste its bitterness, Our Lord acted, by the hands of our dear relations, to sweeten the chalice of grief which He had put to our lips and which I had expected to drink to the very dregs.

O dear Uncle and darling Aunt, if you knew how loving and grateful is the heart of your little Thérèse !

I cannot say all I want to, it is time for Matins; forgive me this

186

jumble of a letter, and my *cat-scratch* handwriting;[1] please have eyes for nothing but your child's heart.

Thérèse of the Child Jesus,
rel. carm. ind.

PS. Please give Mme Fournet her granddaughter's sincerest greetings.

CXXXIV

To M. GUÉRIN

To give him news of Mother Agnes of Jesus,
who had been ill[2]

J. M. J. T.

My dear Uncle,

Our Mother is much better, but she is very weak, though she says she isn't.

Thank you, thank you, for all the kindnesses you are doing for her. I hope she will be completely obedient, it would be very wrong not to obey so *paternal* an Uncle ! . . . . Mother Marie de Gonzague is much moved by your kindness, she thanks you by giving all her maternal cares to our dear little Prioress.

Forgive me, dear Uncle, I am in such a rush that I don't know what I'm saying, but I hope you will realise our gratitude. We say many prayers for Mme Fournet.

I send a kiss to you, and to Aunt also, from your three little Carmelites.

Sister Thérèse of the Child Jesus,
rel. carm. ind.[3]

[1] Thérèse was too hard on her small, sloping, very legible handwriting. In the following year, on the advice of Mother Agnes, she adopted the upright hand found in the reproductions of her autograph.

[2] Undated; written in 1893.

[3] At the end of this letter, Mother Marie de Gonzague added: "Our little Mother Prioress will write tomorrow to thank her beloved uncle for the rice, which has this moment arrived."

1894

TWENTY-SECOND YEAR

29 July : Death of M. Martin at the Château de la Musse.
14 September : Céline enters the Lisieux Carmel. Thérèse, as assistant novice-mistress, has the joy of being entrusted with her sister's formation as a Carmelite.
December : Reverend Mother Agnes of Jesus, at the suggestion of Sister Marie of the Sacred Heart, orders Thérèse to write her memories of childhood, for the Prioress alone.

CXXXV

To REVEREND MOTHER AGNES OF JESUS

For her first feast-day as Prioress—21 January 1894—Thérèse gave her a picture she had painted, representing " The Dream of the Child Jesus"
The child is holding flowers in His hand ; in the background is seen the Holy Face, a chalice surmounted by a Host and the instruments of the Passion
The picture was accompanied by the following from Thérèse :

J. M. J. T.

THE DREAM OF THE CHILD JESUS

Playing with the flowers His dearest spouse has brought Him in the crib, Jesus thinks of what He will do to thank her . . . above, in the gardens of Heaven, the angels, servants of the divine Child, are already weaving the wreaths His heart has laid up for His beloved.

But night has come. The moon sheds its silvery light and the sweet Child Jesus sleeps. . . . His little hand does not leave the flowers which gave Him such pleasure during the day and His heart goes on dreaming of the happiness of His beloved bride.

Soon, He catches glimpses in the distance of strange objects bearing no resemblance to spring flowers. A cross ! . . . a lance ! . . . a crown of thorns ! Yet the divine Child does not tremble. All this He chooses, to show His bride how He loves her ! But it is still not enough, His child face is so beautiful, He sees it distorted and bleeding ! . . . out of all likeness ! . . . Jesus knows that His spouse will always recognise Him, will be at His side when all abandon Him, and the divine Child smiles at this blood-streaked image. He smiles again at the chalice, filled with the "wine that springs forth virgins". He knows that in His Eucharist the thankless will neglect Him, but Jesus thinks of His bride's love, of her loving attentions. He sees the flowers of her virtues filling the sanctuary with fragrance, and the Child Jesus continues to sleep sweetly . . . He is waiting till "the shadows retire"[1] . . . till the night of life gives place to eternity's radiant day! . . .

Then Jesus will restore to His beloved the flowers she gave Him for His consolation upon earth. Then He will bring His divine Face, all radiant with glory, down to hers, and He will give His bride to taste eternally the unutterable sweetness of His divine kiss ! ! ! . . .

Dearest Mother,

You have read the dream your child tried to picture for your feast. But alas, it is only your brush that could have painted so sweet a mystery ! I hope you will see nothing save the goodwill of one who would be so happy to give you pleasure.

It was you, Mother, it was your virtues, that I meant to represent by the little flowers Jesus is pressing to His heart. The flowers are indeed for Jesus alone ! yes, my dearest Mother's virtues will always remain hidden with the tiny Child in the crib; yet in spite of the humility that would like to conceal them, the mysterious fragrance breathing from these flowers gives me here on earth some faint sense of the marvels I shall see one day in the eternal Homeland, when I shall be allowed to gaze on the treasures of love you now lavish upon Jesus.

O Mother ! you know that never shall I be able to tell you all my gratitude for the way you have guided me, like an angel from Heaven, along the pathways of life; it was you who taught me to know Jesus and love Him; now that you are my Mother

[1] Cant. of Cant. iv. 6.

twice over, ah! lead me still towards the Beloved, teach me to practise virtue, that in heaven I may be placed not too far from you, and that you may recognise me as your child and your little sister.

Thérèse of the Child Jesus of the Holy Face,
rel. carm. ind.

CXXXVI

To LÉONIE[1]

J. M. J. T.

Jesus †

My dear Léonie,

I cannot tell you how happy I am to learn of your being accepted for Clothing. . . . I realise how happy you must be and I take a large share in your joy. Darling Sister, how the good God has rewarded your efforts ! I remember what you told me in the parlour before your entry into the ark of holiness. It meant nothing to you to remain always the last, to be taking the habit with no ceremony. You were seeking Jesus only, and for Him you renounced every joy. But as our dearest Father told us so often: God never lets Himself be outdone in generosity; so He did not want you to be deprived of the joy of being betrothed to Him publicly, until such time as you could become His spouse. I feel that the years of exile you spent in the world served to robe your soul in a precious garment for the day of your betrothal. The sad days of winter are over for you, and the lovely days of spring have come, and Jesus says to you, as to the spouse of the Canticles: "The winter is now past, the rain is over and gone. Arise, my love, my dove, and come . . . Behold I am at the door, open to me, my sister, my love, for my Face is full of dew and my locks of the drops of the night."[2] For long you sighed for Jesus' coming, and like the spouse you said to Him: "Who shall grant me, my love, that I may find thee alone without, and kiss thee, and now no man may despise me."[3]

And now He is here, on this day so long desired. You had not yet, darling Sister, met Jesus in the face of the world, but you

---

[1] Written in February or March.
[2] Cant. of Cant. ii. 10, 11, 12, 13; v. 2.
[3] Ibid., viii. 1.

searched for Him so diligently, and behold Him now coming to you ! . . . You consented to "find Him *alone without*" but He desires to give you His *kiss* before *the whole world*, so that none may fail to know that He has placed His sign upon your forehead and that never shall you receive any other Lover than Himself.[1]

Dear Léonie, I am forgetting to thank you for your letter; that is what I should have begun with, but you realise, don't you, that it's nothing but the joy I feel at your great happiness that makes me guilty of such an oversight.

I hope your wishes will soon be fulfilled and that your good Chaplain will be well again very soon. Please, darling Sister, offer my respectful greetings to your good and venerated Mother. Like you, I rejoice that it is she who is to give you the holy Habit.

I leave you, but I remain closely united to you in the divine Heart of Jesus.

Your unworthy little sister,

Thérèse of the Child Jesus of the Holy Face,
rel. carm. ind.

CXXXVII

To CÉLINE[2]

J. M. J. T.

The "codfiches"[3] gave our Mother great pleasure, she would like to write a short note to thank her dearest Céline[4], but she cannot. She is also very pleased at Marie's letter.[5]

Let the little exile be sad *without sadness*, for if the tendernesses of creatures are not concentrated upon her, the *tenderness* of Jesus is CONCENTRATED upon her whole and entire. Jesus is well-lodged, now that Céline has no home; He does not mind seeing His dearest Spouse *homeless*, it pleases Him ! But why ? . . . I simply don't know. . . . It is Jesus' secret, but I think He is preparing very lovely things in her little house. . . . He has

---

[1] Office of St. Agnes, antiphon of the first nocturne.
[2] Letter undated, unsigned. Probably written March 1894.
[3] Scallops.
[4] See note to Letter CXXVII.
[5] Marie Guérin.

so much to work at there, that He apparently forgets His poor Céline. . . . But no, unseen by her, He watches her through the window. . . . He likes to see her in the desert, "with no other thing to do save love",[1] suffering without even the *feeling* that she *loves*! . . . Jesus knows, of course, that life is only a dream, so He rejoices to see His spouse weeping by the river of Babylon! Soon the day will come when Jesus will take His Céline by the hand, and bring her into her little house, which by then will be an eternal palace . . . Then He will say "My turn now".[2] On earth you gave me the *one refuge* no human heart wants to renounce—*yourself*—and now I give you my eternal substance—Myself—and that is your home for eternity. During the night of life, you have been homeless and alone, now you shall have a companion; and it is I—Jesus, your Spouse, your Friend, for whom you gave up all—who will be the companion who will fill you with joy to overflowing unto ages of ages! . . .

CXXXVIII

To MLLE CÉLINE MAUDELONDE

For her approaching marriage

J. M. J. T.

Carmel, 26 March 1894.

My darling Céline,

I should have liked to be able to send an earlier answer to your letter, which gave me great joy; Lent prevented me; but now it is Paschal time and I can tell my dear little cousin[3] how much I shall share in her happiness.[4]

The great peace you feel seems to me a most manifest sign of God's will, for it is He alone who can fill your soul with peace, and the happiness you taste under His divine gaze can come only from Him. Darling Céline, I cannot give you such proofs of my affection as if I were still in the world, but it is no less warm for that; on the contrary, I feel that in solitude I shall be of more

---

[1] St. John of the Cross, *Spiritual Canticle*, strophe xxviii.
[2] C. Arminjon, loc. cit.
[3] They were not cousins in fact; they had an uncle and aunt in common.
[4] Céline Maudelonde was engaged to be married.

use to you than if I had the joy of being with you. The grilles of Carmel are not made to separate souls which love each other only in Jesus; they serve rather to strengthen the bonds that unite them.

While you are following the path that God has marked out for you, I shall be praying for my Céline, my childhood companion,[1] I shall be praying that all her joys may be so pure that she can taste them always under God's eye. Especially I shall pray that she may taste the incomparable joy of bringing back a soul to Our Lord, and that soul the one which is soon to make one single soul with hers. I do not doubt that this grace will soon be granted and I should be glad if my weak prayers had played some small part.

I hope my darling Hélène[2] is now cured, it would be an ill-chosen moment to be sick! Please give her a big kiss from me and I charge her to give my dearest Céline all my tenderest kisses; I am quite sure I could not make a better choice for so sweet a mission.

Mother Marie de Gonzague is wholly one with your three Carmelite cousins in rejoicing at your happiness; they ask you, darling Céline, to give their respectful greetings to M. and Mme Maudelonde.

I leave you, now, dearest Céline, but I remain still close to you in heart.

Your little cousin who will love you all her life and will never cease to pray for your happiness,

Sister Thérèse of the Child Jesus,
rel. carm. ind.

PS. The Mother Prioress of the Carmel at Saïgon[3] sent us a great many Chinese things, including a charming miniature drawing-room suite, so our Mother had the idea of raffling them for the benefit of our community. The tickets are 50 centimes. We are offering them to all the friends of our Carmel. If you want some, we shall be glad to send them.

[1] See Letter V.
[2] Céline Maudelonde's younger sister.
[3] The first Carmel established in the Missions. It was founded in 1861, at the request of Mgr Lefebvre, Vicar Apostolic of Western Cochin-China, by his cousin, Sister Marie-Philomène of the Immaculate Conception of the Lisieux Carmel.

CXXXIX

To SISTER MARIE ALOYSIA VALLÉE

Visitation Nun at Le Mans[1]

J. M. J. T.

Jesus †   3 April 1894.

My very dear Sister,

I am quite incapable of telling you how touched I am at your kind letter. It was a great happiness merely to know that the picture of the Child Jesus had given you pleasure,[2] I was repaid far beyond all my hopes . . . Dear *Aunt*[3]—please let me call you so too—I was thinking of you while I was planning the present I wanted to give our Reverend Mother for her first feast as Prioress.

I knew of course that she would be pleased to send you a small souvenir, so I put all my heart into painting "The Dream of the Child Jesus"; but alas! my unskilled brush was unable to reproduce what my soul had *dreamed*, and I *watered* with my *tears* the white robe of my little Jesus—which did *not* bring down a ray from heaven upon His tiny face! . . . Then, in my disappointment, I vowed to say nothing of the idea which had made me set about the work. In fact it was only when I saw how kindly our good Mother received it, that I told her my little secret. She was good enough to consider the heart and the intention rather than the skill of her child, and, to my great joy, my Child Jesus went off *for me* to make the acquaintance of *my kind Aunt* at Le Mans. I painted the divine Child to show what He is in regard to me. . . . In plain fact He is almost always *asleep*. . . . Poor Thérèse's Jesus does not caress her as once He caressed her saintly Mother. That of course is natural, since the daughter is so unworthy of the Mother! . . . All the same the closed eyes of little Jesus speak deep things in my soul, and, if He does not caress me, I try to

---

[1] Class mistress of Marie and Pauline Martin at the Visitation in Le Mans. She was professed 1 July 1868 and died 1 May 1903.

[2] The picture was "The Dream of the Child Jesus" described in Letter CXXXV.

[3] From affection for this nun and to give her pleasure, Mother Agnes of Jesus had asked Thérèse to call her Aunt, in memory of Sister Marie-Dosithée, Mme Martin's eldest sister, who had been a nun in the same convent (see notes to Letters CXXVI and CXLII).

give *Him* pleasure. I realise that "His heart watches"[1] always, and that in Heaven our homeland He will deign to open His divine eyes. Then, seeing Jesus, I shall also have the joy of seeing my dear Mothers of the Visitation close to Him. I hope they will be kind enough to acknowledge me as their child. Are they not really my Mothers, seeing that they formed the hearts of the *two angels* on earth who acted as my mothers in fact ?

I remember perfectly my journey to the Visitation at Le Mans at the age of three;[2] I have repeated the visit again and again in my heart, and Carmel's grille is no obstacle to my paying many a visit to my *dear aunt* and all the venerated Mothers who, in their goodness, love little Thérèse of the Child Jesus without knowing her.

Please, *kind Aunt*, pay your *little niece's* debt of gratitude by thanking your Reverend Mother and all your dear sisters on her behalf, especially Sister Joseph de Sales[3] whose affectionate greeting touched me deeply. My *very dear Aunt*, I wish I could go on and on talking to you, but I am at the end of my paper and I am forced to leave you, asking your pardon ! . . .

Sister Thérèse of the Child Jesus,
Your unworthy little niece.

CXL

To CÉLINE

For her twenty-fifth birthday

J. M. J. T.

Jesus †   26 April 1894.

Darling Lyre of Jesus,

To hymn your twenty-fifth birthday, I send you a little poem I composed while thinking of you ![4] Céline ! I am sure you will understand all my song is trying to tell you. Alas ! It would

---

[1] Cant. of Cant. v. 2.

[2] Easter Monday, 29 March 1875. Thérèse was in fact only two years and three months. See p. 2 of this book.

[3] Former friend of Mother Agnes of Jesus in the school, now a nun in the Convent.

[4] "La Mélodie de Sainte Cecile", published in *Poésies de sainte Thérèse de l'Enfant-Jésus.*

need a tongue not of this earth to express the beauty of the total abandonment of a heart in Jesus' hands; my heart could do no more than stammer what it felt. . . . *Céline*, the story of *Cecilia* (*Saint* of ABANDONMENT) is your story too.

Jesus has placed at your side an angel from heaven to guard you always, he "bears you in his hand lest you dash your foot against a stone";[1] you do not see him, yet he it is who for twenty-five years has preserved your soul, has kept it in its *virginal whiteness*, who helps you avoid occasions of sin. . . . It was he who showed himself to you in a mysterious dream he sent you while you were a child. You saw an angel carrying a torch walking before our dearest father. Obviously he meant to indicate to you the mission you would have later to accomplish; *you* now are the visible angel of one who will soon go to join the angels of the heavenly city ! . . . Céline, have no fear of earth's storms. . . . Your angel guardian covers you with his wings, and in your heart Jesus, the purity of virgins, takes His rest. You do not see your treasures, Jesus sleeps and the angel stays in his mysterious silence; but all the same they are there with Mary, who hides you too beneath her veil.

Have no fear, dearest Céline, while *your lyre* keeps on singing for Jesus, it will never *be broken*. . . . Of course it is fragile, more fragile than crystal; if you gave it to a musician of no experience, it would soon break, but it is Jesus who moves the strings of your heart's lyre. . . . He is glad that you feel your weakness ; *it is He* who imprints upon your soul its feeling of self-distrust. Thank Jesus. He *is filling* you to overflowing with His *graces* of election. If you always stay faithful to pleasing Him in *small* things, He will be under OBLIGATION to aid you in GREAT. . . .

Without Our Lord, the apostles laboured all night, and caught no fish, but their labour was pleasing to Jesus. He wanted to prove to them that He alone can give us anything. He wanted the apostles to *be humbled*. . . . "Sons," He said to them, "have you nothing to eat ?"[2] "Lord," answered Peter, "we have fished all night and taken nothing."[3] Maybe, if he had caught a few *small fish*, Jesus would not have worked a miracle, but he had *nothing*, so Jesus soon filled his net so that it almost broke.

There you have Jesus' *character*: as God He gives, but He requires *humbleness* of *heart*.

[1] Ps. xc. 12.　　　[2] John xxi. 5.　　　[3] Luke v. 5.

"The whole world before thee is as the least grain of the balance, or as a drop of the morning dew that falls down upon the earth"[1] (Wisdom, ch. xi). (Céline dearest, if you can read my writing, it's quite wonderful, but I haven't time to look over what I write. . . .)

Time passes like a shadow, soon we shall be together again above. Did not Jesus say during His passion: "But you shall see the Son of Man sitting at the right hand of God and coming on the clouds of heaven. . . ."[2]

We shall be there ! . . .

Thérèse of the Child Jesus.

CXLI

To CÉLINE

For 28 April 1894, on an envelope containing a tiny picture, Thérèse wrote :

Little picture painted by
little Thérèse
for the 25th birthday of *little* Céline
with the permission of
little Mother Prioress.

CXLII

To LÉONIE

Who had received the Habit at the Visitation in Caen the month before

J. M. J. T.

Jesus †   Sunday, 20 May 1894.

Darling Sister Thérèse,[3]

Your letter gave me so much joy ! . . . I cannot thank the good God enough for all the graces He is pouring out upon you.

---

[1] Wisdom xi. 22.
[2] Matt. xxvi. 64; Mark xiv. 62; Luke xxii. 69.
[3] Léonie had received the name of Sister Thérèse-Dosithée, the latter name in honour of her mother's sister of whom Thérèse speaks a few letters back. Later she was called Sister Françoise-Thérèse.

Céline has described the beautiful feast of 6 April[1] down to the smallest details. How our little mother in Heaven must have rejoiced that day. And my Aunt who was at Le Mans[2]—with what love she must have fixed her gaze on you. I am very happy that my Holy Mother, Teresa, has become yours. It seems to me that that is a bond binding us still closer.

I cannot say all I would like to, darling Sister, my heart cannot translate its most intimate feelings into the cold language of this world. . . . But one day in Heaven, in our beautiful Homeland, I shall *look* at you and in my *look* you will see all I want to say, for *silence* is the language of the blissful inhabitants of heaven. Meanwhile our heavenly Homeland has to be won ! . . . We must suffer, fight. . . . Oh ! I beg you, pray for your little Thérèse, that she may profit from her exile upon earth and from the abundant means given her to merit Heaven.

Céline has told us the result of your elections. I was sad to see you lose a Mother you loved, but I consoled myself with the thought that the one who takes her place is truly worthy of her saintly predecessor, and I am quite sure that now you have *two Mothers* worthy of that sweet name to guide you to Jesus.

I leave you now, darling Sister, though in my heart I am never far from you, please give my respectful greetings to your good Mothers.

Sister Thérèse of the Child Jesus of the Holy Face,
rel. carm. ind.

CXLIII

To LÉONIE[3]

J. M. J. T.

Jesus †   22 May 1894.

My darling Sister,
My little note of Sunday will reach you at the same time as this and you will see that I had already been rejoicing in your happiness.

---

[1] Her Clothing.
[2] Sister Marie-Dosithée, nun at the Visitation, who died 24 February 1877 in her eighty-ninth year and who had prayed especially for Léonie's future (see Letter CXXVI).
[3] On the first blank page of this letter were written the two words "Soeur Thérèse".

. . . Thank you for your little letter which gives me much, much pleasure. . . .

You are fortunate, darling Sister, that Jesus is so jealous of your heart. He says to you as to the spouse of the Canticles: "You have wounded my heart, my sister, my spouse, with one of your eyes and with one hair of your neck."[1]

I feel that Jesus is very much pleased with you; if He still lets you see infidelities in your heart, I am quite sure that the acts of love He gathers up are more numerous. Which of the Thérèses will be the more fervent? The one who is the more humble, the more united to Jesus, the more faithful in carrying out all her acts through love. Ah! let us pray for each other to be equally faithful. "Let us wound" Jesus "with our eye and with one hair", that is, the greatest thing and the smallest. Let us not refuse Him the least sacrifice, everything is so big in religion. . . . To pick up a pin through love could convert a soul! How mysterious it is! Ah! only Jesus can give such a value to our acts, so let us love Him with all our might.

Your little sister who loves you,

Thérèse of the Child Jesus,
rel. carm ind.

CXLIV

To CÉLINE

At La Musse

Jesus †   7 July 1894.

My dearest Céline,

Léonie's letter makes us very anxious.[2] Ah! how unfortunate for her if she returns to the world! But I confess I hope it is only a temptation, we must pray hard for her. The good God can easily give her what she lacks. . . .

Our Mother is in retreat, which is why she is not writing to you, she often thinks of you and Marie,[3] she will say many prayers for her two little girls.

---

[1] Cant. of Cant. iv. 9.
[2] It made them fear that Léonie might once again find herself unable to remain in the Visitation.
[3] Marie Guérin.

I don't know if you are in the same spiritual disposition as the other day, but anyhow I shall set down for you a passage in the *Canticle of Canticles* which expresses perfectly the state of a soul which is sunk in aridity and to which nothing can bring joy or consolation: "I went into the garden of nuts, to see the fruits of the valley, and to look if the vineyard had flourished and the pomegranates budded. I knew not where I was; my soul troubled me for the chariots of Aminadab" (Chap. VI, v. 10 and 11).[1]

There you have the very image of our souls. Again and again we come down into the fertile valleys where our hearts love to pasture; the *vast field of Scripture*,[2] which had so often opened before us to spread its rich treasures for our profit, that *vast field* seems like an arid and waterless *desert*; we *no longer even know where we are:* instead of peace, light, we find only trouble or at least darkness. . . .

But, like the spouse, we know the cause of our trial: our soul is troubled "for the chariots of Aminadab. . . ." We are not yet in our Homeland and *trials* are to purify us as gold in the crucible. At times we think ourselves deserted, alas! Are the chariots, the vain noises that afflict us, within us or outside us? We do not know, but Jesus knows, He sees our sadness, and suddenly His sweet voice is heard, a voice sweeter than the breath of spring: "Return, return, O Sulamitess, return, return, that we may behold thee" (Cant. Ch. VI, v. 12).[3]

How marvellously our spouse calls us! Think! we did not dare even to *look at ourselves*, so utterly dull and unadorned we felt: and Jesus calls us. He wants to *gaze on* us at leisure, but He is not alone, with Him come the other two Persons of the Blessed Trinity to take possession of our soul. . . . Jesus promised it long ago when He was on the point of ascending to *His Father and our Father*.[4] He said with tenderness unutterable: "If anyone love me, he will keep my word and my Father will love him and we will come to him and will make our abode with him."[5]

To keep Jesus' *word*—that is the sole condition of our happiness, the proof of our love for Him. But what *is* this word? . . . It

---

[1] Cant. of Cant. vi. 11, 12. The reference in the text was inserted by the Saint herself.
[2] *Imitation of Christ*, bk. iii, ch. li, 2.
[3] The reference in text was inserted by the Saint herself.
[4] John xx. 17.
[5] John xiv. 23.

seems to me that Jesus' *word* is *Himself, Jesus, the Word,*[1] the *Word of God*! . . . He says so further on, in the same Gospel of St. John. Praying to His Father for His disciples, He expresses Himself thus: "Sanctify them by thy *word*, thy word is *truth*."[2] In another place Jesus tells us that He is the *Way* and the *Truth* and the *Life.*[3] We know then what the *Word* is that we must keep, we do not, like Pilate, ask Jesus "What is truth?"[4] We possess *Truth*, we *keep* Jesus in our *hearts*! . . .

Often we can say with the Spouse[5] that our Beloved is a *bundle of myrrh,*[6] that he is for us a "betrothed in blood"[7] but how sweet it will be one day to hear that most loving word proceed from Jesus' mouth: "And you are they who have continued with me in my temptations: and I dispose to you, as my Father has disposed to me, a kingdom!" (Gospel[8]).

The temptations of Jesus, what mystery is there! So He too has His temptations! He has indeed. And often He "*treads the winepress alone.* He seeks for those who may give Him aid and finds none".[9] Many serve Jesus when He consoles them, but *few* are willing to keep company with *Jesus sleeping* on the waves or suffering in the garden of agony! . . . Who then will be willing to serve Jesus for Himself? Ah! it must be you and I. . . . Céline and Thérèse will grow ever more and more united, in them will be fulfilled the prayer of Jesus, "Father, that they may be one as we are one".[10] Yes, Jesus is already *preparing* for us a kingdom as His Father prepared a kingdom for Him.[11] He prepares it for us by leaving us in *temptation.* He wants *our face to be seen* by creatures, but that it should be *as though hidden,*[12] that none may recognise us save Him alone. But then what a happiness to think that the *good God*, the whole Trinity, regards us, that It is within us and rejoices to *gaze upon* us. But what does It

[1] John i. 1.
[2] John xvii. 17.
[3] John xiv. 6.
[4] John xviii. 38.
[5] Of the Canticle.
[6] Cant. of Cant. i. 13.
[7] Exod. iv. 25.
[8] Luke xxii. 28, 29. (The word *Gospel* was inserted by the Saint herself.)
[9] Isa. lxiii. 3, 5.
[10] John xvii. 21.
[11] Luke xxii. 29.
[12] Isa. lxiii. 3.

want to see in our heart, save "choirs of music in the camp of an army" (Cant. Ch. VII, v: 1).[1]

"How shall we sing the songs of Sion in a strange land ? For long we have hung up our harps on the willows by the river,"[2] for we cannot play on them ! . . . Our *God*, our heart's *Guest* knows it well, so He comes within us in the intent of finding a dwelling place, an EMPTY *tent*, in the midst of the world's battle-field. He asks no more than that, and He is Himself the divine Musician who is responsible for the *harmony*. Ah ! if we could hear that unutterable harmony, if one single vibration could reach our ears ! . . .

"We know not what we should pray for as we ought, but the spirit Himself asks for us with unspeakable groanings" (Saint Paul).[3] So all we have to do is deliver up our soul, *abandon* it to our great God. What does it matter then if it is without any exteriorly brilliant gifts, since, within, the King of Kings stands brilliant in all His glory ! . . .

How great must a soul be to be able to contain a God ! Yet the soul of a *day-old* child is for Him a paradise of delights; what then will our souls be, that have fought and suffered *to ravish the Heart of their Beloved* ? . . .

Dearest Céline, I assure you that I don't know what I am saying; it cannot have any coherence, but I feel you will understand all the same ? . . . So many things I want to say to you ! . . .

Don't send back a long letter to tell me of your soul, a single brief word will suffice, I should prefer you to write a *very amusing* letter for *everybody*.[4] The good God wants me to forget myself to give pleasure.

I send a kiss to my good Uncle, my dearest Aunt and my little sister.[5] For my dearest *Papa*, I smile at him, and I guard him through his visible *angel*,[6] to whom I am united so closely that we make but one !

Thérèse of the Child Jesus of the Holy Face,
rel. carm. ind.

---

[1] The reference is inserted by the Saint herself.
[2] Ps. cxxxvi. 4, 2.
[3] Rom. viii. 26.
[4] For the whole Community, to whom the Prioress would read it at recreation.
[5] Marie Guérin.
[6] Céline, of course.

CXLV

To MME POTTIER[1]

Who had told Thérèse of her husband's return to the practice of his religion

J. M. J. T.

Jesus †   Carmel, 16 July 1894.

My darling Céline,

Your letter gave me great joy; I am lost in wonder at the way the Blessed Virgin has pleased to grant all your desires. Even before your marriage, she wanted the soul, to which you were to be united, to be but one soul with yours through identity of feeling. What a grace to feel yourself so completely understood ! and above all to know that your union will be immortal, that after this life you will still be able to love the husband who is so dear to you ! ...

So for both of us the blest days of our childhood are over ! We are now in the serious stage of life; we are following very different roads, but the end is the same. Each of us must have but one same purpose: to sanctify ourselves in the road God has marked out for us.

I feel, darling Friend, that I can speak to you freely, you understand the language of faith better than the language of the world, and the Jesus of your first Communion has remained the Master of your heart; it is in Him that you love the beautiful soul which now is but one soul with yours; it is because of Him, that your love is so tender and strong. Oh ! how lovely our religion is, instead of constricting hearts (as the world fancies) it lifts them up and gives them the capacity to love, to love with a love almost infinite, since it is to continue after this mortal life—which is given to us only that we may win the homeland of Heaven, where we shall find once more the dear ones we have loved upon earth.

I had asked Our Lady of Mount Carmel, dear Céline, for the grace you obtained at Lourdes. I am so happy that you are wearing the Blessed Scapular ! it is a sure sign of predestination and, over and above that, it unites you more intimately with your little sisters in Carmel. You ask me, darling Cousin, to pray for your

[1] Née Céline Maudelonde. See Letter CXXXVIII.

dear husband; do you think I could fail in that ? No, I could not possibly separate you in my poor prayers. I ask Our Lord to be as generous towards you as to the bride and bridegroom at Cana. May He always change water into wine—that is, continue to make you happy, and lighten as far as possible the trials to be met with in this life. Trials ! How could I put that word in a letter at a moment when I know that for you all is happiness. Forgive me, darling Friend, enjoy the joy God gives you in peace and don't worry about the future. He has, I am certain, new graces and new joys in store for you.

Our good Mother Marie de Gonzague is much touched at the kind memory you keep of her; nor does she forget her dear little Céline. Our Mother and Sister Marie of the Sacred Heart are also very happy in your happiness; they ask me to assure you of their affection.

I venture, darling Cousin, to ask you to give my respectful greetings to M. Pottier, whom I cannot help regarding as my cousin too. I leave you, dearest Céline, but I remain always with you in heart, and all my life I shall be happy to call myself
Your little sister in Jesus,

Thérèse of the Child Jesus,
rel. carm. ind.

CXLVI

To CÉLINE

In the probability of M. Martin's early death and the quasi-impossibility of a fourth member of the same family entering the Lisieux Carmel—the Superior of the Convent having on a previous occasion interposed his veto—Père Pichon had asked Céline to come to Canada, as soon as she was free from her duty of tending her father, to found a work he had in mind. He had enjoined her to say nothing to the Carmel. Céline, without betraying his secret, began to prepare her sisters for a final separation, telling them that it seemed better to sacrifice her family feelings by embracing the religious life elsewhere than in the Lisieux Carmel. She did not conceal the suffering this caused her . . . Whence this letter from Thérèse.

J. M. J. T.

Jesus †   18 July 1894.

My dearest Céline,

I am not surprised at your trials, I went through them last year and I know what it means ! . . . The good God wanted me to make my sacrifice,[1] I made it and then, like you, I felt serenity in the midst of suffering.

But I felt something else, that often God only wants *our willingness*. He asks *all*, and if we refuse Him the least thing, He loves us too much to give way; but the moment our will is conformed to His, the moment He sees that we seek Him alone, He behaves towards us as once towards Abraham. . . . That is the feeling Jesus gives me in the depth of my heart, so I think you are under *trial*, that the cutting-off of which you feel the need is taking place *now*. . . . "It is *now* that Jesus is breaking your *nature*, giving you the cross and tribulations." The more I go on, the more inner certainty I have that one day you will come here.[2] Mother Marie de Gonzague advises me to tell you this, she was so kind reading your letter, if you had seen her you would have been moved ! . . . Fear nothing, here more than anywhere you will find the cross and *martyrdom* ! We shall be suffering together, like the Christians long ago, who kept together to give themselves more courage in the hour of trial. . . .

And then Jesus will come, He will take one of us and the others will remain for *a little while* in exile and tears. . . . Céline, tell me, would the suffering be as great if one of us were in Lisieux, the other in Jerusalem ? . . . Would the Blessed Virgin have suffered as much if she had not been at the foot of her Jesus' cross ? . . .

You think, perhaps, that I don't understand ? . . . I assure you that I read your soul. . . . I read that you are faithful to Jesus, willing only His *will*, seeking only His love, fear nothing; in the

---

[1] The sacrifice of family feelings in the intention of going to a Carmel in missionary country.

[2] Upon this desire to see her sister with her in the cloister, Thérèse made her mind clear to Reverend Mother Agnes of Jesus: "I had made the complete sacrifice of Sister Geneviève, but I cannot say that I did not desire it. Often during the summer, in the evening silence, sitting on the terrace, I said to myself: 'Ah ! if my Céline were here with me . . . but no, it would be too great a happiness. . . .' And it seemed to me beyond possibility, but it was *not* by nature that I desired this happiness, it was for her soul, that she might walk in our way. . . . And when I saw her entered here, and not only entered but given over wholly to me for her instruction in all things, when I saw that the good God went so far beyond my desires, I realised what an immensity of love He had for me . . ." (*Derniers Entretiens*, 16 July 1897).

present trial God is purging away anything in our affections that might be too much of the senses, but the actual *foundation* of that affection is too pure to be broken. Listen closely to what I am going to tell you. Never, never will Jesus separate us. If I die before you, don't be afraid that I shall be far from your *soul*, we shall never have been more united ! That perhaps is what *Jesus wants* to make you realise in thus talking to you of separation. But above all do not be alarmed, I am not ill, as a matter of fact I have iron health, though the good God can break iron like clay. . . . All this is childish fancy, let us stop thinking of the future (I'm talking of myself, I do not regard the trial that is visiting the soul of my dearest Céline as childish fancy).

Exterior crosses—what do they amount to ? . . . We could be far from each other without suffering, if Jesus consoled our hearts. . . . What *is* a real cross is the martyrdom of the heart, the deep suffering of the soul, and that, unseen by any, *we* can undergo without ever being apart.

I know of course that all I am saying amounts to absolutely nothing at all, your inner trial will cease only on the day set by Jesus, but since in His kindness He uses me sometimes to do good to your soul, perhaps my words are the expression of His will. . . . It is incredible how invariably we have the same trials ! A little sooner or a little later, each of us must drink of the same cup.

When the storm is at its height on land, people say: "No need now to fear for ships, the storm can't be raging at sea."[1] All right ! I say to Céline: the storm has passed over my soul, it has gone on to yours, but fear not, soon it will be calm again, "a great calm will follow after the tempest".[2]

You want news of my daughter ?[3] Well, I think she will stay . . . she is good . . . she is very fond of me, but I try to touch her only with "white silk gloves". I have a title which gives me a good deal of trouble, I am a "little hunting dog",[4] I

---

[1] Thérèse was fond of this saying.

[2] Cf. Matt. viii. 26.

[3] Sister Marie of the Trinity, who entered the Lisieux Carmel 16 June 1894. Formed in the religious life from the beginning of her Postulancy by Thérèse, who taught her her way of spiritual childhood, she was one of the most telling witnesses at the Process. She died 16 January 1944.

[4] She had been acting as assistant-mistress of novices since the previous year, though she did not have the title. Two novices had been entrusted to her: Sister Marthe of Jesus (entered 23 December 1887) and Sister Marie-Madeleine of the Blessed Sacrament (entered 22 July 1892), both lay sisters. Sister Marie of the Trinity, Céline and Marie Guérin, who entered a little later, brought to five the number of novices placed in her charge.

am the one who runs after the game all day. You know, the hunters (novice-mistresses and Prioresses) are too big to hide in the bushes; but a little dog . . . well, it has a *sharp nose*, and naturally it can *slip in* anywhere ! . . . So I keep a close watch on "my daughter" and the "hunters" are not dissatisfied with their little dog. . . . I don't want to damage my "little rabbit", but I *lick* her and tell her *compassionately* that her fur is not sleek enough, that she has too much the look of a *wild rabbit*, in short I try to make her what my hunters want her to be: a very simple little rabbit, occupied only with the small patch of grass it must crop.

I'm jesting, of course, but fundamentally I think the rabbit is worth more than the little dog, had I been in her place I should long since have been *lost* forever in the vast forest of the world ! . . .

Thank you for your two little photographs. They are charming.

Thérèse of the Child Jesus.

PS. Please give a thousand kind messages from me to all the dear travellers who are having such a good time out there.[1] I understand what you tell me about the young men. But it is only a passing moment, one day you won't be seeing too many of them, so don't worry ![2]

I send you two little hymns I've composed,[3] show them to my darling Marie, tell her I love her and pray for her. . . . Oh ! may suffering enlarge her soul and bring it nearer its goal. . . . Mother Marie de Gonzague is not writing to her, because her letter is addressed to Aunt, but next time she will. Ask Aunt for "Mon Chant d'aujourd'hui", Sister Marie of the Sacred Heart sent it to her.

[1] Céline was with her father at La Musse, where the many guests of the Guérins came and went.

[2] Allusion to Céline's desire to enter Carmel.

[3] "Cantique pour obtenir la glorification de Jeanne d'Arc", composed 8 May; and "Mon Chant d'aujourd'hui", composed in June. They are in the main edition of *Histoire d'une âme* and in the Saint's *Poésies*.

CXLVII

To CÉLINE

M. Martin made a holy death at La Musse, 29 July. Céline thought it her duty to tell her Carmelite Sisters her whole mind upon her plans for the future, and to let Père Pichon know she was not coming to Canada (see Letter CXLVI). Her entry at the Lisieux Carmel was then settled.

J. M. J. T.

Jesus †   August 1894.

My dearest Céline,

Your letter is *enchanting*, it caused us to shed very happy tears. . . .

Fear nothing, Jesus will not disappoint you; if you knew how your *docility* and childlike *candour* charm Him ! . . . They move me most poignantly. . . . I have suffered so much for you that I hope not to be an obstacle to your vocation; surely our affection has been purified like gold in the crucible ? . . . "We wept casting our seeds and now we shall soon be coming together, carrying our sheaves."[1]

I shall not write to the Father,[2] I think it is better to await his letter and see what he has to say. If you would rather I wrote to *justify* you, tell me so when you come and I shall not be the least *embarrassed* ! . . . I feel it so *profoundly* ! . . . But I thank God for this trial. He has willed it, I am certain, for it is impossible that Jesus should disappoint *a little child* like you.

All three of us love you even better than before, if possible, your *look* affected us so deeply ! I assure you Sister Marie of the Sacred Heart would astonish you if you could hear her. . . . She does not hesitate to say that her beloved Father was mistaken. . . . But he was only the obedient instrument of Jesus, so his little Thérèse does not hold it against him ! . . .

Please thank Aunt for her letter; if she *knows* I have written to you, tell her that we are deeply moved.

(Mother Marie de Gonzague wept also on reading your letter; poor Mother, she knows nothing, you see how discreet we are !)[3]

---

[1] Ps. cxxv. 6–8.   [2] Père Pichon.   [3] This letter is not signed.

CXLVIII

To CÉLINE

Who was preparing to enter

J. M. J. T.

Jesus †   19 August 1894.

My darling Sister,

So this is the last time I have to write to you in the world ! . . . I did not know how truly I spoke in the letter I sent you at La Musse, promising that you would soon be in Carmel.

I am not surprised at the storm that is raging in Caen.[1] F. and J.[2] have chosen a road so different from ours that they cannot realise the sublimity of our vocation ! . . . But he laughs longest who laughs last. . . . After this life of a day, they will see whether *we* or *they* were the more privileged. . . .

Your miraculous draught of fish[3] touched us tenderly. These little delicacies make us feel that our dearest Father is very close to us ![4] After five years of *death*, what a joy to find him still the same, still looking as he used to for ways of giving us pleasure. Oh ! what a return he will make to Céline for the care she lavished upon him ! . . . It is he who has brought your vocation about in such quick time; now that he is a pure spirit it is easy for him to hunt up priests and bishops, so he did not have as much trouble over his dearest Céline as over his poor little queen !

I am very glad, darling Sister, that you feel no sense of natural pleasure[5] in coming to Carmel. That is Jesus' *delicacy*, He wants to receive a *present* from you. He knows that "it is much more blessed to give than to receive".[6] We have only the brief instant of life that we can *give* to the good God . . . already He is preparing to say: "My turn now." . . . What a happiness to suffer for Him who loves us even to *folly*, and to pass for *fools* in

---

[1] Dr. and Mme La Néele were against Céline's entry and let her see it.
[2] Francis and Jeanne.
[3] Céline had spent a day at Luc-sur-Mer with the Guérins and sent back some fish to Carmel.
[4] It used to be M. Martin's pleasure, when his fishing went well, to send some of his catch to the Carmelites.
[5] Thérèse writes "attrait sensible".
[6] Acts xx. 35.

the eyes of the world. One judges others by oneself, and as the world is stupid it naturally thinks that we are the stupid ones ! . . .

But after all, we are not the first ! The one crime charged against Jesus by Herod was that He was *mad* . . . and I agree with him ! . . . Yes, it was *folly* to seek the poor little hearts of mortals to make them His *thrones*, He, the King of Glory, Who is throned above the Cherubim ! He Whose presence is mightier than the Heavens can contain ! Our Beloved was *mad* to come down to earth seeking sinners to make them His friends, His intimates, to make them *like unto Himself*, when He was perfectly happy with the two adorable Persons of the Trinity ! . . . We shall never be able to commit the follies for Him that He has committed for us, nor do our actions deserve the name of folly, for they are in fact most reasonable acts, far below what our love would like to accomplish. So that it is the world which is stupid, not realising what Jesus has done to save it. It is the world which is the *all-devouring* thing, seducing souls and leading them to fountains without water.[1] . . .

Nor are we the *lazy* ones, the thriftless ones. Jesus defended us, in the person of Magdalen. He was at table, Martha was waiting upon Him, Lazarus eating with Him and His disciples. Mary never gave a thought to her food, but only how she might *give pleasure* to One she loved; so she took a vessel filled with perfume of great price and breaking the vessel poured it upon Jesus' head,[2] and all the house was filled with the odour of the ointment,[3] but the Apostles murmured against Magdalen.[4] . . .

It is very much the same with us, the most fervent *Christians*, the *priests*, consider that we are *too extreme*, that we ought to *serve* with Martha instead of consecrating to Jesus the *vessels* of our *lives* with the perfumes contained in them . . . but after all, what matter that our *vessels* are broken, since Jesus is *consoled*, and since, in spite of itself, the world is forced to *awareness* of the perfumes they breathe forth, perfumes which serve to purify the poisoned air the world is ever breathing.

The infirmarian would be glad if you could find in Caen a half bottle of Tisserand water—2 francs 50—if there are only whole bottles don't get one, they can be had here in Lisieux.

[1] Cf. Jer. ii. 13.
[2] Mark xiv. 3.
[3] John xii. 3.
[4] Matt. xxvi. 8; Mark xiv. 4.

Sister Marie of the Sacred Heart[1] would like seven or eight nut-crackers.[2]

CXLIX

To LÉONIE

J. M. J. T.

Jesus †   20 August 1894.

My darling Sister,

I should like to write you a long letter, but I have only a few minutes at my disposal, they are waiting for my little note to take it to the post.

Since our dearest Father has ascended to Heaven, I think of you more than ever. I am sure your feelings are the same as ours. Papa's death does not feel like a death but like a real *life*. I have found him again after six years' absence, I feel him near me, looking at me, protecting me. . . .

Darling Sister, are we not still more united, now that we can look toward Heaven and there find a Father and a Mother who offered us to Jesus? . . . Soon[3] their desires will be fulfilled, and all the children God gave them will be united to Him forever. . . .

I realise the void that Céline's departure will make for you, but I know how generous you are for Our Lord and, after all, life will pass so rapidly . . . afterwards we shall be united never again to part, and we shall be glad to have suffered for Jesus. . . . Darling Sister, forgive this wretched letter. Have eyes only for the heart of your Thérèse who would like to say so many things that she cannot express. . . .

Please give my respects to the Superior and your dear Mistress.

I shall be glad if you will give the letter to Céline, when she comes to see you, as soon as possible. Goodbye, darling Sister, do not forget to pray for the *smallest* and *unworthiest* of your sisters.

Thérèse of the Child Jesus of the Holy Face,
rel. carm. ind.

[1] At that time provisor of the community.
[2] Letter unsigned.
[3] Upon Céline's entry into Carmel.

211

CL

To LÉONIE

To sustain her in her trials

J. M. J. T.

Jesus †   11 October 1894.

My darling Sister,

I am so happy that your feast is now on the same day as mine. I am sure that St. Teresa will fill you with her graces on the 15th. I shall say so many prayers to her for you, and to Blessed Margaret Mary. . . . If you knew, darling Sister, how we pray for you ! . . . and above all how we offer *sacrifices*, I think you would be very much touched. . . . Since we have learned of your trials our fervour is very great, I assure you all our thoughts and our prayers are for you. I have the strongest confidence that my dear little Visitandine will emerge victorious from all her *great trials* and that one day she will be a model religious. The good God has already granted her so many graces; could He possibly abandon her now when she seems to have come into port ? No, Jesus sleeps while His poor bride struggles against the waves of temptation, but we shall call upon Him so tenderly that soon He will awaken, and command the winds and the sea, and again will come calm.[1]

Dearest little Sister, you will see that joy will follow trial, and later on you will be glad for having suffered; after all, God is upholding you visibly in the person of your *kind* Mothers who never cease to lavish upon you their tender maternal cares and counsels.

Please, *dearest* Sister, remember me to them in Our Lord, and to you, my dear *Thérèse*, be assured of the ever-growing love of your little sister,

Thérèse of the Child Jesus,
rel. carm. ind.

[1] Matt. viii. 26; Mark iv. 39; Luke viii. 24.

CLI

To MME GUÉRIN

For her feast

J. M. J. T.

Jesus †   17 November 1894.

My dear Aunt,

It is with my soul still so filled with the fragrance of Uncle's beautiful letter to sister Marie-Madeleine[1] that I am writing to wish you a happy feast.

O my darling Aunt, if you knew how proud I am to have relations like you ! . . . I am happy to see God so well served by those I love, and I wonder to what end He gave me the grace to belong to so wonderful a family.

I feel that Jesus comes to take His rest joyfully in your house, as long ago in Bethany. He is indeed "the divine Mendicant of love", asking hospitality and saying "Thank you" by always asking more, in proportion to the gifts He receives. He feels that the hearts He approaches realise "that the greatest honour God can do a soul is not to give it much but to ask much of it".

So, dearest Aunt, how sweet it will be for you one day to hear the name of *Mother* given you by Jesus Himself ! . . . Yes, you are in very truth His *mother*, He assures you so in the gospel when He says : "He who does the will of My Father, he is My mother".[2] And you have not only done His will, but you are giving him six of your children to be his brides ![3] . . . Thus you are His mother six times over, and to you the angels in Heaven might well address the beautiful words : "But thou shalt rejoice in thy children because they shall all be blessed and shall be gathered together to the Lord."[4] Yes, they shall all be blessed, and

---

[1] See note 4, page 206. Her Profession was to take place 20 November. M. Guérin, as a benefactor and friend of the community, had led Sister Marie-Madeleine to the altar—she having no family—on the day of her Clothing, 7 September 1893.

[2] Matt. xii. 50.

[3] Her five nieces and her daughter Marie who wished to enter Carmel.

[4] Tobias xiii. 17.

in heaven, O my dearest Aunt, your crown will be of roses and lilies.

The two roses[1] which will shine in the middle will not be the least of its glories. They are the ones who, upon earth, have copied your virtues, that the sad world may be filled with their sweetness, and that God may still find here upon earth a few flowers to delight Him and stay His arm, raised to punish the wicked.

Darling Aunt, I meant to say so much to you, but they have come for my letter, I have only time to give you once more the assurance of all my love. I am thinking also of the feast of our dear Grandmama;[2] please give her a big kiss from me.

Your little *girl,*
Thérèse of the Child Jesus,
rel. carm. ind.

CLII

To SISTER MARTHE OF JESUS[3]

Who was making her private retreat

J. M. J. T.

Dearest little *Sister*, yes I understand everything . . . I am begging Jesus to let the sun of His grace shine upon your soul. Ah ! don't be afraid to tell Him that you *love Him*, *even though you have no feeling of love*, that is the way to *force* Jesus to come to your help, to carry you like a little child too weak to walk.

It is a great trial to see everything *black*, but this is a matter not wholly within your control, do what you *can*. Detach your heart from the *cares* of the world and especially from creatures, then be sure that Jesus will do the *rest*. He cannot let you fall into the *slough* that you fear. Stop worrying, dearest little Sister, in Heaven you won't see *everything black*, you'll see *everything white*. . . . Yes, everything will be clothed in the divine *whiteness* of our Spouse, the Lily of the valleys. *Together* we shall go with Him wherever He may go. . . . Ah ! let us make good use of the

---

[1] Jeanne and her husband.
[2] Mme Fournet, Mme Guérin's mother.
[3] See notes to Letters LVI and CXLVI. The present note, undated, was perhaps written in 1894.

brief instant of life . . . *together* let us give pleasure to Jesus, save souls for Him by our sacrifices . . . above all, *let us be small, so small that everybody may trample us underfoot,*[1] without our having the least air of noticing or minding.

Goodbye for now, dearest little Sister, I look forward to seeing you. . . .

[1] *Imitation of Christ*, bk. iii, ch. xiii, 3.

1895

TWENTY-THIRD YEAR

During this year Thérèse, on the order of the Prioress, Mother Agnes of Jesus, writes the memories of childhood and of life in the Convent which later form the first eight chapters of her Autobiography.

5 February : Céline is clothed in the Carmel at Lisieux.[1]

9 June : On the feast of the Blessed Trinity, Thérèse "receives the grace to understand better than ever how much Jesus desires to be loved".[2] *In response to this grace she offers herself as a holocaust to the merciful Love of the good God.*

CLIII

To LÉONIE[3]

New Year wishes

J. M. J. T.

Jesus †

My darling Sister,

It is with great joy that I bring you my good wishes at the beginning of this new year. The one that has just ended has been very fruitful for Heaven, our dearest Father has seen what "the eye of man cannot gaze upon". He has heard the harmony of the angels . . . and his heart realises, his soul enjoys, the rewards "God has prepared for those who love Him"[4]. . . .

Our turn will come too. . . . Perhaps we shall not see the end of the year that is beginning ! Perhaps one of us will soon hear Jesus' call. . . .

---

[1] Thérèse did not write a letter to her sister upon this occasion, but composed some verses for her, which appeared in the first editions of her poetry under the title: "Chant de reconnaissance de la Fiancée de Jésus."

[2] *Histoire d'une âme,* ch. viii.

[3] Letter undated, written early in January 1895.

[4] 1 Cor. ii. 9.

216

Oh ! how sweet it is to realise that we are skimming along towards the eternal shore ! . . .

Darling Sister, don't you find, like me, that our dearest Father's departure brings us nearer to Heaven ? More than half the family is now enjoying the vision of God, and the five exiles of earth will not be long in taking flight to their Homeland. This thought of the shortness of life gives me courage to bear the fatigue of the road. "What matters," says the Imitation, "a little labour upon earth. . . . We pass, and have here no permanent dwelling".[1] "Jesus has gone before to prepare a place for us in His Father's house, later He will come and take us with Him, that where He is, we may be also[2]. . . ." Let us wait and suffer in peace, the hour of rest approaches, for "the light tribulations of this momentary life produce in us an eternal weight of glory".[3]

Darling Sister, your letters have pleased me so much and have done so much *good* to my *soul*. I rejoice to see how God loves you and fills you with His graces. . . . He finds you worthy to suffer for His love, and that is the greatest proof of tenderness He can give you, for it is suffering that makes us like to Him. . . .

O my dearest little Sister, do not forget the last and *poorest* of your sisters, ask Jesus that she may always be *utterly faithful*, that, like you, she may be happy in being everywhere the littlest and last ! . . .

Please give my New Year greetings to your good Mothers and assure them that I am wholly united with them in the Heart of Jesus.

Your poor little sister,

Thérèse of the Child Jesus,
rel. carm. ind.

CLIV

To SISTER GENEVIÈVE

Upon her entry into Carmel 14 September 1894, Céline had received the name of Sister Marie of the Holy Face, chosen for her by Thérèse as far back as 1889.[4] In the beginning of 1895 the

[1] *Imitation of Christ*, Lamennais' translation with reflections at the end of each chapter (Mame, 1824), bk. iii; "reflection" following ch. xlvii.
[2] John xiv. 3.
[3] Cf. 2 Cor. iv. 17.
[4] See Letter LXXVI.

Superior of the Convent, Canon Delatroëtte, expressed the view that it would be preferable to give her the name of the saintly foundress of the Lisieux Convent, "Mother Geneviève de Sainte Thérèse", so that the title "Holy Face" was moved back into second place.[1] The change was announced at the evening recreation in January 1895. Coming out of recreation Thérèse wrote in pencil, on a scrap of paper she found in her pocket:

> Sister Geneviève de Sainte Thérèse
> Little Thérèse was the first to write it ! . . .

She gave this scrap of paper to her sister to console her, but she too had felt disappointment, in spite of her veneration for the saintly Mother Geneviève.[2]

CLV

To LÉONIE

J. M. J. T.

Jesus †   24 February 1895.

My dear Léonie,

I was very glad to get news of you, I hope that you continue to keep well and that your dear sisters are getting better.

I have only the smallest scrap of time that I can devote to you, but I want to commend myself to your prayers before Lent, and to promise that I for my part will think of you even more if that is possible, and then I shall come and sing the Alleluia with you at great length, to make up for being unable to do it today. . . .

I mean, of course, after Easter, but I put it so badly that you might think I was going to sing the Alleluia in Lent. . . . Oh ! . . . no, I shall be content to follow Jesus in His sorrowful way, I shall "hang my harp on the willows by the banks of the rivers of Babylon".[3] But after the Resurrection, I shall take up my harp, forgetting for a moment that I am in exile; with you I shall hymn

---

[1] See Letter CIX.

[2] It was only in 1916 that the title Holy Face was once more brought back for Sister Geneviève, many people spontaneously giving her the title when she painted the Holy Face as a copy of the Shroud at Turin. From that time she was known as Sister Geneviève of the Holy Face and St. Teresa.

[3] Cf. Ps. cxxxvi. 2.

the joy of serving Jesus and dwelling in His house, the joy of being His Bride for time and for eternity ! . . .

Darling Sister, please give my religious respects to your good Mothers, and believe in my *great* love.

Your very little sister,
Thérèse of the Child Jesus,
rel. carm. ind.

PS. When you write, will you please tell me the *year* of your first Communion.[1]

CLVI

To LÉONIE

J. M. J. T.

Jesus †   28 April 1895.

My darling Sister,

I should have liked to thank you sooner for your letter, which gave me great pleasure, but our Mother wrote to you at once and I could not write at the same time.

Darling Sister, I am profoundly persuaded that you have found your true vocation, not only as a Visitandine, but also as a Visitandine at *Caen*. God has given us so many proofs, that we must not doubt it.[2] I regard your notion of going to Le Mans[3] as a temptation and I beg Jesus to deliver you from it. Oh ! I do understand that the postponement of your Profession must be a trial for you, but Profession is so great a grace that the more time one has to prepare for it, the more reason to be glad. It pleases me to recall what happened in my own soul some months before my Profession. I saw my year of novitiate gone by and no one taking any notice of me (because of our Father Superior, who thought me too young); I felt great pain, I assure you, but one day God showed me that in my desire to pronounce my sacred vows, there was a good deal of self-seeking,[4] so I said to myself: "For my Clothing, I was dressed in a lovely white robe

---

[1] Léonie had made her first Communion 23 May 1875.
[2] The future was wholly to confirm this certainty. After leaving the Visitation in Caen for the second time (see Letter CLVII) she returned there on 28 January 1899 and remained till she died in 1941. She edified the other nuns by her long and saintly religious life of forty-two years.
[3] To the Visitation Convent there.
[4] See *Histoire d'une âme*, ch. vii.

219

adorned with lace and flowers; but who has thought to give me a robe for my espousals? That robe I must prepare myself, *by myself*; Jesus wants no one but Himself to aid me; so with His help I shall set about the task and work ardently at it. Creatures will not see my efforts, for they will be hidden in my heart. Trying to be *forgotten*, I shall wish to be seen by none save Jesus. . . . What matter if I appear poor and totally lacking in intelligence and talent. . . . I want to put into practice this counsel from the *Imitation*: 'Let this one glorify himself for one thing, and that one for another, do you put your joy only in contempt of yourself, in My will and My glory,'[1] or again: 'Do you wish to learn something that may serve you: love to be ignored and counted as nothing !'"[2]

Thinking of all this, I felt a great peace in my soul, I felt it was *truth* and *peace* ! . . . I worried no more about the date of my Profession, realising that on the day my *wedding-garment* was finished Jesus would come for His poor little bride. . . .

Darling Sister, I was not wrong; and indeed Jesus was satisfied with my desires, with my total abandonment; he deigned to unite Himself with me much sooner than I dared to hope. . . . Now God continues to guide me along the same road, I have but one desire, to do His will. You remember, perhaps, there was a time when I liked to call myself *Jesus' little toy*.[3] Now I am happy still to be His toy, but I have realised that the divine Child has many other souls, filled with sublime virtues, who also call themselves His toys; so I decided that they were His *fine toys* and that my poor little soul was only a small toy of no value. For my consolation, I told myself that children often get more pleasure from *little toys* that they can *pick up* or *lay down*, *break* or *kiss* at their fancy, than from others of greater value which they hardly dare touch.

Then I was glad to be *poor*, I desired to become every day poorer, that every day Jesus might find more pleasure in *playing* with me.

Darling Sister, now that I have given you my advice, do please pray for me that I may put into practice the lights Jesus gives me.

Please give my respectful greeting to your good Mothers.

Your very little sister who loves you,
Thérèse of the Child Jesus,
rel. carm. ind.

---

[1] *Imitation of Christ*, bk. iii, ch. lxix, 7.   [2] Ibid., bk. i, ch. ii, 3.
[3] See *Histoire d'une âme*, ch. vi.

CLVII

To MME GUÉRIN

*Written soon after Léonie's leaving the Visitation and
some time before Marie Guérin's entry into the
Lisieux Carmel*

J. M. J. T.

Jesus †   20 July 1895.

My darling Aunt,

I was indeed touched to see that you were thinking of your little Thérèse. She too thinks of you a great deal, and if she has not yet written to her dearest Aunt, it is not through want of feeling but because her heart is so full of tenderness and veneration that she cannot express her thoughts.

But I must try, at the risk of saying to my little Aunt things that will not please her—does not truth come "out of the mouth of babes"? Very well then, you must forgive me if I speak the truth, for I am and always want to remain a child. . . . I shall give you a brief account of myself to show you how *good* to me the *good* God is. I love reading the lives of the Saints, and the account of their heroic actions sets my courage on fire and rouses me to imitate them; but I admit that occasionally I have found myself envying the happy lot of their relations, who had the good fortune to live in their company and enjoy their holy conversation. But now I have nothing to envy them, for I can see saints in action close, see their struggles and the generosity with which they submit to God's will.[1]

Darling Aunt, I know you would be annoyed if I told you that you are a saint, all the same I should very much like to . . . anyhow, if I don't tell you that, I *can* tell you something that you must not tell Uncle, because he would not like me any more; this fact you know better than I, namely that he is a saint, as few upon earth are saints, and that his faith can be compared to Abraham's. . . . Ah! if you knew with what sweet emotion my soul was filled

---

[1] M. Guérin was preparing to make the sacrifice of his daughter Marie, who was to enter the Lisieux Carmel on the following 15 August.

yesterday to see my Uncle with his angelic little Marie. We were plunged into very great grief because of our poor Léonie,[1] it was like a deathbed. The good God, wishing to try our faith, sent us no consolation and I at least could find no other prayer than that of Our Lord on the Cross: "My God, my God, why hast thou forsaken us";[2] or again, as in the Agony in the Garden: "My God, not my will but thine be done".[3] And then for our consolation, our Divine Saviour sent us, if not the angel who comforted him in Gethsemani, at least one of his saints, still a pilgrim upon the earth and filled with His divine power. . . . Seeing his calmness, his resignation, our grief melted away, we felt the sustaining power of a Father's hand. . . . O my darling Aunt ! how great are the good God's mercies towards His poor children ! . . . If you knew the tears of consolation I shed, listening to the heavenly conversation of my saintly Uncle. . . . He seemed to me already transfigured; his speech was not the speech of the faith that hopes, but of the love that possesses. At a moment when trial and humiliation were visiting him, he seemed to forget all things else and think only of blessing the divine hand which was stealing his *Treasure* from him, and for recompense, trying him as saints are tried. St. Teresa was quite right when she said to our Lord, who was laying crosses upon her at a time when she was undertaking mighty works for Him: "Ah ! Lord, I am not surprised that you have so few friends, you treat them so ill !" Another time she said that the good God gives some trials to the souls He loves with ordinary love, but upon those he loves with a love of predilection he *heaps* crosses as a most certain mark of His love.[4]

21 July.

I had left my letter unfinished yesterday, for Marie arrived with Léonie; our emotion at sight of her was very great, we could not get her to say a word, she was weeping so; at last she was able to

[1] Léonie, to her great sorrow, had just left the Visitation in Caen for the second time. When she died in 1941, the Mother Superior of the Convent wrote in a biographical notice: "At that time our older Mothers required of our young Sisters the integral carrying out of the rule, and did not use the mitigations now seen indispensable in the formation of subjects. So a number of them, of delicate health, had to confess themselves beaten, and our poor child was of the number." Léonie received the most paternal welcome from M. Guérin.

[2] Matt. xxvii. 46; Mark xv. 34.

[3] Matt. xxvi. 29; Mark xiv. 36; Luke xxii. 42.

[4] Cf. *Way of Perfection*, ch. xxxiv. p. 279 (edited P. Grégoire).

look at us, and all went well. I am not giving you any other details, little Aunt, because you will learn them all from Marie, who was truly a "valiant woman" in the sorrowful situation of that moment. We told her so, but I saw plainly that the compliment did not please her, so I called her "*Little Angel*"; she laughed and said she liked that better than "valiant woman". She is merry enough to make stones laugh, and this is a distraction for the poor girl with her; we served them in earthenware dishes like Carmelites, which made them laugh. [1]

Ah! what virtue your little Marie has! Her self-control is astonishing, yet she has enough *energy* to become a saint; and energy is the most necessary virtue, with energy one can easily arrive at the summit of perfection.

If she could give a little to Léonie, your "little angel" would still have enough for herself, and it would do her no harm. . . . Darling Aunt, I see that my phrases are not very clear; I am rushing, to give my letter to Marie: she didn't want me to write to you, because she said she would give all my messages; she didn't even want to give me *three sous* for a stamp, but I did not feel like waiting any longer to send so dear an Aunt something more than "a look", however expressive the look might be, for she could not see it from so far!

I wanted to speak to you about Jeanne and Francis, but I haven't time; all I can say is that I reckon them among the saints I am privileged to contemplate close at hand upon earth, and whom I rejoice that I shall soon see in heaven, in the company of their children whose shining crowns will increase their own glory. [2]

Dearest little Aunt, if you cannot read this, it is Marie's fault. Kiss her for me to scold her, and tell her to give you a very big kiss from me.

Your *very little* girl,
Thérèse of the Child Jesus,
rel. carm. ind.

[1] Léonie and Marie had accidentally taken their meals with some of the Sisters on duty at the turning-box.

[2] Dr. La Néele was a valiant defender of religion. As we have seen, he desired a large family.

CLVIII

To MARIE GUÉRIN[1]

A few days before her entry into Carmel

To my dearest little sister, from her little Thérèse who *thinks* of her a *great deal* ! . . . and who above all things hopes, in fear and trembling, that her dear Marie may keep her promises, staying as quiet as a small child in its Mother's arms.

I keep praying for you, darling Sister, and for all the dear family at La Musse who must at this moment be making rapid advances in perfection, since they are accepting the sacrifice of separation so generously ! . . .

I love . . . I pray for my *dearest Uncle* and my *dearest Aunt more* and *more*, I don't know where it will end, for my love grows greater day by day ! . . .

CLIX

To MME LA NÉELE

J. M. J. T.

Jesus †   14, 15, 17 October 1895.

My dear Jeanne,

Reading your letter I seem to see you and hear you; it gives me very great pleasure to learn of the amiable malady Uncle and Aunt have brought you from Lisieux, I hope you have not yet got over your "attack of gaiety" ! . . . Probably you haven't, since the celebrated Member of the Faculty,[2] in spite of his universal knowledge, can find no remedy for his darling Jeanne. If he does chance to discover one, I beg him not to forget our Carmel, the whole novitiate has caught the contagion[3]. . . .

---

[1] This note is undated and unsigned; it was written early in August 1895.
[2] Dr. Francis La Néele.
[3] Since Marie Guérin's entry.

It is a great consolation for me, the *elderly* senior of the novitiate,[1] to see so much gaiety surrounding my last days; it rejuvenates me, and in spite of my seven years and a half of religious life, my gravity often breaks down in presence of the charming imp, she is the joy of the community. If you had seen her the other day with the photographs of you and Francis, it would have amused you considerably! Our Mother had brought them to recreation, and was having them passed round from sister to sister. When it came to Sister Marie of the Eucharist's turn, she took the photographs one by one, and gave them her most gracious smiles! . . . All the Carmelites are very happy to have so pleasing a postulant.

Her lovely voice makes us happy and is the delight of our recreation; but what especially rejoices my heart much more than all the talents and exterior qualities of our dear angel, is her disposition to virtue.

The sacrifice the good God has just asked of you, dear Jeanne, is very great; but has He not promised "to everyone that has left father or mother or sister for His sake a reward a hundredfold in this life?"[2] Well then: for His sake you did not hesitate to endure separation from a sister you loved far beyond the power of words to express. Ah! Jesus will *have* to keep his promise. I know of course that ordinarily these words are applied to souls in religion; all the same, I feel in the depths of my heart that they were uttered for generous relations who make the sacrifice of children dearer than themselves.

Have you not already received the hundredfold promised? . . . Yes, already the sweet peace and happiness of your little Marie have flowed out through the cloister grille and poured into your soul. Soon, I have an intimate conviction that you will receive a more abundant hundredfold, a little angel will come to bring joy to your heart and receive your maternal kisses.[3] . . .

My darling Sister, I should have begun by thanking you for the present you are kind enough to be giving me for my feast;

---

[1] Thérèse should have emerged from the novitiate, according to the custom at that time, three years after her Profession, that is, in September 1893. But, according to a current interpretation of the laws, more than two sisters from the same family were not admitted as chapter nuns. Reverend Mother Agnes of Jesus and Sister Marie of the Sacred Heart were chapter nuns, and their younger sister never occupied the place that rightly belonged to her in the convent chapter. She was charged with the formation of the novices, as we have seen, but she remained among them as their senior until her death.

[2] Matt. xix. 29; Mark x. 29.

[3] See Letter CCXXVII.

I am very much moved, I assure you, but forgive me if I tell you in all simplicity what my taste is. Since you want to give me pleasure, what I should really like is not fish, but flowers to copy.[1] You will think me very selfish but, you see, Uncle spoils his dear Carmelites, they are in no risk of dying of hunger. Though little Thérèse has never *liked the things you eat*, she does like things useful for her community, she knows that with designs one can earn money to buy fish. It is rather like the story of Perrette,[2] isn't it? Anyhow, if you give me a branch of *eglantine*, I shall be quite happy; if there isn't any, then I'd like periwinkles or buttercups or indeed any other *common* flower.

I fear all this is hardly proper: if so, pay no attention to my request, and I shall be very grateful for the fish you give me, especially if you are kind enough to add the *beads* you spoke of the other day. You see, dear Jeanne, that I am converted, and far from keeping silent I am talking like a *magpie* and making over-bold requests—it is so difficult to keep the golden mean! . . . Luckily a sister forgives everything, even the importunities of a little Benjamin.

I have broken off my letter so often that it is all a jumble. I thought of very *beautiful things* about the hundredfold I was talking of at the beginning, but I have to keep those beautiful things at the bottom of my heart and simply ask the good God to do them for you, for I haven't the time to set them down. I must be off to the laundry, to scrub the clothes and listen to the darling "imp"; she will probably be singing "Ce lavage doit nous conduire au rivage, sans orage.[3] . . ."

Our two good Mothers and all your little sisters send you and Francis a thousand kind messages. I have not forgotten that tomorrow is the feast of St. Luke, one of his patrons,[4] so I shall offer Holy Communion for him, and I shall ask Jesus to repay him for the trouble he has taken to find me remedies.

I kiss you warmly, Jeanne darling, and I assure you of the affection and gratitude of your *very little* sister.

Thérèse of the Child Jesus,
rel. carm. ind.

[1] In order to do painting for the Community.
[2] From La Fontaine.
[3] A jesting rhyme composed by Sister Marie of the Eucharist.
[4] As a doctor.

CLX

To MME LA NÉELE

A few lines written at the end of a letter from
Sister Marie of the Eucharist

End of October 1895.

†

Our Mother has not time to write to her darling Jeanne. She thanks her warmly for her letter and her pretty designs.[1]

Little Thérèse sends all loving greetings to her dear travellers!

CLXI

To MME GUÉRIN

For her feast

J. M. J. T.

Jesus †

16 November 1895.

My darling Aunt,

Here comes your very little girl to join her feeble voice to the lovely harmony with which her big sisters celebrate your feast.

What remains for me to wish you, dearest Aunt? . . . After all the wishes that have been sent you I feel I have only to say with all my heart, Amen.

I say it every year. Upon earth I cannot find words to express the feelings of my soul, so I am happy to join with my three elder sisters and above all with our dearest Benjamin[2] in bringing you my feast wishes.

I haven't time to write to you at greater length, darling Aunt, but I am quite certain that you will know without telling all the feelings of tenderness that overflow from my heart.

On your feast day I shall offer my Communion for you and our dear Grandmama.[3]

---

[1] See previous Letter.   [2] Sister Marie of the Eucharist.
[3] See note to Letter CLI.

Please, dear Aunt, shower kisses upon all those I love, my dearest Uncle especially, and I charge him to give you a thousand kisses more from your little girl.

Thérèse of the Child Jesus,
rel. carm. ind.

CLXII

To SISTER GENEVIÈVE[1]

On the back of a picture of the Child Jesus scything lilies :

"I say to you : If two of you shall consent upon earth concerning anything whatsoever they shall ask, they shall obtain it from my Father who is in heaven, for where two or three are gathered together in my name there am I in the midst of them" (St. Matthew, ch. XVIII, 19-20).

O my God, we ask You that never may Your two lilies be separated upon earth. May they console You together for the little love You find in this valley of tears, and may their petals glow with the same brilliance for all eternity and shed the same perfume when they bend towards You ! . . .

Céline and Thérèse
Souvenir of Christmas Night 1895.

[1] After midnight Mass, Sister Geneviève found this note in one of her sandals.

1896

TWENTY-FOURTH YEAR

24 February : Céline is professed, as Sister Geneviève of St. Teresa.
21 March : Mother Marie de Gonzague is elected Prioress. She con-
firms Thérèse in her position with the novices.
3 April : Good Friday : first spitting of blood marks the beginning of
the illness from which the Saint was not to recover.
5 April, Easter Sunday : To this day the Saint seems to attach[1] the
beginning of the interior trial of temptations against the faith that
she was to suffer until her death.
14 and 15 September : At the request of Sister Marie of the Sacred
Heart, the Saint writes the pages which form chapter xi of the
Histoire d'une âme.
November : To discover God's will upon the answer to be given to the
Carmelites of Hanoï, who want her to join them, Thérèse makes
a novena to Bl. Théophane Vénard,[2] martyred at Tonking, to
obtain her cure. During this novena she suffers a serious relapse.

CLXIII

To SISTER GENEVIÈVE

On February 23, the eve of her Profession, Sister Geneviève
found in her cell a large envelope with the likeness of the
Holy Face in place of a stamp and addressed thus :

From the Knight Jesus
To my beloved Spouse
Geneviève of St. Teresa
Living on love upon the Mountain of Carmel

Land of Exile.

Inside the envelope there was an imitation parchment sheet,
bearing two blazons finely illuminated,[3] Sister Geneviève's motto

---

[1] See *Histoire d'une âme*, ch. ix and xi.
[2] Then Venerable. He was beatified 2 May 1909.
[3] Sister Geneviève had earlier designed armorial bearings and drawn them in pen and ink. Thérèse used the idea to paint the parchment and compose the text; and her sister's initiative gave her the notion of designing a coat of arms for herself.

LETTERS OF ST. THÉRÈSE

"Who loses wins", and the text that follows, artistically written and decorated.

CONTRACT OF MARRIAGE

Of Jesus with Céline

I JESUS, the ETERNAL WORD, the ONLY SON of GOD and of the VIRGIN MARY, today wed CÉLINE, princess in exile, poor and without titles.

I give myself to her under the name of KNIGHT OF LOVE, SUFFERING AND CONTEMPT.

It is not my intention to give my Beloved her Homeland, her titles or her riches yet. I want her to share the lot it pleased me to choose upon earth. . . . Here below, my face is hidden, but she is able to recognise me when others despise me; in return, today I place upon her head the Helmet of salvation and grace, that her face may be hidden as mine is. . . . I want her to conceal the gifts she has received from me, letting me give and take back as I please, attaching herself to none, forgetting all that might magnify her in her own eyes as in the eyes of creatures.

Henceforth my beloved will be called GENEVIÈVE OF ST. TERESA (her most glorious title, MARIE OF THE HOLY FACE,[1] will remain hidden upon earth that it may shine with incomparable brilliance in heaven). She will be shepherdess of the unique Lamb who is to be her Spouse. Our union will bring to birth souls more numerous than the stars of the firmament, and the family of the Seraphic Teresa will rejoice in this its new splendour.

Geneviève will bear patiently the absence of her Knight, letting him fight alone that he alone may have the glory of victory, she will be content to wield only the sword of Love. Like a sweet melody, her voice will charm me in the midst of camps. The slightest sigh of love she utters will inflame my best troops with a wholly new ardour.

I, the Flower of the fields, the Lily of the valleys, will give my Beloved for her nourishment the Wheat of the Elect, the "wine that springs forth Virgins" . . . She will receive this food from the hands of the humble and glorious Virgin Mary, the Mother of us both. . . .

[1] As we have seen, in 1916 the name was in part restored, following her drawings of the Holy Face as seen in the Shroud of Turin.

I wish to live in my Beloved, and for pledge of this life I give her my Name,[1] that royal seal will be the mark of her all-power over my Heart.

TOMORROW, THE DAY OF ETERNITY, I shall raise my vizor . . . My Beloved will see the glory of my adorable Face . . . She will hear the NEW NAME I hold in store for her. . . For her Supreme Reward, she will receive the BLESSED TRINITY ! . . . Having shared the same hidden life, we shall enjoy in our Kingdom the same GLORIES, the same THRONE, the same PALM and the same CROWN. Our two hearts, united for eternity, will love each other with the same ETERNAL LOVE ! . . .

Given on Mount Carmel under our sign-manual and the seal of our arms on the feast of my Agony,[2] the twenty-fourth day of February, in the year of grace one thousand eight hundred and ninety-six.

Th. of the Child Jesus, in the name of the Divine Knight.

CLXIV

To SISTER GENEVIÈVE

For her Profession

24 February 1896.

A note written by Thérèse, but as though it had been written by the venerated Mother Geneviève of St. Teresa, foundress of the Lisieux Carmel.[3]

Accompanying the note was the saintly nun's last tear, gathered up after her death by Thérèse herself.[4]

[1] The monogram IHS had been chosen to mark the clothing worn by Sister Geneviève (see note to Letter LXVII).

[2] The office celebrated on Monday 24 February 1896 was that of Our Lord's Agony. At that time it was the custom to celebrate on each Tuesday of Lent a feast relating to Our Lord's Passion—the Agony, the Nails, the Crown of Thorns, the Shroud, the Cross, etc. But 1896 being a leap year, St. Matthias, apostle, was celebrated the following day, and the Agony brought forward to Monday the 24th.

[3] See Letter CIX.

[4] See *Histoire d'une âme*, ch. viii: "While our venerated Mother was in her death-agony, I observed a tear glistening on her eyelid like a beautiful diamond. This tear, the last of all the tears she shed upon earth, did not fall: I saw it still shining there when her body was lying in the choir. Then, taking a fine linen cloth, I ventured to come to her, in the evening, seen by none, and I now have the happiness of possessing the last tear of a saint." Mother Geneviève died 5 December 1891, and Thérèse wrote these lines at the end of 1895. Very soon after, she gave the relic to Sister Geneviève.

J. M. J. T.

To you, my dearest Child, I give as wedding present the *last tear* I shed in this land of exile. Bear it on your heart, and remember that it is by suffering that a Sister Geneviève of St. Teresa must attain sanctity. You will have no difficulty in loving the Cross and the tears of Jesus, if you think often of the words: "He loved me and delivered Himself up for me."[1]

CLXV

TO SISTER GENEVIÈVE

For her Profession and Veiling

Thérèse had given Sister Geneviève a picture entitled "The Divine Choice", representing the Blessed Virgin with the Infant Jesus standing on her knees ; with one hand He holds a branch of lilies, and with the other traces a cross on the brow of a child, who is pressing a crown of thorns to his heart. Four angels look on. The Saint had written on the front :

Posuit Signum in Faciem Meam ! (St. Agnes, v.m.), *and on the back :*

In memory of the loveliest of days . . . the day which contains and confirms all the graces Jesus and Mary have showered upon their beloved Céline. . . .

For Love, Céline will henceforth press to her heart the thorns of Suffering and Contempt, but she is not afraid, knowing of her own experience that Mary can change into Milk the blood that pours from wounds made by Love. . . .

With her left hand, Céline grasps the thorns, but with her right she continues to keep hold on Jesus, the divine bundle of Myrrh resting upon her heart.

For Him alone will Céline bring forth children, she will water the seeds with her tears, and Jesus will be always joyous, bearing sheaves of lilies in His hands. . . .

The four little cherubim whose wings barely skimmed the earth

---

[1] Gal. ii. 20. When Céline was still in the world, Mother Geneviève had sent her this phrase as a message from Jesus.

come close and gaze enraptured upon their dearest sister; they hope, by approaching her, to participate in the merits of her sufferings, and in return they reflect back upon her the immaculate light of the innocence and all the gifts which the Lord has freely lavished upon them.

24th February—17th March 1896.[1]

> *Thérèse of the Child Jesus of the Holy Face,*
> *rel. carm. ind.*

CLXVI

To LÉONIE

For her feast

J. M. J. T.

10 April 1896.

My dear Léonie,

Your very little sister simply must write too, to tell you how much she loves you and thinks of you, on this your feast day[2] especially. I have nothing to give you, not even a *picture* ! but I am wrong, tomorrow I shall offer the divine *Reality* for you, Jesus-Victim, your SPOUSE and mine.

Darling Sister, how sweet it is that all five of us can call Jesus "our Beloved"; but what will it be when we shall see Him in Heaven, when we shall be everywhere with Him, singing the same canticle which none but Virgins may sing ! . . . Then we shall understand the price of suffering and trial, like Jesus we shall say : "It was truly necessary for suffering to try us and bring us to glory."[3]

My darling Sister, I cannot tell you all the profound thoughts about you that my heart contains; the one thing I want to tell you again is this: I love you a thousand times more tenderly than ordinary sisters love each other, since I can love you with the *Heart* of our heavenly Spouse.

It is in Him that we live the same life, in Him that I shall remain for eternity

> Your very little sister,
> *Thérèse of the Child Jesus,*
> *rel. carm. ind.*

---

[1] Date of Taking the Veil.   [2] The feast of St. Leo the Great.
[3] Cf. Luke xxiv. 26.

233

CLXVII

To SISTER MARIE OF THE TRINITY[1]

On the day of her Profession

This note was placed by Thérèse on the young nun's bed, on which she had strewn forget-me-nots.

30 April 1896.

My dearest little Sister,

I should like to have flowers that will not die to give you in memory of this beautiful day, but it is only in Heaven that flowers will never fade.

But at least these forget-me-nots will tell you that, in your little sister's heart, the memory will always remain deeply graven of the day on which Jesus gave you the kiss of the *union* which must be completed, or rather, realised, in Heaven.[2]

Thérèse of the Child Jesus of the Holy Face.

CLXVIII

To PÈRE ROULLAND[3]

Of the Foreign Missions

J. M. J. T.

Jesus †   Carmel at Lisieux, 23 June 1896.

Reverend Father,

I thought I should please our dear Mother by giving her for her feast, June 21, a corporal and a purificator with a pall, so that

[1] See note 4, page 206.

[2] Sister Marie's Profession was a great joy for Thérèse, who had been her support during a novitiate complicated by many difficulties. "I feel like Joan of Arc at the coronation of Charles VII," she said to her delighted novice on the day she uttered her vows. Sister Marie was in no doubt that she owed this inestimable grace to her young Mistress.

[3] Adolphe-Jean-Louis-Eugène Roulland, born at Cahagnolles, near Bayeux, 13 October 1870, entered the seminary of the Society of Foreign Missions in Paris. A month before his ordination he asked the Mother Prioress of the Lisieux Carmel (through Père Norbert of the Premonstratensions of Mondaye) to select one of her

she might have the pleasure of sending them to you for the 29th.[1]
It is to this venerated Mother that I owe the profound happiness
of being united to you by the apostolic bonds of prayer and
mortification, so I beg you, Reverend Father, to aid me at the
Holy Altar to pay my debt of gratitude.

I feel very unworthy to be thus associated with one of the
Missionaries of our adorable Jesus; but since obedience entrusts
this sweet task to me, I am sure my heavenly Spouse will make
up for my feeble merits (upon which I place no reliance at all)
and grant the desires of your soul by making your apostolate
very fruitful. I shall be truly happy to work with you for the
salvation of souls, it was for that that I became a Carmelite;
since I could not be a missionary in action, I wanted to be one by
love and penance like my seraphic Mother, St. Teresa.

I beg you, Reverend Father, on the day when Jesus deigns
for the first time to come down from Heaven *at your voice*, ask
Him to inflame me with the *fire of His love* so that I may aid you
to kindle that fire in hearts.

For a long time I have desired to know an *apostle* who would
utter my name at the holy Altar on the day of his first Mass. . . .
I desired to prepare the sacred linen myself and the *white host*
destined to veil the King of Heaven. . . . Our God of Kindness
has willed to fulfil my dream and show me once again what delight
He takes in accomplishing the desires of souls that love Him
alone.

If I did not fear to seem overbold, I should ask you further,
Reverend Father, to remember me every day at the Holy Altar. . . .

When the ocean lies between you and France, you will remember,
as you look at the pall I painted so joyfully, that upon the

---

daughters to associate herself with his future missionary apostolate. Mother Marie
de Gonzague selected Thérèse (see *Histoire d'une âme*, ch. x) and wrote to Père
Roulland: "Of my good ones she is the best"; and again: "You have a very fervent
auxiliary who will neglect nothing that is for the salvation of souls, the dear little
creature is wholly God's." Père Roulland left for China in 1896. He was a missionary at Su-Chuen, but was recalled by his superiors in 1909 and was given the post
first of Director, then of Procurator, at the Seminary of the Foreign Missions in
Paris. He was a witness at the Process. In 1922 he became Chaplain at the Convent
of La Reconnaissance at Dormans and died 12 May 1934. Through modesty, he
had refused in 1917 the Bishopric for which he had been chosen unanimously by
the voters of the Society of Foreign Missions.

[1] This was the day on which Père Roulland was to celebrate his first Mass in Paris.
A few days later he came to offer the Holy Sacrifice in the chapel of the Lisieux
Carmel and conversed in the parlour with Thérèse.

Mountain of Carmel, a soul prays without ceasing to the divine Prisoner of Love for the success of your glorious conquest.

I desire, Reverend Father, that our union in the apostolate may be known to *none* but Jesus;[1] and I claim one of your first blessings for one who will be happy to style herself eternally

Your unworthy little sister in Jesus-Victim,

Thérèse of the Child Jesus of the Holy Face,
rel. carm. ind.

CLXIX

To MME GUÉRIN

A little note written at the end of a letter from
Sister Marie of the Eucharist

Thank you, darling Aunt, for your letter. It gave me so much pleasure. It seems that there is no place for me today, which is why I am reduced to hiding in this corner of your Benjamin's letter. I kiss my Uncle and everybody I love at La Musse.

CLXX

To MOTHER MARIE DE GONZAGUE[2]

Mother Marie de Gonzague was very much upset because she was elected Prioress (on 21 March 1896) only on the seventh ballot. She confided her feelings to Thérèse, who sent her this letter for her consolation. The "Shepherdess" represents Mother Marie de Gonzague, and the "little lamb" is Thérèse herself.

Thérèse places herself at the Prioress's point of view, seeming to apply to herself the reproaches she addressed to certain of her daughters. It was not that the Saint actually saw things in this manner, which was very far from the reality. She merely used this

[1]Mother Marie de Gonzague had ordered Thérèse to tell no one, not even Mother Agnes of Jesus, that Père Roulland was her spiritual brother. Extracts were sometimes read at recreation from his letters, without saying to whom they were addressed.

[2] Born at Caen in 1834, Mother Marie de Gonzague entered the Lisieux Carmel 29 September 1860, received the habit 30 May 1861, was professed 27 June 1862, and was Prioress for sixteen years (in two terms), until Mother Agnes of Jesus filled the office for a three year period (February 1893 to March 1896).

means to bring Mother Marie de Gonzague to judge the facts more supernaturally, to detach herself from whatever was too human in her feelings, above all to see in this trial the hand of Christ, the sign of the Cross. Nowhere else, perhaps, does Thérèse's charity reach such a combination of daring and delicacy.

J. M. J. T.

Legend of a very Little Lamb

In a smiling fertile meadow lived a happy Shepherdess; she loved her flock with all the tenderness of her heart, and ewes and lambs loved their Shepherdess too.

. . . But perfect happiness is not to be found in the valley of tears; one day the lovely blue sky of the meadow was covered with clouds, and the Shepherdess grew sad; she no longer found joy in guarding her flock and, dare one whisper, the thought of leaving it for ever occurred to her mind. . . . Fortunately, she still loved a very small lamb; she often took it in her arms, caressed it and, as if the lamb had been her equal, the Shepherdess confided her woes to it and sometimes wept with it. . . .

Seeing its Shepherdess weep, the poor little creature was afflicted and in its very small heart it sought, but in vain, a way to console one whom it loved *more than itself.*

One evening the little lamb fell asleep at the Shepherdess's feet; then the meadow . . . the clouds . . . everything disappeared. It found itself in a great plain infinitely vaster and more beautiful. In the midst of a flock whiter than snow, it perceived a Shepherd resplendent in glory and sweet majesty. . . . The poor lamb dared not advance, but the good, the divine Shepherd came to it, took it on His knees, kissed it as once its loving Shepherdess did, and said: "Little lamb, why are tears glistening in your eyes, and why does your Shepherdess *whom I love* shed so many tears? Speak, I want to console you both."

"If I weep," replied the lamb, "it is only at seeing my dearest Shepherdess weep; listen, divine Shepherd, to the cause of her tears. There was a time when she believed herself loved by her dear flock and would have given her life for its happiness; but by your order, she was obliged to be away for a few years; on her return it seemed to her that she no longer found the spirit she had loved so in her sheep. You know, Lord, You have given

237

the flock the power and the privilege of choosing its Shepherdess. Well, this time she was not chosen unanimously as she used to be, it was only after a sevenfold deliberation that the crook was placed in her hands . . . Once You *wept* upon our earth, do You not realise how the heart of my dearest Shepherdess must suffer ?"

The Good Shepherd smiled and bending over the lamb said: "Yes, I realise . . . but let your Shepherdess be consoled; the great trial which has caused her such suffering was not merely *permitted* by Me, it was *willed* by Me." "Is it possible, Jesus !" answered the little lamb. "I thought you were so good, so kind. . . . Surely you could have given the crook to another, as my dearest Mother desired, or, if You were absolutely determined to put it back in her hands, why not have done it upon the *first* ballot ?" "Why, little lamb ? Because I *love* your Shepherdess ! All her life I have guarded her with jealous care, she had already suffered much for me, in her soul, in *her heart*; all the same, she still lacked the *chosen trial* I have just sent her, the trial I had *prepared* from all *eternity*."

"Ah ! Lord, I see plainly that You do not know the thing that is my Shepherdess's greatest grief . . . or else You do not wish to confide in me ! You, too, think that the original spirit of our flock is going . . . Alas ! how could my Shepherdess not think so ? So many Shepherdesses are deploring the same disasters in their folds. . . ." "It is true," Jesus answered, "the spirit of the world creeps even into the most remote meadows; but it is easy to be wrong in the discernment of motives. I see all, I know the most secret thoughts, and this I tell you: the Shepherdess's flock is *dear to me among all*, I have simply used it as an *instrument* to accomplish My work of sanctification in the soul of your dearest Mother."

"Ah ! Lord, I assure You that my Shepherdess does not realise all that You tell me . . . and how should she, since people do not judge things as You have taught me to see them. . . . I know sheep who give my Shepherdess much trouble with their *worldly-wise* reasonings. . . . Jesus, why do You not tell those sheep the secrets You have confided to me, why do You not speak to the heart of my Shepherdess ?"

"If I spoke to her, her *trial would disappear*, her heart would be filled with joy so great that her crook would never have seemed so light. . . . But I do not want *to take her trial from her*, I only want her *to grasp the truth* and realise that *her cross* comes to her from Heaven not from earth."

"Then, Lord, speak to my Shepherdess; how can You expect her to *grasp* the *truth* when all around her she hears nothing but falsehood. . . ."

"Little Lamb, are you not your Shepherdess's favourite ? . . . Very well then, tell her the words I have uttered to your heart."

"Jesus, I shall do it, but I wish You would give the commission to one of those sheep with the *worldly-wise* reasoning. . . . I am so little . . . my voice is so feeble, how will my Shepherdess believe me ?"

"Your Shepherdess knows that it pleases Me *to hide My secrets* from the wise and prudent, she knows that I *reveal them to the little ones*,[1] to the simple lambs whose white wool has taken no stain from the dust of the way . . . She will believe you . . . and if tears still flow from her eyes, those tears will no longer have the same bitterness, they will make her soul beautiful with the austere splendour of suffering loved and accepted with gratitude."

"I understand, Jesus, but there is still a mystery I should like to fathom. Tell me, I beg You, why You have chosen the *sheep beloved* of my Shepherdess to try her. . . . If You had chosen strangers, the trial would have been less harsh."

Then, showing the lamb His feet and hands and heart all adorned with luminous wounds, the Good Shepherd answered, "Look upon these wounds, I received them in *the house of those who loved me* !²[2] . . . That is why they are so beautiful, so glorious, that is why for all eternity their brightness will ravish angels and saints with joy.

"Your shepherdess wonders what she has done to drive her sheep from her, and *My people, what have I done to you? In what have I caused you grief?*[3]

"So your dearest mother must rejoice to be sharing in my sorrows. . . . If I rob her of human support, it is that I alone may fill that most *loving* heart of hers. . . .

"*Blessed is the man whose help is from me. In his heart he has disposed steps*[4] to ascend to Heaven. Note well, little lamb, I

---

[1] Matt. xi. 25; Luke x. 21.
[2] Zach. xiii. 6.
[3] The Reproaches from the Mass of the Presanctified.
[4] Cf. Ps. lxxxiii. 6.

did not say to separate oneself *completely* from creatures, to despise their love, their kind thoughtfulness, but on the contrary to *accept* them in order to give me pleasure, *to use them as so many steps*; for to go aside from creatures would have only one result, that one would walk and lose one's way in the pathways of the world. . . . To ascend, one must *place one's foot* upon the steps of creatures, and attach oneself to none but Me. . . . Do you really understand, little lamb?"

"Lord, I believe, even more I *feel*, that Your words are truth, for they put *peace* and joy into my small heart; ah! may they sweetly penetrate the very *great* heart of my Shepherdess! . . .

"Jesus, before going back to her, I have a prayer to make to You. Do not leave us to languish long on this earth of exile, summon us to the joy of the fields of Heaven, where eternally You will lead our dear little flock by flowering paths."

"Dear little lamb," replied the good Shepherd, "I shall grant your prayer *soon*; yes, soon; I shall take the Shepherdess[1] and her lamb; then through all eternity you will bless the fortunate suffering that merited so much happiness, and I, EVEN I, will wipe all tears from your eyes. . . ."

[1] Mother Marie de Gonzague died 17 December 1904, in the most edifying sentiments of humility and confidence in the intercession of her one-time lamb. Upon Thérèse's sanctity she had given this beautiful testimony written in her own hand on the register of the Convent, alongside the Saint's act of Profession:

"This Flower, more of Heaven than earth, was plucked by the Divine Gardener, at the age of 24 years 9 months on 30 September 1897.

"The nine and a half years she spent among us leave our souls fragrant with the most beautiful virtues with which the life of a Carmelite can be filled.

"A perfect model of humility, obedience, charity, prudence, detachment and regularity, she fulfilled the difficult discipline of Mistress of Novices with a sagacity and affection which nothing could equal save her love for God.

"We call to witness the dear manuscript which will edify the whole world while leaving the most perfect examples to us all.

"This angel on earth had the happiness of taking flight to her Beloved in an Act of Love.

"Oh, dear loved one, watch over your Carmel."

CLXXI

To LÉONIE

She expounds her Little Way of Spiritual Childhood

J. M. J. T.

Jesus †   12 July 1896.

My darling Léonie,

I should have answered your *charming* letter last Sunday, had it been given to me; but there are five of us and you know that I am the smallest . . . I am the one who runs the risk of seeing letters long after the others, or even not at all. . . . It was only on Friday that I saw your letter, so, darling sister, I am not late through my own fault. . . .

If you could know how happy I am to see you in such good dispositions. . . . I am not surprised that the thought of death is sweet to you since you no longer care for anything on earth.

I assure you that God is even kinder than you think. He is satisfied with a look, a sigh of love. . . . Personally, I find perfection quite easy to practice because I have realised that all one has to do is *take Jesus by the heart.* Consider a small child who has displeased his mother, by flying into a rage or perhaps disobeying her; if he sulks in a corner and screams in fear of punishment, his mother will certainly not forgive his fault; but if he comes to her with his little arms outstretched, smiling and saying: "Kiss me, I *won't do it again,*" surely his mother will immediately press him tenderly to her heart, forgetting all that he has done. . . . Of course she knows quite well that her dear little boy *will do it again* at the first opportunity, but that does not matter, if he takes her *by the heart,* he will never be punished. . . .

In the time of the law of fear, before the coming of Our Lord, the prophet Isaias, speaking in the name of the King of Heaven, could say: "Can a mother forget her child? and if she should forget, yet will not I forget thee."[1] What ecstasy in that promise! Ah! and we who live under the law of love, how can we fail to put to profit the loving advances our Spouse makes to us? How

[1] Isa. xlix. 15.

can we fear One "who lets himself be held by a hair of our neck ?"[1] So we must learn to hold Him prisoner, this God who makes Himself a mendicant for our love. In telling us that a hair can work so great a marvel, He is showing that the *smallest actions* done for love are the actions which win His heart. Ah ! if we had to do great things, how much to be pitied we should be ! . . . But how fortunate we are, since Jesus lets Himself be held by the *smallest* ! . . . You have no lack of small sacrifices, my dear Léonie, is not your life made up of them ? I rejoice to see you with such a treasure before you, especially when I realise that you know how to put it to profit, not only for yourself, but even more for souls. It is so sweet a thing to *aid Jesus* by our slight sacrifices, to aid Him to save the souls He has redeemed at the price of His blood, souls which await only our help not to fall into the abyss.

It seems to me that if our *sacrifices* are hairs to hold Jesus prisoner, so are our *joys*; to make them so, it is enough that we are not concentrated in a selfish happiness but that we *offer* our Spouse the *small joys* He sows in life's path to win our souls and *raise* them to Him. . . .

I meant to write to Aunt today, but I haven't time, it must be next Sunday; please tell her[2] how much I love her, and of course dear Uncle. I think of Jeanne and Francis, too, very often.

You ask me about my health. As to that, darling Sister, I no longer cough at all. Are you satisfied ? This will not stop the good God taking me when He will. Since all my effort is to be a very little child, I have no preparations to make. Jesus must Himself pay all the expenses of the journey and the price of admission into Heaven ! . . .

Goodbye, dearest little Sister. I love you, I think, more and more.

Your little sister,

Thérèse of the Child Jesus,
rel. carm. ind.

Sister Geneviève was very pleased with your letter, she will answer next time we write.

All five of us send kisses.

---

[1] Cant. of Cant. iv. 9.
[2] Léonie had been living with the Guérins since leaving the Visitation.

CLXXII

To MME GUÉRIN

J. M. J. T.

Jesus †   16 July 1896.

My dear Aunt,

I should have liked to be the first to write to you: but all that remains to me is the altogether pleasant duty of thanking you for your lovely letter. How kind you are, dearest Aunt, to think of your little Thérèse. Anyhow, I assure you that you have to do with a most grateful daughter.

I should like to give you some sort of news, but I search my mind in vain, absolutely nothing emerges save love for my dear relations . . . and there's nothing new in that, it's *as old as me*!

You ask me, dear Aunt, to give you, as a mother, news of my health. And that is what I shall do. But if I tell you that I am in marvellous health, you won't believe me, so i shall let the famous Doctor de Cornière[1] speak for me: I had the *signal honour* of being presented to him in the parlour yesterday. This illustrious person, after having *honoured* me with a glance, declared that I looked well! . . . This *declaration* does not stop me thinking I shall soon be allowed to go to Heaven with the little Angels, not because of my health, but because of another *declaration* made today in the chapel of Carmel by the Abbe Lechêne. . . . Having reminded us of the illustrious origins of our Holy Order, having compared us with the prophet Elias striving with the priests of Baal, he *declared* "That times similar to those of Achab's persecution were about to come again". To us he seemed already poised for martyrdom.

What happiness, darling Aunt, if our whole family went to heaven the same day. I fancy I see you smile, perhaps you think it an honour not reserved for us. . . . What is certain is that all together, *or* one by one, we shall one day leave exile for the Homeland and there we shall rejoice at all these things of which "heaven will be the reward. . . ."[2]

---

[1] Friend and doctor of the community. He attended Thérèse until her death, and often expressed his admiration for her heroic courage amid her great sufferings.
[2] From a hymn Sister Marie of the Eucharist often sang.

I had wanted to write many things to my little Aunt, for I love her so. Fortunately Sister Marie of the Eucharist will supply for my poverty; that is my one consolation in my utter destitution. We are always at our work,[1] and we understand each other perfectly. I assure you that neither of us is a breeder of melancholy. We have to take great care not to utter unnecessary words, for after each *necessary* phrase, some small amusing tag suggests itself which must be kept for recreation.

Dear Aunt, please give my greetings to all the dear people at La Musse especially my dear Uncle, I call upon him to give you a big kiss from me.

Your little girl who loves you,

Thérèse of the Child Jesus,
rel. carm. ind.

CLXXIII

To PÈRE ROULLAND

On the point of leaving for the Mission

J. M. J. T.

Jesus †   Lisieux, 30 July 1896.

My Brother,

I hope you will allow me from now on to call you by no other name, seeing that Jesus has deigned to unite us in the bonds of the apostolate. It is very sweet to think that from all eternity our Lord formed this union, which is to save Him souls, and that He created me to be your sister. . . . Yesterday we got your letters; it was with joy that our good Mother brought *you* into the cloister. She has allowed me to keep *my brother's photograph*, it is a *very special* privilege, a Carmelite has not even the portraits of her nearest relations; but Our Mother realises that yours, far from reminding me of the world and earthly affections, will raise my heart to regions far above, will make it forget self for the glory of God and the salvation of souls. So, Brother, while I shall

---

[1] In the sacristy.

cross the sea with you, you will remain with me, hidden in our poor cell[1]. . . .

I am surrounded by things that remind me of you. I have pinned the map of Su-Chuen[2] on the wall of the room in which I work, and the picture you gave me[3] lies always on my heart in the book of the Gospels, which never leaves me. I thrust it in haphazard, and this is the passage it came to: "Whoever has left all to follow me, shall receive a hundredfold in this world, and in the world to come eternal life."[4] Jesus' words are already fulfilled in you, for you tell me: "I start out happy."[5]

I realise that this joy must be wholly spiritual. It is impossible to leave father, mother, native land without feeling all the rending of separation. . . . O my brother! I suffer with you, I offer your great sacrifices with you, and I beg Jesus to pour His abundant consolations upon your dear family, until the union in heaven where we shall see them rejoicing in your glory, a glory which will dry their tears forever, and fill them with joy overflowing for a blissful eternity.

This evening, at prayer, I meditated on passages of Isaias which seemed to me so appropriate to you that I felt I simply must copy them out for you:

"Enlarge the place of thy tents. Thou shalt spread out to the right hand and to the left, and thy seed shall inherit the Gentiles and shall inhabit the desolate cities. . . . Lift up thy eyes round about and see: all these are gathered together, they are come to thee, thy sons shall come from afar and thy daughters will rise up at thy side. Then shalt thou see and abound, and thy heart shall wonder and be enlarged when the multitude of the sea shall be converted to thee, the strength of the Gentiles will come to thee."[6]

---

[1] After Thérèse's death, Père Roulland's photograph was found in her writing-case with a paper on which she had written:

"This photograph does not belong to me, our Mother told me to *keep it for her* in our writing-case, she will take it when she needs it

"*Th. of the Child Jesus,*
"*rel. carm. ind.*"

[2] The province in China to which he had been sent.

[3] Père Roulland's ordination card. On the back he had written for his spiritual Sister the following lines:

"Let us work together here below; in Heaven we shall share the reward."

[4] Cf. Luke xviii. 29–30.

[5] He embarked at Marseilles 2 August.

[6] Isa. liv. 2–3; lx. 4–5. The translation here and next page is from the Douay, which differs in many—not important—points from the French quoted by the Saint.

Is not that the hundredfold promised ? And can you not cry out in your turn: "The spirit of the Lord is upon me, because the Lord has anointed me. He has sent me to announce his word; to heal the contrite of heart, to preach a release to the captives, and console those who are in chains."[1]

"I shall rejoice in the Lord, for He has clothed me with the garments of salvation and with the robe of justice he has covered me. As the earth brings forth her bud, so shall the Lord God make justice to spring forth and praise before all the nations. My people will be a people of the just, they will be the shoots that I have planted . . . I shall go unto the islands afar off, to those who have never heard of the Lord. I shall announce his glory to the nations and shall give them as a gift to my God."[2]

If I wanted to copy all the passages that touched me most, it would take too long. I conclude, but first I have one more request to make. When you have a moment free I should be very glad if you would write me the principal dates of your life, thus I could unite myself especially with you to thank the good God for the graces He has given you.

Goodbye, Brother . . . distance can never separate our souls, even death will only make our union closer. If I go to Heaven soon, I shall ask Jesus' permission to visit you in Su-Chuen, and we shall continue our apostolate together. Meanwhile I shall always be united to you by prayer, and I ask our Lord never to let me be joyful when you are suffering. I would even wish that my Brother should always have joys and I trials, but perhaps that is selfish ! . . . but no, because my only *weapon* is love and suffering, and you have the sword of the word and of apostolic labours.

Goodbye once more, Brother, deign to bless her whom Jesus has given you for a Sister,

Thérèse of the Child Jesus and the Holy Face,
rel. carm. ind.

To the fourth page of this letter, Mother Marie de Gonzague had added the following lines:

Dear Child,

Man proposes and God disposes: I had meant to write you a long letter, and here Jesus gives me a minor indisposition which

[1] Isa. lxi. 1 ff. Our Lord read these verses and applied them to Himself in the synagogue at Nazareth; cf. Luke iv. 18 ff.
[2] Isa. lxi. 10, 11 ; lxvi. 19–20.

246

makes me unable to write, I am now an old crock, my chest plays tricks from time to time, but I shall offer all to win the souls our dear apostle is going to evangelise; you have a very fervent auxiliary who will neglect nothing necessary to the salvation of souls, the dear little thing is all God's ! . . .

We are with you, the ocean will not separate our souls. If you go by Saïgon, do not forget the Carmel or to tell the Reverend Mother Prioress and Sister Anne of the Sacred Heart that our hearts are always with them.[1]

To God *in* God, in Heaven meeting, and on this foreign earth union of souls.

Your old Mother,

Sister Marie de Gonzague, r. c. i.

CLXXIV

To SISTER GENEVIÈVE[2]

A jesting note written in pencil. Thérèse returns to the language of her childhood when, in memory of a story well known to her and Céline, she was called "M. Toto" and her sister "Demoiselle Lili"

J. M. J. T.

"Poor thing, poor thing,"[3] you must not be all upset because M.T.[4] has been caught in the trap ![5] . . . When he has wings,[6] there will be no point in spreading snares for him, he won't fall into them, nor you either, poor D.[7] He will stretch out his hand to you, will fix two little white wings on you, and together we shall fly very high and very far, we shall flutter our little silvery wings as far as Saïgon[8]. . . . That is the very best thing we can do for

---

[1] See Letter CCII and note.
[2] Undated.
[3] From a song sometimes sung at Les Buissonnets.
[4] Short for M. Toto.
[5] She is alluding to the possibility of her departure for a Carmel in the Far East. Having let her secret escape, she had drawn many questions from Sister Geneviève in veiled terms.
[6] i.e. when he has left this world.
[7] Short for Demoiselle Lili.
[8] The Carmel at Saïgon, the first to be established in the Far East (see note to

Jesus, because its His own wish that we should be two cherubim and not two foundresses. That is certain, at the moment; if He changes His mind, we shall change ours too, that's all !

CLXXV

To SISTER MARIE OF THE SACRED HEART

14 September 1896.

Sister Marie of the Sacret Heart had asked Thérèse to set down in writing for her "all the feelings of her heart" and what she called her "little doctrine". On 14 and 15 September the Saint, with Mother Prioress's permission, composed in her free time the pages which later appeared as chapter xi of her Autobiography.[1]

As it was there published, there seems no point in reproducing it here in full. We give only the following passages, containing "the story of the little bird" to which Thérèse alludes in her Letter CLXXV below.

These passages had been abridged and summarised in certain parts through the need to preserve the balance of chapter xi. They are here set out in their totality.

How can a soul as imperfect as mine aspire to possess the plenitude of love ?

O Jesus, *my first, my only Friend,* You Whom *I love* SOLELY, tell me what the mystery is ? Why do you not reserve these measureless aspirations to great souls, to the eagles flying in the upper air ?

I see myself as a feeble little bird, with only a light down to cover me; I am not an eagle, yet I have an eagle's *eyes* and an eagle's *heart*, for in spite of my extreme littleness, I dare to gaze upon the divine Sun, the Sun of Love, and my heart feels within it all the eagle's aspirations.

The little bird wants to *fly* toward that radiant Sun which

Letter CXXXVIII). From it issued the Carmel at Hanoï and several others. For a moment there was an idea that Mother Agnes of Jesus and Sister Geneviève might go to Saïgon, but nothing came of it (see *Histoire d'une âme,* ch. ix).

[1] But she dated them 8 September, anniversary of her Profession, because it was during the retreat she made a few days earlier that she had received decisive lights upon her "little doctrine".

charms its eye, it would imitate the eagles its brothers, as it sees them mounting up to the divine Fire of the Blessed Trinity. . . .

Alas ! all it can do is to *lift up* its *little* wings, but to fly—that is not in its *small* power.

What will it do ? Die of grief to see itself thus impotent ? Oh ! no, the little bird will not grieve at all. With reckless abandon, it wants to stay gazing upon its divine Sun; nothing can affright it, not wind nor rain, and if dark clouds come and hide the Star of Love, the little bird does not move, it knows that beyond the clouds its Sun shines still, that its radiance is not for a single instant eclipsed.

Sometimes, of course, the little bird's heart is beaten upon by the storm, it feels as if it believed that nothing exists save the clouds wrapping it round. . . . Then is the moment of *perfect joy* for the *poor feeble little creature.* What happiness for it to *stay there* just the same ! to gaze steadily at the invisible light which stays hid from its faith ! ! !

Jesus, so far I understand Your love for the little bird, for it has not gone away from You. . . . But I know, and You know too, that the imperfect little creature—though it stays where it is (that is under the rays of the Sun)—does let itself be distracted a little from its sole business, takes a little grain on this side or that, runs after a small worm . . . again it finds a little pool of water and *wets* its barely formed plumage; it sees a flower that pleases it, and its little mind is occupied about the flower. . . . In a word, not being able to soar like the eagles, the poor little bird still bothers with the trifles of this earth.

But even now, after all its misdeeds, the little bird doesn't go and hide in a corner to bewail its wretchedness and die of contrition, but turns to the Sun its Beloved, presents its little *wet* wings to its kindly rays and "cries like the swallow";[1] and in its sweet song, it confides its infidelities, tells them in detail, thinking, in the audacity of its total trust, to win in greater plenitude the love of Him "who came not to call the just but sinners"[2]. . . .

If the adored Star remains deaf to the plaintive twitter of its little creature, if it remains *veiled* by cloud . . . in that event the little creature stays *wet*, it accepts to be numb with cold, and rejoices in the suffering, which of course it has deserved. . . .

---

[1] Isa. xxxviii. 14.
[2] Matt. ix. 13.

O Jesus, how happy Your *little* bird is to be *feeble* and *little* ! What would become of it if it were big ? It would never have the boldness to appear in Your presence, to *sleep* before You. . . . Yes, for that too is a weakness of the little bird. . . . When it wants to gaze upon the divine Sun and the clouds keep it from seeing a single ray, its little eyes close in spite of itself, its little head is hid under its little wing, and the poor little thing sleeps, still fancying that it is gazing upon its dearest Star ! When it awakes, it is not all desolate, its little heart stays at peace; it resumes its task of *love*; it invokes the Angels and the Saints who mount up like eagles toward that consuming Fire, which it so much desires. And the Eagles take pity on their little brother, protect it, defend it, and put to flight the vultures that would devour it. These vultures are the demons, and the little bird has no fear of them, it is not destined to become their *prey* but the prey of the *Eagle* it contemplates in the very centre of the Sun of Love.

O divine Word, You are the adored Eagle, I love You, and You *draw* me to You. It is You, descending into this earth of exile, who have chosen to suffer and die to *draw* souls to the heart of the eternal Fire of the Blessed Trinity. It is You, ascending again to the inaccessible Light which is ever after to be Your dwelling-place, who remain still in the valley of tears under the appearance of a white host. . . . Eternal Eagle, You will to nourish me with Your divine substance, me, a poor little thing who would return to nothingness if Your divine gaze did not give me life from instant to instant. . . .

O Jesus ! let me, in the excess of my gratitude, tell You that Your love reaches the point of folly ! In face of this folly, how could You not want my heart to leap upward to You ? How can my trust have *any* limits ?

Ah ! for You, I know, the saints have committed *follies* too, they have done big things, because they were Eagles. . . . Jesus, I am too little to do big things, and *my* folly is to hope that your Love may accept me as a victim. . . . My folly consists in begging the Eagles, my brothers, to obtain for me the favour of flying upward to the Sun of Love with the divine Eagle's own wings.

As long as You will, O my Beloved, Your little bird will remain without strength of wings; it will stay with its eyes fixed upon You, its desire is to be *fascinated* by Your divine gaze, to become the *prey* of Your love. One day, so I hope, adored Eagle, You will come for Your little bird, and mounting with it to the Fire of Love, You will plunge it for eternity in the burning Abyss of the Love to which it has offered itself as victim. . . .

.   .   .   .[1]

O Jesus ! why can I not tell all *little souls* that Your condescension is beyond utterance . . . I feel that if, by an impossibility, You found a soul feebler and smaller than mine, You would take delight in showering upon it favours greater still, if it abandoned itself with entire trust to Your infinite mercy. . . .

But why desire to communicate Your secrets of love, O Jesus ! Was it not You alone who taught them to me, and can You not reveal them to others ? Yes, I know it and I conjure You to do it, I beg You to bend down Your divine gaze upon a great mass of *little* souls; I beg You to choose in this word a legion of *little* victims worthy of Your LOVE ! . . .

The *very little*
> *Sister Thérèse of the Child Jesus of the Holy Face,*
> *rel. carm. ind.*

Sister Marie of the Sacred Heart, having read the whole letter, wrote to Thérèse:

Jesus †   16 September 1896.

Darling Sister,

I have read your pages, with their burning love for Jesus. Your little Marie is *very happy* to possess this treasure and very grateful to her dearest little girl for thus unveiling the secrets of her soul. Oh ! how much I shall have to say to you about these lines, so marked with the seal of Love ! . . .

A single word about myself: Like the young man in the Gospel, I am seized with a certain sadness at your extraordinary desire for martyrdom. That is indeed the proof of your love. Yes, love you do possess: but not I ! You will never make me believe I can attain the desired goal, for I fear all that you love. That of course is a proof that I do not love Jesus as you do.

Ah ! you say that you do nothing, that you are a poor miserable little bird, but what about your desires ? How do you reckon them ? The good God certainly regards them as works.

---

[1] This line of dots was inserted by Thérèse herself.

I cannot say more: I began this short note this morning, and I have not had a minute to finish it. It is five o'clock, I wish you would write down for your little Godmother whether she can love Jesus as you love Him, but only two words, what I have is sufficient for my happiness and my pain: for my happiness, since I see to what an extent you are loved and privileged; for my pain since I have a presentiment of Jesus' desires to pluck His dearest little flower. Oh! I was very close to weeping as I read lines which are not of earth, but an echo from the Heart of God. . . . May I tell you? I will: you are possessed by God: literally *possessed*, exactly as the wicked are by the devil. I wish I could be possessed by Jesus as you are, but I love you so much that I rejoice, after all, to see you more privileged than I am.

A brief word for your little Godmother.

Thérèse replied with the following letter:

CLXXVI

To SISTER MARIE OF THE SACRED HEART

J. M. J. T.

Jesus †   17 September 1896.

My dearest Sister,

I am not embarrassed to answer you. . . . How can you ask me if it is possible for you to love the good God as I love Him? . . . If you had understood the story of my little bird, you would not ask me such a question. My *desires* for martyrdom *are nothing*, it is not they that give me the limitless confidence I feel in my heart. In fact they are the spiritual riches which *make* us *unjust*—when we rest in them complacently and think they are *something great*.

These desires are a *consolation* that Jesus sometimes grants to weak souls like mine (and such souls are numerous), but when He does not give this *consolation* it is a grace of *privilege*. Remember the words of the Father:[1] "Martyrs have suffered with joy, and the King of Martyrs suffered with sorrow."

[1] Père Pichon, S.J.: during a retreat he gave the Carmelites in October 1887.

Yes, Jesus said: "Father, take away this chalice from me."[1] Dearest Sister, after that how can you say that my desires are the mark of my love? Ah! I realise that what pleases God in my little soul is not that. What pleases Him is *to see me love my littleness and poverty, the blind hope I have in His mercy.* . . . That is my sole treasure, dearest Godmother; why should not this treasure be yours? . . .

Are *you* not ready to suffer whatever the good God wants? I know well that you are; then, if you want to feel joy in suffering, to be drawn to it, what you seek is your own consolation, for when one loves a thing, the pain vanishes. I assure you that if we went together to martyrdom in the dispositions in which we now are, you would have great merit and I none, unless it pleased Jesus to change my dispositions.

O my dearest Sister, *please* understand your little sister, understand that to love Jesus, to *be* His *victim of love*, the weaker one is, without desires or virtues,[2] the more apt one is for the operations of that consuming and transforming Love. The *desire* to be a victim is enough of itself, but one must consent to stay always poor and without strength, and that's the difficulty, for where are we to find the man truly poor in spirit? He must be sought afar, says the psalmist.[3] He does not say we must look for him among great souls, but "afar", that is in *lowliness, nothingness.* Ah! do let us stay *very far* from all that is brilliant, let us love our littleness, love to feel nothing, then we shall be poor in spirit, and Jesus will come for us, *far off* as we are, He will transform us in love's flames. . . . Oh! how I wish I could make you realise what I mean! . . . It is trust, and nothing but

---

[1] Matt. xxvi. 39.

[2] To understand these words aright, it must be remembered that Thérèse addresses them to a fervent Carmelite, striving for perfection. The expression "with no desires" cannot be taken literally, as she says in the next sentence: "The desire to be a victim is enough in itself"—which presupposes that one is not "without virtues" either, but already animated by a very great supernatural charity. "God preserve us from isolating this text and leaving it in the hands of some ill-intentioned commentator, who would deform it," says Père Lucien-Marie de St.-Joseph, in his study of "La Pauvreté Spirituelle de Ste. Thérèse de l'Enfant-Jesus" (*Journal d'etudes thérésiennes*, Paris, July 1947). "This daring affirmation of the Saint is in line with the severest texts of *The Ascent of Carmel* upon human virtues which are very fine in appearance but pharisaic, and of which St. John of the Cross proclaims the uselessness (bk. iii, ch. xxvii). In a sense the Saint was 'without desires or virtues'. She did not rely for support upon those which God had gratuitously granted her. She was truly poor."

[3] Thérèse is mistaken. The passage is from the *Imitation of Christ*, bk. ii, ch. xi, quoting Prov. xxxi. 10.

trust, that must bring us to Love. . . . Fear brings us only to Justice.*

Since we see the *way*, let us run *together*. Yes, I feel that Jesus wants to grant us the same graces, wants to give us His Heaven *as a free gift*. O, my dearest little Sister, if you don't understand me, it is because you are too great a soul . . . or rather because I explain myself badly, for I am sure that the good God would not give you the desire to be *possessed* by Him, by His *merciful Love*, if He did not have this favour in store for you; or rather He has already given it to you since you are given over to *Him*, since you *desire* to be consumed by *Him*, and the good God never gives desires that He cannot fulfil. . . .

9 o'clock is sounding, I must leave you; ah! what things I should like to say to you! But Jesus will put into your heart all that I cannot write. . . .

I love you with all the tenderness of *the little heart of a* GRATEFUL *child*.

Thérèse of the Child Jesus,
rel. carm. ind.

* To *strict justice* as it is shown to sinners, but that is not the *Justice* Jesus will have for those who love Him.[1]

CLXXVII

To ABBÉ BELLIÈRE[2]

Her first "spiritual brother"

J. M. J. T.

Jesus †   Lisieux, Carmel, 21 October 1896.

Monsieur l'Abbé,

Our Reverend Mother, who is ill, has confided to me the duty of answering your letter. I regret that you are deprived of the

---

[1] Note added by the Saint herself. She had struck out the words "to justice".

[2] The Abbé Maurice-Barthélemy Bellière, born 10 June 1874 was, a second-year student at the Major Seminary of Sommervieu (Calvados) and aspiring to be a missionary when he wrote, 15 October 1895, to the Prioress of the Lisieux Carmel, Mother Agnes of Jesus, to ask her "in the name and on the feast of the great St. Teresa" the aid of the prayers and sacrifices of a religious of her community for his

holy words our good Mother would have written you, but I am happy to be her mouthpiece[1] and to tell you her joy at learning of the work Our Lord has just wrought in your soul. She will continue to pray that He may bring His divine work in you to completion.

It is, I fancy, unnecessary to tell you, Monsieur l'Abbé, how much I share in our Mother's happiness. Your letter of July had very much grieved me, since I attributed the struggles you had to wage[2] to my lack of fervour; I never ceased imploring for you the aid of the sweet Queen of Apostles, so my joy was very great to receive, as a bouquet for my feast, the assurance that my poor prayers had been granted.

Now that the storm is over, I thank the good God for having made you go through it, for we read in our Holy Books the beautiful words: "Blessed is the man that endures temptation"[3] and again "He who has not been tried, what does he know?"[4] The fact is that when Jesus calls a man to guide and save multitudes of other souls, it is most necessary that He make him experience the temptations and trials of life. Since He has given you the grace to come forth victorious from the struggle, I hope, Monsieur l'Abbé, that our sweet Jesus will fulfil your great desires. I ask Him that you may be, not a *good* missionary merely, but a *saint*, all aflame with love for God and love for souls. Obtain

---

soul and his apostolate: Mother Agnes chose Thérèse (see *Histoire d'une âme*, ch. x). Thérèse sustained him by prayers, then for two years by letters as well. Abbé Bellière left France for the Novitiate of the White Fathers in Algiers, on 29 September 1897, the day before the death of his spiritual Sister. He had learnt to appreciate her virtues, for he wrote to Mother Marie de Gonzague before taking ship at Marseilles: "And Sister Thérèse? What a saint!" The year following, having read the *Histoire d'une âme* which Mother Marie de Gonzague had sent, he wrote to her, 14 November 1898, a letter in which he told her "that he felt the continual action of his beloved sister on his soul". After several years as a missionary in Africa, he was stricken with sleeping sickness (which was not diagnosed at the time), returned to France and died in the home of his family at Langrunes (Calvados) on 14 July 1907, aged thirty-three.

[1] It may seem surprising that a year should have elapsed between her designation as his spiritual Sister and this first letter. The Saint thus explains it in her *Souvenirs inédits*: "It must be admitted that at first I had no consolations to stimulate my zeal. After having written a charming letter full of heart and noble sentiments to thank Mother Agnes of Jesus, my Brother gave no sign of life till the month of July following, except a card in November to say that he was going into barracks to do his military service."

[2] Struggles against himself, to remain faithful to his missionary vocation as soon as circumstances should allow.

[3] Jas. i. 12.

[4] Ecclus. xxxiv. 10.

that love for me too, I beg, that I may help you in your apostolic labour. You know that a Carmelite who was not an apostle would be losing sight of the goal of her vocation and would cease to be a daughter of the Seraphic St. Theresa, who would have given a thousand lives to save a single soul.

I am sure, Monsieur l'Abbé, that you will be kind enough to join your prayers to mine that Our Lord may cure our venerated Mother.

In the Sacred Hearts of Jesus and Mary, I shall always be happy to be called

Your unworthy little sister,
Thérèse of the Child Jesus of the Holy Face,
rel. carm. ind.

CLXXVIII

To PÈRE ROULLAND

In China

Jesus †   Carmel at Lisieux, 1 November 1896.

My Brother,

Your most interesting letter, which has arrived under the patronage of all the Saints, causes me great joy. I thank you for treating me as a real sister: with the grace of Jesus I hope to become worthy of a title so dear to me.

I thank you also for sending us *L'Ame d'un Missionaire*. The book interested me keenly, it enabled me to accompany you in your long voyage. The life of Père Nempon has the exactly right title, it is indeed "the soul of a missionary" that it reveals, or rather the souls of all apostles truly worthy of the name.

You ask me (in the letter written in Marseilles) to pray to Our Lord to spare you the cross of being appointed to a Seminary or even of returning to France. I realise that such a prospect is not agreeable to you: with all my heart I ask Jesus in His goodness to let you carry out the laborious apostolate as your soul has always dreamt it. But I add, with you, "May God's will be done". Only in that lies rest; outside that loving *will* we should do *nothing* either for Jesus or for souls.

I cannot tell you, Brother, how happy I am to see you so completely surrendered into the hands of your superiors; it seems to me sure proof that one day your desires will be accomplished —that is, you will be a great saint.

Let me tell you a secret just revealed to me by the page containing the memorable dates of your life.

On 8 September 1890, your vocation to the missions was saved by Mary, Queen of Apostles and Martyrs;[1] on that same day a little Carmelite became the spouse of the King of Heaven. Bidding goodbye to the world forever, her one object was to save souls, especially the souls of apostles. She particularly asked Jesus, her divine Spouse, for an apostolic soul; since she could not be a priest, *she wanted a priest to receive in her stead the Lord's graces, to have the same aspirations, the same desires as she.* . . .

My Brother, you know the unworthy Carmelite who made that prayer. Don't you agree with me that our union, confirmed on the day of your ordination to the priesthood, began on September 8 ?

I thought that only in Heaven should I meet the apostle, the brother, I had asked Jesus for; but our beloved Saviour, raising a corner of the mysterious veil which hides the secrets of eternity, deigned to give me, still in exile, the joy of knowing the brother of my soul, of working with him for the salvation of poor infidels.

Oh ! how great is my gratitude when I consider the delicacy of Jesus' gifts ! What has He in store for us in Heaven, seeing that even here below His love gives us such delightful surprises.

More than ever I realise that the smallest happenings of our life are guided by God, He makes us desire, then grants our desires. . . . When our good Mother proposed that I become your auxiliary, I confess to you, Brother, that I hesitated.[2] Considering the virtues of the holy Carmelites all round me, it seemed to me

---

[1] Here is what Père Roulland has to say on the matter: "On 8 September 1890 I had hesitations as to my vocation and my entry into the Major Seminary. While I was praying in the chapel of Notre Dame de la Délivrande [a shrine in Normandy to which many come on pilgrimage] I was suddenly and definitively fixed in my mind. Now I learnt later that on that same day, which was the day of the Servant of God's Profession, she had asked Our Lord to give her a priest's soul, and she informed me of the link between the two events in her letter of 1 November 1896" (*Summarium* of the Process, No. 1523). It is to be noted that Thérèse loved to give the Blessed Virgin the title Queen of Apostles and Martyrs. She had composed a poem (16 July 1896) entitled "To Our Lady of Victories, Queen of Virgins, Apostles and Martyrs", in which she sings her joy at being associated by prayer and sacrifice with the work of Père Roulland, of her apostolic desires and her hope to be "the sister of a martyr".

[2] See *Histoire d'une âme*, ch. x.

that our Mother would have served your interests better by choosing for you some Sister other than me: only the thought that Jesus would regard, not my imperfect works but my good will, made me accept the honour of sharing in your apostolic labours. I did not know then that Our Lord Himself had chosen me, He who uses the weakest instruments to accomplish marvellous things. I did not know that for six years I had had a brother preparing to become a Missionary. Now that this brother is an apostle in fact, Jesus reveals the mystery to me, surely in order to increase still more the desire in my heart to love Him and make Him loved.

Do you know, Brother, if the Lord continues to grant my prayer, you will obtain a favour that your humility keeps you from asking. You guess what that incomparable favour is, *martyrdom*. . . . Yes, I have the hope, that after *long years* spent in apostolic labours, having given Jesus love for love, life for life, you will also give Him *blood for blood*.

As I write these lines, it occurs to me that they will reach you in January, a month when good wishes are exchanged. I am pretty sure the wishes your little sister sends will be the only ones of their sort. . . . Truth to tell, the world would see such wishes as follies; but for us the world lives no more, "our conversation is already in Heaven",[1] our one desire is to resemble our adorable Master, whom the world did not wish to recognise because "He annihilated Himself, taking the form and nature of a slave".[2] O my Brother, how blessed you are to be following so closely the example of Jesus. Realising that you have put on Chinese clothes, I think naturally of the Saviour putting on our poor humanity and becoming like one of us, to redeem our souls for eternity. You will perhaps think me very childish, but no matter: I confess that I committed a sin of envy, to read that your hair was to be cut and replaced by a pigtail. That of course was not what I coveted, but simply a little lock of hair that is of no further use to you. I imagine you laugh and ask what I should do with it? It's quite simple, really. When you are in Heaven, the martyr's palm in your hand, those hairs will be *relics*. Doubtless you think I am setting about it a long time ahead, but I know that it's the one way to get what I want, for your little sister (known to be such only by Jesus) will certainly be forgotten in the distribution of *your relics*. I'm quite sure you're laughing at me, but I don't mind

[1] Phil. iii. 20.   [2] Cf. ibid., ii. 7.

a bit. If, for the small entertainment I give you, you are willing to *pay* with *the hair of a future martyr*, I shall be very well paid !

On December 25, I shall not fail to send my Angel to lay my intentions beside the host that will be consecrated by you. From the very depths of my heart I thank you for offering your dawn Mass for our Mother and me; while you are at the Altar we shall be chanting the Matins of Christmas which immediately precede the midnight Mass.[1]

Brother, you made no mistake when you said that my intention would surely be "to thank Jesus for the day of graces beyond all others". As a matter of fact it was not on that day that I received my religious vocation: Our Lord, wishing my first glance to be for Him alone, deigned to ask me for my heart actually in the cradle, if I may put it so.

The *night* of Christmas 1886 was, it is true, decisive for my vocation, but to give it a more exact name I should call it *the night of my conversion*. On that blest night, of which it is written that it *illumines God's own delights*,[2] Jesus, who became a child for love of me, deigned to bring me forth from the swaddling clothes and imperfections of infancy. He transformed me so utterly that I no longer recognised myself. But for this change, I should have had to remain many years longer in the world. St. Teresa—who said to her daughters "I want you in nothing to be women but in everything to equal strong men"[3]—St Teresa would have been unwilling to acknowledge me as her child, if the Lord had not clad me in His divine strength, if He had not Himself armed me for war.

I promise, Brother, to commend to Jesus quite specially the girl you speak of, who is finding obstacles in the way of her vocation. I sympathise sincerely in her trouble, knowing from experience what an affliction it is to be unable to answer God's call at once. My wish for her is that she may not be forced to go to Rome, as I was . . . I imagine you did not know that your sister had the audacity *to speak to the Pope* ? . . . But it's true, and if I hadn't had that audacity, perhaps I should still be in the world.

[1] Reckoning on the difference of time between France and Su-Chuen. As it turned out, he was not able to say Mass that day as he had promised, upon which the Saint made this sad comment some months later: "And I, who had united myself with it in such happiness at the exact hour ! Ah ! all is uncertain on earth !"

[2] Cf. Ps. cxxxviii. 10: "Et nox illuminatio mea in deliciis meis."

[3] *Way of Perfection*, ch. viii.

Jesus said that "the Kingdom of heaven suffers violence and the violent take it by storm".[1] It was the same for me with the kingdom of Carmel. Before I could be Jesus' prisoner, I had to journey very far to capture the prison I loved more than all earth's palaces: I had no desire whatever to make a journey for my personal pleasure, and when my incomparable father proposed to take me to Jerusalem, if I would be willing to postpone my entry by two or three months, I did not hesitate (in spite of the natural inclination which led me to want to visit the places hallowed by the Saviour's life) to choose *rest in the shadow of him I had desired*:[2] I realised that in all truth "one day in the house of the Lord is better than a thousand elsewhere".[3]

Perhaps, Brother, you would like to know what was the obstacle in the way of my fulfilling my vocation? That obstacle was nothing but my youth. Our good Father Superior absolutely refused to receive me under the age of twenty-one, saying that a child of fifteen was incapable of realising what she was undertaking. His conduct was prudent, and I doubt not that, in testing me, he was carrying out the will of the good God, who wanted to make me conquer the fortress of Carmel at the sword's point: perhaps, too, Jesus allowed the demon to impede my vocation, for I imagine it could not have been much to the taste of that *loveless* wretch, as our Holy Mother Teresa called him.

Fortunately all his tricks turned to his shame, serving only to render a child's victory more spectacular. If I were to write to you all the details of the combat I had to wage, I should need much time, ink and paper! Told by a skilful pen, these details would interest you, I think; but mine is not the pen to give charm to a long recital, please forgive me for having perhaps bored you already.

You promise me, Brother, to go on saying at the altar every day: "My God, inflame my sister with Your love." I am profoundly grateful and I readily assure you that your conditions are and will *always* be accepted. All I ask Jesus for myself, I ask for you too; when I offer my feeble love to the Beloved, I venture to offer your love as well.

Like Josue you are fighting in the plain, I am your little Moses, and ceaselessly my heart is raised to heaven to gain the victory. O my Brother! how much to be pitied you would be if Jesus

---

[1] Matt. xi. 12.   [2] Cant. of Cant. ii. 3.   [3] Ps. lxxxiii. 11.

Himself did not bear up the arms of "your Moses" ![1] But with the help of the prayers you offer for me daily to the "divine Prisoner of love",[2] I hope that you will never be *to be pitied*, and that after this life in which we have sown together *in tears*, we shall be found "joyous, bearing sheaves in our hands".[3]

I loved the little sermon you sent to our good Mother, exhorting her to remain upon earth a while longer: it is short, but, as you say, it is unanswerable. Obviously you won't have much trouble convincing your listeners when you preach, and I hope that an abundant harvest of souls will be reaped and offered by you to the Lord.

I see that I am at the end of my paper, which forces me to put a stop to my scribbling. The one thing I still have to say is that I shall celebrate your anniversaries faithfully. July 3 will be particularly dear because on that day you *received Jesus* for the first time and on that same date I *received Jesus* from your hand and was present at your first Mass in Carmel.

My Brother, bless your unworthy sister,

Thérèse of the Child Jesus,
rel. carm. ind.

(I commend to your prayers a young seminarian who wants to be a *missionary*; his vocation has been shaken by his year of military service.)[4]

CLXXIX

To MME GUÉRIN

For her feast

J. M. J. T.

Jesus †

16 November 1896.

Dear Aunt,

It is very sad for your little girl to have to depend on a cold pen for the expression of her heart's feelings . . . Perhaps you will

---

[1] The expression was Père Roulland's, but Thérèse had of her own motion used it years before, writing to Céline: cf. Letter CXIV.
[2] Another expression of Père Roulland's, also used by Thérèse earlier, in her Letter CLXVIII.
[3] Ps. cxxv. 5.
[4] The Abbé Bellière.

smile and say: "But, little Thérèse, would you express them any
more easily in words?" Dearest Aunt, I have to admit it: no,
of course, I cannot find phrases to satisfy the feelings of my heart.

The poet who had the daring to say

> What is well thought is clearly uttered
> And the words to say it come easily[1]

certainly never felt what I feel in the depths of my heart! . . .
Fortunately I have for my consolation the profound insight of
Father Faber : he at least understood that the words and phrases
of this world cannot express the heart's feelings, and that *full*
hearts are hearts which can least utter all that lies within them.[2]

Dear Aunt, I shall bore you with my quotations, all the more so
as the letters of my four nice sisters are there to give the lie to
what I am saying. But at any rate, dearest Aunt, rest assured that
for all their eloquence they do not love you any more than I,
though I cannot say it in well-chosen terms. . . . If you do not
believe me now, one day, when we are all together in the beauty
of Heaven, you will be obliged to admit that the *littlest* of your
children was not the littlest in tenderness and gratitude, but only
in age and wisdom.

Please, dear Aunt, pray to God that I may grow in wisdom
like the divine Child Jesus;[3] that is not what I am doing, I
assure you. . . . Ask our dear little Marie of the Eucharist,
she will tell you that I'm not lying: yet I have been almost *nine
years* in the house of the Lord. So I ought by now to be far
advanced in the ways of perfection, but I am still only at the foot
of the ladder; it does not discourage me, and I am as merry as a
grasshopper; singing away all day, and hoping at the end of my
life to share in the riches of my sisters, who are much more
generous than the ant!

I hope too, dear Aunt, to have a good seat at the heavenly
banquet, for this reason: when the Saints and Angels realise that
I have the honour to be your little girl they won't want to disappoint you by putting me a long way off. So I shall enjoy

[1] Boileau, *Art poétique.*
[2] It is difficult to discover the source of the second part; of the first there is more
than one possible source. The idea occurs several times in ch. iv, and again in
ch. vi and vii, of *All for Jesus.*
[3] Luke ii. 52.

eternal rewards because of your virtues. Ah! I was indeed born under a lucky star, and my heart melts with gratitude to the good God for giving me such relations as are nowhere else to be found on earth.

And, darling Aunt, since I am a *poor grasshopper* with nothing but its songs—nor can it really sing save in the depths of its heart, its voice being so unmelodious—I shall sing my finest tune the day of your feast, and I shall try to do it with a note so touching that all the saints, taking pity on my poverty, will give me treasures of grace that I shall be enchanted to present to you. And of course I shall use those treasures, too, to celebrate my dear Grandmama's feast.[1] The saints will be so generous that my heart will have nothing more to desire, and I assure you, Aunt, that that is no light thing to say, for my desires are very great.

I ask my dear Uncle to kiss you very tenderly for me. If Francis, Jeanne and Léonie will very kindly do the same, I shall sing a little song to thank them (naturally Uncle will not be forgotten in my gay song).

Forgive me, dearest Aunt, for saying so many things with neither rhyme nor reason, and take my word that I love you with all my heart.

Thérèse of the Child Jesus,
rel. carm. ind.

CLXXX

To REVEREND MOTHER AGNES OF JESUS[2]

J. M. J. T.

4 December 1896.

Little Mother is much too darling ! . . . If she *doesn't know* what *she is*, I do, and I LOVE[3] her ! . . . yes ! . . . but how pure my affection is ! . . . it is the affection of a child marvelling at its *mother's humility*. You do me more good than all the books in the world ! . . .

---

[1] See note to Letter CLI.
[2] This note is unsigned and written in pencil.
[3] The word is underlined three times.

CLXXXI

To REVEREND MOTHER AGNES OF JESUS[1]

Who, subject to many worries in her work as Depositrix,[2] had called herself the "little ass" and the "little servant" of the Holy Family, in imitation of Sister Marie of St. Peter, of the Carmel at Tours

J. M. J. T.

18 December 1896.

The Blessed Virgin is so pleased to have a "little ass" and a "little servant", that she has them running right and left *for her pleasure*, so it is not surprising that the little Mother sometimes stumbles . . . of course ! . . . But when the *Child* Jesus is grown-up and no longer needs to learn "how to keep shop",[3] He will prepare a *little* place for the *little* Mother in His Kingdom which is not of this world;[4] and then, in his turn, He will *minister* to her.[5]

How many will have to stand up to look at one who had no other ambition than to be *the Child Jesus' donkey* !

CLXXXII

To SISTER GENEVIÈVE

On the envelope :

Sent by the Blessed Virgin

TO MY DEAREST CHILD
WITH NO PLACE OF REFUGE
IN FOREIGN LAND.

Inside the envelope, this note :

Christmas 1896.

My darling Daughter,

If you knew how you rejoice my heart, and the heart of my little Jesus, how happy you would be ! . . .

[1] Unsigned; written in pencil.
[2] Nun charged with the material administration of the convent.
[3] "Le petit métier de la boutique", a jesting expression used at Les Buissonnets.
[4] John xviii. 36.
[5] Luke xii. 37.

But you do not know, you do not see, and your soul is in gloom. I wish I could console you. If I do not, it is because I know the value of suffering and anguish of heart, O my dearest child ! If you knew in what affliction my heart was plunged when I saw my husband St. Joseph coming back to me all sad, having found no inn to take us.

If you are willing to bear serenely the trial of being displeasing to yourself, you will be to me a pleasant place of shelter; you will suffer, of course, for you will be outside the door of your own home; but have no fear, the poorer you are, the more Jesus will love you. He will journey far, so far, to seek you, if at times you stray. He would rather see you striking your foot against the stones of the way by night, than walking in broad daylight along a road gemmed with flowers which could easily slow your advance. I love you, O my Céline, I love you more than you can possibly realise. . . .

I am delighted to see you desiring great things, and I am preparing greater still for you . . . One day you will come with your *Thérèse* into the beauty of Heaven, you will take your place on the knees of my beloved Jesus, and I too shall take you in my arms and shower caresses upon you, for I am your *Mother*.

Your dearest *Mama*,

Mary, Queen of little *Angels*.

CLXXXIII

To SISTER MARIE OF THE TRINITY

Sister Marie of the Trinity writes thus in the anonymous " Souvenirs" published at the end of the Histoire d'une âme *:*

" As I was very young in disposition, the Child Jesus, to help me in the practice of virtue, inspired me to play with Him. *I chose the game of skittles. I figured the skittles to myself as of all sizes and colours, to personify the souls I wanted to reach. The bowl was* my love.

In December 1896, the novices received various small objects for a Christmas tree, in aid of the missions. At the bottom of the magic box was an object very rare at Carmel, a top. *My companions said 'Isn't it ugly ! What can it be for ?' I, who knew the game well, picked up the top, crying : 'But it's most amusing ! it could go for a whole day without stopping, all you have to do is whip it !' Then I gave them a demonstration which absolutely astonished them.*

Sister Thérèse of the Child Jesus watched me without making any comment ; at Christmas, after Midnight Mass, I found in our cell the famous top, with the following letter."

On the envelope :

Personal

TO MY DEAREST LITTLE BRIDE
SKITTLES-PLAYER ON MOUNT CARMEL

In the envelope, this note :

Christmas Eve, 1896.

My dearest little Bride,

Oh! how pleased I am with you . . . All through the year you have entertained me vastly with your *skittles.* I enjoyed it so much that the angelic court was surprised and delighted, more than one of the smaller Cherubim asked me why I had not made him a child . . . more than one went on to ask me if I didn't like the melody of his harp better than your joyous laugh when you knocked down a *skittle* with the ball you called *love* ? I answered my little Cherubim that they must not worry about not being children, because one day they would be able to play with you in the fields of heaven, and I told them that certainly your smile was lovelier to me than their melodies, because you could not play and smile except by *suffering*, by forgetting *yourself.*

Beloved little Bride, I have a request to make, you will not refuse me ? . . . Oh, no! you love me too well. So—I confess I should like a change of *game*; skittles are great fun, but now I want to play at *tops*, and *you* shall be my *top*. I give you one for a model, it isn't beautiful, anyone who didn't know what to do with it would kick it out of his way, but a child would leap for joy to see it; he would say: "Ah ! isn't it fun, it can keep on going all day and never stop."

I, the Child Jesus, love you, though you *have no charm*, and I beg you to *keep on going* to *entertain* me. . . But to keep the *top* going, it must be whipped. . . . So, let the sisters do you this favour, and be grateful to those who are most assiduous in keeping you from slowing down. When I have had enough pleasure from you, I shall bring you up there, and we can play with no suffering.

Your little Brother Jesus.

CLXXXIV

To ABBÉ BELLIÈRE

J. M. J. T.

Jesus †   Lisieux Carmel, 26 December 1896.

Monsieur l'Abbé,

I should have liked to answer sooner, but the rule of Carmel does not allow me to write or receive letters during Advent; our Venerated Mother did allow me, as an exception, to read yours, because she knew that you had especial need to be sustained by prayer.[1]

I assure you, Monsieur l'Abbé, that I am doing all that lies in my power to obtain the graces you need; those graces will surely be granted, for Our Lord never asks us for a sacrifice beyond our strength. Sometimes, of course, that divine Saviour lets us taste all the bitterness of the cup He is holding to our soul. When He asks the sacrifice of all that is dearest to us in this world, it is impossible, short of a quite special grace, not to cry out as He did in the garden of His agony: "My Father, let this chalice pass from me . . . Nevertheless not as I will, but as Thou wilt."[2]

It is very consoling to remember that Jesus, the *God of Might*, knew our *weaknesses*, that He shuddered at sight of the bitter cup, the cup that earlier He had so ardently desired to drink. . . .

Your lot is very beautiful, Monsieur l'Abbé, for Our Lord chose it for Himself, because He first tasted the cup He is now offering you.

A saint has said: "The greatest honour God can do a soul is not to give much to it, but *to ask much of it* !" So Jesus is treating you as a privileged person. He wants you to begin your missionary work *now* and save souls by suffering. Was it not by suffering

[1] In his November letter, Abbé Bellière, then at Langrunes (Calvados) with his family, spoke of his missionary vocation and of the pain he felt at the prospect—distant as it still was—of parting from his own people.
[2] Matt. xxvi. 39.

and dying that He redeemed the world ? I know you aspire to the happiness of sacrificing your life for the Divine Master, but the martyrdom of the heart is no less fruitful than the shedding of blood, and that first martyrdom is yours already. So I am right in saying that your lot is beautiful, is worthy of an apostle of Christ.

You look for encouragement, Monsieur l'Abbé, to one whom Jesus has given you as your sister, and you are entitled to.[1] As our Reverend Mother permits me to write to you, I am very glad to fulfil the pleasant task entrusted to me ; but I feel that the surest way to reach my goal is by prayer and suffering. . . . Let us work together for the salvation of souls, we have only the single day of this life to save them and thus give Our Lord proofs of our love. The morrow of this day will be eternity ; then Jesus will return you a hundredfold the lovely, rightful joys that you are sacrificing for him ; He knows that the suffering of people dear to you makes your own greater still ; but He too suffered that martyrdom to save our souls, He left His Mother, He saw the Immaculate Virgin at the foot of the Cross, her Heart pierced by a sword of sorrow ; so I hope that our divine Lord will comfort your dear Mother, and my prayer for that is most urgent. Ah ! if the divine Master would give those you are leaving for love of Him even a glimpse of the glory He has in store for you, the multitude of souls who will enter heaven in your train, they would even now be repaid for the great sacrifice that losing you will mean to them.

Our Mother is still ill, but a little better these last few days, I hope the divine Child Jesus will give her back the strength she will expend for His glory. That venerated Mother sends you a picture of St. Francis of Assisi ; he will teach you how to find joy amid the trials and warfare of life. I hope, Father, that you will continue to pray for me ; I am not an angel, as you seem to think, but a poor little Carmelite, very imperfect but, for all her poverty, bent, as you are, upon working for the glory of the good God.

Let us remain, united in prayer and suffering, by Jesus' crib.
Your unworthy little Sister,

Thérèse of the Child Jesus of the Holy Face,
rel. carm. ind.

---

[1] The Abbé Bellière had written to her : "Your last month's letter encouraged me and did me good. If your charity moves you to write again, it will be a great consolation and an added strength."

CLXXXV

To SISTER MARIE OF THE TRINITY[1]

The good God *wants* you to bear your trial alone. He shows this in many ways. . . . but . . . I suffer with you ! and I love you dearly . . .

Don't worry, I shall come to you for a few minutes tomorrow morning, and on the day after the laundry I shall go with you to the altar-breads.[2]

[1] This letter, undated, belongs to 1896 or 1897.
[2] Sister Marie of the Trinity had the task of baking altar-breads.

TWENTY-FIFTH AND LAST YEAR

During the winter of 1896–1897, Thérèse's physical powers had gradually declined. By the end of Lent 1897 her condition had become alarming. But she was not excused any of the Community exercises. The body's martyrdom was accompanied by temptations against faith. It was the ascent of Calvary.

On 3 June Mother Marie de Gonzague ordered Thérèse to go on with the manuscript of her life. The Saint began the task and continued till the pen dropped from her hands. On 2 July she gave the Prioress the pages she had managed to write ; they form chapters ix and x of the Histoire d'une âme.

On 8 July she left her cell for the infirmary, received Extreme Unction on 30 July and made her last Communion on 19 August.

From May onwards Reverend Mother Agnes of Jesus noted down the things her sister said on her daily visits.[1]

On Thursday, 30 September, at the end of a long and most painful agony, of unrelieved desolation, Thérèse uttered in the night of faith the words : "OH ! . . . I LOVE HIM ! . . . MY GOD, I LOVE YOU," and died in an ecstasy of love. It was seven-twenty in the evening. She was buried in the Lisieux Cemetery on 4 October.

CLXXXVI

To REVEREND MOTHER AGNES OF JESUS

J. M. J. T.

Jesus †   9 January 1897.

My dearest Little Mother,

If you knew how touched I am at the degree of your love for me ! Oh ! never shall I be able here below to show you my gratitude. . . . I hope soon to be going above, then I shall be rich, I shall have all the treasures of the good God and He Himself will be *my wealth*; then I shall be able to repay a hundredfold all I owe you.

[1] They were published in a small volume entitled *Novissima Verba*.

Oh ! *how* I look forward to it. . . . I feel so much pain to be always receiving, never giving. . . . The little Mother's way (to the eyes of *little* Thérèse) is like the way He chose for Himself when He journeyed in this land of exile. . . . Then *His look* was as it were *hidden,* none *recognised* Him, *He was despised.*[1] My little Mother is not despised, but very few recognise her, because Jesus has hidden her face ![2] . . .

O Mother, how splendid is your lot ! It is truly worthy of *you,* the favoured one of our family, who show us the way, like the small swallow one always sees ahead of his companions, tracing in the air the path that is to lead them to their new homeland. Oh ! do realise the affection of YOUR[3] little girl, who would love to say *so many, many* things to you ! . . .

CLXXXVII

To BROTHER SIMÉON

Of the Christian schools. Director of the College of St. Joseph, Piazza di Spagna, Rome[4]

Jesus †   Lisieux Carmel, 27 January 1897.

Monsieur le Directeur,

I am glad to join my sister Geneviève in thanking you for the precious favour you have obtained for our Carmel.[5]

Since I cannot tell you in words how grateful I am, I mean to show you, at Our Lord's feet, by my poor prayers, how deeply I am touched by your kindness to us. . . .

A feeling of sadness mingled with my joy as I learnt that your health had been less good, so with my whole heart I am asking Jesus to prolong for as many years as possible a life so precious to the Church. I realise that the divine Master must be eager to give you your crown in heaven, but I hope He will leave you still

---

[1] Isa. liii. 3.
[2] Since she was no longer Prioress.
[3] The word is underlined five times.
[4] Brother Siméon was also founder of the College. He died in 1899 at the age of eighty-five. See *Histoire d'une âme*, ch. vi and vii, *Histoire d'une famille*, p. 294, and Letters LXXXIX and XCIX above.
[5] A spiritual favour ; probably a blessing from the Holy Father.

in exile, so that you may go on working for His glory as you have from your youth upward, and the immense mass of your merits may make up for other poor souls who will appear before God empty-handed.

I dare to hope, most dear Brother, that I shall be one of the fortunate souls who will share in your merits. I think my course here below will not be long. . . . When I appear before my beloved Spouse, I shall have nothing to offer Him but my desires; but if you go before me into the Homeland, I hope you will come to meet me, and offer the merit of your most fruitful works for me. . . . You see, your little Carmelites can never write to you without asking some favour and appealing to your generosity ! . . .

Monsieur le Directeur, you are so *powerful* in *our* behalf upon earth, you have already got us the blessing of our Holy Father Leo XIII so often, that I feel certain that in Heaven God will grant you very great power over His heart. I beg you not to forget me in His presence if you have the good fortune to see Him before I do. . . . The one thing I beg you to ask for my soul is the grace to *love* Jesus and *make Him loved* as much as lies in my power.

If Our Lord comes for *me* first, I promise to pray for your intentions and for all who are dear to you. Of course I am not waiting till I get to heaven to offer that prayer, even here I am glad that I have this way of proving my profound gratitude.

In the Sacred Heart of Jesus, I shall always be happy to call myself, Monsieur le Directeur,

> Your grateful little Carmelite,
> *Sister Thérèse of the Child Jesus of the Holy Face,*
> *rel. carm. ind.*

CLXXXVIII

To the ABBÉ BELLIÈRE

J. M. J. T.

Jesus †

Lisieux Carmel, Wednesday
evening, 24 February 1897.

Monsieur l'Abbé,

Before entering upon the hallowed forty-day silence, I should like to add a brief word to our venerated Mother's letter to thank you for the one you sent me last month.

If you feel it a consolation that there is a sister in Carmel praying for you without ceasing, my own gratitude to Our Lord is no less than yours for giving me a younger brother whom He destines for His priest and His apostle. Truly, only in heaven will you know how dear you are to me. I feel that our souls are made to understand each other. Your style, which you call "rough and unpolished", reveals to me that Jesus has given your heart such aspirations as He gives only to souls called to the highest sanctity. Since it is He who chose me for your little sister, I hope that He will not consider my weakness, or rather that He will use that very weakness for the accomplishment of His work, since the God of Might loves to show His power by making use of nothingness.

United in Him, our souls will be able to save many others, for our sweet Jesus has said: "If two of you shall consent together concerning anything they shall ask my Father, it shall be done to them".[1] Ah! what we ask Him is that we may work for His Glory, that we may love Him and make others love Him! How could our union and our prayer fail to be blessed?

Since the poem upon Love[2] gave you pleasure, Monsieur l'Abbé, our good Mother has told me to copy out several others for you; but you won't receive them for some weeks, as I have very few free moments, even on Sunday, because of my work as sacristan.[3] These

[1] Matt. xviii. 19.
[2] The poem "Vivre d'amour" which she had written on 26 February 1895.
[3] Thérèse had been relieved of this work the year before, but had had to resume it. On the matter of her very scarce free time, it is interesting to read the unpublished testimony of Sister Geneviève of the Holy Face: "My darling sister never did

273

poor poems will show you, not what I am, but what I want to be and ought to be. . . . In writing them, I was more concerned with the substance than the form, so the rules of versification are not always respected. My aim was to express my feelings (or rather a Carmelite's feelings) in response to the desires of my sisters. The verses apply to a nun rather than to a seminarian, I hope all the same that they will please you.[1] For your soul is the betrothed of the Lamb of God, and it is soon to be His spouse, on the day of your ordination to the sub-diaconate.

Thank you, Monsieur l'Abbé, for choosing me as godmother of the first child you have the joy of baptising. So it is for me to choose the name of my future godchild. I desire to give him as protectors the Blessed Virgin, St. Joseph and St. Maurice, my dear little brother's patron-saint.[2] I imagine the child does not yet exist, save in the mind of the good God, but I am already praying for him and fulfilling my duty as godmother in advance. I pray too for all the souls that will be entrusted to you and I especially beg Jesus to adorn your own soul with every virtue, His love above all.

You tell me that you pray very often for your sister. Since you have that charity, I should be very glad if every day you would say this prayer for her, it includes all her desires: "Merciful Father, in the name of our sweet Jesus, of the Virgin Mary and the saints, I ask you to inflame my sister with Your spirit of Love and grant her the grace to make You greatly loved."

You have promised to pray for me *all your life*. I am sure it will be longer than mine: and you are not allowed to sing with me: "It is my hope, my exile will be short!" But neither are you allowed to forget your promise. If Our Lord takes me soon

---

anything for herself; her free time, her Sundays . . . all were spent in giving others pleasure. I noticed that when she was sacristan and her share of the work was finished, she made a point of going by the sacristy in order to be called upon. She would go where her assistant would see her so that she would be asked to do some task or other—as happened invariably. Knowing that in reality all this cost her a great deal, I signed to her not to go that way . . . I made it possible for her not to, but in vain."

[1] At Easter, Abbé Bellière replied: "I was enchanted with your poems. You wrote them for Carmelite nuns, but the angels must surely sing them with you, and men like me, less fine of feeling as we are, find a real charm in reading and singing such poetry of the heart. I liked them all, especially perhaps 'Mon chant d'aujourd'hui', 'A Théophane Vénard' (naturally), 'Rappelle-toi', 'A mon Ange gardien' . . ." Later the Abbé alludes to "Mes Armes" and to the "Cantique pour obtenir la glorification de Jeanne d'Arc".

[2] The Abbé's Christian name was Maurice.

to Himself, I ask you to go on saying the same little prayer daily, for in heaven I shall want the same thing as on earth: to love Jesus and make men love Him. Monsieur l'Abbé, you must find me very strange. Perhaps you regret having a sister apparently so anxious to go off and enjoy eternal rest, leaving you to work on alone. . . . But you need not worry, the only thing I desire is the good God's will, and I confess that if I could no longer work for His glory in heaven, I should like exile better than the Homeland. I do not know the future, but if Jesus brings to pass what I feel lies before me, I promise to remain your little sister up above. Our union will certainly not be broken, it will be closer than ever; then there will be no more cloister, no more grille, my soul can fly off with you to the remotest missions.

Our rôles will still be the same: for you the weapons of the apostolate, for me prayer and love.

I see that I have lost count of time, Monsieur l'Abbé, it is late, in a few minutes the bell will ring for divine office; but I have one further request. I should like you to set down for me the memorable dates of your life, that I may unite myself with you, in a very special way, in thanking our sweet Saviour for the graces He has granted you.

In the Sacred Heart of Jesus-Host, who will soon be exposed for our adoration,[1] I am happy to style myself for ever
Your very small and unworthy sister,

Thérèse of the Child Jesus of the Holy Face,
rel. carm. ind.

CLXXXIX

To SISTER MARIE OF THE SACRED HEART [2]

J. M. J. T.

The dear Jesus loves you with all His Heart and so do I, dearest Godmother ! ! : . . .

Thérèse of the Child Jesus,
rel. carm. ind.

---

[1] Quinquagesima Sunday, 28 February, and the Monday and Tuesday before Ash Wednesday, for the Forty Hours.
[2] Undated, written early in 1897.

CXC

To REVEREND MOTHER AGNES OF JESUS[1]

*One of the first predictions the Saint seems to have
made as to what her mission would be after death*

J. M. J. T.

19 March 1897.

Thank you, little Mother: Oh ! yes, Jesus loves you. . . . And
so do I ! He gives you proofs of it daily, and I don't. . . . True,
but when I am up there, my little arm will reach very far, and my
little Mother will hear of it. . . .

CXCI

To PÈRE ROULLAND

Jesus †   Lisieux Carmel, 19 March 1897.

Brother,
 Our good Mother has just given me your letters, in spite of Lent
(a time when we in Carmel do not write). She most kindly permits
me to answer you today, for we fear that our November letter
has paid a visit to the depths of the Blue River. Your letters,
dated September, made a prosperous journey and arrived to
rejoice your Mother and your little Sister on the feast of All
Saints; the one of January 20 reaches us under the protection of
St. Joseph. Since you follow my example and write on every
line, I must not lose so good a habit, but it makes my wretched
writing still harder to decipher.
 Ah ! how long must we wait till we have no need of ink and paper
to tell one another our thoughts ? You very nearly went, Brother,
to that magic country where they convey what is in their mind
without writing or even speech;[2] I thank God with all my
heart for leaving you on the battlefield, that you may win Him
many a victory. . . . Already your sufferings have saved many

---

[1] This note is written in pencil and unsigned.
[2] Père Roulland just escaped drowning on his arrival in China.

276

souls. St. John of the Cross says: "The smallest movement of pure love is more useful to the Church than all works put together".[1] If so, how profitable to the Church must your pains and trials be, since for the sole love of Jesus you suffer them with joy.

Truly, Brother, I cannot pity you, because in you are fulfilled the words of the *Imitation*: "When you find suffering sweet and love it for the love of Jesus Christ, you have found Paradise upon earth."[2] That is, in fact, the Paradise of the Missionary and the Carmelite; the joy the worldly seek from pleasure is a fleeting shadow, but our joy, sought and savoured in labour and suffering, is a most sweet reality, a foretaste of the bliss of heaven.

Your letter, shot through with holy gaiety, interested me deeply; I followed your example and laughed heartily at your cook: I can see him bashing in his saucepan. . . . Your visiting-card amused me too, I don't even know which way up to turn it, I am like a child trying to read a book upside down.[3]

But, to come back to your cook, would you believe that we too sometimes have amusing incidents in Carmel? Carmel, like Su-Chuen, is to the world a foreign country where the world's most elementary usages are lost; here is a small example. A charitable person recently made us a present of a *little* lobster, all tied up in a hamper. Naturally no such marvel had been seen in the Convent for a very long time; but our dear Sister Cook did remember that the little thing had to be put into water to be cooked; she did it, with much lamentation at having to treat an innocent creature so cruelly. The innocent creature was apparently asleep and let itself be handled without protest; but the moment it felt the heat, its mildness turned to fury. It knew its innocence and, without so much as a by-your-leave, leaped out onto the kitchen floor, for its soft-hearted executioner had not yet put the lid on the pot.

So poor Sister armed herself with tongs and rushed after the lobster which was leaping about frantically. The struggle lasted quite a time: at last, weary of battle, the Cook, still armed with the tongs, came to our Mother and told her that the lobster was certainly possessed. Her face was even more expressive than her words (poor little creature, a moment ago so mild, so innocent,

---

[1] *Explanation of the Spiritual Canticle*, strophe xxix.
[2] *Imitation of Christ*, bk. ii, ch. xii, 11.
[3] It was in Chinese characters.

now possessed ! Truly you can't trust the praise of "creatures" !).
Our Mother couldn't help laughing to hear the judge demanding
justice ; she went straight to the kitchen, seized the lobster—which,
not having made a vow of obedience, offered some resistance—
put it in its prison and went off after closing the door—that is,
the lid—tight. In the evening at recreation the whole Community
laughed till the tears ran at the little lobster possessed by the devil,
and next day everyone was able to enjoy *a mouthful.* . .

The donor wanted to give us a treat, and certainly succeeded ; for
the famous lobster, or rather its story, will serve again and again
as a feast not in the refectory but at recreation. Maybe my little
story does not strike you as very funny, but I can assure you that
had you been present you would not have kept your gravity.[1] . . .
Still, Brother, if I bore you please forgive me.

I now begin to speak more seriously. Since your departure, I
have read the lives of several missionaries (in the letter you may
not have received, I thanked you for the life of Père Nempon).
Among others I read Théophane Vénard's, which interested me
and touched me more than I can say ;[2] under the impression it
left on me I composed some verses, which are entirely personal ;[3]
I am sending them to you, all the same ; our good Mother told
me she thought these verses would please my brother in Su-
Chuen. The last stanza but one requires certain explanations : I
say I should be happy to set out for Tonking. . . . No, indeed !
it is not a dream ; in fact I can assure you that if Jesus doesn't
come soon and get me for the Carmel of Heaven, I'll start off one
day for the Carmel of Hanoï—there is one in that city now, founded
from the Saïgon Carmel. You have visited the last-named, and
you know that in Cochin-China an Order like ours cannot
maintain itself without French subjects ; but alas ! vocations are
very rare, and often Superiors are unwilling to let sisters go whom
they think capable of being useful to their own community. Thus
in her youth our good Mother was prevented, by the will of her

---

[1] It is noteworthy that, at this moment when she showed such gaiety, Thérèse
was growing seriously ill. During this Lent she began to find difficulty in swallowing
her food. Every day she ran a temperature. Her treatment included very painful
cauterisations.

[2] It was at Père Roulland's suggestion that she read this book. It was the beginning
of her great devotion to the young martyr—or rather of a "heavenly friendship"—
one of the greatest graces and consolations of her last days on earth.

[3] The poem "A Théophane Vénard". She wrote it, not at anyone's suggestion,
but of her own motion, from devotion to the martyr.

Superior, from going to help the Saïgon Carmel; I am the last one to complain of that ! I thank the good God for giving so true an inspiration to His representative; but I remember that the desires of mothers are often fulfilled in their children and I should not be surprised if I went off to the infidel shore to pray and suffer as our Mother wanted to. . . . It must be admitted, however, that the news we get from Tonking is not very comforting: at the end of last year, thieves got into the poor monastery, and made their way into the Prioress's cell; she did not wake, but in the morning she could not find her crucifix beside her (at night a Carmelite's crucifix lies always near her head, attached to the pillow), a small cupboard had been broken open and the handful of money which was all the Community's material treasure was gone. The Carmels of France, touched by the distress of Hanoï, clubbed together to give her the money for a wall high enough to keep thieves from getting into the Monastery.

Perhaps you are wondering what our Mother thinks of my desire to go to Tonking ? She believes in my vocation (truly a rather special one is needed, not every Carmelite feels the call to go into exile); but she does not believe my vocation can ever be fulfilled: for that, the scabbard would have to be as strong as the sword and perhaps (thinks our Mother) the scabbard would be thrown into the sea before it got to Tonking. . . . As a matter of fact, it's no great convenience to be composed of a body and a soul ! miserable Brother Ass, as St. Francis of Assisi called the body, often hinders his noble sister and prevents her from darting off where she would. . . . Still, I won't abuse him, for all his faults; he is still good for something, he helps his companion to get to heaven, and gets there himself. I am not in the least worried about the future, I am sure the good God will do what He wills: that is the one and only grace I desire—one must not be more royalist than the King. . . .

To accomplish His work, Jesus needs no one, and if He accepted me it would be sheer kindness; but to tell you the truth, Brother, I think it more likely that Jesus will treat me as a little idler; I don't want that, for I should be most happy to work and suffer for Him a long time: so I ask Him to act in me for His own satisfaction—that is, to pay no attention to my wishes, whether my wish to love Him in suffering, or my wish to come and enjoy Him in heaven. I do hope, Brother, that if I were to leave this exile, you would not forget your promise to pray for me; you have received all my requests so kindly that I venture to make this one more. I don't want you to ask God to deliver me from the flames of Purgatory. St. Teresa said to her daughters, when they wanted to pray for themselves: "What care I if I stay in Purgatory till the end of the world, if I save a single soul by my prayers."[1] That phrase finds an echo in my heart, I want to save souls and forget self for them; I want to save them even after my death, so I should be happy if—instead of the little prayer you say, which will be eternally fulfilled—you would say: "My God, permit my sister to go on making you loved." If Jesus hears you, I shall be well able to show you my gratitude.

You ask me, Brother, to choose between the two names, Marie or Thérèse, for one of the girls you are to baptise; since the Chinese don't want two saints to protect them but only one, they must have the more powerful, so the Blessed Virgin wins. Later, when you baptise a great many children, you would give great pleasure to my sister (a Carmelite, like me) by calling two little sisters Céline and Thérèse, the names we bore in the world.

Céline, nearly four years older than I, joined me here, after she had closed our good Father's eyes; this dear sister of mine does not know the close relation that exists between you and me;[2] but as we often speak at recreation of Our Mother's missionary (the name you bear at the Lisieux Carmel), she recently told me of her desire that, through you, Céline and Thérèse might go to China to start life over again.

Please, Brother, forgive my requests and my too lengthy chatter, and in your goodness bless your unworthy little sister,

Thérèse of the Child Jesus of the Holy Face,
rel. carm. ind.

[1] *Way of Perfection*, ch. iii.
[2] See note to Letter CLXVIII.

CXCII

To SISTER MARIE OF ST. JOSEPH

A professed nun at the Lisieux Carmel[1]

J. M. J. T.[2]

The little verses are charming ! . . . How shameful it is to go begging from others when one's own purse is full ![3] But it is not shameful to sleep, to be kind and gay; that is "the little art of keeping shop",[4] and the shop must never close, not even on Sundays and holydays—the days Jesus reserves to Himself to test our souls. . . . Sing your lovely songs like a finch;[5] as for me, I moan away in my corner *like a* poor little *sparrow*,[6] singing, like the Wandering Jew "la mort ne me peut rien, je m'en aperçois bien".[7]

I have heard no further talk of the famous cloth;[8] has the idea been dropped ?

[1] She was fifteen years older than Thérèse and died some time after her. The usual biographical notice was not sent to the Convents of the Order. She was neurotic but showed great confidence in Thérèse who, knowing that she was difficult to bear on account of her psychological ailment, had asked to be her assistant in looking after the linen and did her best to comfort and encourage her most charitably. Sister Marie of St. Joseph retained a feeling of veneration and great gratitude to Thérèse.

[2] This note and those that followed are undated. They are certainly of the beginning of the year, but lacking more precise information, it seemed best to publish them one after the other, about this period. Only one is signed.

[3] The reference is to some verses written by the Sister.

[4] From a song sung at Les Buissonnets.

[5] Sister Marie had a very fine voice.

[6] Ps. ci. 8.

[7] "Death can do nothing to me, I see"—from a song Thérèse knew as a child.

[8] The reference is to a mending job that was to have been done by the Sisters in charge of the linen.

CXCIII

To THE SAME

J. M. J. T.

Is it wicked to keep awake,[1] "little brother" ?[2] *No*, a thousand times *no* ! . . . I am not surprised that p.f.[3] has his struggles, but only that he wastes his small strength by surrendering his arms to the first corporal he meets and even chasing him up the barrack-stairs to force him to take his armour, down to the smallest piece. Is it surprising, after that, if a burning sun—ordinarily borne with fortitude—falling on the defenceless little soldier, burns him and gives him fever ? . . .

For punishment his p.f. condemns him to be shut up in the prison of love and *sleep* all carefree . . . otherwise p.f. will be disappointed.

(Above all, don't stay awake ! tomorrow, we'll really go to work together ![4] . . .)

CXCIV

To THE SAME

J. M. J. T.

All goes well, the Small Boy[5] is a hero and deserves *gold* epaulettes. But let him never again lower himself to fight with little stones, it is unworthy of him. His weapon should be Charity.

Everything else goes well too, since the Small Boy laughs at *Messire Satanas* and always sleeps on the Great General's Heart. . . . Close to that heart, one learns valiance, and above all *confidence*. Grapeshot, the roar of cannon, what is any of it when one is upheld by the General ? . . .

---

[1] Sister Marie wanted to stay awake to work.

[2] A nickname Thérèse gave Sister Marie to draw her out of her gloom. It is to be noted that these gay, pleasant lines were written at a time when Thérèse was stricken with a grave illness and was suffering internal pains which she calls a *torment* (cf. *Histoire d'une âme*, ch. ix). This gay heroism was to show itself in many ways up to Thérèse's death.

[3] Short for *petit frère*, little brother.

[4] A reference to work on the linen.

[5] So Sister Marie called herself.

CXCV

To THE SAME

J. M. J. T.

The little brother agrees with the Small Boy.

The most *pain-filled*, the most LOVE-FILLED martyrdom is ours, since it is seen by Jesus alone.

It will never be revealed to creatures upon earth, but when the Lamb opens the *book of life*, what a surprise for the Court of heaven to hear, along with the names of missionaries and martyrs, the names of poor little children who have never done anything outstanding.

I am going on mending the worst damaged toques.[1]

CXCVI

To THE SAME

Jesus †

I am enchanted with the Small Boy, and *He* who holds him in His arms is even more enchanted than I. . . . Ah ! how beautiful is the Small Boy's vocation ! It is not *a* mission he is to evangelise but *all missions*. How ? By *loving*, *sleeping*, STREWING FLOWERS upon Jesus while He sleeps. Then Jesus will take the flowers and, conferring upon them an inestimable value, will strew them in His turn, will send them flying off to all shores and will save souls with the flowers, with the love of the *Small Boy* who will see none of this, but will keep smiling even through his tears ! . . . (How marvellous a thing is a child missionary and warrior.)

---

[1] She says "soigner les toques très malades". "Toques" are white guimpes worn by Carmelites under their veils.

CXCVII

To THE SAME

J. M. J. T.

What a wretched thing it is to spend one's time worrying miserably about oneself instead of sleeping on Jesus' Heart.

If the night terrifies the Small Boy, if he complains at not *seeing* the One who bears him up, *let him close his eyes*: let him *willingly* make the sacrifice asked of him and then wait for sleep to come ! . . . So he remains at peace, and the night, which he no longer notices, cannot frighten him: and soon serenity, if not joy, will be born again in his heart. Is it too much to ask him to close his eyes ? Not to struggle with the chimeras of the night ? No, it is not too much, and the Small Boy is going to let himself go, believe that he is in Jesus' arms, be content with not seeing Him and leave far behind the sterile fear that he is unfaithful (a fear which does not go with childhood).

Signed: An Ambassador.

CXCVIII

To THE SAME

The little A.[1] has no thought of jumping off the boat, he is there to make the Small Boy[2] look at heaven; he wants all the Small Boy's gaze to be upon Jesus and all his attentions for Him. So he would be very glad to see the Small Boy do without consolations that are too childish and below the dignity of a missionary and warrior. . . . I love my p.E.[3] deeply . . . and Jesus loves him even more.

[1] Ambassador of Jesus.
[2] Thérèse writes "petit Enfant".
[3] Initials of "petit Enfant".

284

CXCIX

To THE SAME

I hope Sister Geneviève reassured you;[1] the thought that you have stopped worrying makes me stop worrying !

Ah ! how happy we shall be in heaven; there we shall participate in the divine perfections and shall be able to give to everybody without depriving those dearest to us. . . . The good God was right not to give us this power on earth; perhaps we should not have wanted to leave it; and anyhow it is so good for us to realise that He alone is perfect, that He alone should suffice us, when He pleases to take away the branch the little bird was sitting on.

The bird has wings, it is meant to fly!

CC

To REVEREND MOTHER AGNES OF JESUS[2]

J. M. J. T.

5 April 1897.

I'm afraid I've hurt my little Mother; I love her, all the same; I do indeed, but I cannot tell her all that is in my mind, she has to know it for herself.

CCI

To ABBÉ BELLIÈRE

J. M. J. T.

25 April 1897.

Alleluia

My dear little Brother,

My pen, or rather my heart, refuses to go on calling you "Monsieur l'Abbé", and our good Mother told me that in writing to you I could use the name I always use when I speak of you to Jesus. I feel that our divine Saviour in His goodness has united

---

[1] Sister Marie had been much upset to learn that Thérèse was very seriously ill.
[2] This letter is *unsigned* and *written in pencil.*

our souls to work for the salvation of sinners, as long ago He united the souls of the Venerable Père de la Colombière and Blessed Margaret Mary. I recently read in her life: "One day when I was approaching Our Lord to receive Him in Hóly Communion, He showed me His Sacred Heart as a flaming furnace and two other hearts (her own and Père de la Colombière's) joining together and plunging into it: and He said: 'Thus it is that my pure love unites these three hearts for ever.' Further He showed me that this union was all for His glory and that therefore He wanted us to be as a brother and sister with spiritual goods shared equally. At that point, I represented to our Lord my poverty and the inequality there was between a priest of such great virtue and a poor sinful woman like me, but He said: 'The infinite riches of my Heart will supply for all and remove all inequality.'"

Perhaps, Brother, the comparison strikes you as inexact. You, of course, are not yet a Père de la Colombière, but I do not doubt that one day you will be like him, a true apostle of Christ. Nor does it occur to me to compare myself in any way with the Blessed Margaret Mary; I simply note that Jesus has chosen me to be the sister of one of His apostles, and the words the saintly Lover of His Heart addressed to Him through *humility*, *I* repeat to Him in *all truth*. So I hope that His infinite riches will supply for all that is lacking in me that I may accomplish the task He entrusts to me.

I am truly happy that the good God has used my poor verses to do you a little good. I should have been embarrassed to send them to you, if I had not remembered that a sister should keep nothing from her brother. It is with a truly fraternal heart that you have received them and judged them. You must have been surprised to get "Vivre d'amour" again. I did not mean to send it to you twice. I had begun to copy it when it struck me that you had it already, and it was too late to stop.

My dear Brother, I must confess that in your letter there is one thing that pains me—namely that you do not know me as I really am. It is true that to find great souls, you must come to Carmel; just as in virgin forests there grow flowers of a fragrance and brilliance unknown to the world. Jesus in His mercy has willed that among these flowers smaller ones should grow; never shall I be able to thank Him for it enough, for it is owing to this condescension that I, a poor flower of no brilliance, am in the same garden-bed as the roses, my sisters. O my Brother! believe me, I beg you, the good God has not given you a *great* soul for your sister, but a *very small* and very imperfect one.

Do not believe that it is humility that keeps me from realising the good God's gifts, I know that "He has done great things in me",[1] and I sing it daily, with joy. I know that one "to whom more is forgiven should love more";[2] so I try to make my life an act of love, and I no longer worry because I am a *little* soul, indeed I rejoice at it; it is why I venture to hope that "my exile will be short"; but this is not because I am *ready*, I feel I never shall be, unless Our Lord Himself deign to transform me. He can do it in an instant; after all the graces He has showered upon me, I still await the grace of His infinite mercy.

You tell me, Brother, to ask the grace of martyrdom for you. I have often begged that grace for myself, but I am not worthy of it, and truly one can say with St. Paul: "It is not of him that wills, nor of him that runs, but of God that shows mercy".[3]

Since Our Lord seems willing to grant me only the martyrdom of love, I hope He will allow me to gather the *other palm* of our ambition, *through you*. I see with pleasure that the good God has given us the same tastes, the same desires. I made you smile, dear little Brother, by my poem "Mes Armes"; but—I shall make you smile even more when I tell you that as a child I dreamt of fighting on battlefields. When I began to learn the history of France, the story of Joan of Arc's exploits entranced me; I felt in my heart the desire and the courage to imitate her; it seemed to me that Our Lord meant me for great things too. I was not mistaken, but in place of voices from heaven calling me to war, I heard in the depths of my soul a voice sweeter, more powerful still, the voice of the Spouse of virgins calling me to other exploits, conquests more glorious, and in the solitude of Carmel I realised that my mission was not to get a mortal King crowned but to get the King of Heaven loved, to bring the realm of hearts under His sway.

It is time to stop; but I have still to thank you for the dates you sent me;[4] I should be glad if you would add the years, as I don't know your age.

That you may excuse my simplicity, I am sending you the

[1] Luke i. 49.
[2] Cf. Luke vii. 47.
[3] Rom. ix. 16.
[4] His anniversaries.

memorable dates of my own life—this, too, to the end that we may be especially united by prayer and gratitude on those blest days.

If the good God gives me a little goddaughter, I shall be very happy to grant your wish by giving her for protectors the Blessed Virgin, St. Joseph and my holy Patroness.

And so, dear little Brother, I end with a plea for your forgiveness for my lengthy scrawl and the disjointedness of my letter.

In the sacred Heart of Jesus I am, for eternity, your unworthy little Sister,

> *Thérèse of the Child Jesus of the Holy Face,*
> *rel. carm. ind.*

In the margin the Saint added:

(It is understood, of course, that our relation remains secret. No one, except your Director, is to know the union Jesus has formed between our hearts.)

CCII

To SISTER ANNE OF THE SACRED HEART[1]

A Carmelite nun of Saïgon

J. M. J. T.

Jesus †

2 May, Feast of the Good Shepherd, 1897.

My very dear Sister,

I am sure you will be surprised to get a letter from me. So that you may forgive me for disturbing the silence of your solitude, I shall tell you how it comes that I have the pleasure of writing to you. The last time I went to our good Mother for direction, we spoke of you and of the dear Carmel at Saïgon. Our Mother told me that I had her permission to write to you if it gave me pleasure. I received the suggestion with joy, and I am profiting

---

[1] She was born in Indo-China in 1850, of a Portuguese father and an Annamite mother, and entered the Carmel at Saïgon, where she was professed 8 September 1876. Later she asked permission to enter the Carmel at Lisieux. In June 1883 she was received there "with happiness"—we read in the book of the Foundations of the Lisieux Carmel—"as a link uniting our Carmel to our beloved foundation at Saïgon". She went back to Saïgon in 1895; so that Thérèse had lived with her several years. She died 24 July 1920.

by the "licence",[1] on the feast of the Good Shepherd, to come and chat with you for a few moments.

I hope, dear Sister, that you have not forgotten me; I certainly think very often of you, I remember with happiness the years I spent in your company, and as you know, for a Carmelite, thinking of a person one loves means praying for him. I ask God to fill you to overflowing with His graces, and daily to increase His holy love in your heart, though I do not doubt that you possess that love in an eminent degree. The burning sun of Saïgon is as nothing to the fire that flames in your soul. O Sister, please ask Jesus that I too may love Him and make Him loved; I want to love Him, not with ordinary love, but like the Saints who committed follies for Him. Alas ! how far I am from resembling them ! . . . Ask Jesus, too, that I may always do His will; for that, I am ready to cross the world . . . and I am ready to die, too !

Silence[2] will finish in a moment, I must end my letter and I see that I haven't yet told you anything of interest; fortunately our Mother's letters are there to give you news of our Carmel. Our "licence" has been very short, but, if you don't find it a nuisance, I shall come for a longer talk another time.

Will you please, my very dear Sister, give my respectful and filial greeting to your Reverend Mother, she does not know me, but I often hear *her* spoken of by our good Mother, I love her and I beg Jesus to comfort her in her trials.

I leave you, dear Sister, but remain very close to you in the Heart of Jesus, there I am happy to style myself for ever[3]

Your very little Sister,

Thérèse of the Child Jesus of the Holy Face,
rel. carm. ind.

---

[1] So Carmelites call a conversation they are allowed to have, on a day of extraordinary recreation, with the permission of the Prioress.
[2] The hour of free time between Compline and Matins.
[3] A copy of this letter was sent by Sister Anne to the Lisieux Carmel, dated 3 July 1910.

CCIII

To PÈRE ROULLAND

The Saint was alluding to this letter when she said to Reverend Mother Agnes of Jesus on 16 July following: "Mother, in my copybook [the manuscript of her life] I have said only a word or two on the good God's Justice. But, if you wish, you will find the whole of my thought in a letter to Père Roulland in which I have made my view clear."

J. M. J. T.

Lisieux Carmel, 9 May 1897.

Brother,

I received with joy, or rather with emotion, the relics[1] you were kind enough to send me. Your letter is almost a "Goodbye till heaven" letter. Reading it, I felt I was hearing the story of the trials of your ancestors in the apostolate. On this earth where everything changes, one thing alone remains stable, the conduct of the King of Heaven to His friends; "Since He has raised the standard of the Cross" it is in its shadow that all must fight and gain the victory.[2] "The life of every missionary is founded in the cross," said Théophane Vénard, and again: "True happiness is to suffer, and to live we must die."

Brother, the beginning of your apostolate is marked with the seal of the Cross, Our Lord treats you as one privileged: it is much more by persecution and suffering than by brilliant sermons that He wills to establish His Kingdom in souls. You say "I am still a little child, unable to speak".[3] Père Mazel, who was ordained the same day as you, could not speak either, yet he has already gathered the palm[4]. . . .

Oh! how far above our thoughts are God's! Learning of the death of this young missionary, whose name I was hearing for the

---

[1] The lock of hair Thérèse had asked for (see Letter CLXXVIII).
[2] *Meditations sur les Mystères de la Foi et sur les Epîtres et les Evangiles*, by a Solitary of Sept-Fons: Meditation for the Thursday of the twenty-fourth week after Pentecost.
[3] He did not know Chinese.
[4] Père Mazel (of the Society of Foreign Missions) had not been long in China. On his way to the post his superiors had assigned him he was killed, April 1897, by brigands *because he was a European and a Frenchman.*

first time, I felt drawn to invoke him, I seemed to see him in heaven, in the glorious choir of martyrs. I know that in the eyes of men his martyrdom does not bear the name, but, in the sight of God, such a sacrifice without glory is no less fruitful than that of the first Christians, confessing their faith before tribunals. Persecution has changed its form. Christ's apostles have not changed their feelings, so their divine Master cannot change His rewards, unless to increase them in recompense for the glory refused them here below.

I do not understand, Brother, why you seem to doubt of your immediate entry into heaven, if the infidels took your life. I know one must be most pure to appear before he God of all holiness, but I know too that the Lord is infinitely just; and it is this justice, which terrifies so many souls, that is the basis of my joy and trust. To be just means not only to exercise severity in punishing the guilty, but also to recognise right intentions and reward virtue. I hope as much from the good God's justice as from His mercy—because He "is compassionate and merciful, long-suffering and plenteous in mercy. For He knows our weakness. He remembers that we are but dust. As a father has compassion on his children, so the Lord has compassion on us ! . . ."[1] O my Brother, hearing those lovely consoling words of the Prophet-King, how can we doubt that the good God will open the gates of His kingdom to His children who have loved Him to the point of sacrificing all for Him, who not only have left family and country to make him known and loved, but also desire to give their life for the One they love . . . Rightly did Jesus say that "there is no greater love"[2] than that ! How then can He possibly let Himself be outpassed in generosity ?

How can He purify in the flames of Purgatory souls consumed in the fires of divine love ? Of course no human life is free from faults, only the immaculate Virgin presents herself in absolute purity before God's Majesty. What a joy to remember that

[1] Ps. cii. 8, 14, 13.

[2] John xv. 13. In his letter of 24 February, to which the Saint was replying, Père Roulland has written : "At this moment we are not in imminent danger of death, but from one day to the next, we might be stabbed ; we should not be martyrs in the full sense of the term, but if we direct our intention aright—if we say, for instance 'My God, it is for love of you that we have come here, accept the sacrifice of our lives and convert souls'—should we not be martyrs enough to go to Heaven ? . . . Anyhow, we are at the good God's disposal ; if the brigands murder me and I am not admitted into Heaven at once, you will get me out of Purgatory and I shall go and wait for you in Paradise."

she is our Mother ! Since she loves us and knows our weakness, what have we to fear ? What a lot of phrases to express my thought, or rather to manage not to express it; I simply wanted to say that it seems to me that all missionaries are *martyrs* by desire and will, and that, in consequence, not one should go to Purgatory. If, at the moment they appear before God, some traces of human weakness remain in their souls, the Blessed Virgin obtains for them the grace to make an act of perfect love, and then gives them the palm and the crown they have so truly merited.

That, Brother, is my idea of the good God's justice, my way is all of trust and love, I don't understand souls who are afraid of so loving a Friend. Sometimes, when I read spiritual treatises, in which perfection is shown with a thousand obstacles in the way and a host of illusions round about it, my poor little mind grows very soon weary, I close the learned book, which leaves my head muddled and my heart parched, and I take the Holy Scripture. Then all seems luminous, a single word opens up infinite horizons to my soul, perfection seems easy; I see that it is enough to realise one's nothingness, and give ourself wholly, like a child, into the arms of the good God.

Leaving to great souls, great minds, the fine books I can't understand, I rejoice to be little, because "only children, and those who are like them, will be admitted to the heavenly banquet."[1] I am so happy that "in the Kingdom of God there are many mansions",[2] for if there were but the one, the description of which and the way to which seem to me incomprehensible, I could not get in. All the same I should like to be not too far from *your mansion*; in consideration of your merits, I hope the good God will grant me the grace to share in your glory, just as on earth the sister of a conqueror, though she lack all natural gifts, does, in spite of her poverty, share in the honours paid her brother.

The first act of your ministry in China seems to me delightful. The little soul whose mortal remains you blessed must surely be smiling down on you and promising its protection to you and yours. How grateful I am to you for counting me among them. I am deeply moved and grateful, too, for your remembrance of my dearest parents at Holy Mass. I hope they are now in possession of Heaven, for to it tended all their actions and desires.

[1] Cf. Matt. xix. 14.   [2] John xiv. 2.

This does not mean that we are not to pray for them, for it seems to me that the souls of the blest must receive great glory from the prayers offered for their intention, prayers which they can use for other souls still suffering.

If, as I believe, my Father and Mother are in Heaven, they must look upon the brother Jesus has given me and bless him. They had so desired a son, to be a missionary! I have been told that before my birth they hoped that their wish was at last to be fulfilled. Had they been able to pierce the veil of the future, they would have seen that it was indeed through me that their wish was to be fulfilled; since a missionary has become my brother, he is also their son and in their prayers they cannot separate the brother from his unworthy sister.

You pray, Brother, for my parents in Heaven; I say many prayers for yours, still on earth; I find it a most sweet obligation and I promise you always to fulfil it faithfully, even if I leave this exile—even more so perhaps, for I should better know the graces they need; and then, when their course here below is finished, I shall come and seek them out in your name and introduce them to Heaven. How pleasant will be the family life we shall enjoy for all eternity! While awaiting that blissful eternity, which will open to us so soon since life is but a day, let us work together for the salvation of souls; I of course can do very little, absolutely nothing in fact, alone; what encourages me is the thought that by your side I can be of *some* use; after all zero, by itself, has no value, but put alongside *one* it becomes potent, always provided it is put on the *proper side*, after and not before! . . . That in fact is where Jesus has put me, and I hope to remain there always, following you afar off by prayer and sacrifice.

If I listened to my heart, I should not end my letter today, but the end of silence is about to ring, I must take my letter to our good Mother, who is waiting for it. So please, Brother, be good enough to send your blessing to the *little zero* the good God has put beside you.

Sister Thérèse of the Child Jesus of the Holy Face,
rel. carm. ind.

CCIV

To REVEREND MOTHER AGNES OF JESUS[1]

Who had written in pencil on a scrap of paper :

I cannot tell you what passes in my soul about you, it is unutterable. Can I, in spite of your vagabond walks, manage to get a bare quarter-hour's conversation with you ?[2]

Thérèse answered on the back of the same scrap, also in pencil :
I must "keep walking till my last moment—that is what will end my torment"[3]—like the poor Wandering Jew.

CCV

To SISTER GENEVIÈVE

For the anniversary of her first communion

13 May 1897.

Jesus is pleased with His little Céline, to whom He gave Himself for the first time seventeen years ago. He is prouder of what He has done in her soul, of her littleness and poverty, than of having created millions of suns and the whole expanse of the heavens. . . .

CCVI

To REVEREND MOTHER AGNES OF JESUS

Who was grieved to see the Saint's health grow daily worse

J. M. J. T.

23 May 1897.

I am much afraid I have given my little Mother pain ! Oh !
I so wanted to be her little joy, and now I feel I am her little

---

[1] Undated.
[2] In obedience to her first infirmarian and at the cost of very heavy fatigue, the Saint took walks in the garden (cf. *Histoire d'une âme*, ch. xii. "I'm walking for a missionary.").
[3] From a song they used to sing at Les Buissonnets.

sorrow. . . . That is so, but—when I am far from this sad earth where flowers fade and birds fly away, I shall be very near my dearest Mother, the angel that Jesus sent before me to *prepare the way*[1] for me, the way that leads to heaven, the lift to raise me without fatigue to the infinite regions of love. . . . Yes, I shall be very near her, and that without leaving the Homeland, for *I* shall not *descend* but my little Mother will *ascend* where I am. Oh ! if I could express my thoughts as she does, if I could tell her how my heart overflows with gratitude and love for her, I think I should be her little joy even now, without waiting till I am far from this sad earth.

Dearest little Mother, the good you have done to my soul, you have done to Jesus, for He says: "What you shall do to *the least of* these my brethren, you shall do it unto me".[2] And *I* am the *least* ! . . .

CCVII

To REVEREND MOTHER AGNES OF JESUS

That day, while Thérèse was suffering with a very high tempera-ture, one of the sisters came and asked her immediate assistance in a piece of painting of considerable difficulty ; for a moment Thérèse's face betrayed her inner struggle, and Mother Agnes of Jesus saw it. In the evening Thérèse wrote this letter :

J. M. J. T.

28 May 1897.

Dearest little Mother,

Your little girl has just been shedding more tears; tears of repentance, but even more of gratitude and love. Ah ! this even-ing, I showed my virtue, my TREASURES *of patience* ! And I, who am so good at preaching to others ! ! ! I am glad you saw my imperfection. Ah ! what good it does me to have been bad ! You have not scolded your little girl, though she deserved it; but the little girl is used to that, your mildness affects her more deeply than stern words; for her you are the image of the good God's *mercy*.

[1] Cf. Mark i. 2.   [2] Matt. xxv. 40.

Yes, but on the other hand Sister ———— is *usually* the image of the good God's *severity*. Well, I have just met her. Instead of passing me coldly by, she kissed me, saying (exactly as if I had been the dearest little girl in the world): "Poor little Sister, you stirred me to pity ! I don't want to tire you, I was wrong, etc. etc."

In my own heart I felt perfect contrition, and I could not get over her uttering no reproach. I realise that in actual fact she must find me very imperfect: it is because she thinks I'm going to die that she has spoken to me like that. No matter, I heard none but kind and loving words from her mouth; so I find her very good and myself very bad !

Entering my cell, I began to wonder what Jesus was thinking of me. Immediately I recalled the words He addressed one **day** to the adulterous woman: "Does any one condemn you ?"[1] And with tears in my eyes I answered Him: "No one, Lord . . . neither my little Mother, the image of Your love, nor Sister ————, the image of Your justice; and I feel that I may surely go in peace, for You do not condemn me either!"

Little Mother, *why* is dear Jesus so gentle to me ? Why does He never scold me ? Ah ! truly I might well die of gratitude and love.

I am happier for having been imperfect than if, upheld by grace, I had been a model of sweetness. . . . It does me so much good to see that Jesus is always so sweet, so loving to me ! . . . Ah ! from this moment I realise that all my hopes will indeed be fulfilled . . . the Lord will do marvels for us, infinitely beyond our *immeasurable desires* ! . . .

Little Mother, Jesus does well to hide, to speak to me only now and then, and "through the bars" at that (Cant. of Cant.);[2] for I feel that I could not bear any more, my heart would break, powerless to contain so much happiness. . . . Ah ! you, who are the sweet echo of my soul, will realise that this evening the vessel of divine mercy has overflowed for me ! . . . you will realise that you have been, and will always be, the angel charged to guide me and announce the Lord's mercies to me ! . . .

Your *very little girl*,

Thérèse of the Child Jesus of the Holy Face,
rel. carm. ind.

[1] John viii. 10.
[2] The reference in the text is given by Thérèse herself. She is quoting ch. ii. 9.

CCVIII

To REVEREND MOTHER AGNES OF JESUS

As Thérèse had not received from Mother Marie de Gonzague, then Prioress, permission to tell her own sisters of her spitting of blood on Good Friday (3 April 1896), Mother Agnes of Jesus had just learnt of it, and was much afflicted at having been so long unaware, though she had known that her sister was ill. The Saint is consoling her.

J. M. J. T.

30 May 1897.

Do not be grieved, my dearest little Mother, that *your* little girl has *seemed* to be hiding something from you; I say "seemed", for, you realise, if she has hidden a small corner of the *envelope*,[1] she has never hidden from you a single line of the *letter*, so who knows better than you the little letter you love so much? To others, one can show all of the envelope, since that is all they can see, but to you !!! . . . Oh, little Mother, you know now that it was on Good Friday that Jesus began to make a slight tear in the envelope of *your* little letter. Are you not pleased that He is getting ready to read it, the letter you have been writing this twenty-four years? Ah ! . . . . it will indeed tell Him of your love for all eternity.

CCIX

To REVEREND MOTHER AGNES OF JESUS

J. M. J. T.

30 May 1897.

(2nd brief note).

I put my first brief word[2] into Sister Geneviève's hand[3] as she was giving me yours, now I regret[4] having "posted" my note, I am going to pay excess postage to tell you that I perfectly understand

---

[1] The Saint used to call her body "the envelope", her soul "the letter".
[2] The previous letter.
[3] As infirmarian she carried messages to and from the sick.
[4] Spelt "gé raîgrette"—an allusion to a comic story in which one of the characters pronounced the words so.

how hurt you are; I was more anxious than you, perhaps, to hide nothing from you, but it seemed to me that I must wait; if I did wrong, forgive me and believe that I have *never* lacked confidence in you ! . . . Ah ! I love you too much for that ! . . . I do not remember ever having hidden anything else about the *envelope* from my little Mother and beg her, after my death, simply not to believe what may be told her. Oh ! little Mother, the *letter* is *yours*, please continue to read it till the day when Jesus tears up the little envelope which has caused you so much trouble since it was made ! . . .

CCX

To REVEREND MOTHER AGNES OF JESUS[1]

Who had written her a few lines

†

J. M. J. T.

1 June 1897.

It is *too* touching, *too* melodious ! . . . I would rather stay silent than make a vain effort to sing what is passing in my little soul ! . . . Thank you, little Mother.

CCXI

To REVEREND MOTHER AGNES OF JESUS

Who had lovingly scolded Thérèse for wanting to leave her for heaven

2 June 1897.

No, the little dove does not want to leave its little Mother, it wants always to *fly and take its rest*[2] in the enchanting little world of her heart. Tomorrow I shall say thank you to my little Mother. This evening I say nothing, so as not to pierce her heart and because it is too late. Baby go to sleep.[3]

[1] This letter and the next are in pencil. [2] Cf. Ps. liv. 6.
[3] Bébé va faire dodo.

CCXII

To SISTER MARIE OF THE EUCHARIST

She was taking the Veil:[1] *Thérèse gave her a picture of the Child Jesus which she had had for some time in her breviary. She had written on the back :*

In memory of the lovely day of my dearest little Sister's taking the veil: 2 June 1897.

May Thérèse's Child Jesus always caress Marie of the Eucharist.

The following note accompanied the picture :

J. M. J. T.

2 June 1897.

To my dearest little Sister, in memory of the lovely day on which the Spouse of her soul deigned to place His sign on the brow that He intends one day to crown, in the presence of all the Elect. . . .

Years ago, the whole of Heaven assembled on June 2 to contemplate this mystery of love—Jesus, the loving Jesus of the Eucharist, giving Himself for the first time to Marie. It is there again today, the splendid Heaven of Angels and Saints, it is there, in ecstasy contemplating Marie, as she gives herself to Jesus in face of a world startled at a sacrifice it does not understand. Ah ! if it had understood the *look* that Jesus cast upon Marie on the day of His first visit, it would also understand the *mysterious sign* she wills to receive today from Him who has wounded her with love. . . . No longer is the graceful snow-white veil with its long folds to enwrap Marie of the Eucharist, but a dark veil, to recall to Jesus' spouse that she is an exile, that her Spouse is a Spouse who will not lead her to festivals but up the hill of Calvary. Henceforth, Marie must consider *nothing* here below, *nothing* but the *God of mercy*, the *Jesus of the* EUCHARIST ! . . .

Little *Sister Thérèse of the Child Jesus of the Holy Face*,
rel. carm. ind.

[1] On the anniversary of her First Communion.

CCXIII

To SISTER MARIE OF THE TRINITY

Jesus †   6 June 1897.

My darling Sister,

Your nice little letter rejoices my soul; I see that I was certainly not wrong in thinking that God calls you to be a great saint, while still remaining *little*, and becoming more so every day. I understand the pain you feel at not being able now to talk to me, but you can be sure that I suffer too from my powerlessness, and that I have never felt so much that you hold an *immense* place in my *heart* !

One thing that gives me pleasure is to realise that sorrow does not make you melancholy; I could not keep from laughing as I read the end of your letter. Ah ! so that's how you laugh at me ! And who has told you of *my writing*! to what folios do you allude ?[1] I see that you are asserting the false to find out the true. All right, you will know it one day,[2] if not on earth, then in Heaven: but it certainly won't trouble you much, we shall have other things to think about then. . . .

You ask if I am joyful at going to Paradise ? I should be very joyful *if* I went there, but . . . I don't rely on sickness, it is too slow a *guide*. I now *rely only* on *love*; ask the good Jesus that all the prayers offered for me may serve to build up the Fire which is to consume me.

I fancy you won't be able to read this; I am sorry,[3] but I had only a few minutes.

[1] The reference is to the manuscript (begun 3 June at the request of Mother Marie de Gonzague) which was to be ch. ix and x of her *Histoire d'une âme.*

[2] Naturally Sister Marie came to know it, along with the whole community, but also by a special title: for it was her task, until her death, to aid the Prioress and Thérèse's sisters in the publication of her writing.

[3] See note to Letter CCIX.

CCXIV

To SISTER MARIE OF THE TRINITY[1]

*Who wished to go without Holy Communion because of
an imperfection which she had repented*

J. M. J. T.

Little flower beloved of Jesus, I understand the whole thing perfectly. Realise that it is unnecessary to tell me everything in detail, the *tiny eye* in your calyx shows me what to think of the whole little flower.[2] . . . I am very pleased, very much consoled, but you must no longer *want* to *eat* earth, the forget-me-not[3] need only open, or rather upraise its petals for the *Bread of angels* to come like a divine Dew to strengthen it and give it all it lacks. . . .

Good night, poor flowerlet, take my word that I love you more than you think ! . . .

CCXV

To SISTER GENEVIÈVE

*Who had expressed her admiration at Thérèse's patience
during a long and fatiguing session before the camera
(see note to Letter CCXXIX) and her own fear that she
would be unable to imitate so perfect an example*

J. M. J. T.

7 June 1897.

Beloved little Sister, never seek after what seems great to the eyes of creatures. Solomon, the wisest king there ever was upon the earth, having considered all the various labours that occupy men under the sun—painting, sculpture, all the arts—realised that *all* these *things* were *subject to envy* and cried out that they are nought but "vanity and affliction of spirit".[4]

---

[1] Undated, written in June 1897.
[2] In other words, a look is enough.
[3] Sister Marie of the Trinity (see Letter CLXVII).
[4] Eccles. i. 14.

The one thing that is not *envied* is the last place; the *last place* is the one thing that is not vanity and affliction of spirit.

Yet "the way of man is not his own"[1] and sometimes we surprise ourselves by wanting something that catches the eye. Then we must number ourselves humbly with the imperfect, see ourselves as *little souls* which God must uphold from instant to instant. The moment He sees us convinced of our nothingness, He reaches out His hand: if we still want to try some *great* thing, even under colour of zeal, the good Jesus leaves us to ourselves: "If I said: My foot is moved; thy mercy, O Lord, assisted me" (Ps. XCIII).[2] Yes, it is enough if we humble ourselves and bear our imperfections patiently: that is true sanctity. Let us take each other's hand, darling Sister, and run to the last place, no one will dispute it with us.

CCXVI

To ABBÉ BELLIÈRE

On June 9, the Saint, finding herself much worse, wrote this letter, which was not sent.[3]

J. M. J. T.

Jesus †   9 June 1897.

My dear little Brother,

I received your letter this morning, and take advantage of a moment when the infirmarian is out of the room to write you a last short word of farewell; when you get it, I shall have come out of exile. Your little sister will be united to Jesus for ever; then she will be able to obtain graces for you and fly with you to distant Missions.

Oh! my Brother, how glad I am to die! . . . Yes, I am glad, not because I shall be delivered from sufferings here below (on the contrary, suffering is the one thing I see as desirable in the valley of tears), but because I realise that so the good God wills.

Our good Mother would like to keep me on earth; at this moment a novena of masses is being said for me to Our Lady of

[1] Jer. x. 23.   [2] Ps. xciii. 18.
[3] This explains why Letter CCXXIV contains many of the same ideas.

Victories. She has already cured me once, in my childhood,[1] but
I fancy the only miracle she will work now is to console the Mother
who loves me so tenderly.

Dear little Brother, on the point of appearing before the good
God, I realise more than ever that there is but one thing necessary,
to work *solely for Him* and do nothing either for oneself or for
creatures.

Jesus wants to possess your heart completely, He wants you to
be a great saint. For that you will have to suffer greatly, but, when
all that is over, bliss will come flooding into your soul when you
arrive at the joyous moment of your arrival in eternal life ! . . .

To all your friends in Heaven, Brother, I shall soon be bringing
your love, praying them to protect you. I should like to say the
thousand things I realise, now that I am at the gate of eternity;
but I am not dying, I am entering into life, and all that I cannot
say to you here below I shall make clear to your understanding
from the height of Heaven.

Goodbye, pray for your little sister, who says : I'll see you soon,
I'll see you in Heaven !

Thérèse of the Child Jesus of the Holy Face,
rel. carm. ind.

CCXVII

To M. AND MME GUÉRIN[2]

J. M. J. T.

Little Thérèse thanks her dear Aunt very much for the letter
she sent her, she also thanks her dear Uncle for wanting to
to write her, and her little sister Léonie, who enchants her by her
resignation and *true* affection.

Little Thérèse sends presents to all her relations (alas ! they are
flowers as ephemeral as herself . . .).

(*Very important instructions* for the distribution of the flowers.)
There is a *pansy*[3] for my Uncle, a *pansy* for my Aunt (not

[1] See Prologue, last page.
[2] This letter, undated, was written a few days after Pentecost, which fell that
year on 6 June.
[3] "Pensée."

303

counting all those that blossom for them in the little garden of my heart).

The two rosebuds are for Jeanne and Francis, the one by itself is for Léonie.

With her flowers, little Thérèse would like to send all the fruits of the Holy Spirit to her dear Relations, especially "*Joy*" !

CCXVIII

To SISTER MARIE OF THE TRINITY

On the back of a picture of the Child Jesus

"May the divine Child Jesus find in your soul a dwelling all fragrant with the roses of love; may He find the burning lamp of fraternal charity to warm His frozen limbs and rejoice His small heart, making Him forget the ingratitude of souls which do not love Him enough."

Sister Thérèse of the Child Jesus of the Holy Face,
r. c. i.

(13 June 1897).

CCXIX

To her Sisters,

REVEREND MOTHER AGNES OF JESUS
SISTER MARIE OF THE SACRED HEART
and SISTER GENEVIÈVE

June 1897.

As a farewell card, she wrote the following words round a picture, stuck on thin cardboard, of the Child Jesus scything lilies:[1]
Above the picture: Do not weep for me, for I am in heaven with the LAMB and the consecrated Virgins ! . . .

On both sides of the picture: The slightest movement of pure love is more useful to the Church than all other works put together ![2] It is, then, of the highest importance that the soul should

---

[1] Beneath the picture (number 1563, published by Bouasse-Lebel) is the printed text: "Happy the lily that has remained without spot until the reaping, its whiteness will shine eternally in Paradise."

[2] St. John of the Cross: *Explanation of the Spiritual Canticle*, strophe xxix.

exercise itself much upon LOVE, that, coming to speedy consummation, it may linger but a moment here below and arrive with the least delay at the vision of its God FACE TO FACE[1] (St. John of the Cross).

Below the picture: I see what I have believed. I possess what I have hoped. I am united with HIM whom I have LOVED with all my power of LOVING.

On the back, she copies some passages from the last letters of Théophane Vénard.[2] *Of these extracts the Saint said:* "*They are my thoughts, my soul resembles his*" (*Histoire d'une âme, ch. xii*)*:*

"I find nothing on earth to make me happy; my heart is too great, nothing that is called happiness on earth can satisfy it. My thoughts fly to eternity, time will end.[3] My heart is peaceful, like a great lake or a clear sky;[4] I do not regret the life of this world; my heart thirsts for the waters of eternal life[5]. . . . Only a little while, and my soul will leave the earth, end its exile, finish its warfare. . . . I am going up to Heaven ! . . . I am close to the Homeland, the victory is mine ! . . . I am to enter the abode of the elect, see beauties that the eye of man has never seen, hear harmonies that the ear has never heard, enjoy joys that the heart of man has never savoured[6]. . . . So I have come to the hour that each one of us has so desired ![7] It is most true that the Lord chooses the *weak* to confound the strong things of this world. I am not relying on my own strength, but on the strength of One who on the Cross conquered the powers of hell.[8] I am a spring flower that the Master of the Garden is about to pick for his pleasure. We are all of us flowers planted on this earth, to be picked by God in His own time: a little sooner, a little later. . . . I am a little creature of a day, I go first.[9] One day we shall meet again in Paradise and shall enjoy true happiness[10]. . . .

Thérèse of the Child Jesus,
borrowing the words of the angelic martyr Théophane Vénard.

---

[1] *The Living Flame of Love*, Explanation of strophe i, line 6.
[2] See Letter CXCI to Père Roulland, and note.
[3] Letter of 3 January 1861 to Mgr Theurel.
[4] 28 December 1860, to the same.
[5] 2 January 1861, to his family.
[6] 20 January 1861, to his sister.
[7] 3 January 1861, to Mgr Theurel.
[8] 3 December 1860, to his family.
[9] 20 January 1861, to his father.
[10] 2 January 1861, to his family.

CCXX

To ABBÉ BELLIÈRE

J. M. J. T.

Jesus †   Carmel, Lisieux, 21 June 1897.

My dear little Brother,

With you I have thanked Our Lord for the great grace He deigned to give you on the day of Pentecost; it was also on that great feast (ten years ago) that I obtained—not from my Director but from my Father—permission to become an apostle in Carmel. That is one more link between our souls.

O Brother, *please*, never think you "weary me or distract me", by talking much of yourself. Would it be possible for a sister not to take interest *in all* that concerns her brother ? As to distracting me, you have nothing to fear; on the contrary, your letters unite me still closer to the good God, bringing the marvels of His mercy and love very near for my contemplation. Sometimes Jesus delights "to reveal His secrets to the little ones":[1] as an example, when I had read your first letter of 15 October 1895, I thought the same thing as your Director. You cannot be half a saint, you must be a whole saint or no saint at all. I felt that you must have a soul of great energy, and I was happy to become your sister. Don't think you can frighten me with talk of "your best years wasted". I simply thank Jesus for looking on you with a *look of love*, as once He looked on the young man in the Gospel.[2] More fortunate than he, you loyally answered the Master's call, you left all to follow Him, and that at the *best age* of life, eighteen. . . .

Ah ! my Brother, like me you can hymn the mercies of the Lord ! They shine in you in all their spendour. . . . You love St. Augustine, St. Magdalen, those souls to whom "many sins have been forgiven because they loved much";[3] I love them too, love their repentance and above all . . . their daring in love ! When I see Magdalen come forward in face of the crowd of guests, and water with her tears the feet of her adored Master as she touches Him for the first time, I feel that *her heart* realised the fathomless depths of love and mercy in *Jesus' Heart*, realised,

[1] Matt. xi. 25.   [2] Mark x. 21.   [3] Luke vii. 47.

despite her sins, that that Heart was ready not only to pardon her but actually to lavish on her the treasures of His divine intimacy and raise her to the highest summits of contemplation.

Ah! my dear little Brother, since it has been given me too to realise the love of Jesus' Heart, I own that it has driven from my own heart all fear! The remembrance of my faults humiliates me, leads me never to rely at all on *my* strength, which is only weakness; but the remembrance speaks to me still more of mercy and love. When one casts one's faults into the consuming flame of Love, how could they fail to be consumed past return?

I know there are saints who spent their lives in the practice of astonishing mortifications to expiate their sins, but what of it? —"In my Father's house there are many mansions".[1] Jesus has told us so, which is why I follow the path He marks out for me. I try not to think about myself in anything whatsoever; and what Jesus in His goodness effects in my soul, I give over to Him; for I chose an austere life, not to expiate my own sins but the sins of others.

I have just read over my brief note and I wonder if you will understand me, for I have put it very badly. Do not think I am blaming you for repenting of your sins and wanting to expiate them. Oh, no! far from it; but you know, now that there are *two* of us the work will go faster (and I, with *my way*, will get more done than you), so I hope that one day Jesus will set you on the same way as me.

Forgive me, Brother, I don't know what is the matter with me today, I hadn't really meant to say all this.

I have no more room to answer your letter. I shall do so another time. Thank you for the dates of your life. I have already celebrated your twenty-third birthday. I am praying for your dear parents whom God has taken from this world, and I am not forgetting the mother[2] you love.

Your unworthy little Sister,

Thérèse of the Child Jesus of the Holy Face,
rel. carm. ind.

[1] John xiv. 2.   [2] The aunt who had brought him up.

CCXXI

To SISTER MARTHE OF JESUS[1]

To console her

J. M. J. T.

Jesus' little bride must not be sad, for Jesus would be so too; she must keep singing in her heart the canticle of love. She must forget her small trouble to bring consolation to the *great* troubles of her Spouse. . . .

Dearest little Sister, do not be a *sad little girl*, because you are not understood, misjudged, forgotten, but win everybody by trying to do like the rest, or rather by treating yourself as the rest treat you—I mean, forget all that is not Jesus, forget *yourself* for His love ! . . . Dearest little Sister, don't say it's difficult; if I speak like this, it's your fault; you told me you loved Jesus *greatly*, and nothing seems impossible to the soul that loves.

Rest assured that your little note pleased me very much ! . . .

CCXXII

To SISTER GENEVIÈVE[2]

Who, as infirmarian, apologised for having to leave her patient too often, to carry out her other duties

J. M. J. T.

Don't worry, poor "Demoiselle",[3] obliged to carry little cups to right and left; one day Jesus in His turn "will come and go to minister to you",[4] and that day will be here soon.

[1] This note, in pencil, is not dated. The shaky handwriting suggests that the Saint was much enfeebled by her illness.
[2] This note is undated.
[3] A jesting name given Sister Geneviève in memory of Les Buissonnets (see Letter CLXXIV).
[4] Luke xii. 37.

CCXXIII

To REVEREND MOTHER AGNES OF JESUS

13 July 1897.

I love you deeply, little Mama. You will see it soon ! . . . You will indeed.

CCXXIV

To ABBÉ BELLIÈRE[1]

J. M. J. T.

Jesus †

13 July 1897.

My dear little Brother,

Perhaps when you read this note, I shall be no longer on earth, but in the bosom of delights without end ! I do not know the future, but I can tell you with certainty that the Spouse is at the door. It would take a miracle to keep me here in exile, and I do not think Jesus will work so pointless a miracle.

Oh ! my Brother, how glad I am to die ! Yes, I am glad ! not at being delivered from sufferings here below (on the contrary suffering joined to love is the one thing I see as desirable in the valley of tears). I am glad to die because I realise that so the good God wills, and because I shall be much more useful than here below to the souls that are dear to me, yours especially.[2]

In your last letter to our Mother, you ask that I write you often during your vacation. If the Lord wills to prolong my pilgrimage by a few weeks more, I shall manage to scrawl more little notes like this, but most probably I shall be doing better than writing to my dear little Brother, better even than speaking the fatiguing speech of earth, I shall be *very near* him, I shall see all he needs, and I shall give the good God no rest till He has given me all I want !

When my dear little Brother sets out for Africa, I shall be with him, and no longer in thought only; by prayer my soul will be

[1] This letter and all that follow in this volume are written in pencil. The Saint had grown too weak to use pen and ink. The writing, still very upright, becomes increasingly tremulous to the end.
[2] Cf. Letter CCXVI.

with him always, and his faith will discover the presence of a little sister given him by Jesus, not to be his stay for a bare two years, but till *the last night of his life.*

All these promises, Brother, may possibly seem to you somewhat fanciful, but you must begin to realise that the good God has always treated me as a spoilt child. It is true that His Cross has gone with me from my cradle, but Jesus has made me love the Cross passionately. He has always made me desire what He willed to give me. Do you think then that in Heaven He will begin *not* to fulfil my desires ? I simply cannot believe it, and I say "Soon, little Brother, I shall be with you".

Ah ! I beg you, pray hard for me, prayers are so necessary for me at this moment, but *especially* pray for *our Mother.* She would have liked to keep me here a long time yet. To this end our venerated Mother is having a novena of masses to Our Lady of Victories, who cured me once before in childhood, but I, feeling that the miracle would not take place, have asked and obtained from the Blessed Virgin that she should give my Mother's heart some small consolation, or rather that she should win her consent to Jesus' carrying me off to Heaven.

Goodbye, little Brother, I'll see you soon, I'll see you in the beauty of Heaven !

Thérèse of the Child Jesus of the Holy Face,
rel. carm. ind.

CCXXV

To PÈRE ROULLAND

Her last letter to him

J. M. J. T.

Jesus †   Carmel, Lisieux, 14 July 1897.

Brother,

You say in your last letter (which I much enjoyed): "I am a *baby*, learning to talk."[1] Well, this last five or six weeks I am a baby too, for I live on nothing but *milk*,[2] but I shall soon

---

[1] He was learning Chinese.
[2] She had been put on a milk diet: even this, as a result of her fever, was sheer torment: one would hardly guess it from her jesting reference.

be taking my seat at the celestial banquet and slaking my thirst with the waters of eternal life ! When you get this letter, I shall pretty surely have left the earth. The Lord in His infinite mercy will have opened His Kingdom to me, and I shall be able to draw upon infinite treasures and shower them on souls dear to me. Be sure, Brother, that your little sister will keep her promises and that her soul, freed from the weight of its mortal envelope, will fly off happily to the distant regions you are evangelising. Ah ! Brother, I feel I shall be much more useful to you in Heaven than on earth, so that it is with joy I announce my approaching entry into that blissful city, sure that you will share my joy and thank the Lord for giving me the means to aid you more effectively in your apostolic labours.

I am perfectly sure I shall not stay inactive in Heaven, my desire is to go on working for the Church and for souls, that is what I keep asking God, and I am certain He will say yes. After all, the angels are continually occupied with us, while yet they never cease to see the Face of God, and are rapt forever in the shoreless ocean of Love. Why should not Jesus permit me to do as they do ?

You see, Brother, that if I am leaving the battlefield thus early, it is with no selfish desire to rest, the idea of eternal beatitude scarcely stirs a vibration in my heart, suffering has long been my heaven here below, and actually I find it hard to conceive how I shall get acclimatised in a Country where joy reigns with no tincture of sadness. Jesus will have to transform my soul and give it the capacity to enjoy, otherwise I shall be quite unable to bear eternal bliss.

What attracts me to the Homeland of Heaven is the call of Jesus, the hope that I may at last love Him as I have so longed to love Him, and the thought that I shall bring a multitude of souls to love Him, who will bless Him for all eternity.

Brother, you will not have time to send me the list of things I can do for you in heaven, but I guess them ; and in any event you will have but to whisper them and I shall hear you and faithfully bear your messages to Our Lord, to our immaculate Mother, to the Angels and the Saints you love. I shall ask for the palm of martyrdom for you, and I shall be near you, sustaining your hand that it may pluck that glorious palm without effort ; and then with joy we shall fly together to the celestial Homeland, thronged round by all the souls you will have won !

Goodbye, Brother, keep praying for your sister, *pray for our Mother* whose sensitive mother's heart cannot easily consent to my going.

I rely upon you to console her. I am for eternity your little sister,

Thérèse of the Child Jesus of the Holy Face,
r.c.i.

CCXXVI

To SISTER MARIE OF THE TRINITY[1]

She had been assistant in the infirmary, but was withdrawn— from fear of contagion—when Thérèse was brought there. The novice's pain was great at being deprived of the consolation of looking after her young mistress. She expressed it one day in the presence of another Sister. The Saint rebuked her and, that evening, wrote her this note:

My darling Sister,

I have pity on your weakness. . . . With you one must say what one thinks *on the spot.* I don't want you to be sad; you know what perfection I dream of for your soul, which is why I spoke to you severely. I should have understood your struggle and lovingly consoled you, if you had not spoken of it aloud but kept it in your heart as long as the good God allows it to continue. I have now only to remind you that our affection must be hidden henceforward. . . . Goodbye, poor little one. . . . I must bring you to Heaven very quickly.

---

[1] The original of this note no longer exists. It has been reconstituted, as far as possible, with the aid of various documents.

CCXXVII

To M. and MME GUÉRIN

Last letter written to them

J. M. J. T.

Jesus †   16 July 1897.

My dear Uncle and Aunt,

I am so glad to be showing you that your little Thérèse has not yet left the land of exile, for I know it will please you. All the same, my dearest Uncle and Aunt, I feel that your joy will be greater still when instead of reading a few lines traced by me with a shaking hand, you feel my soul close to yours.

Ah! I am certain the good God will let me pour His graces abundantly on you, and on my little sister Jeanne and her dear Francis, I shall choose Heaven's loveliest cherub and shall ask the good Jesus to give him to Jeanne, that he may become "a great Bishop and a great Saint".[1] If my prayer is not granted, then my darling sister will have to stop wanting to be a mother here on earth; but she can rejoice to think that in Heaven the Lord will give her the joy of being *the mother of many children*,[2] as the Holy Spirit promised, when through the mouth of the Prophet King He sang the words I have just written.

These children would be souls brought to birth in the life of grace by her right acceptance of her sacrifice; all the same I hope to get *my cherub*—by which I mean a small soul that would be a *copy* of him—for, alas, no one of the cherubim would agree to go into exile, even to receive the loving caresses of a mother! . . .

I see I shall never have room in this letter to say all I should like to. I meant, dear Uncle and Aunt, to tell you in detail of this morning's communion, which you made so moving, or rather so triumphant, by your masses of flowers. I leave it to my dear little sister Marie of the Eucharist to give you the details; all I shall tell you is that, before communion, she sang a little verse I had composed for this morning.[3] When Jesus had come into my heart

---

[1] Allusion to a dream of Jeanne's.
[2] Cf. Ps. cxii. 9.
[3] See *Histoire d'une âme*, ch. xii.

she sang again the verse from "Vivre d'amour"; "To die of love is a most sweet martyrdom." I cannot tell you how high and lovely her voice was, she had promised not to weep (to please me): my hopes were far outpassed. The good Jesus must have *heard* perfectly and understood what I expect of Him, and that is precisely what I wanted ! . . .

I know my sisters have told you of my cheerfulness, and it is true that I am like a finch, except when I have a temperature, luckily it usually comes only at night, at the hour when finches sleep, their head beneath their wing. I should not be as cheerful as I am if the good God did not make me see that the only joy on earth is to do His will. One day M. de Cornière[1] looks so dismayed that I think I am at Heaven's gate, and the next day he goes off all gay saying, "Why, you're on the road to recovery". I am only a small *baby* living on *milk*.[2] What *I* think is that I shall not recover, but that I may *drag on* a long time yet.

Goodbye, my dear Uncle and Aunt, only from Heaven shall I tell you my affection; while I am *dragging on*, my pencil cannot convey it to you.

Your little girl,

Thérèse of the Child Jesus.

CCXXVIII

To LÉONIE

J. M. J. T.

Jesus †   17 July 1897.

My dear Léonie,

I am very happy that I can still chat with you, a few days ago I thought I should never more have that joy on earth; but God seems to mean to prolong my exile a little. I don't mind, for I should not like to enter Heaven a minute sooner by my own will. The only happiness on earth is to train oneself always to find the lot Jesus gives us delightful; yours is very beautiful, darling Sister. If you want to be a saint, it will be easy, because in the depths of your heart the world means nothing to

---

[1] The Community's doctor.
[2] See note to Letter CCXXV.

you. So you, like us, can concentrate upon "the one thing necessary".[1] I mean that while you give yourself devotedly to external works, you have but *one* goal: to give pleasure to Jesus, to be united more intimately with Him.

You want me in Heaven to pray to the Sacred Heart for you; rest assured that I shall not forget to give Him your messages or ask Him for all that is necessary for you to become a *great saint*.

Goodbye, dearest Sister, I want the thought of my entry into Heaven to fill you with joy, for there I can love you still better.

Your little sister Thérèse of the Child Jesus,

I shall write you at greater length another time, I can't now.

CCXXIX

To ABBÉ BELLIÈRE

To console him and explain to him her " Little Way of Spiritual Childhood"

J. M. J. T.

Jesus †   18 July 1897.

My poor[2] dear little Brother,
   Your grief *touches me deeply*; but you see how good Jesus is. He permits me still to be able to write and try to console you, probably not for the last time. That loving Saviour understands your grief and your prayers: that is why He leaves me still on earth. Do not think I mind. Oh, no! my dear little Brother, very much the reverse, for in this conduct of Jesus I see how much He loves you ! . . .

   I feel sure I explained myself very badly in my last little note, because you say that I must "not ask you to feel *the joy* I feel at the approach of *bliss*". Ah ! if for a few moments you could read my soul, what a surprise you would get. The thought of the bliss of Heaven not only causes me no joy, I even wonder whether I

[1] Luke x. 41.
[2] Abbé Bellière, in the letter of 16 July that the Saint is here answering, told her movingly of the grief he felt at her approaching death.

315

can be happy without suffering. Jesus of course will change my nature, otherwise I should look back with longing to suffering and the valley of tears. I have never asked God to let me die young, it would have seemed to me cowardice; but from my childhood He has deigned to give me the intimate conviction that my course here below would be brief. So that the one cause of all my joy is the thought of doing the Lord's will.

O Brother ! how I wish I could pour the balm of consolation into your soul ! I can only borrow Jesus' words at the Last Supper. He will not object, because I am His little bride and therefore all His goods are mine. I say to you then, as He to His friends, "I go to my Father . . . but because I have spoken these things to you, sorrow has filled your heart. But I tell you the truth: it is expedient to you that I go. You now have sorrow, but I will see you again and you shall rejoice; and your joy no man will take from you."[1] Yes, of this I am sure, after my entry into life, my dear little Brother's sorrow will be turned into a *serene joy* that no creature can wrest from him.

I feel that we must go to Heaven by the same road—suffering joined with love. When I am come into harbour, I shall instruct you, dear little Brother of my soul, how you must navigate on the tempestuous sea of the world: with the love and utter trustfulness of a child who knows that his father loves him too much to forsake him in the hour of peril.

Ah ! how I wish I could make you realise the tenderness of Jesus' heart, what It expects of you. As I read your letter of the 14th, my heart thrilled tenderly. More than ever I realised the degree to which your love is sister to mine, since it is called to go up to God by the lift of love, not to climb the rough *stairway* of fear. I am not surprised that the practice of "familiarity" with Jesus seems to you not at all easy to manage; you cannot come to it in a day, but I am certain that I shall aid you better to walk that delightful way when I am free of my mortal envelope, and soon you will be saying with St. Augustine "Love is the weight that draws me".[2]

I should like to try, by a very simple analogy, to make you see how Jesus loves the souls, even the imperfect souls, which trust themselves to Him.

Suppose a father with two sons, mischievous and disobedient.

[1] John xvi. 5–7, 22.   [2] Confessions, xiii, 9.

Coming to punish them, he sees one shaking with terror and trying to get away from him—yet admitting in the bottom of his heart that he deserves punishment; while his brother does the opposite, casts himself into his father's arms, says that he is sorry for having caused him pain, that he loves him and that he will prove it by being good in future. Then, if this child asks his father *to punish him* with a *kiss*, I do not think the heart of the delighted father could resist the filial confidence of his child, for he knows his sincerity and love. He is of course perfectly aware that his son will fall, not once but many times, into the same faults, but he is ready to pardon him every time if every time his son *takes him by the heart.* . . . I say nothing of the first boy, dear little Brother, you must know whether the father can love him as much or treat him as forgivingly as the other.

But why do I speak to you of the life of trust and love? I explain myself so badly that I must wait till Heaven to talk with you of that blissful life. What I wanted to do today was console you. Ah! how happy I should be if you could take my death as Mother Agnes of Jesus is taking it. You probably do not know that she is my sister twice over, and that she was mother to me in my childhood. Our *good* Mother was very much afraid that her sensitive nature and great affection for me would make my going very bitter to her. It has been just the opposite. She speaks of my death as of a feast, and this is a great consolation to me.

Please, dear little Brother, try like her to realise that you will not be losing me but *finding* me, and that I shall never more leave you.

Ask the same grace for our Mother whom you love, and whom I love even more because she is Jesus visibly present to me. I should give you what you ask[1] with joy, if I had not taken the vow of poverty; but, because I have, I cannot even give away a holy picture. Only our Mother can satisfy your wish and I know that she will do so in full measure. Actually, in view of my approaching death, a sister has photographed me for our Mother's feast.[2] When the novices saw me they cried that I had put on my grand look; it seems that I am ordinarily more smiling; but take my word for it, Brother, that if my photograph does not

[1] Abbé Bellière had written, 16 July: "Leave me, I beg, something of you, your crucifix, if you will."
[2] Sister Geneviève had taken three photographs on the previous 7 June (see Letter CCXV).

smile at you, my soul will never cease to *smile on you* when it is with you.

Goodbye, *dear* little Brother, be assured that for eternity I shall be your *true little* sister.

Thérèse of the Child Jesus,
r.c.i.

CCXXX

To SISTER GENEVIÈVE

To sustain her in a time of interior trials

J. M. J. T.

22 July 1897,
Feast of St. Magdalen.

Jesus †

"Let the just man break me in mercy for sinners; but let not the oil wherewith their head is scented make mine grow soft."[1]

I cannot be broken, tried, save by the just, for all my sisters are pleasing to God. It is less bitter to be broken by a sinner than by one who is just; but *in mercy for sinners*, to obtain their conversion, I ask you, O my God, to let me be broken for them by the just souls round about me. I ask you, too, that the *oil of praise*, so sweet to my nature, *may not make my head*—that is my mind—*soft*, by getting me to think I possess virtues which on several occasions I did not practise very notably. . . .

O Jesus! "Your name is as oil poured out",[2] in that divine perfume I would bathe myself wholly, far from the eye of creatures . . .

[1] Cf. Ps. cxl. 5. [2] Cant. of Cant. i. 3.

CCXXXI

To ABBÉ BELLIÈRE

J. M. J. T.

Jesus †

26 July 1897.

My dear little Brother,

What pleasure your letter gave me! If Jesus has heard your prayers and prolonged my exile a little, He has also heard mine, since you are resigned to losing "my presence, my visible action", as you say. Ah! Brother, let me tell you : the good God has many a sweet surprise in store for your soul. You write that it is "not much habituated to supernatural things"; and I, who am not your little sister for nothing, promise when I have gone into life everlasting to make you taste the joy that lies in feeling a friend's soul close at hand. It will not be an exchange of letters—more or less remote, always so very incomplete—which you seem to regret losing; it will be a conversation of brother and sister which will delight the Angels, a conversation of which creatures cannot disapprove, for it will be hidden from them.

Ah! how good it will feel to be delivered from this mortal body, which would oblige me—if *by an impossibility* I were in my dear little brother's company when others were present—to treat him as a stranger, one who meant nothing to me ! . . .

Please, Brother, do not follow the example of the Hebrews who looked back with longing to "the onions of Egypt". For long I have served you only too many of those vegetables which make you *weep* when you bring them, raw, too near your eyes. Now I dream of sharing with you "the hidden manna" (Apocalypse[1]) that the Almighty has promised "the victors".

Precisely because it is *hidden* this heavenly *manna* attracts less than "the onions of Egypt"; but, I am certain, once I am permitted to offer you a wholly spiritual food, you will never more regret the food I would have given you, had I still remained long on earth.

Ah! your soul is too great to be attached to any joy of earth ! You must live by anticipation in heaven, for it is said "Where a

[1] Apoc. ii. 17.

319

man's heart is, there is his treasure".[1] Is not your *sole* treasure Jesus ? Since He is in Heaven, that is where your heart must dwell. And I tell you quite simply, dear little Brother, I feel it will be easier for you to live with Jesus when I am with Him for ever.

You must know me very imperfectly, to fear that a detailed account of your faults would lessen my affection for your soul. O Brother! do believe I shall not need to "put my hand over Jesus' mouth".[2] He has long forgotten your infidelities, only your desires for perfection are present to give joy to His Heart.

Please, I beg you, never again "*drag* yourself to His *feet*", follow the "first impulse which would draw you into His arms": that is where you belong, and I see, even more clearly than in your other letters, that you are *barred* from going to Heaven by any other way than your poor little sister's.

I am altogether of your opinion that "the divine Heart is more grieved at the thousand small discourtesies of His friends than by the faults, even the grave faults, committed by people in the world"; but, dear little Brother, surely it is *only* when his friends, not noticing their repeated discourtesy, let it become habitual, and do not ask pardon, that Jesus can say the touching words that are put into the Church's mouth during Holy Week: "The wounds in the midst of my hands are those I received in the house of them that loved me."[3] For those who love Him and, after each discourteous act, cast themselves into His arms and ask pardon, Jesus is vibrant with joy. He says to His angels what the prodigal son's father said to his servants: "Put on him the first robe, put a ring on his hand, and let us make merry." Ah ! Brother, how little are Jesus' *kindness* and *merciful love* realised ! . . . It is true, that, to enjoy his riches, we must humble ourselves, see our own nothingness, which is what many souls will not do; but, little Brother, you do not act like them, so the way of simple loving confidence is indeed the way for you. I would have you to be *simple* with the good God—and with me too. You are startled at that phrase ? I say it, dear little Brother, because you ask me to *forgive* "your indiscretion" in wanting to know if *your sister's* name in the world was Geneviève. Actually the question strikes

---

[1] Matt. vi. 21; Luke xii. 34.
[2] From the Abbé Bellière's letter, as are the passages in quotation marks that follow.
[3] Zach. xiii. 6.

me as perfectly natural. To prove it, I am going to give you details about my family, for you have not been told a great deal.

God gave me a father and mother worthier of Heaven than earth. They asked the Lord to give them many children and take them for Himself. Their desire was fulfilled. Four little angels fled away to Heaven, and the five children who remained in the arena took Jesus for their Spouse. It was with heroic courage that my father, like another Abraham, three times climbed the mountain of Carmel to immolate to God the thing he held most dear. First were his two eldest; then his third daughter, on the advice of her director, was taken by her incomparable father to try her vocation in a Visitation Convent. (God was content with her willingness. *Later* she returned to the world, where she lives as in the cloister.) There remained only two children to God's Elect, one eighteen, the other fourteen. The latter, "little *Thérèse*", asked his permission to fly off to Carmel: she gained it without difficulty, and her good Father in his limitless kindness took her first to Bayeux, then to Rome, to remove the obstacles in the way of the immediate immolation of one whom he called *his Queen*. When he had brought her to the gate, he said to the *one child* remaining to him: "If you want to follow your sisters' example, I consent, don't bother about me."

The angel who was to support the old age of such a saint answered him that *when he had gone to heaven* she too would take flight to the cloister, which filled him with joy, for he lived for God alone.

But so beautiful a life required to be crowned by a trial worthy of it. A little after my departure, the Father we had such good reason to love was seized by paralysis in the legs; it returned on several occasions but did not confine itself to his legs: such a trial would have been too easy, for the heroic patriarch *had offered himself to God as a victim*: so the paralysis changed its course and lodged in the venerable head of the *victim* whom the Lord had accepted. . . .

I have no room for the moving details, I need only say that we had to drink the chalice to the dregs: we were separated from our venerated father for three years, confiding him to the hands of religious, indeed, but strangers.

He accepted the trial, realising all its humiliation, and carried heroism to the point of wanting us not to pray for a cure.

Goodbye, dear little Brother, I hope to write to you again, unless the shaking of my hand grows worse, for I have been forced to write this letter with many pauses between.

Your little sister, not *Geneviève*, but

" Thérèse" of the Child Jesus of the Holy Face.[1]

CCXXXII

To SISTER MARTHE OF JESUS[2]

For her anniversary

J. M. J. T.

Darling Sister,

I suddenly realise that I have not wished you a happy birthday.[3] Ah ! be assured it is an oversight which *wounds my heart*, I was in such great joy over your birthday, I wanted to give you the prayer on humility ;[4] it is not yet finished re-copying, but you will have it soon.

Your little twin,[5] who wouldn't be able to sleep if she had not sent you this little note

Thérèse of the Child Jesus,
rel. carm. ind.

CCXXXIII

To SISTER GENEVIÈVE

3 August 1897.

In a moment of great anguish, Thérèse, very ill, asked for a scrap of paper and wrote these lines in pencil.

O my God, how kind You are to the little victim of Your merciful Love ! Now even when You add bodily suffering to

---

[1] Bent upon observing poverty, the Saint squeezed these pencilled lines as close together as possible. For want of space, she did not sign her name in full, nor add *rel. carm. ind.* This happened in other instances too.

[2] Undated, written a little later than 16 July.

[3] She was born 16 July 1865.

[4] This prayer was composed by the Saint on 16 July 1897. It appears in the main edition of *L'Histoire d'une âme.*

[5] Twin in profession. Thérèse was professed 8 September 1890 and Sister Marthe 23 September 1890 (see Letter XCVII).

my soul's anguish, I cannot say "The sorrows of death surrounded me"[1]; but I cry out in my gratitude "I have gone down into the valley of the shadow of death, yet will I fear no evil, for You, Lord, are with me" ![2]

(To my beloved little Sister Geneviève of St. Teresa—3 August 1897—Ps. XXII.)

CCXXXIV

To PÈRE PICHON, S.J.

On her death bed, Thérèse wrote Père Pichon a long letter in which she told him all that God had done for her, all her thoughts upon His Love and Mercy. She also laid before him her hopes and especially her desire to do good on earth. She based her letter on Psalm xxii on which she made a brief commentary. Lovers of the Saint might very well read the Psalm at this point, since it was the object of her meditations when she was so near death.

It was intended to make a copy of the letter, but the post went before it was done. When Thérèse learnt of this, she said simply "my whole soul was in it" ; and her sisters realised that she would have been glad to leave it to them as a spiritual testament. . . . Like all the other letters sent to Père Pichon, this one was unhappily not preserved.

CCXXXV

To ABBÉ BELLIÈRE

Last Letter

Jesus †   Carmel, Lisieux, 10 August 1897.

My dear little Brother,

I am now all ready to go. I have received my passport for Heaven, and it is my dear father who got me this grace; on the 29th he gave me guarantee that I should soon be with him;[3] the day after, the doctor, startled at the progress the sickness had made in two

---

[1] Ps. xvii. 5.
[2] Ps. xxii. 4.
[3] On 29 July, the third anniversary of M. Martin's death, she had been worse.

days, told our good Mother that the time had come to fulfil my
desires and give me Extreme Unction. So I had that happiness on
the 30th, the happiness too of seeing Jesus-victim leave the tabernacle for me: I received Him as the Viaticum for my *long* journey.
The Bread of Heaven strengthened me. See, my pilgrimage seems
unable to finish. Far from complaining, I rejoice that the good
God lets me suffer still for his love. Ah! how sweet it is to abandon
oneself in His arms, without fears or desires!

I confess, Brother, that you and I do not see Heaven in quite
the same way. It seems to you that, participating in the justice
and holiness of God, I shall not be able, as on earth, to excuse
your faults. Are you forgetting that I shall also be participating
in the *infinite mercy* of the Lord?

I believe that the Blessed in Heaven have a great compassion
for our wretchedness; they remember that when they were frail
and mortal like us they committed the same faults, endured the
same struggles, and their fraternal love becomes greater even than
it was on earth, which is why they do not cease to protect us and
pray for us.

Now, my dear little Brother, I must speak to you of the *inheritance* you will receive after my death. This is what our Mother
will give you:

1. The reliquary which I received on the day of my Clothing
and which has never left me. 2. A small crucifix incomparably
dearer to me than the large one, for the one I have now is not the
first one given me. At Carmel, we sometimes exchange objects of
piety, a good means of keeping us from growing attached to them.

To return to the small crucifix. It is not beautiful, the face of
Christ has almost disappeared, you will not be surprised at that
when I tell you that since I was thirteen this gift from one of
my sisters has accompanied me everywhere. It became especially
precious to me during my Italian journey.

I laid it against all the wonderful relics I had the good fortune
to pray before, the number would be impossible to tell: over and
above, it was blessed by the Holy Father.

Since I have been ill, I have held our dear little crucifix in my
hands practically all the time; looking at it, I remember with joy
that, having received my kisses, it will go off to claim my little
Brother's. So that is what your *inheritance* consists of. Further,
our Mother will give you the *last* picture painted by me.

I shall finish where I should have begun, by thanking you for the *great pleasure* you gave me by sending your photograph.

I congratulate you on your new dignity: on the 25th, the day I celebrate my little Father's feast, I shall also have the happiness of celebrating that of my Brother Louis of France.[1]

God be with you, Brother, may He give us the grace to love Him and save souls, that is the wish of your unworthy little sister,

Thérèse of the Child Jesus of the Holy Face,
rel. carm. ind.

(It was by choice that I became your sister.[2])

CCXXXVI

To LÉONIE[3]

J. M. J. T.

My darling Léonie,

I am *touched beyond all bounds* by your eagerness to give me pleasure. I thank you with all my heart and am enchanted by the coverlet you have made me. It is just what I wanted . . .

[1] The Abbé Bellière bore the name Louis in the Franciscan Third Order which he had recently joined.

[2] This phrase was written in the margin. It was an answer to a question asked by the Abbé in his letter of 6 August: "Will you tell me whether you became my sister by choice or by chance?" It was by the choice of Reverend Mother Agnes of Jesus that Thérèse became his sister.

Now that we are at the end of this correspondence with her spiritual brothers, it is worth nothing the Saint's own view upon it. At the end of June 1897, in the part of her manuscript addressed to Mother Marie de Gonzague, she wrote: "Obviously it is by prayer and sacrifice that one can aid missionaries, but occasionally, when it pleases Jesus to unite two souls for His glory, He permits them to exchange their ideas, and thus incite each other to love God more. I realise that for this the express will of authority is necessary; otherwise, it seems to me, such a correspondence, of one's own seeking, would do more harm than good, if not to the missionary, at least to the Carmelite, whose whole way of life leads her to retire within herself. Instead of uniting her to the good God, such an exchange of letters—even with long intervals between—would occupy her mind uselessly; she might well imagine that she was accomplishing wonders, while actually, under colour of zeal, doing nothing at all but give herself a superfluous distraction" (*Histoire d'une âme,* ch. x). On 8 July, she warned Mother Agnes of Jesus that a great many priests, when later they knew that she had been given as spiritual Sister to two missionaries, would ask the same favour. She said that this might well be a danger for certain souls: "This one or that one would be writing what I write and receiving the same compliments, the same confidence. . . . It is by prayer and sacrifice alone that we can be of use to the Church. Correspondence must be very rare, and should not be permitted at all to certain souls, who would be too much occupied with it, who would think they were accomplishing marvels when in reality they would be merely damaging their souls and perhaps falling into the subtle snares of the devil. Mother, what I say is very important, do not forget it later" (*Novissima Verba,* p. 56).

[3] Undated; see next note.

I shall offer my Communion for you tomorrow.[1] I *love* you and kiss you.

Your little sister,
Thérèse of the Child Jesus,
rel. carm. ind.

CCXXXVII

To SISTER MARIE OF THE TRINITY

Thérèse wrote the following lines on the back of a small picture of the Holy Family.

To my dear little Sister, in memory of her 23rd birthday.— 12 August 1897.

May your life be all humility and love, that you may soon come where I am going, into the arms of Jesus! . . .

Your little sister,
Thérèse of the Child Jesus of the Holy Face.

CCXXXVIII

To the MOST HOLY VIRGIN MARY
(The last lines Thérèse wrote)

Thérèse tells in the Histoire d'une âme *that when her father heard of her intention to enter Carmel, he picked a little white flower and gave it to her, asking her to note "with what care the Lord had brought it to blossom and preserved it till that day". The Saint adds: "I felt I was hearing my own story, so striking was the resemblance between the little flower and little Thérèse. I accepted the flower as a relic; and I noticed that in picking it Papa had pulled out all the roots without breaking them: it looked as if it were meant to have a further life in another more fertile soil. My darling Father had just done the same thing for me, by giving me permission to leave the sweet valley, that had seen the beginning of my life, for the mountain of Carmel. I stuck my little white flower*

---

[1] As Thérèse offered her last communion, on 19 August, for the ex-priest Hyacinthe Loison, this note must have been written a few days earlier. As we know (from *Novissima Verba*, p. 137) that she received communion on 12 August, it is possible that these lines were written on 11 August.

on a picture of Our Lady of Victories ; the Blessed Virgin is smiling at it, the Child Jesus seems to hold it in his hand. It is still there, only the stalk has broken close to the root. The good God clearly means by this that He will soon break the ties that hold His little flower and will not leave it on earth to wither . . ."

Thérèse wrote these lines in 1895. On 8 September 1897, three weeks before her death, she wrote in ink, on the back of the same little picture of Our Lady of Victories,[1] the following lines :

Mary, if I were the Queen of Heaven, and you were Thérèse, I should want to be Thérèse that you might be the Queen of Heaven ! ! ! . . .

8 September 1897

[1] It has been placed in a precious reliquary which allows both sides to be seen.

EPILOGUE

Suffering almost without respite in mind and body, but serene beneath the suffering and wholly yielded up to God's will, Thérèse came to the last day of her exile, 30th September 1897.

Then, more than ever, it was "sheer suffering, with no single element of consolation".

And she cried, in the terrible death-agony, which lasted twelve hours:

"O my God ! O sweet Virgin Mary ! come to my aid."

"The cup is full to the brim ! I could never have believed it was possible to suffer so much. . . . I cannot account for it save by the extremity of my desire to save souls. . . ."

"O my God ! Whatever you will ! but have pity on me !"

When she seemed driven to the very depths by the storm, she mastered herself to assure those around her that the centre of her soul remained the same :

"All I have written on my desire to suffer terribly for the good God, oh ! it is true."

On the evening before, she had answered her sister Céline, who wanted a word of farewell : "I have said all . . . all is consummated . . . only love counts."

At seven-fifteen in the evening of the 30th, after the Angelus, the Prioress warned her that her agony might go on longer. Thérèse answered courageously, in a voice barely audible : "Very well then ! . . . let it come . . . oh ! I would not want to suffer less ! . . ."

Then, looking at the crucifix she held so tightly in her clasped hands :

"Oh! I love Him ! . . . My God . . . I love you !" She had barely uttered these words in "the night of faith", when she collapsed; then suddenly, as though hearing a voice from heaven, she sat up in ecstasy, her look radiant, gazing above her.

It was the rending of the cloud, the skies opening, illumination; and in that illumination she died.

Act of offering
to the merciful love of the good God
Drawn up by
St.Thérèse of the Child Jesus

St. Thérèse had this act of offering near her heart day and night, in the book of the Gospels.

†
J. M. J. T.
An offering of myself
as a burnt-offering
to the Merciful Love of the
Good God

O my God ! Blessed Trinity, I desire to *love* You and make You *loved,* to work for the glorification of Holy Church by saving souls on earth and delivering souls suffering in Purgatory. I desire to accomplish Your will perfectly and attain the degree of glory You have prepared for me in Your Kingdom. In a word I desire to be a saint, but I feel my powerlessness, and I ask You, O my God, to be Yourself my Sanctity.

Since You have so loved me as to give Your only Son to be my Saviour and my Spouse, the infinite treasures of His merits are mine, I offer them to You with joy, begging You to look at me only with the Face of Jesus between, and in His Heart burning with *Love.*

I offer You too all the merits of the Saints, in Heaven and on earth, their acts of *Love* and those of the Holy Angels; finally I offer You, *O Blessed Trinity,* the *Love* and the merits of the *Blessed Virgin, my dearest Mother,* to her I yield up my offering, asking her to present it to You. Her divine Son, my *Beloved* Spouse, said to us in the days of His mortal life: "Whatsoever you shall ask My Father in My name, He will give it to you !"[1]

[1] John xvi. 23.

So I am certain that You will grant my desires. O my God! I know that "the more You mean to give, the more You make us want".[1] In my heart I feel immeasurable desires, and it is with confidence that I ask you to come and take possession of my soul. Ah! I cannot receive Holy Communion as often as I desire, but, Lord, are You not *all-powerful*? Remain in me, as in the tabernacle, never leave Your little victim. . . .

I want to console You for the ingratitude of the wicked, and I beg You to take away my freedom to displease You, and if at times I fall through weakness, I beg that Your *divine gaze* may purify my soul instantly, consuming all my imperfections, as fire transforms everything into itself. . . .

I thank You, O my God! for all the graces You have granted me, in particular for having made me pass through the crucible of suffering. It is with joy that I shall look upon You on the Last Day, bearing the sceptre of the Cross; since You have deigned to give me that most precious *Cross* as my portion, I hope to be like You in Heaven, and see the sacred stigmata of Your Passion shining in my body.

After earth's exile, I hope that I shall enjoy You in the Homeland, but my wish is not to amass merits for Heaven, but to work *solely for love* of You, with the single aim of giving You pleasure, consoling Your Sacred Heart and saving souls which will love You everlastingly.

In the evening of this life I shall appear before You empty-handed, for I do not ask You, Lord, to count my works. All our justices have stains in Your sight.[2] So I want to be clad in Your own *Justice*, and receive from Your *Love* the possession of *Yourself*. I want no other *Throne* or other *Crown* than *You*, O my *Beloved*! . . .

In your sight, time is nothing. A single day is as a thousand years,[3] so that in an instant you can prepare me to appear before You.

To live in an *act of perfect Love*, I OFFER MYSELF AS A BURNT-OFFERING TO YOUR MERCIFUL LOVE, calling upon You to consume me at every instant, while You let the floods of *infinite tenderness* pent up within You flow into my soul, that so I may become *Martyr* to Your *Love*, O my God! . . .

[1] St. John of the Cross, Letter XI to Mother Eleonora of St. Gabriel.
[2] Isa. lxiv. 5.
[3] Ps., lxxxix, 4.

ACT OF OFFERING

When that *martyrdom* has prepared me to appear before You, may it cause me to die, and may my soul hurl itself in that instant into the eternal embrace of *Your Merciful Love.* . . .

At every heartbeat, O my *Beloved*, I wish to renew this offering an infinite number of times, till the shadows retire[1] and I can tell You my *Love* over again, looking upon you face to face eternally.

Marie Françoise Thérèse of the Child Jesus
and of the Holy Face, rel. carm. ind.

Feast of the Most Holy Trinity,
9 *June in the year of grace* 1895

Indulgences attached in perpetuity to the recitation
of the Act of Offering
composed by St. Thérèse of the Child Jesus

1. A partial indulgence of three years every time the faithful recite, with a contrite heart and with devotion, the above act, at least from the words "To live in an act of perfect love" until the end;

2. A plenary indulgence, every month, on the usual conditions, for anyone who has recited the act every day of that month.

(Given at Rome, at the Sacred Penitentiary, 31 July 1923 and 23 December 1935.)

[1] Cant. of Cant. iv. 6.

IMPORTANT DATES SINCE THE DEATH OF
ST. THÉRÈSE

1898

7 March: Imprimatur for *L'Histoire d'une âme* given by Mgr Hugonin, Bishop of Bayeux.

30 September: Appearance of the first edition of 2,000 copies of *L'Histoire d'une âme*.

1908

8 May: At the request of Mother Marie-Ange of the Child Jesus, prioress of the Lisieux Carmel, Mgr Lemonnier, Bishop of Bayeux, consents to interest himself in the cause of Sister Thérèse of the Child Jesus.

1909

21 January: Father Rodrigue of St. Francis de Paul, a Discalced Carmelite of Rome, is appointed Postulator of the Cause.

28 January: Mgr de Teil is appointed Vice-Postulator at Paris.

1910

16 January: *Feast of the Holy Name of Jesus.* The Servant of God, Sister Thérèse of the Child Jesus, appears to Mother Carmela, prioress of the Carmel at Gallipoli (Italy), and reveals to her that her "Way is certain".

10 February: Letters from the Sacred Congregation of Rites authorising Mgr Lemonnier, Bishop of Bayeux and Lisieux, to open the proceedings of the Cause by examining the writings of the Servant of God.

6 September: The body of the Servant of God, previously buried in the earth, is exhumed and translated to a cement vault in the cemetery at Lisieux.

1911

12 December: Solemn conclusion of this part of the Process by the Ordinary in the Chapel of the Grand Seminaire at Bayeux.

1912

10 December: Decree of approbation given at Rome to the writings of the Servant of God. In Paris, she tells a Seminarian that she is about to let fall a "shower of roses".

IMPORTANT DATES

1914

10 June: The Sovereign Pontiff Pius X signs the Decree for the Introduction of the Cause in the Roman Court.

1915

17 March: Opening of the Apostolic Process at Bayeux.

1917

9 and 10 August: Second Exhumation and official identification of the body of the Servant of God in the cemetery at Lisieux.

30 October: Solemn conclusion of the Apostolic Process in the Cathedral of Bayeux.

1919

22 September: Decree given at Rome authorising the opening of discussions on the Heroism of the virtues of the Servant of God before the expiration of the fifty years after her death required by Canon Law.

1921

14 August: PROMULGATION OF THE DECREE ON THE HEROISM OF THE VIRTUES OF THE VENERABLE SERVANT OF GOD, SISTER THÉRÈSE OF THE CHILD JESUS, AND SERMON BY POPE BENEDICT XV ON SPIRITUAL CHILDHOOD.

1923

11 February: Promulgation of the Decree of Approbation of the Miracles advanced for the Beatification, and Sermon by Pope Pius XI.

19 March: Promulgation of the Decree *de tuto* declaring that the Beatification can go forward, and Sermon by Pope Pius XI.

26–27 March: At Lisieux, translation from the cemetery to the Chapel of the Carmel and veneration of the relics of the Venerable Thérèse of the Child Jesus.

29 April: SOLEMN PROMULGATION IN ST. PETER'S OF THE BRIEF OF BEATIFICATION OF THE VENERABLE THÉRÈSE OF THE CHILD JESUS.

30 April: The Beata is declared Patron of Missions and Missionaries of the Order of Discalced Carmelites.

28–30 May: The Papal Legate, Cardinal Vico, presides over a solemn Triduum at Lisieux.

15 June: The Beata is declared Patron of Noviciates of the Order of Carmel by a Rescript of the Sovereign Pontiff.

25 July: The Sovereign Pontiff Pius XI gives his *Placet* for the resumption of the Cause with a view to Canonisation.

1925

19 March: Promulgation of the Decree of Approbation of the Miracles advanced for the Canonisation, and Sermon by Pope Pius XI.

29 March: Promulgation of the Decree *de tuto* declaring that the Canonisation may go forward, and Sermon by Pope Pius XI.

17 May: SOLEMN CANONISATION IN THE BASILICA OF SAINT PETER AT ROME. PROMULGATION OF THE BULL OF CANONISATION, AND SERMON BY POPE PIUS XI.

29 July: By a Pontifical letter, the Saint is declared Patroness of the work of Saint Peter the Apostle.

24-30 September: Solemn celebrations at Lisieux. The "Golden Rose" blessed by Pope Pius XI is placed in the hands of the Saint by Cardinal Vico, the Papal Legate.

1927

17 May: The statue of St. Thérèse of the Child Jesus installed in the gardens of the Vatican.

13 July: Decree extending the feast of St. Thérèse of the Child Jesus, fixed on 3 October, to the Universal Church.

November: Pius XI approves the project of dedicating a Basilica at Lisieux to St. Thérèse of the Child Jesus, and blesses those who subscribe to it.

14 December: PONTIFICAL DECREE DECLARING ST. THÉRÈSE OF THE CHILD JESUS PRINCIPAL PATRON, WITH ST. FRANCIS XAVIER, OF ALL MISSIONARIES, BOTH MEN AND WOMEN, AND OF MISSIONS THROUGHOUT THE WORLD.

1928

11 February: At Rome, the foundation stone is laid of *Russicum*, the Seminary for Missionaries to Russia. The Seminary, and Russia herself, are placed under the protection of the Saint by the Sovereign Pontiff.

1929

30 September: Cardinal Charost, Archbishop of Rennes and Papal Legate, lays the foundation stone of the Lisieux Basilica.

3 October: The Apostolic Delegation of Mexico is consecrated to St. Thérèse of the Child Jesus, to whom Pius XI had several times dedicated Mexico.

1931

17 May: Opening of the Square in front of the Basilica at Lisieux and blessing of the first bell.

1932

26 June-3 July: Theresian Congress at Lisieux and Blessing of the Crypt by Mgr Maglione, Apostolic Nuncio in Paris.

1933

6 April: Clothing at Lisieux of the first Oblates of St. Thérèse of the Child Jesus.

IMPORTANT DATES

20 June: The Pious Union set up at Lisieux under the patronage of St. Thérèse of the Child Jesus is raised by Pope Pius XI to the dignity of *Primaria*.

1934

2 April: Opening of the memorial Way of the Cross at Lisieux by Cardinal Liénart, Bishop of Lille.

1936

3 October: Foundation of the "Petits Clercs de Sainte Thérèse" at Lisieux.

1937

30 March–8 April: Theresian pilgrimage at Rome to commemorate the fiftieth anniversary of the Saint's own pilgrimage (1887).

7–11 July: Eleventh National Eucharistic Congress held at Lisieux.

11 July: OPENING AND BLESSING OF THE BASILICA AT LISIEUX BY THE LEGATE OF POPE PIUS XI, CARDINAL PACELLI, WHO WAS TO SUCCEED HIM AS POPE PIUS XII. Message broadcast by Pope Pius XI.

1939

11 July: The Cross is blessed and set on the dome of the Basilica by Cardinal Piazza, O.D.C., Patriarch of Venice.

1941

7 September: Foundation of the Mission de France at Lisieux.

1944

3 May: LETTER OF HIS HOLINESS POPE PIUS XII DECLARING ST. THÉRÈSE OF THE CHILD JESUS SECONDARY PATRON OF FRANCE WITH ST. JOAN OF ARC.

1945

27 February–8 March: Great celebrations at Paris of the new Patronage of "Thérèse of France", before the Shrine containing the Relics of the Saint, surrounded by many Cardinals, Archbishops, Bishops, Prelates and vast crowds.

1946

During this year and the following one the Institut Catholique de Paris devotes its course on history and Christian spirituality to the doctrine of St. Thérèse of the Child Jesus.

30 September: Solemn opening of the Jubilee Year of the fiftieth anniversary of the death of St. Thérèse of the Child Jesus.

November: Progress of the Shrine containing the Relics of the Saint through Alsace, Rheims, Domrémy and the Eastern region of France.

LETTERS OF ST. THÉRÈSE

1947

Fiftieth anniversary of the death of the Saint. In almost all dioceses throughout France the Bishops preside over the solemn veneration of the Relics of St. Thérèse. Ceremonies in honour of the Saint are held throughout the world.

10–13 July: Theresian days of study are held in Paris.

23–28 September: National Congress at Paris in honour of St. Thérèse and veneration of her Relics.

29 and 30 September: Solemn conclusion at Lisieux of the Theresian year.

1948

4–11 March: A week of study is held at Rome, in continuation of the Theresian year, on the doctrine of St. Thérèse.

3 May: Canonical erection at Bassac (in the diocese of Angoulême) of the Congregation of Missioners of St. Thérèse of the Child Jesus.

INDEX OF LETTERS

L (7 or 8 January 1889)
LI (8 January 1889)
LIV (9 January 1889)
LXVII (May 1889)
LXVIII (May 1889)
LXIX (May 1889)
LXXXI (end of April or beginning of May 1890)
LXXXII (beginning of May 1890)
LXXXIV (May 1890)
LXXXV (May 1890)
LXXXIX (end of August 1890)
XC (1 September 1890)
XCI (beginning of September 1890)
XCIII (4 or 5 September 1890)

CXIX (20 February 1893)
CXXXV (21 January 1894)
CLXXX (4 December 1896)
CLXXXI (18 December 1896)
CLXXXVI (9 January 1897)
CXC (19 March 1897)
CC (5 April 1897)
CCIV (1897)
CCVI (23 May 1897)
CCVII (28 May 1897)
CCVIII (30 May 1897)
CCIX (30 May 1897)
CCX (1 June 1897)
CCXI (2 June 1897)
CCXIX (June 1897)
CCXXIII (13 July 1897)

4. *Léonie (Sister Françoise Thérèse):*

CXXVI (13 August 1893)
CXXX (5 November 1893)
CXXXII (27 December 1893)
CXXXVI (February or March 1894)
CXLII (20 May 1894)
CXLIII (22 May 1894)
CXLIX (20 August 1894)

CL (11 October 1894)
CLIII (beginning of January 1895)
CLV (24 February 1895)
CLVI (28 April 1895)
CLXVI (10 April 1896)
CLXXI (12 July 1896)
CCXXVIII (17 July 1897)
CCXXXVI (11 August (?) 1897)

5. *Céline (Sister Geneviève of St. Teresa):*

(Childhood note: 1879)
XXVI (8 May 1888)
XXXI (17 June 1888)
XXXII (23 July 1888)
XL (20 October 1888)
LVII (January 1889)
LVIII (February 1889)
LIX (28 February 1889)
LXI (12 March 1889)
LXII (15 March 1889)
LXIII (4 April 1889)
LXV (26 April 1889)
LXVI (27 April 1889)
LXXIII (14 July 1889)
LXXIV (15 October 1889)
LXXVI (22 October 1889)
LXXIX (31 December 1889)
LXXX (26 April 1890)

LXXXIII (May 1890)
LXXXVI (May 1890)
LXXXVIII (18 July 1890)
XCVIII (23 September 1890)
CII (14 October 1890)
CIV (20 October 1890)
CVI (3 April 1891)
CVII (26 April 1891)
CVIII (8 July 1891)
CIX (23 July 1891)
CXI (20 October 1891)
CXIII (26 April 1892)
CXIV (15 August 1892)
CXVI (19 October 1892)
CXX (25 April 1893)
CXXI (6 July 1893)
CXXII (18 July 1893)
CXXIII (23 July 1893)

INDEX OF LETTERS

339

LETTERS OF ST. THÉRÈSE

XLIV (October or November 1888) LXXXVII (July 1890)
LXIV (24 April 1889) CXV (16 October 1892)
LXXI (30 May 1889) CLVIII (beginning of August 1895)
LXXII (14 July 1889) CCXII (2 June 1897)

11. *Mother Marie de Gonzague:*
(Childhood note : end of 1882) CLXX (29 June 1896)

12. *Sister Marie of the Trinity:*
CLXVII (30 April 1896) CCXIV (June 1897)
CLXXXIII (Christmas 1896) CCXVIII (13 June 1897)
CLXXXV (1896) CCXXVI (1897)
CCXIII (6 June 1897) CCXXXVII (12 August 1897)

13. *Sister Marie of St. Joseph:*
CXCII (1897) CXCVI (1897)
CXCIII (1897) CXCVII (1897)
CXCIV (1897) CXCVIII (1897)
CXCV (1897) CXCIX (1897)

14. *Sister Marthe of Jesus:*
LVI (10 January 1889) CCXXI (1897)
XCVII (23 September 1890) CCXXXII (July 1897)
CLII (1894)

15. *Her sisters in religion and her family:*
CI (October 1890)

16. *Sister Anne of the Sacred Heart:*
CCII (2 May 1897)

17. *Sister Marie-Josèphe of the Cross:*
XCIX (28 September 1890)

18. *Sister Marie-Aloysia Vallée:*
CXXXIX (3 April 1894)

19. *Mother Saint-Placide, O.S.B.:*
XLVI (beginning of December 1888)

20. *Père Roulland, missionary priest:*
CLXVIII (23 June 1896) CXCI (19 March 1897)
CLXXIII (30 July 1896) CCIII (9 May 1897)
CLXXVIII (1 November 1896) CCXXV (14 July 1897)

INDEX OF LETTERS

III.   CHRONOLOGICAL LIST OF LETTERS

Notes written in childhood:

LETTERS OF ST. THÉRÈSE

INDEX OF LETTERS

LETTERS OF ST. THÉRÈSE

INDEX OF LETTERS

INDEX OF LETTERS